CIVIL WAR II

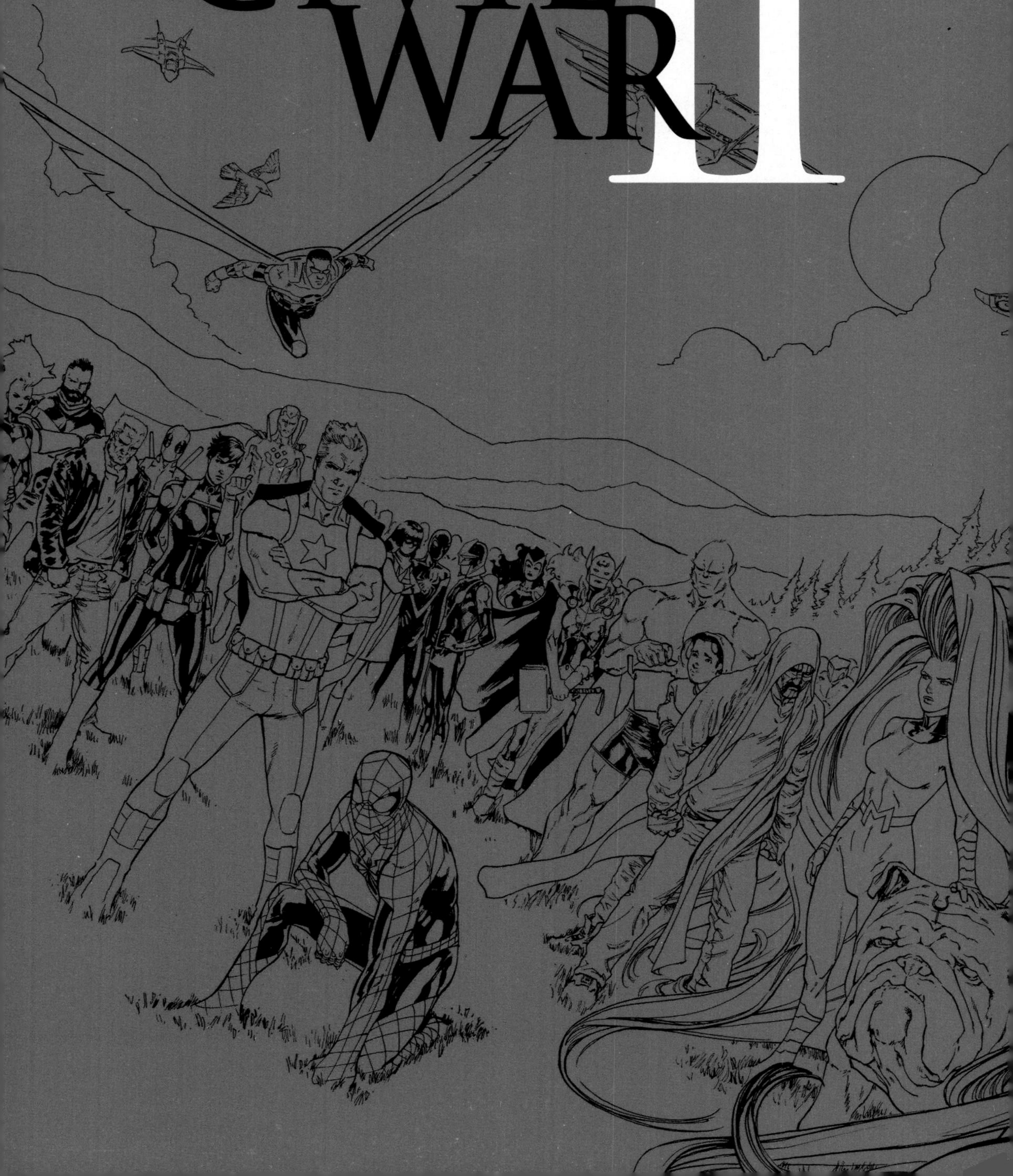

CIVIL WAR II

COLLECTION EDITOR: **JENNIFER GRÜNWALD**
ASSISTANT EDITOR: **CAITLIN O'CONNELL**
ASSOCIATE MANAGING EDITOR: **KATERI WOODY**
EDITOR, SPECIAL PROJECTS: **MARK D. BEAZLEY**
VP PRODUCTION & SPECIAL PROJECTS: **JEFF YOUNGQUIST**
SVP PRINT, SALES & MARKETING: **DAVID GABRIEL**
BOOK DESIGNER: **JAY BOWEN**

EDITOR IN CHIEF: **C.B. CEBULSKI**
CHIEF CREATIVE OFFICER: **JOE QUESADA**
PRESIDENT: **DAN BUCKLEY**
EXECUTIVE PRODUCER: **ALAN FINE**

CIVIL WAR II. Contains material originally published in magazine form as CIVIL WAR II #0-8 and FREE COMIC BOOK DAY 2016 (CIVIL WAR II) #1. Second printing 2018. ISBN 978-1-302-90157-8. Published by MARVEL WORLDWIDE, INC., a subsidiary of MARVEL ENTERTAINMENT, LLC. OFFICE OF PUBLICATION: 135 West 50th Street, New York, NY 10020. Copyright © 2017 MARVEL No similarity between any of the names, characters, persons, and/or institutions in this magazine with those of any living or dead person or institution is intended, and any such similarity which may exist is purely coincidental. **Printed in the U.S.A.** DAN BUCKLEY, President, Marvel Entertainment; JOHN NEE, Publisher; JOE QUESADA, Chief Creative Officer; TOM BREVOORT, SVP of Publishing; DAVID BOGART, SVP of Business Affairs & Operations, Publishing & Partnership; DAVID GABRIEL, SVP of Sales & Marketing, Publishing; JEFF YOUNGQUIST, VP of Production & Special Projects; DAN CARR, Executive Director of Publishing Technology; ALEX MORALES, Director of Publishing Operations; DAN EDINGTON, Managing Editor; SUSAN CRESPI, Production Manager; STAN LEE, Chairman Emeritus. For information regarding advertising in Marvel Comics or on Marvel.com, please contact Vit DeBellis, Custom Solutions & Integrated Advertising Manager, at vdebellis@marvel.com. For Marvel subscription inquiries, please call 888-511-5480. **Manufactured between 9/5/2018 and 9/25/2018 by LSC COMMUNICATIONS INC., KENDALLVILLE, IN, USA.**

10 9 8 7 6 5 4 3 2

WRITER
Brian Michael Bendis

CIVIL WAR II #0

ARTIST
Olivier Coipel

COLOR ARTIST
Justin Ponsor

COVER ART
Olivier Coipel & Justin Ponsor

FREE COMIC BOOK DAY 2016 (CIVIL WAR II)

PENCILER
Jim Cheung

INKER
John Dell

COLOR ARTIST
Justin Ponsor

CIVIL WAR II #1-8

ARTIST
David Marquez

COLOR ARTIST
Justin Ponsor

BANNER CONVERSATION ARTIST
Olivier Coipel

ART ASSIST, #5
Sean Izaakse

OLD MAN LOGAN ARTISTS
Andrea Sorrentino & Marcelo Maiolo

FUTURE ARTISTS
Adam Kubert, Leinil Francis Yu, Daniel Acuña,
Alan Davis & Mark Farmer, Marco Rudy,
Mark Bagley & John Dell and Esad Ribić

COVER ART
Marko Djurdjević

LETTERER
VC's Clayton Cowles

ASSISTANT EDITOR
Alanna Smith

EDITORS
Tom Brevoort with Wil Moss

CIVIL WAR II #0

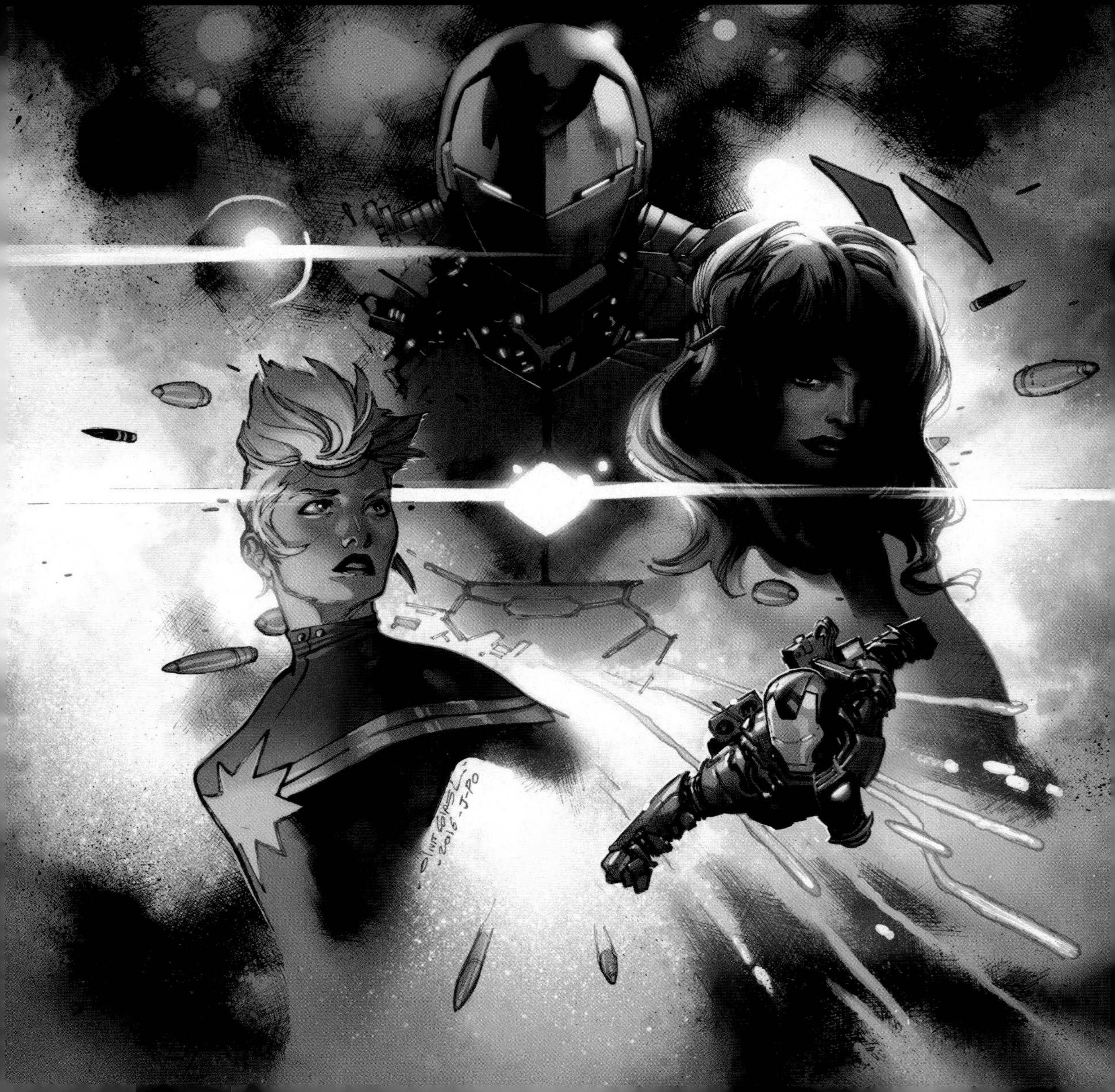

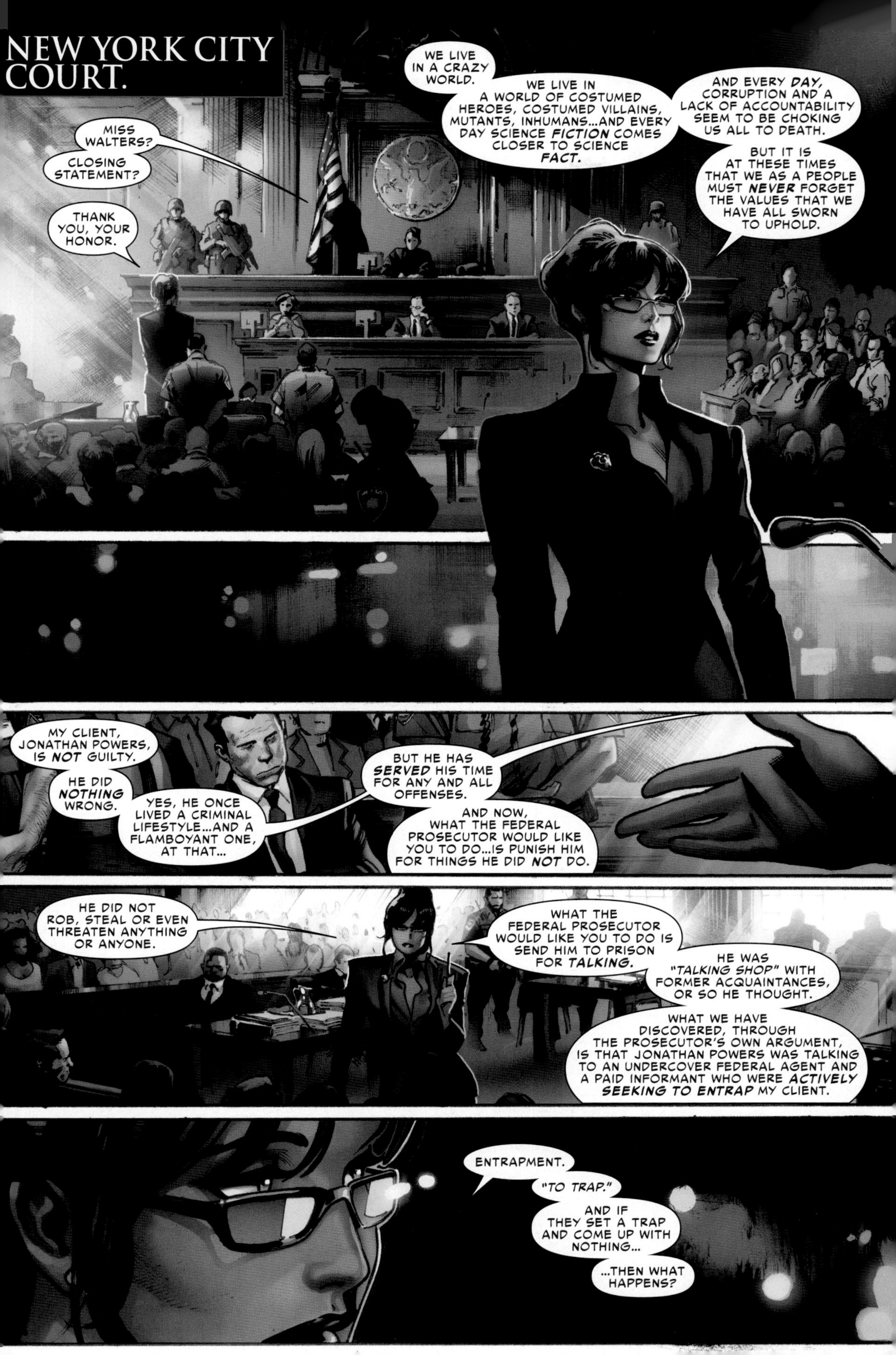
NEW YORK CITY COURT.
MISS WALTERS?
CLOSING STATEMENT?
THANK YOU, YOUR HONOR.
WE LIVE IN A CRAZY WORLD.
WE LIVE IN A WORLD OF COSTUMED HEROES, COSTUMED VILLAINS, MUTANTS, INHUMANS...AND EVERY DAY SCIENCE FICTION COMES CLOSER TO SCIENCE FACT.
AND EVERY DAY, CORRUPTION AND A LACK OF ACCOUNTABILITY SEEM TO BE CHOKING US ALL TO DEATH.
BUT IT IS AT THESE TIMES THAT WE AS A PEOPLE MUST NEVER FORGET THE VALUES THAT WE HAVE ALL SWORN TO UPHOLD.
MY CLIENT, JONATHAN POWERS, IS NOT GUILTY.
HE DID NOTHING WRONG.
YES, HE ONCE LIVED A CRIMINAL LIFESTYLE...AND A FLAMBOYANT ONE, AT THAT...
BUT HE HAS SERVED HIS TIME FOR ANY AND ALL OFFENSES.
AND NOW, WHAT THE FEDERAL PROSECUTOR WOULD LIKE YOU TO DO...IS PUNISH HIM FOR THINGS HE DID NOT DO.
HE DID NOT ROB, STEAL OR EVEN THREATEN ANYTHING OR ANYONE.
WHAT THE FEDERAL PROSECUTOR WOULD LIKE YOU TO DO IS SEND HIM TO PRISON FOR TALKING.
HE WAS "TALKING SHOP" WITH FORMER ACQUAINTANCES, OR SO HE THOUGHT.
WHAT WE HAVE DISCOVERED, THROUGH THE PROSECUTOR'S OWN ARGUMENT, IS THAT JONATHAN POWERS WAS TALKING TO AN UNDERCOVER FEDERAL AGENT AND A PAID INFORMANT WHO WERE ACTIVELY SEEKING TO ENTRAP MY CLIENT.
ENTRAPMENT.
"TO TRAP."
AND IF THEY SET A TRAP AND COME UP WITH NOTHING...
...THEN WHAT HAPPENS?

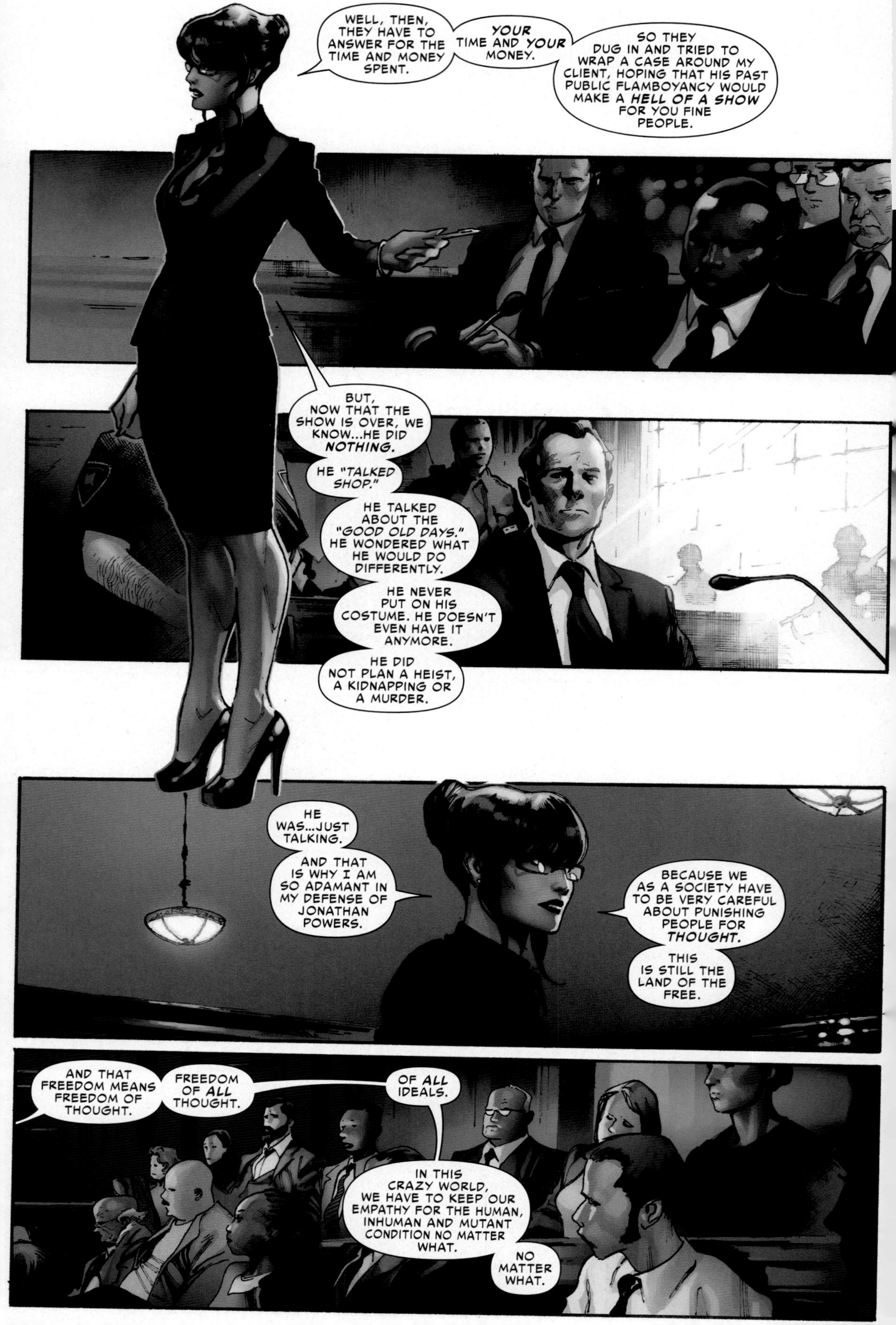

WELL, THEN, THEY HAVE TO ANSWER FOR THE TIME AND MONEY SPENT.
YOUR TIME AND YOUR MONEY.
SO THEY DUG IN AND TRIED TO WRAP A CASE AROUND MY CLIENT, HOPING THAT HIS PAST PUBLIC FLAMBOYANCY WOULD MAKE A HELL OF A SHOW FOR YOU FINE PEOPLE.
BUT, NOW THAT THE SHOW IS OVER, WE KNOW...HE DID NOTHING.
HE "TALKED SHOP."
HE TALKED ABOUT THE "GOOD OLD DAYS." HE WONDERED WHAT HE WOULD DO DIFFERENTLY.
HE NEVER PUT ON HIS COSTUME. HE DOESN'T EVEN HAVE IT ANYMORE.
HE DID NOT PLAN A HEIST, A KIDNAPPING OR A MURDER.
HE WAS...JUST TALKING.
AND THAT IS WHY I AM SO ADAMANT IN MY DEFENSE OF JONATHAN POWERS.
BECAUSE WE AS A SOCIETY HAVE TO BE VERY CAREFUL ABOUT PUNISHING PEOPLE FOR THOUGHT.
THIS IS STILL THE LAND OF THE FREE.
AND THAT FREEDOM MEANS FREEDOM OF THOUGHT.
FREEDOM OF ALL THOUGHT.
OF ALL IDEALS.
IN THIS CRAZY WORLD, WE HAVE TO KEEP OUR EMPATHY FOR THE HUMAN, INHUMAN AND MUTANT CONDITION NO MATTER WHAT.
NO MATTER WHAT.

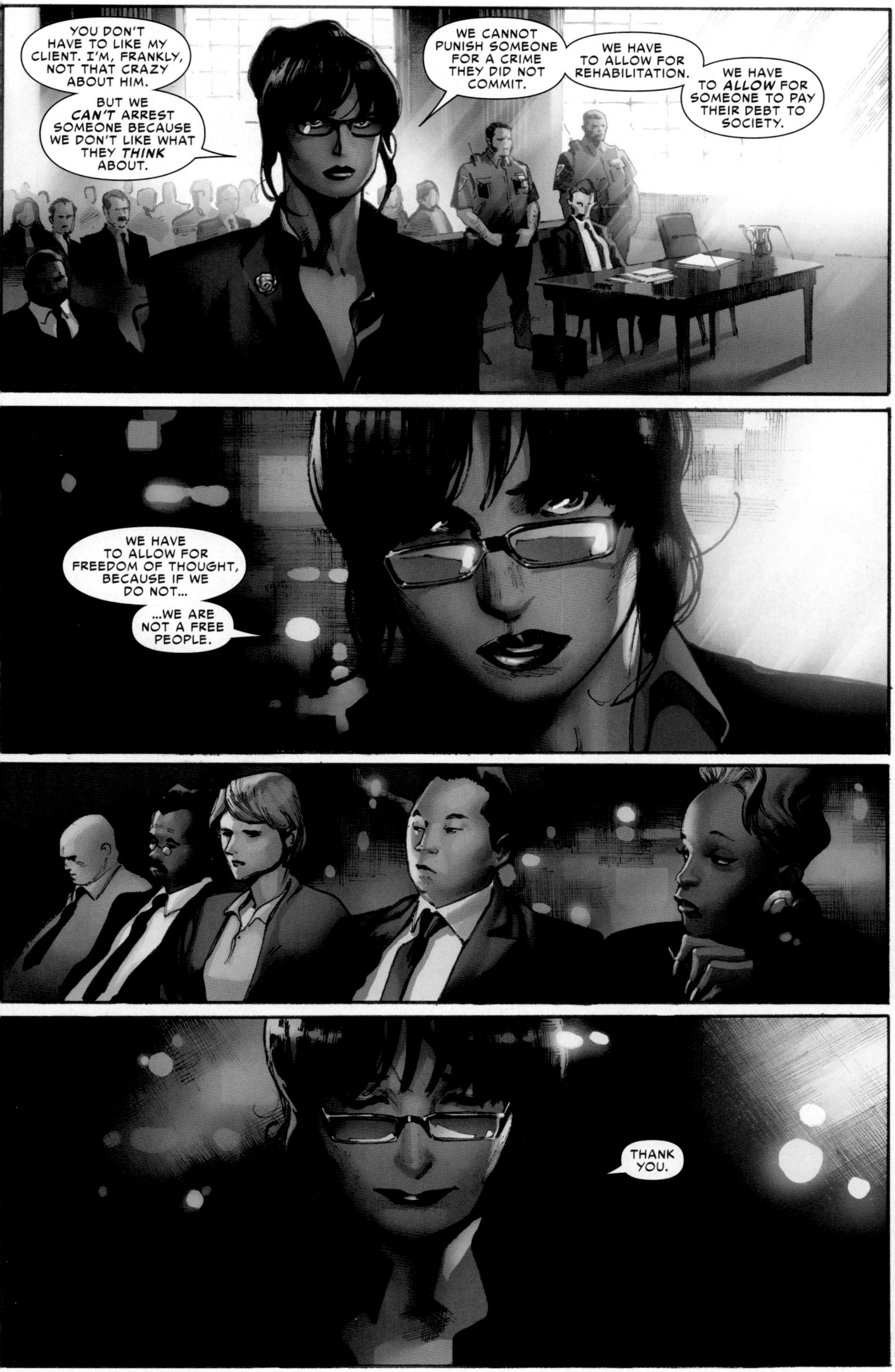
YOU DON'T HAVE TO LIKE MY CLIENT. I'M, FRANKLY, NOT THAT CRAZY ABOUT HIM.
BUT WE *CAN'T* ARREST SOMEONE BECAUSE WE DON'T LIKE WHAT THEY *THINK* ABOUT.
WE CANNOT PUNISH SOMEONE FOR A CRIME THEY DID NOT COMMIT.
WE HAVE TO ALLOW FOR REHABILITATION.
WE HAVE TO *ALLOW* FOR SOMEONE TO PAY THEIR DEBT TO SOCIETY.
WE HAVE TO ALLOW FOR FREEDOM OF THOUGHT, BECAUSE IF WE DO NOT...
...WE ARE NOT A FREE PEOPLE.
THANK YOU.

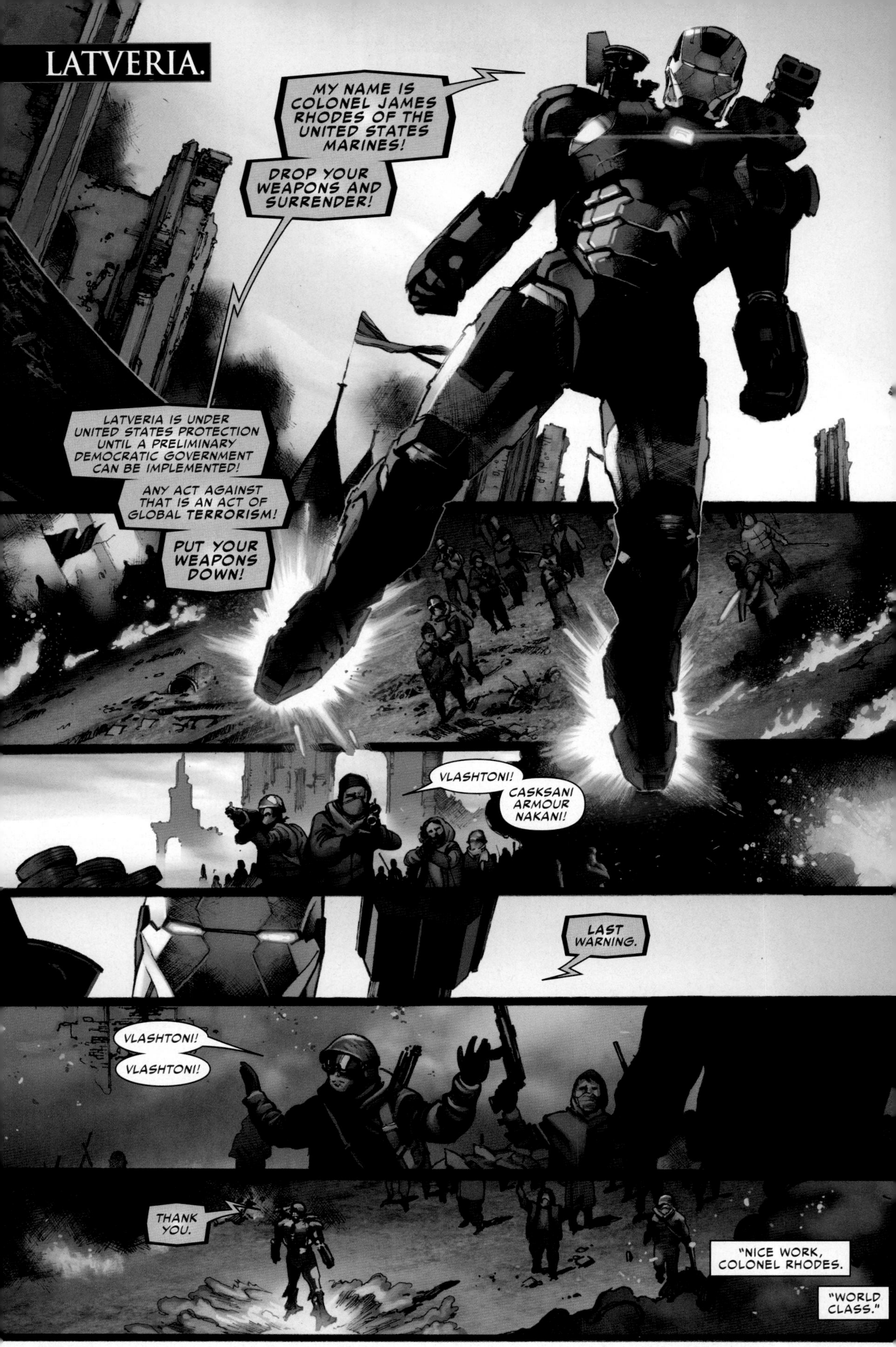
LATVERIA.
MY NAME IS COLONEL JAMES RHODES OF THE UNITED STATES MARINES!
DROP YOUR WEAPONS AND SURRENDER!
LATVERIA IS UNDER UNITED STATES PROTECTION UNTIL A PRELIMINARY DEMOCRATIC GOVERNMENT CAN BE IMPLEMENTED!
ANY ACT AGAINST THAT IS AN ACT OF GLOBAL TERRORISM!
PUT YOUR WEAPONS DOWN!
VLASHTONI!
CASKSANI ARMOUR NAKANI!
LAST WARNING.
VLASHTONI!
VLASHTONI!
THANK YOU.
"NICE WORK, COLONEL RHODES.
"WORLD CLASS."

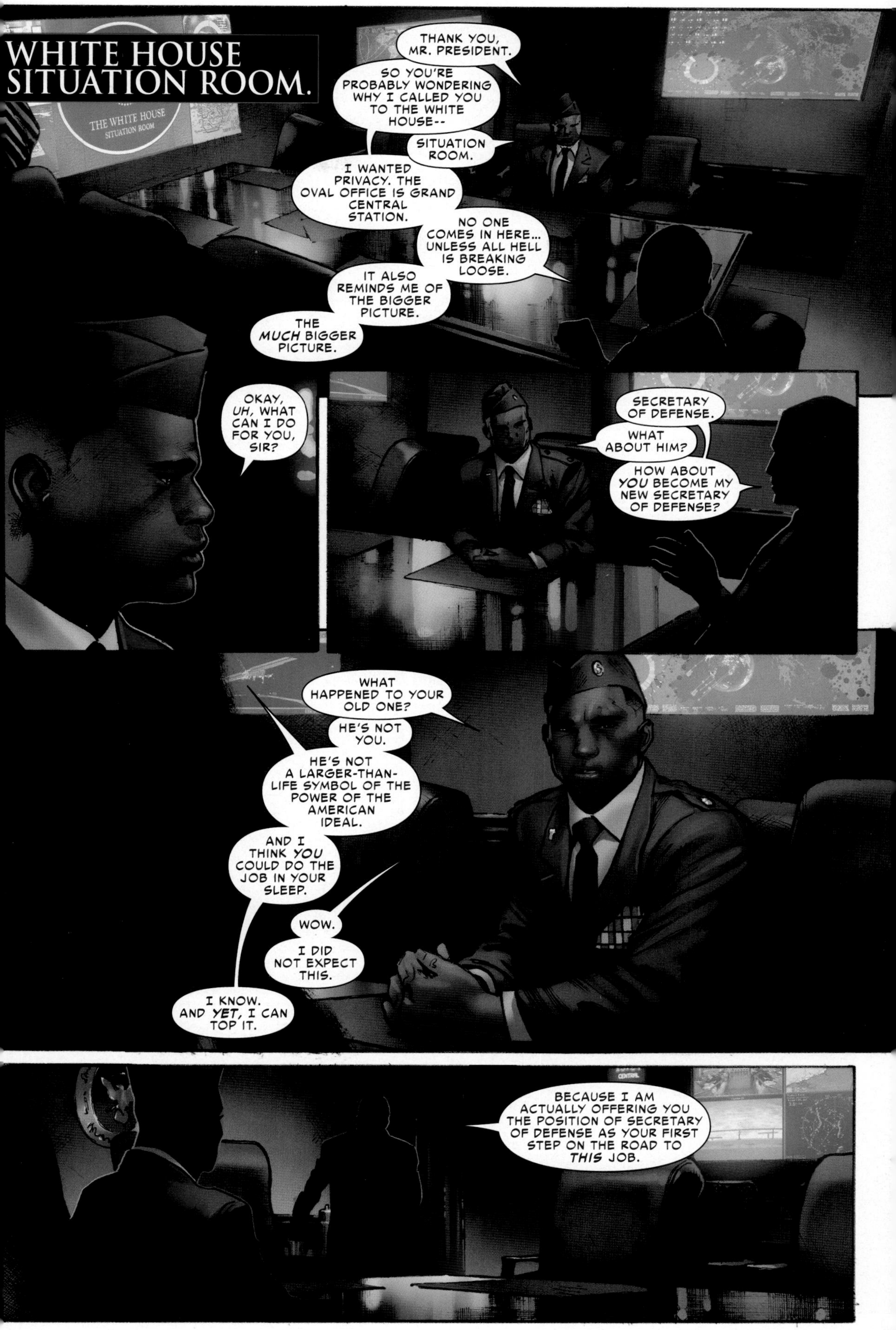
WHITE HOUSE SITUATION ROOM.
THE WHITE HOUSE SITUATION ROOM
THANK YOU, MR. PRESIDENT.
SO YOU'RE PROBABLY WONDERING WHY I CALLED YOU TO THE WHITE HOUSE--
SITUATION ROOM.
I WANTED PRIVACY. THE OVAL OFFICE IS GRAND CENTRAL STATION.
NO ONE COMES IN HERE... UNLESS ALL HELL IS BREAKING LOOSE.
IT ALSO REMINDS ME OF THE BIGGER PICTURE.
THE *MUCH* BIGGER PICTURE.
OKAY, *UH*, WHAT CAN I DO FOR YOU, SIR?
SECRETARY OF DEFENSE.
WHAT ABOUT HIM?
HOW ABOUT *YOU* BECOME MY NEW SECRETARY OF DEFENSE?
WHAT HAPPENED TO YOUR OLD ONE?
HE'S NOT YOU.
HE'S NOT A LARGER-THAN-LIFE SYMBOL OF THE POWER OF THE AMERICAN IDEAL.
AND I THINK *YOU* COULD DO THE JOB IN YOUR SLEEP.
WOW.
I DID NOT EXPECT THIS.
I KNOW. AND *YET*, I CAN TOP IT.
BECAUSE I AM ACTUALLY OFFERING YOU THE POSITION OF SECRETARY OF DEFENSE AS YOUR FIRST STEP ON THE ROAD TO *THIS* JOB.

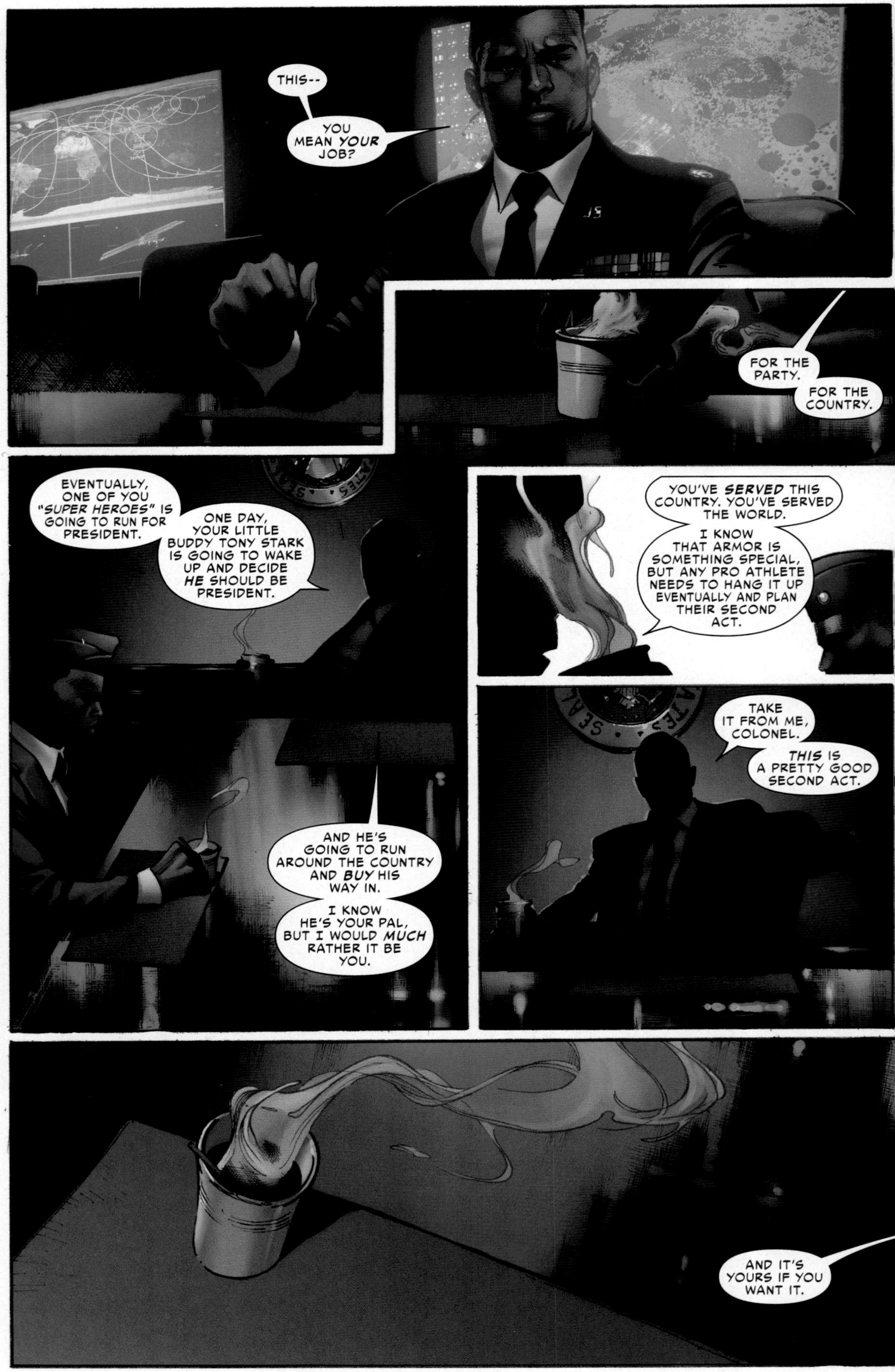
THIS--
YOU MEAN *YOUR* JOB?
FOR THE PARTY.
FOR THE COUNTRY.
EVENTUALLY, ONE OF YOU "*SUPER HEROES*" IS GOING TO RUN FOR PRESIDENT.
ONE DAY, YOUR LITTLE BUDDY TONY STARK IS GOING TO WAKE UP AND DECIDE *HE* SHOULD BE PRESIDENT.
AND HE'S GOING TO RUN AROUND THE COUNTRY AND *BUY* HIS WAY IN.
I KNOW HE'S YOUR PAL, BUT I WOULD *MUCH* RATHER IT BE YOU.
YOU'VE *SERVED* THIS COUNTRY. YOU'VE SERVED THE WORLD.
I KNOW THAT ARMOR IS SOMETHING SPECIAL, BUT ANY PRO ATHLETE NEEDS TO HANG IT UP EVENTUALLY AND PLAN THEIR SECOND ACT.
TAKE IT FROM ME, COLONEL.
THIS IS A PRETTY GOOD SECOND ACT.
AND IT'S YOURS IF YOU WANT IT.

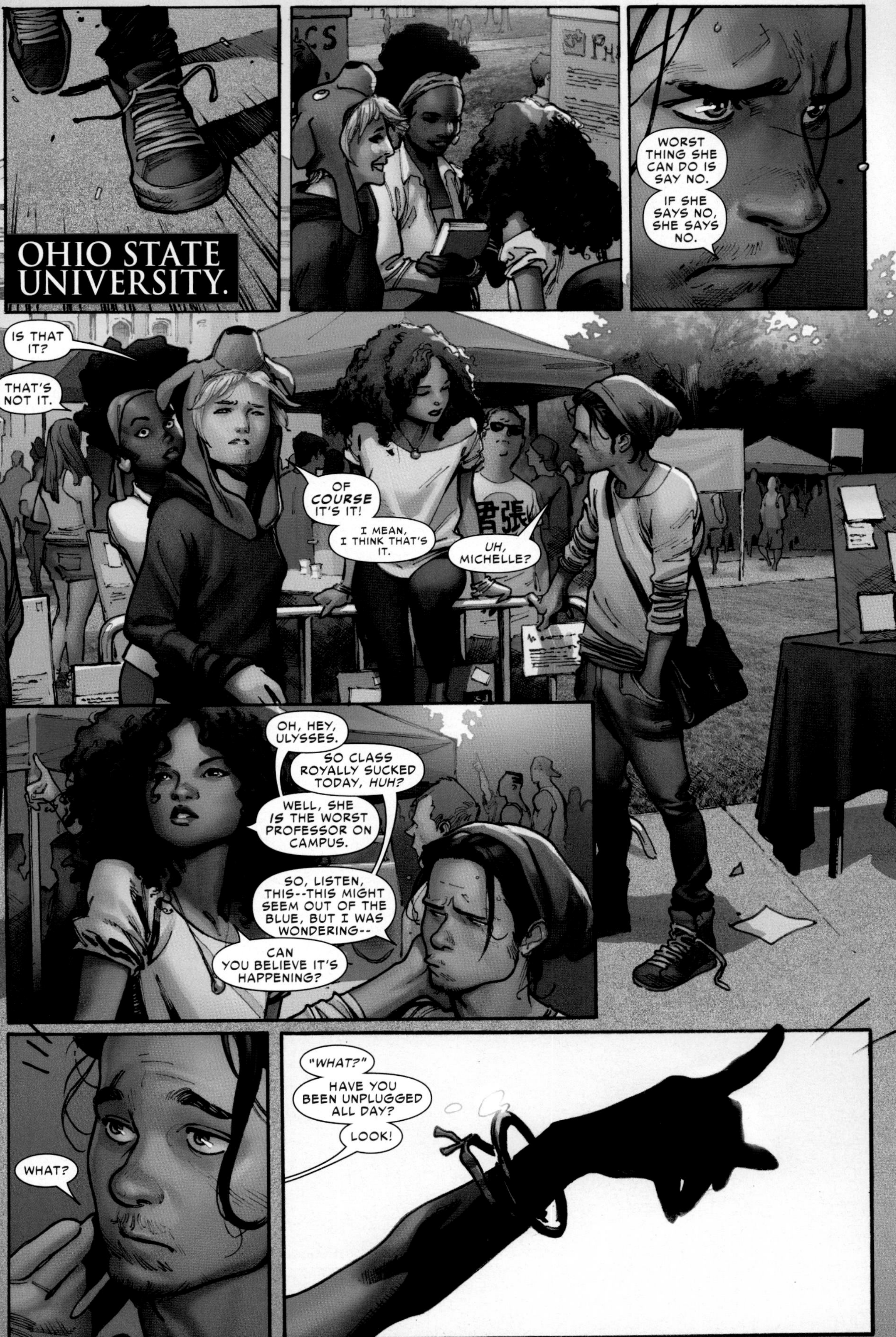
OHIO STATE UNIVERSITY.
WORST THING SHE CAN DO IS SAY NO.
IF SHE SAYS NO, SHE SAYS NO.
IS THAT IT?
THAT'S NOT IT.
OF COURSE IT'S IT!
I MEAN, I THINK THAT'S IT.
UH, MICHELLE?
OH, HEY, ULYSSES.
SO CLASS ROYALLY SUCKED TODAY, HUH?
WELL, SHE IS THE WORST PROFESSOR ON CAMPUS.
SO, LISTEN, THIS--THIS MIGHT SEEM OUT OF THE BLUE, BUT I WAS WONDERING--
CAN YOU BELIEVE IT'S HAPPENING?
WHAT?
"WHAT?"
HAVE YOU BEEN UNPLUGGED ALL DAY?
LOOK!

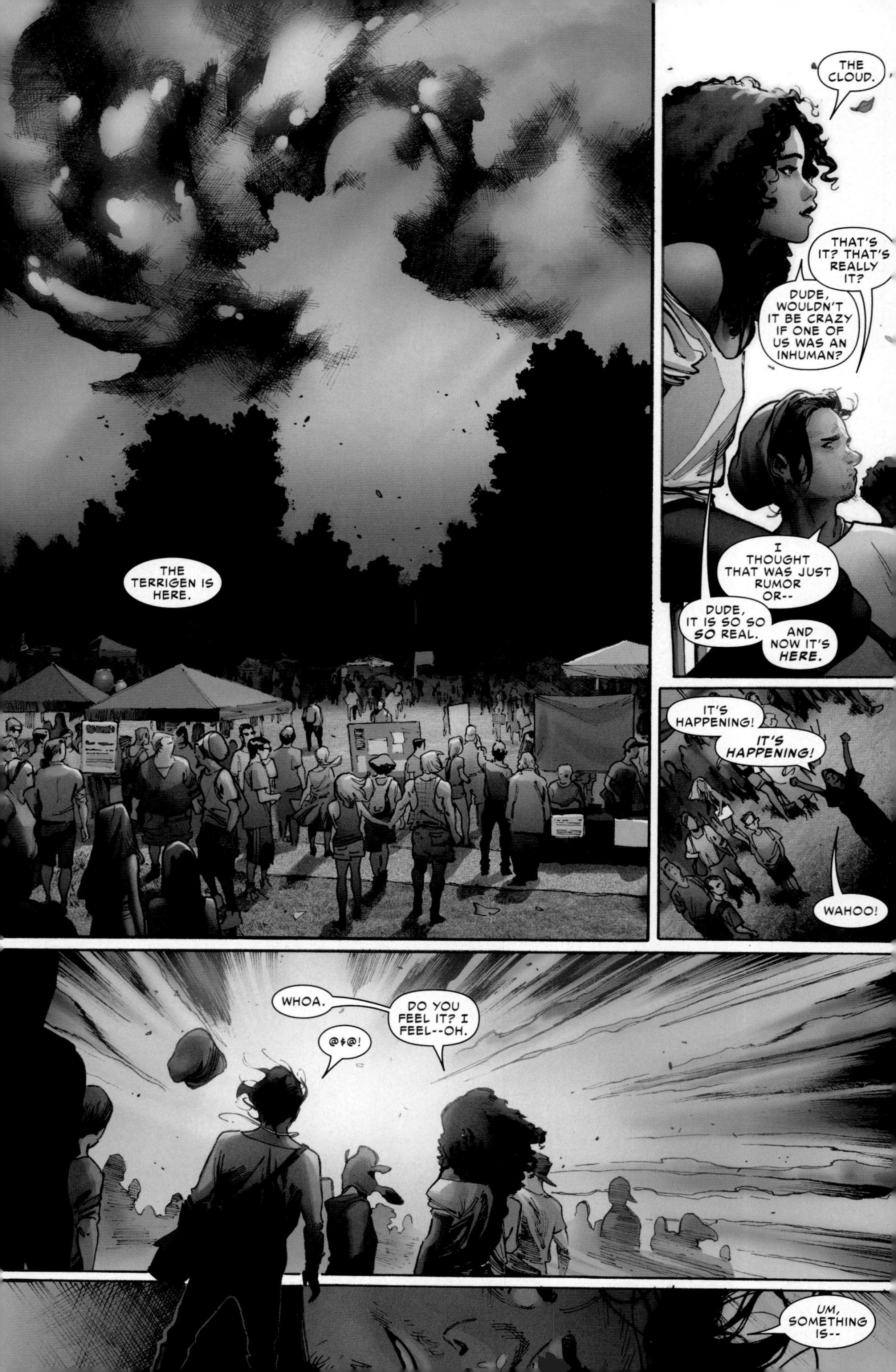
THE TERRIGEN IS HERE.
THE CLOUD.
THAT'S IT? THAT'S REALLY IT?
DUDE, WOULDN'T IT BE CRAZY IF ONE OF US WAS AN INHUMAN?
I THOUGHT THAT WAS JUST RUMOR OR--
DUDE, IT IS SO SO SO REAL.
AND NOW IT'S HERE.
IT'S HAPPENING!
IT'S HAPPENING!
WAHOO!
WHOA.
DO YOU FEEL IT? I FEEL--OH.
@$@!
UM, SOMETHING IS--

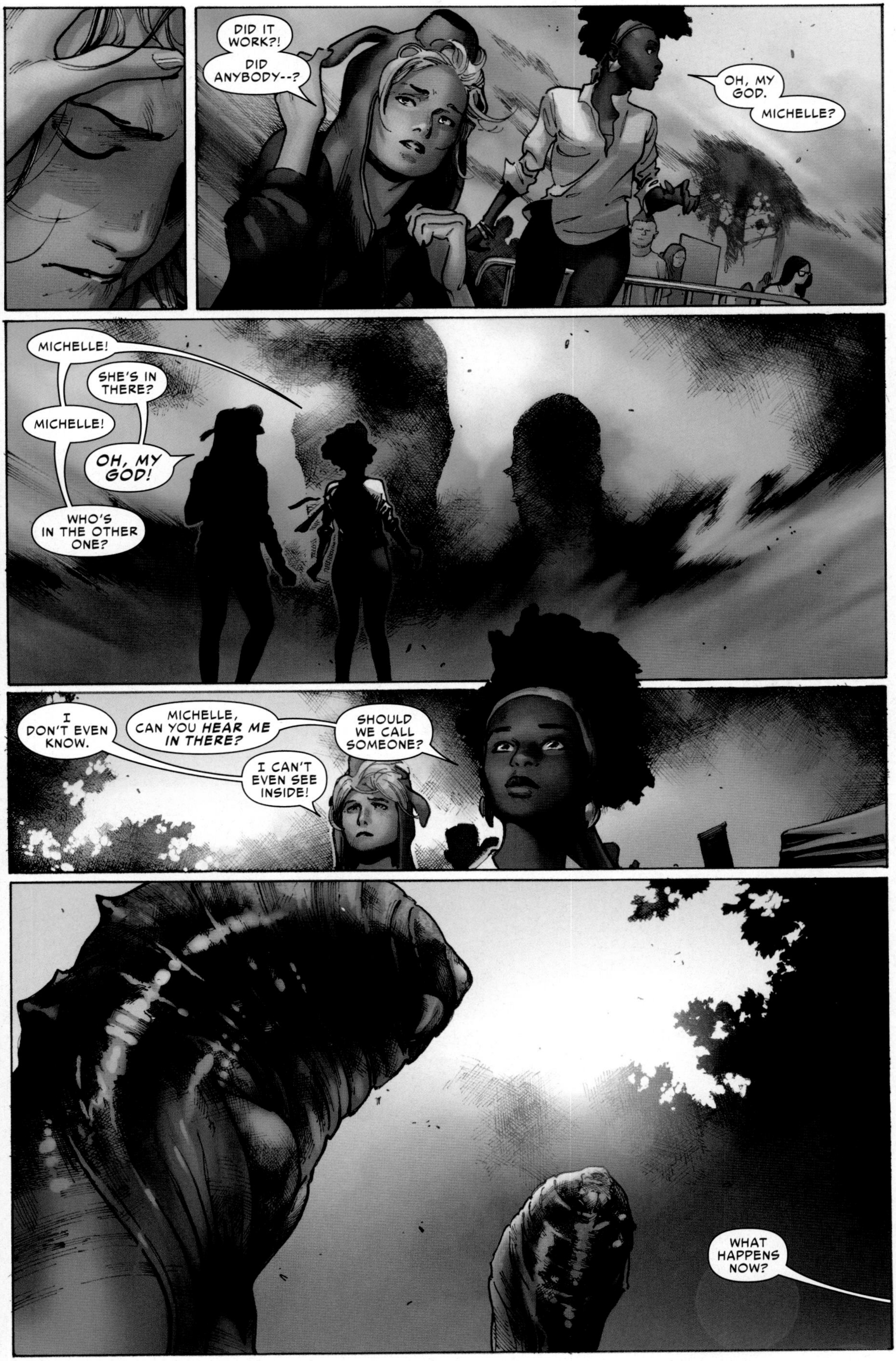
DID IT WORK?!
DID ANYBODY--?
OH, MY GOD.
MICHELLE?
MICHELLE!
SHE'S IN THERE?
MICHELLE!
OH, MY GOD!
WHO'S IN THE OTHER ONE?
I DON'T EVEN KNOW.
MICHELLE, CAN YOU HEAR ME IN THERE?
SHOULD WE CALL SOMEONE?
I CAN'T EVEN SEE INSIDE!
WHAT HAPPENS NOW?

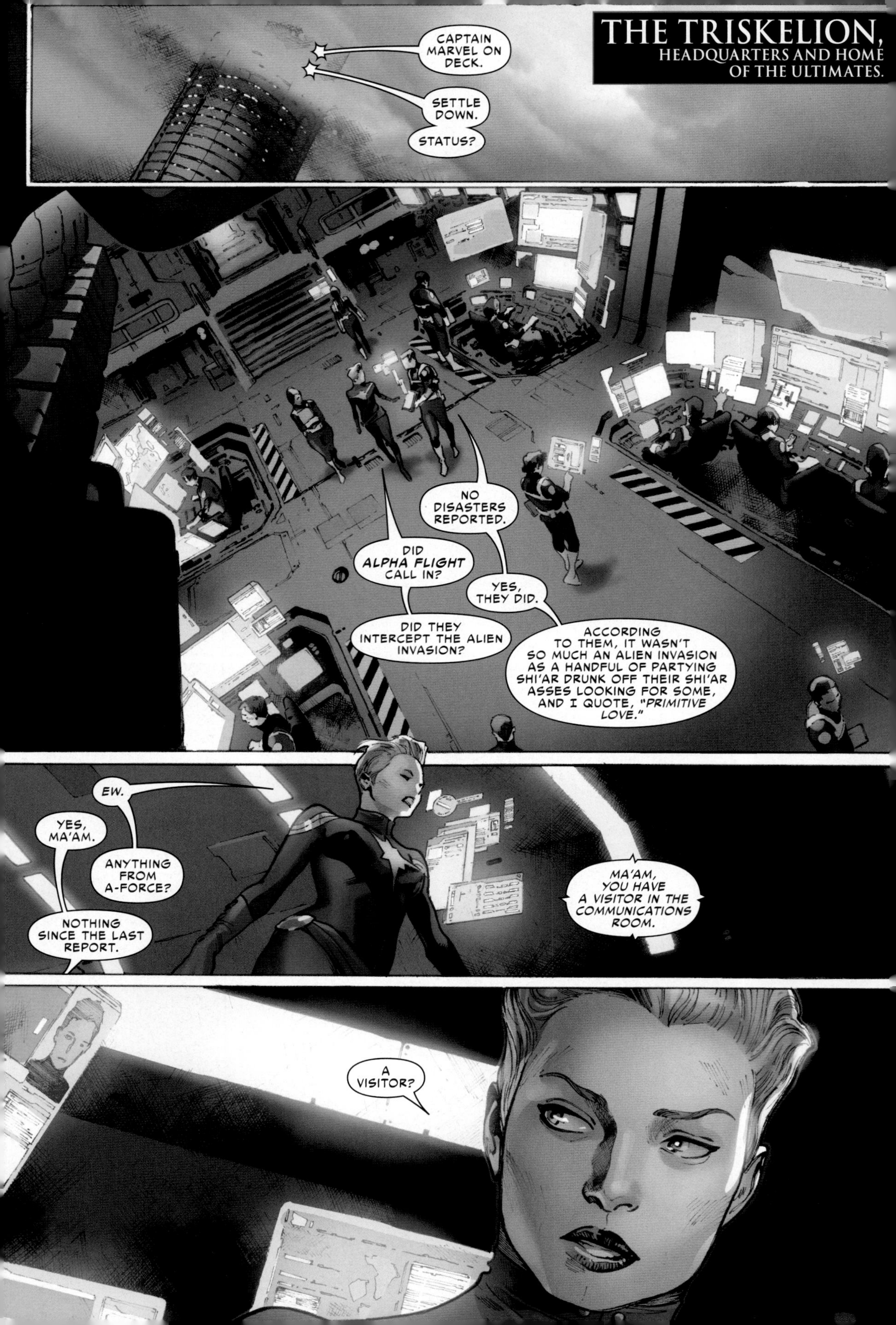
THE TRISKELION,
HEADQUARTERS AND HOME OF THE ULTIMATES.
CAPTAIN MARVEL ON DECK.
SETTLE DOWN.
STATUS?
NO DISASTERS REPORTED.
DID *ALPHA FLIGHT* CALL IN?
YES, THEY DID.
DID THEY INTERCEPT THE ALIEN INVASION?
ACCORDING TO THEM, IT WASN'T SO MUCH AN ALIEN INVASION AS A HANDFUL OF PARTYING SHI'AR DRUNK OFF THEIR SHI'AR ASSES LOOKING FOR SOME, AND I QUOTE, "*PRIMITIVE LOVE.*"
EW.
YES, MA'AM.
ANYTHING FROM A-FORCE?
NOTHING SINCE THE LAST REPORT.
MA'AM, YOU HAVE A VISITOR IN THE COMMUNICATIONS ROOM.
A VISITOR?

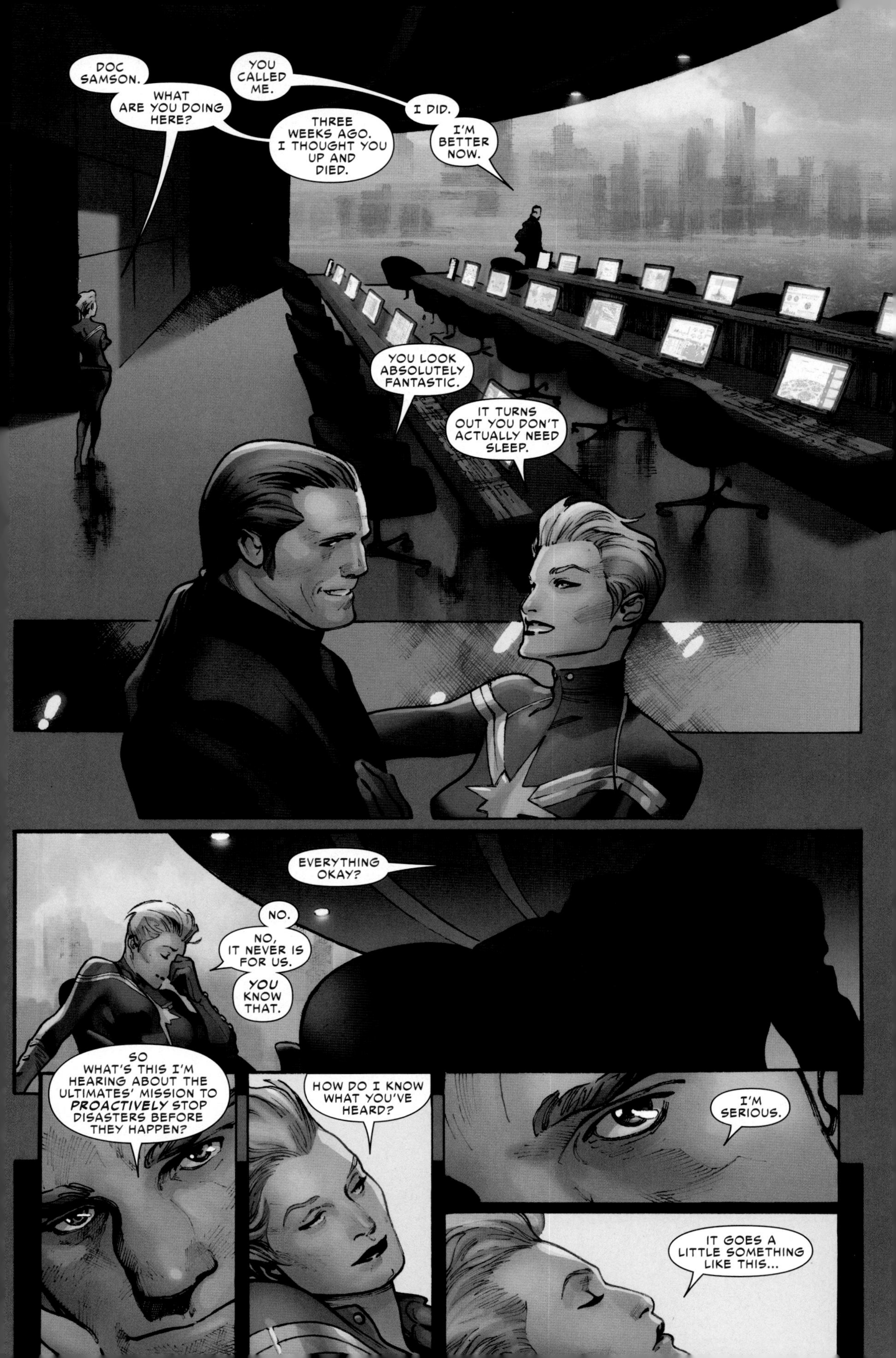
DOC SAMSON.
WHAT ARE YOU DOING HERE?
YOU CALLED ME.
THREE WEEKS AGO. I THOUGHT YOU UP AND DIED.
I DID.
I'M BETTER NOW.
YOU LOOK ABSOLUTELY FANTASTIC.
IT TURNS OUT YOU DON'T ACTUALLY NEED SLEEP.
EVERYTHING OKAY?
NO.
NO, IT NEVER IS FOR US.
YOU KNOW THAT.
SO WHAT'S THIS I'M HEARING ABOUT THE ULTIMATES' MISSION TO *PROACTIVELY* STOP DISASTERS BEFORE THEY HAPPEN?
HOW DO I KNOW WHAT YOU'VE HEARD?
I'M SERIOUS.
IT GOES A LITTLE SOMETHING LIKE THIS...

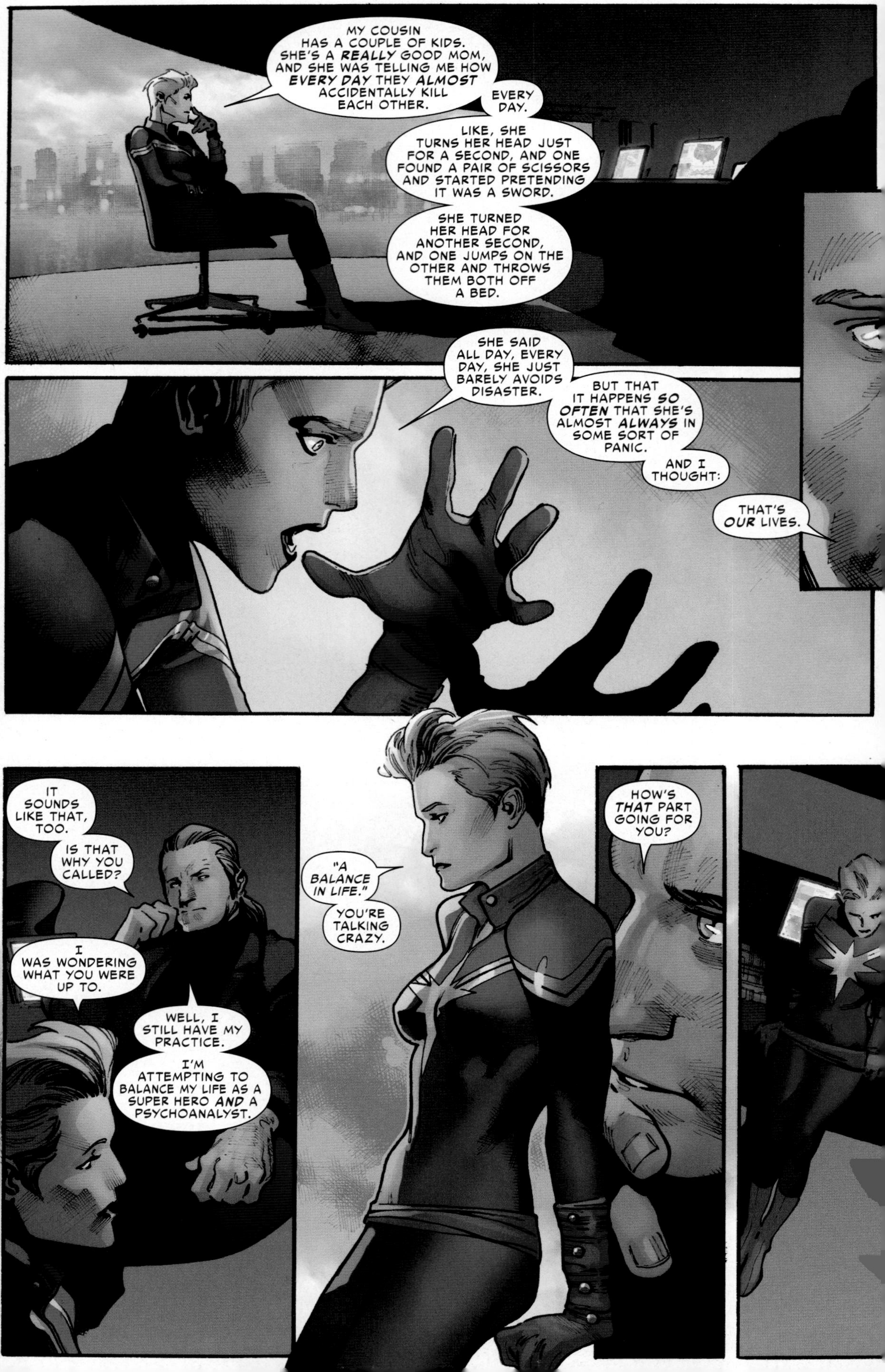

MY COUSIN HAS A COUPLE OF KIDS. SHE'S A **REALLY** GOOD MOM, AND SHE WAS TELLING ME HOW **EVERY DAY** THEY **ALMOST** ACCIDENTALLY KILL EACH OTHER.
EVERY DAY.
LIKE, SHE TURNS HER HEAD JUST FOR A SECOND, AND ONE FOUND A PAIR OF SCISSORS AND STARTED PRETENDING IT WAS A SWORD.
SHE TURNED HER HEAD FOR ANOTHER SECOND, AND ONE JUMPS ON THE OTHER AND THROWS THEM BOTH OFF A BED.
SHE SAID ALL DAY, EVERY DAY, SHE JUST BARELY AVOIDS DISASTER.
BUT THAT IT HAPPENS **SO OFTEN** THAT SHE'S ALMOST **ALWAYS** IN SOME SORT OF PANIC.
AND I THOUGHT:
THAT'S **OUR** LIVES.
IT SOUNDS LIKE THAT, TOO.
IS THAT WHY YOU CALLED?
I WAS WONDERING WHAT YOU WERE UP TO.
WELL, I STILL HAVE MY PRACTICE.
I'M ATTEMPTING TO BALANCE MY LIFE AS A SUPER HERO **AND** A PSYCHOANALYST.
"A BALANCE IN LIFE."
YOU'RE TALKING CRAZY.
HOW'S **THAT** PART GOING FOR YOU?

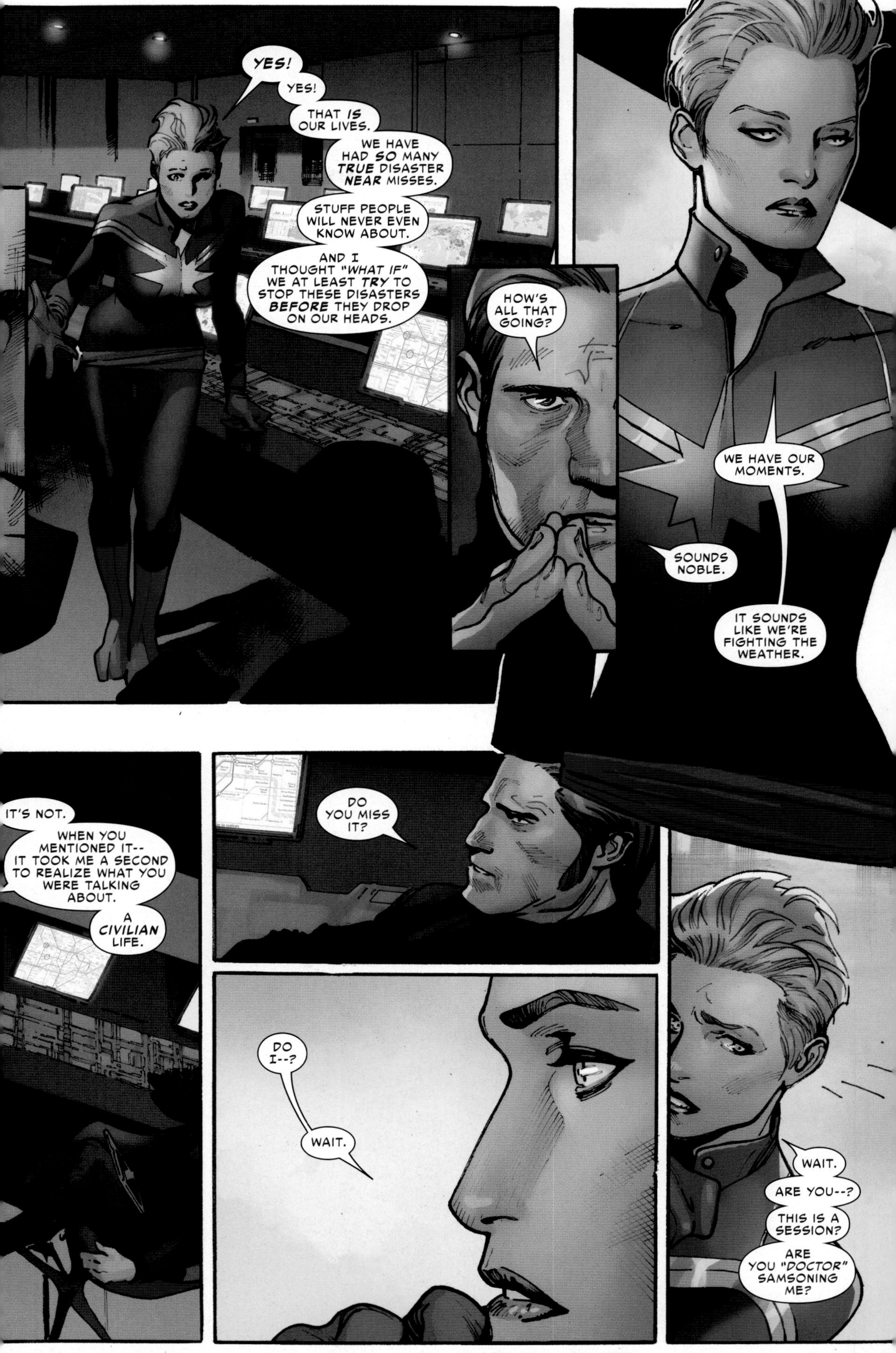
YES!
YES!
THAT *IS* OUR LIVES.
WE HAVE HAD *SO* MANY *TRUE* DISASTER *NEAR* MISSES.
STUFF PEOPLE WILL NEVER EVEN KNOW ABOUT.
AND I THOUGHT "*WHAT IF*" WE AT LEAST *TRY* TO STOP THESE DISASTERS *BEFORE* THEY DROP ON OUR HEADS.
HOW'S ALL THAT GOING?
WE HAVE OUR MOMENTS.
SOUNDS NOBLE.
IT SOUNDS LIKE WE'RE FIGHTING THE WEATHER.
IT'S NOT.
WHEN YOU MENTIONED IT-- IT TOOK ME A SECOND TO REALIZE WHAT YOU WERE TALKING ABOUT.
A *CIVILIAN* LIFE.
DO YOU MISS IT?
DO I--?
WAIT.
WAIT.
ARE YOU--?
THIS IS A SESSION?
ARE YOU "*DOCTOR*" SAMSONING ME?

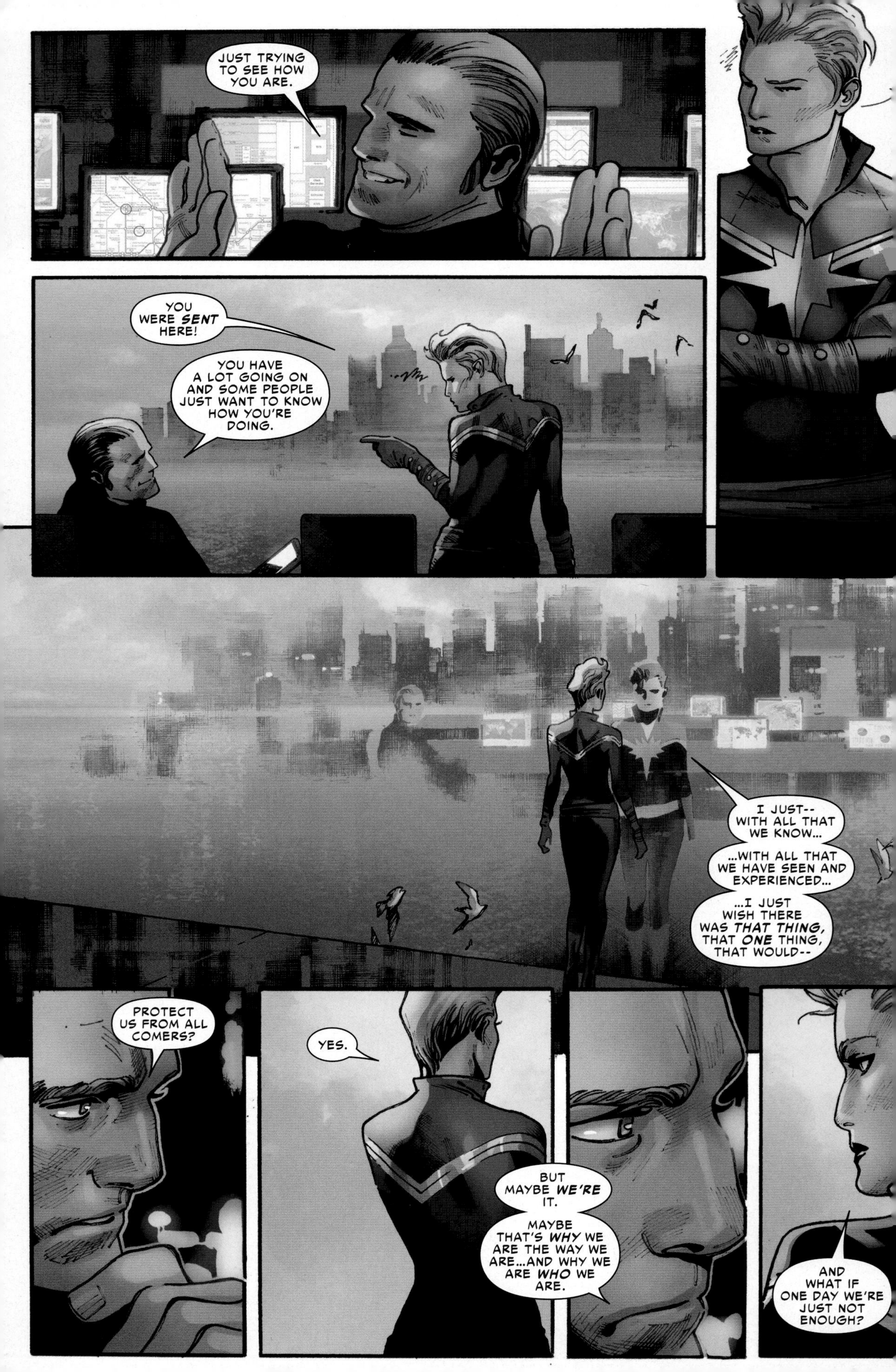
JUST TRYING TO SEE HOW YOU ARE.
YOU WERE *SENT* HERE!
YOU HAVE A LOT GOING ON AND SOME PEOPLE JUST WANT TO KNOW HOW YOU'RE DOING.
I JUST-- WITH ALL THAT WE KNOW...
...WITH ALL THAT WE HAVE SEEN AND EXPERIENCED...
...I JUST WISH THERE WAS *THAT THING,* THAT *ONE* THING, THAT WOULD--
PROTECT US FROM ALL COMERS?
YES.
BUT MAYBE *WE'RE* IT.
MAYBE THAT'S *WHY* WE ARE THE WAY WE ARE...AND WHY WE ARE *WHO* WE ARE.
AND WHAT IF ONE DAY WE'RE JUST NOT ENOUGH?

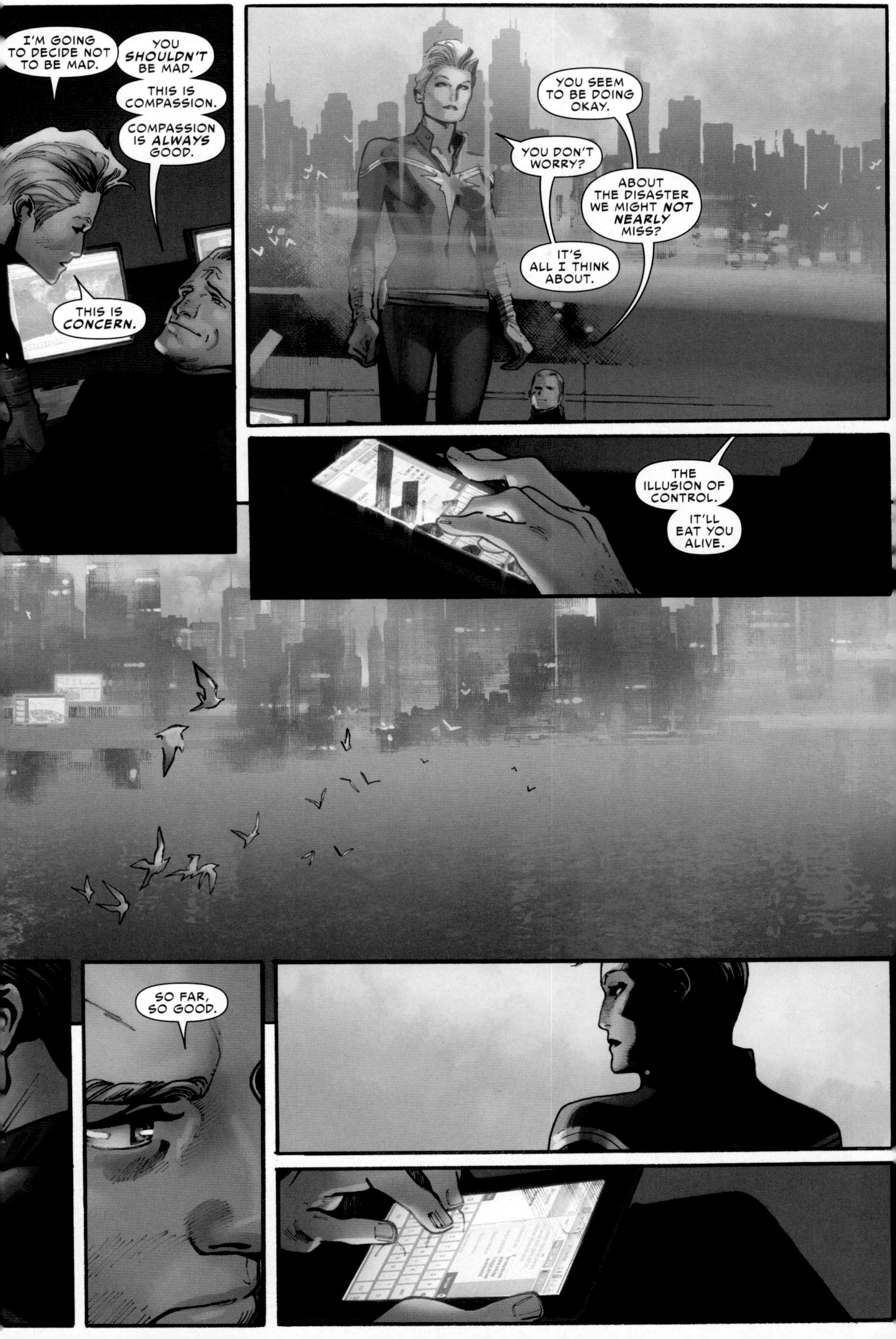
I'M GOING TO DECIDE NOT TO BE MAD.
YOU SHOULDN'T BE MAD.
THIS IS COMPASSION.
COMPASSION IS ALWAYS GOOD.
THIS IS CONCERN.
YOU SEEM TO BE DOING OKAY.
YOU DON'T WORRY?
ABOUT THE DISASTER WE MIGHT NOT NEARLY MISS?
IT'S ALL I THINK ABOUT.
THE ILLUSION OF CONTROL.
IT'LL EAT YOU ALIVE.
SO FAR, SO GOOD.

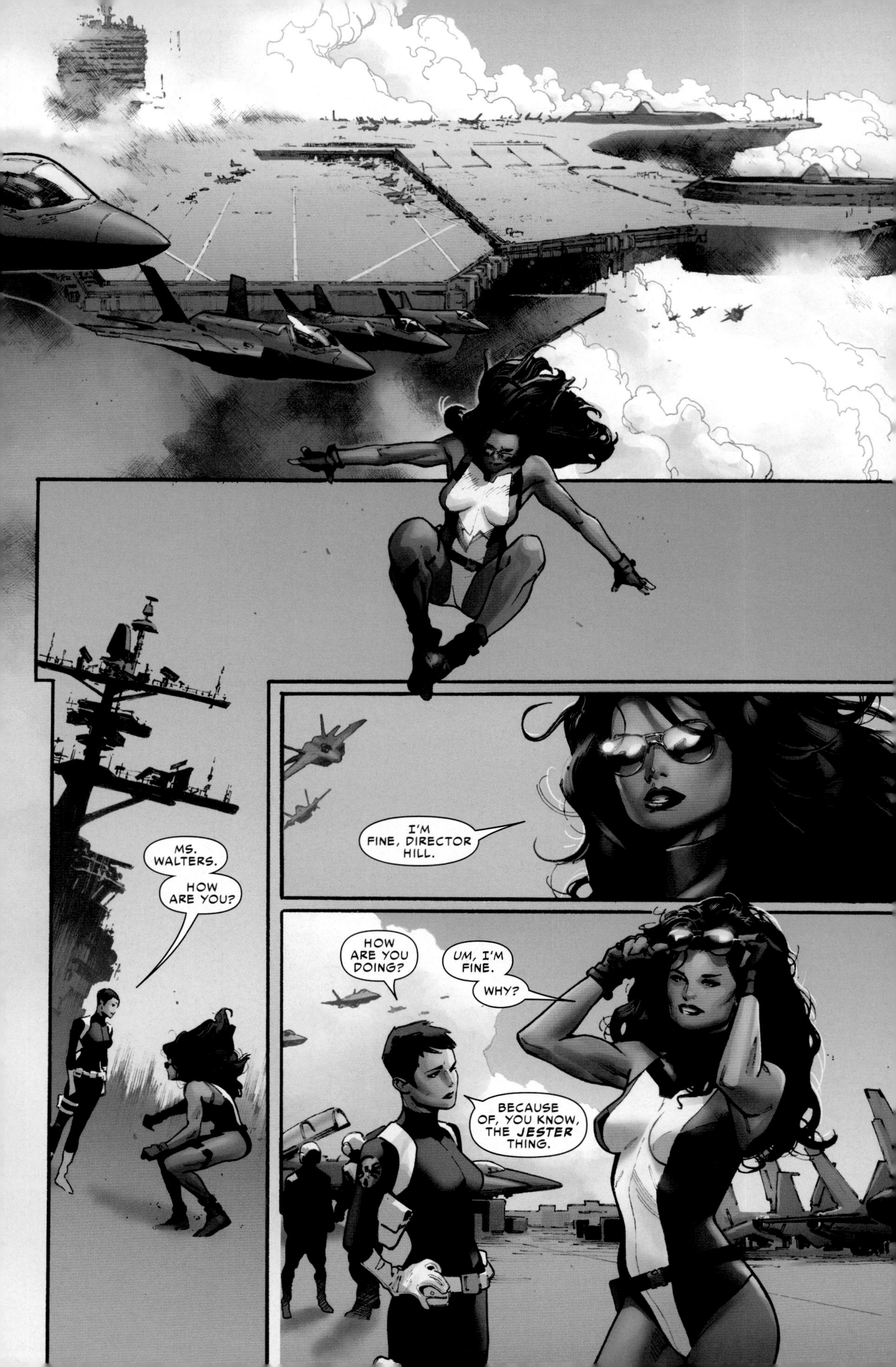
MS. WALTERS.
HOW ARE YOU?
I'M FINE, DIRECTOR HILL.
HOW ARE YOU DOING?
UM, I'M FINE.
WHY?
BECAUSE OF, YOU KNOW, THE JESTER THING.

... WHAT?

NOTHING.

ARE YOU OKAY?

IT'S JUST THAT, FIVE WORDS AGO, THIS BECAME THE LONGEST CONVERSATION WE'VE EVER HAD.

THAT CAN'T BE TRUE.

IS THERE SOMETHING I CAN DO FOR YOU, MA'AM?

THE JESTER. JONATHAN POWERS.

OH, THAT? WELL, YEAH. I'M UPSET.

I LOST A CASE.

I'M SURE.

BUT IT IS REALLY HARD TO GET A JURY TO SEE PAST THE IDEA THAT SOMEONE ONCE DECIDED TO DRESS UP LIKE A PLAYING CARD CHARACTER AND ROB BANKS.

IT'S A HARD IMAGE TO GET PAST.

SO YOU'RE OKAY.

I'VE LOST CASES BEFORE... BUT NOW THIS GUY IS IN JAIL AGAIN.

I'M GOING TO APPEAL THE HOLY HELL OUT OF THIS BECAUSE--

JENNIFER... HE'S DEAD.

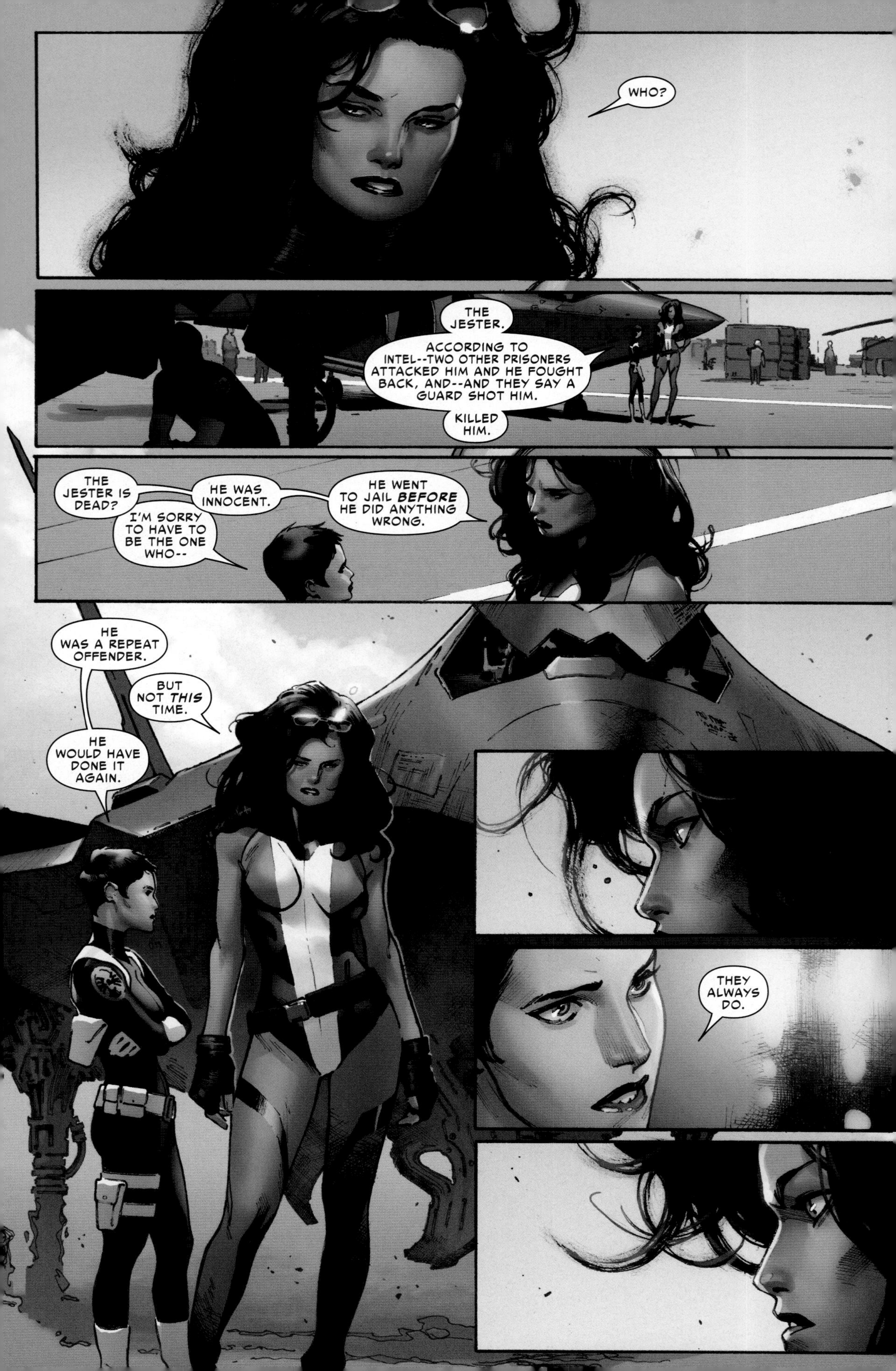
WHO?
THE JESTER.
ACCORDING TO INTEL--TWO OTHER PRISONERS ATTACKED HIM AND HE FOUGHT BACK, AND--AND THEY SAY A GUARD SHOT HIM.
KILLED HIM.
THE JESTER IS DEAD?
I'M SORRY TO HAVE TO BE THE ONE WHO--
HE WAS INNOCENT.
HE WENT TO JAIL *BEFORE* HE DID ANYTHING WRONG.
HE WAS A REPEAT OFFENDER.
HE WOULD HAVE DONE IT AGAIN.
BUT NOT *THIS* TIME.
THEY ALWAYS DO.

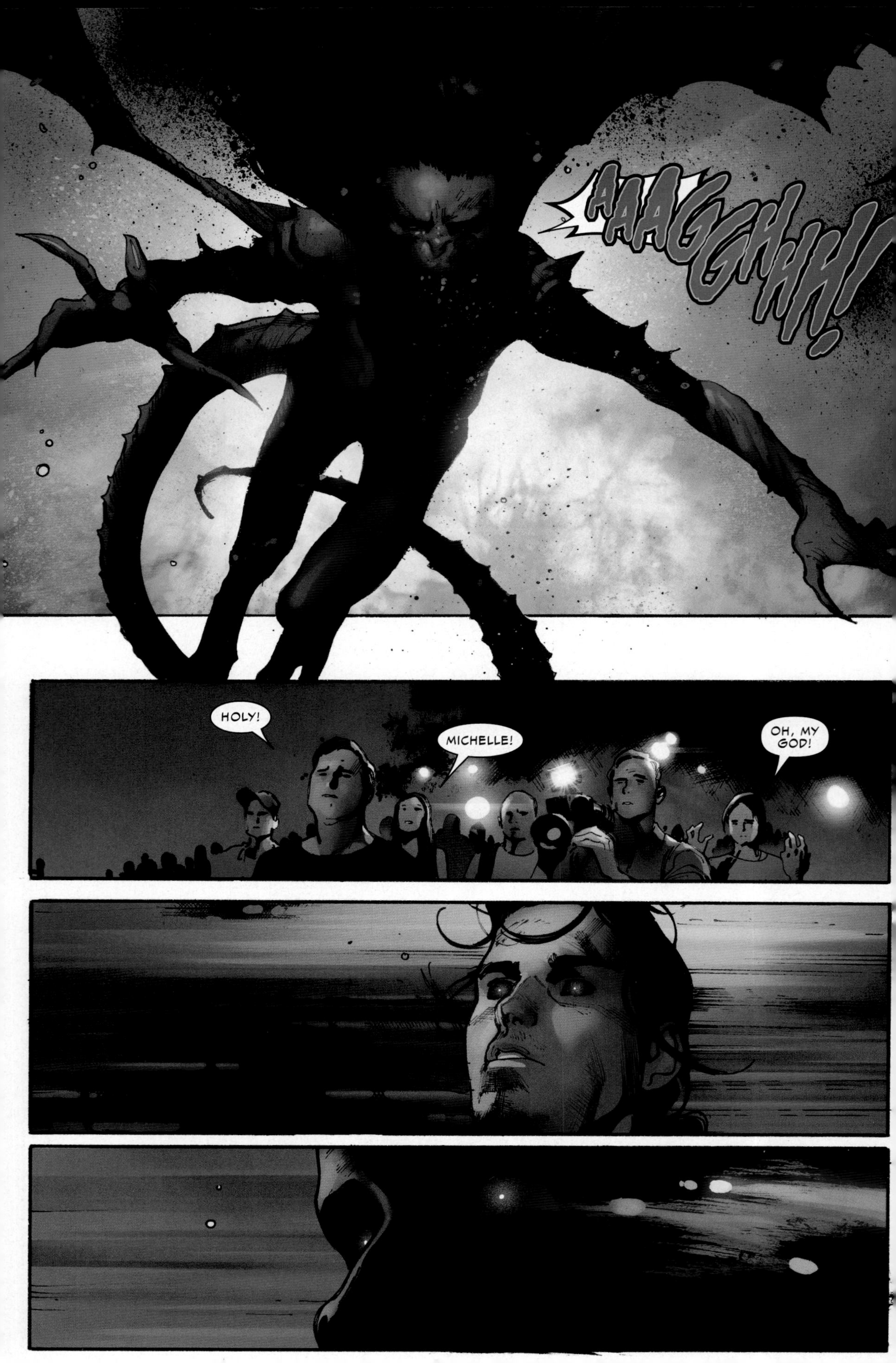
AAAGGHHH!
HOLY!
MICHELLE!
OH, MY GOD!

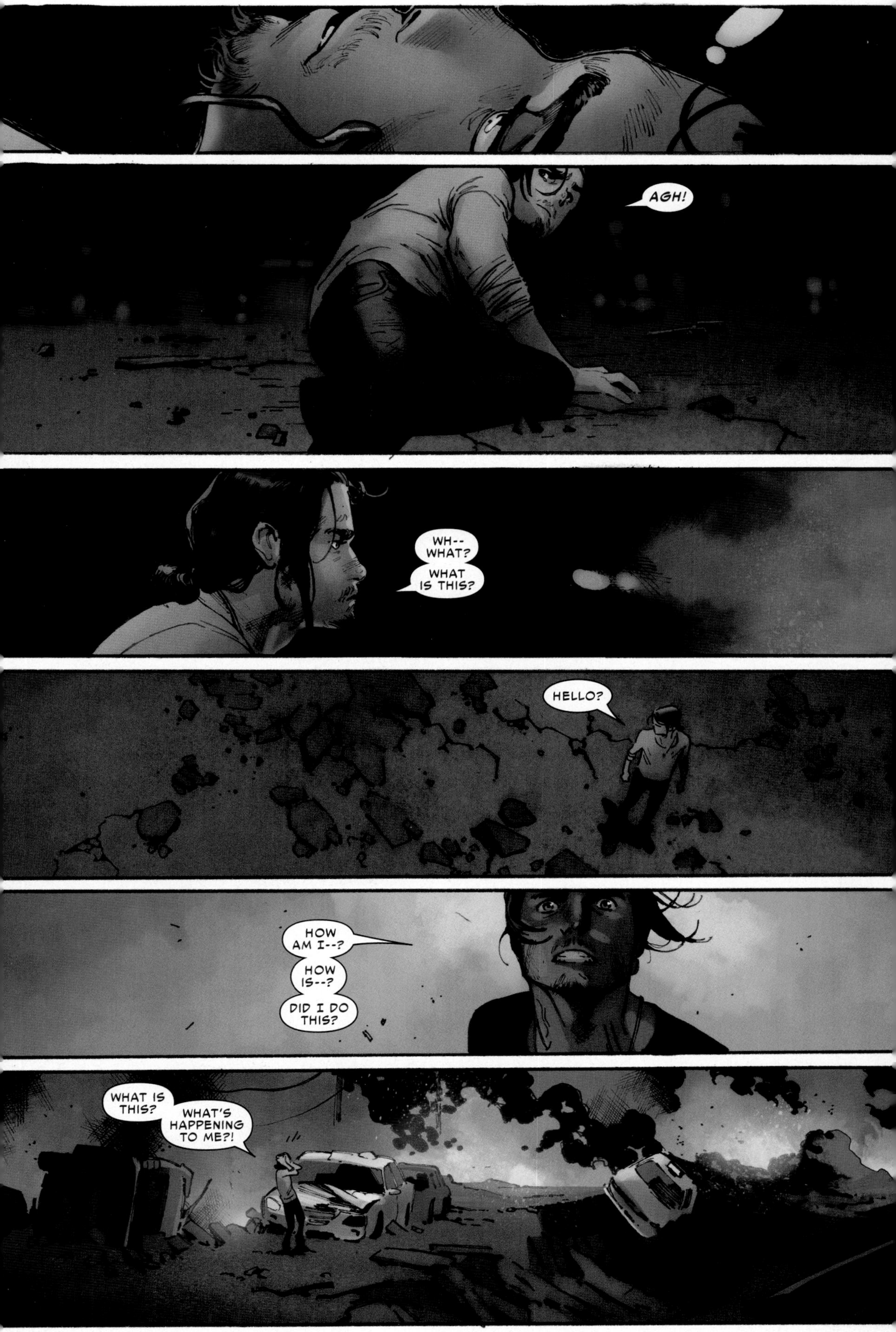

AGH!
WH-- WHAT?
WHAT IS THIS?
HELLO?
HOW AM I--?
HOW IS--?
DID I DO THIS?
WHAT IS THIS?
WHAT'S HAPPENING TO ME?!

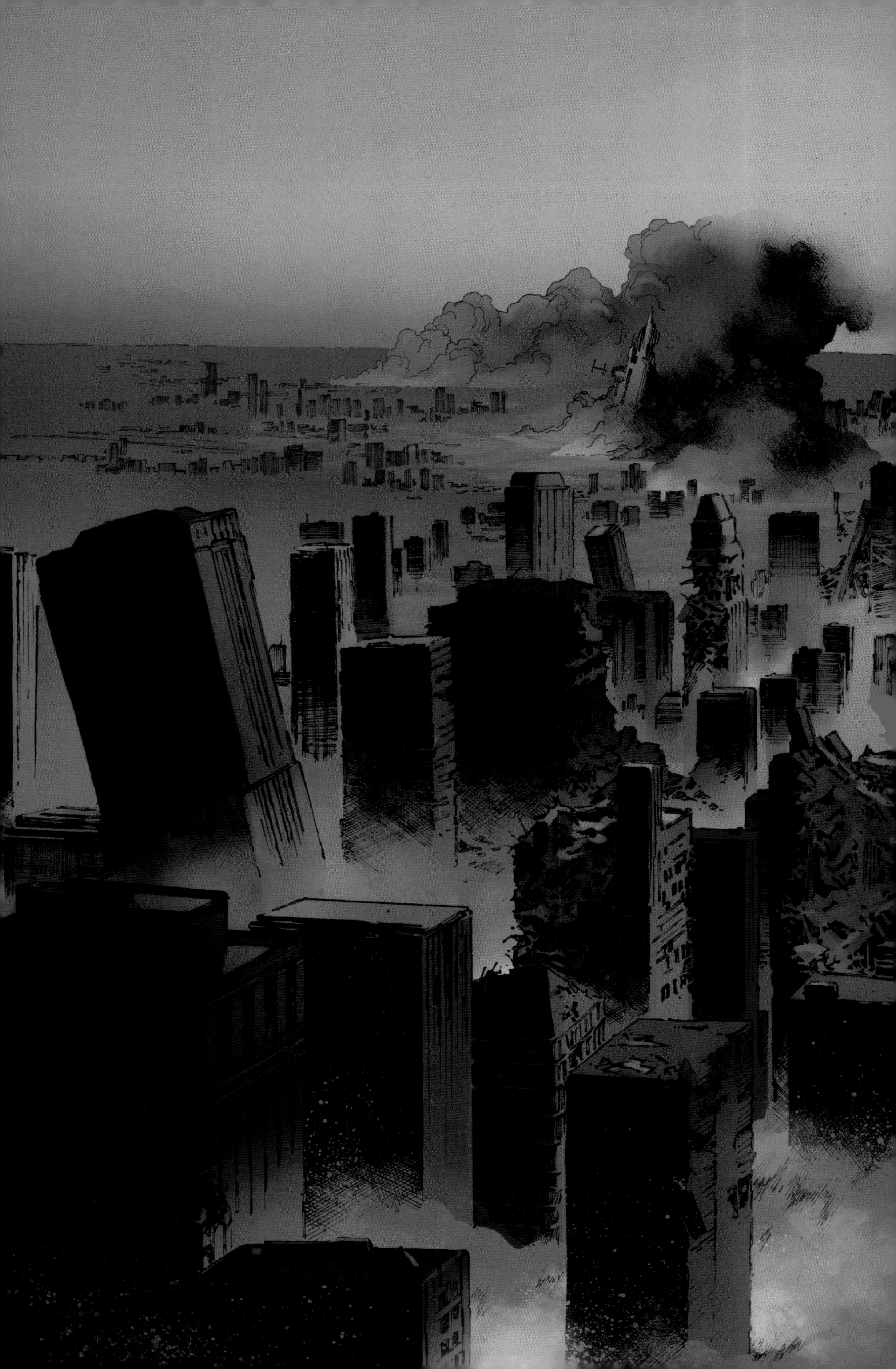

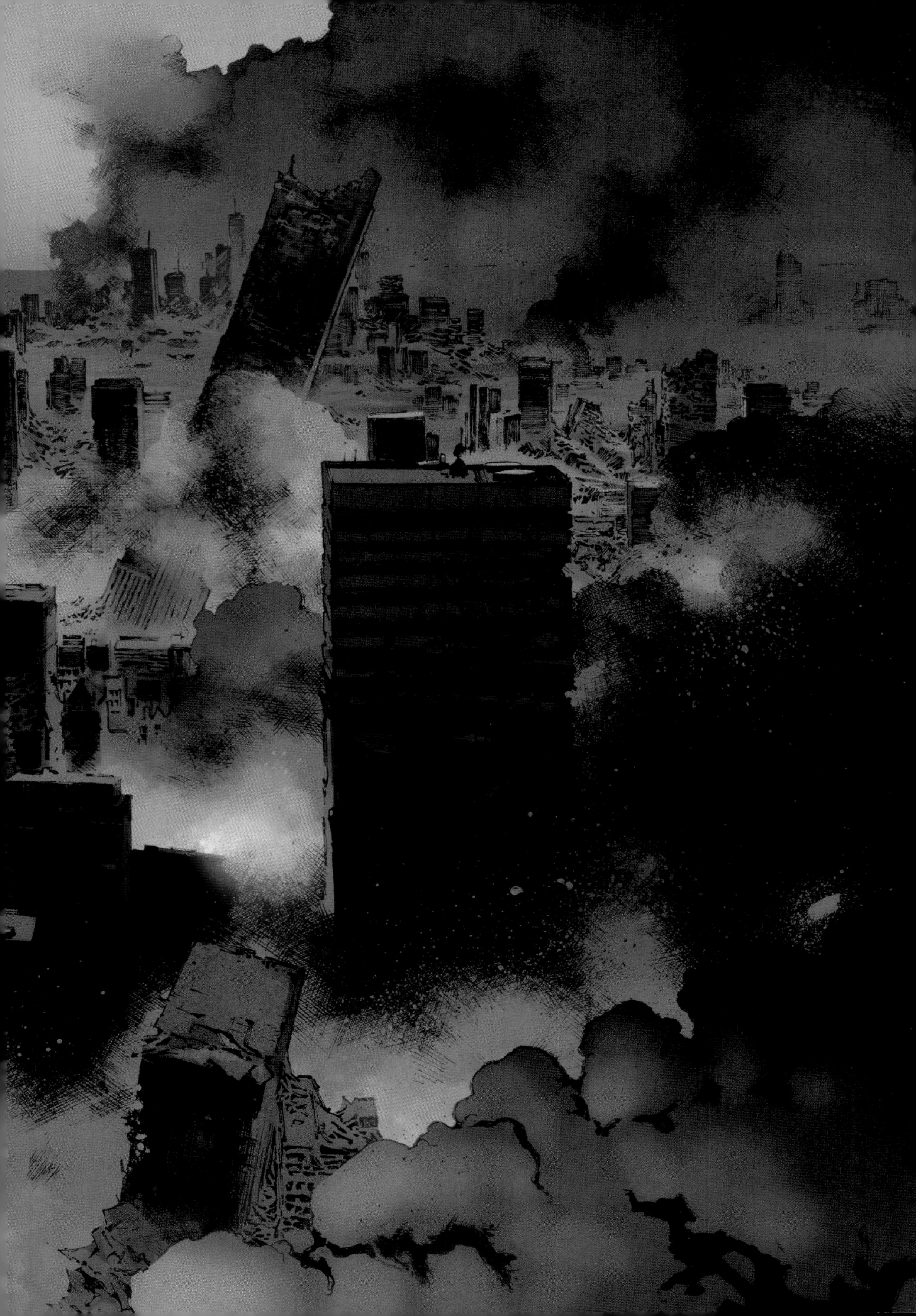

FREE COMIC BOOK DAY

CIVIL WAR II

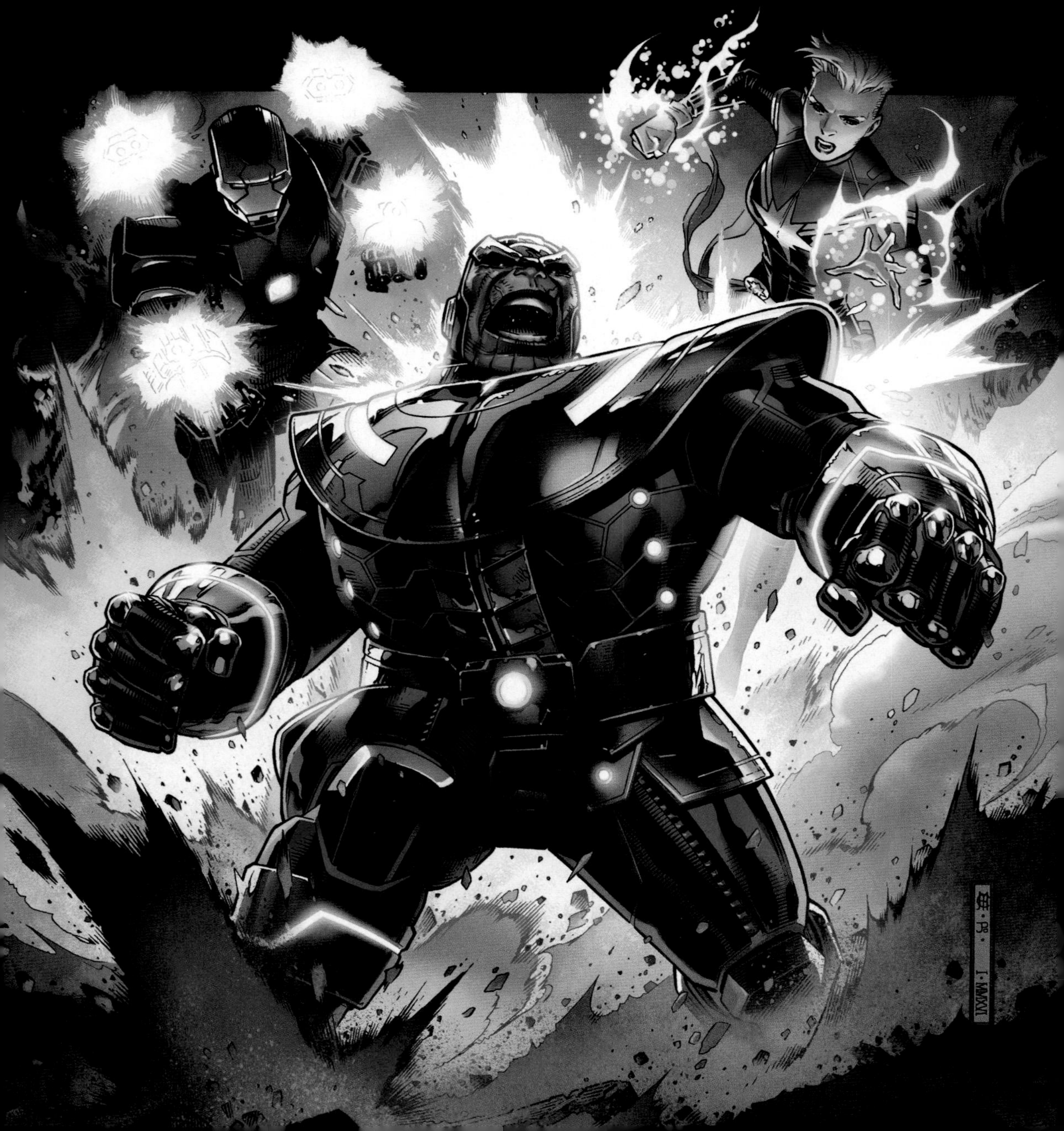

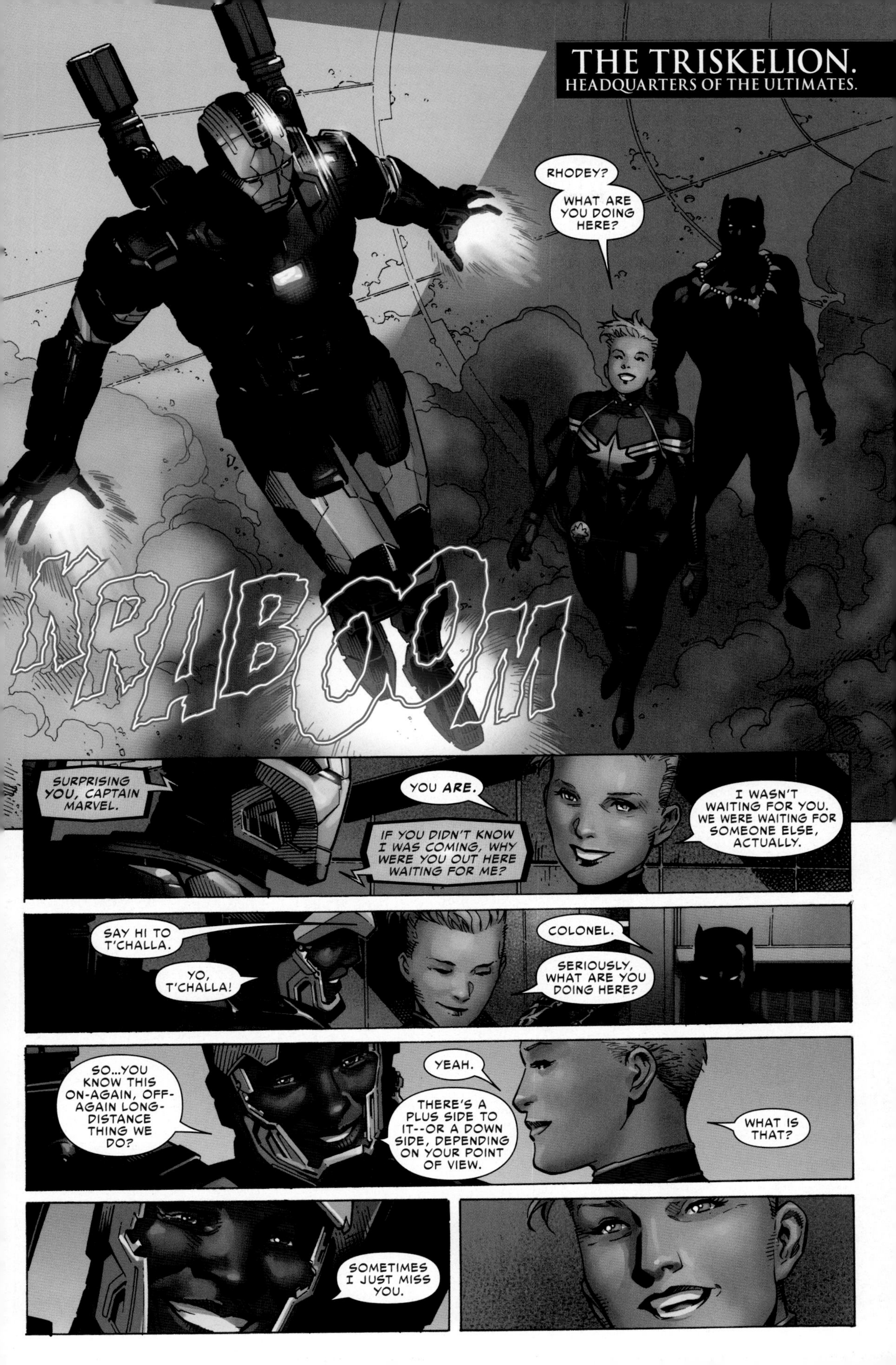
THE TRISKELION.
HEADQUARTERS OF THE ULTIMATES.
RHODEY?
WHAT ARE YOU DOING HERE?
KRABOOM
SURPRISING YOU, CAPTAIN MARVEL.
YOU ARE.
IF YOU DIDN'T KNOW I WAS COMING, WHY WERE YOU OUT HERE WAITING FOR ME?
I WASN'T WAITING FOR YOU. WE WERE WAITING FOR SOMEONE ELSE, ACTUALLY.
SAY HI TO T'CHALLA.
YO, T'CHALLA!
COLONEL.
SERIOUSLY, WHAT ARE YOU DOING HERE?
SO...YOU KNOW THIS ON-AGAIN, OFF-AGAIN LONG-DISTANCE THING WE DO?
YEAH.
THERE'S A PLUS SIDE TO IT--OR A DOWN SIDE, DEPENDING ON YOUR POINT OF VIEW.
WHAT IS THAT?
SOMETIMES I JUST MISS YOU.

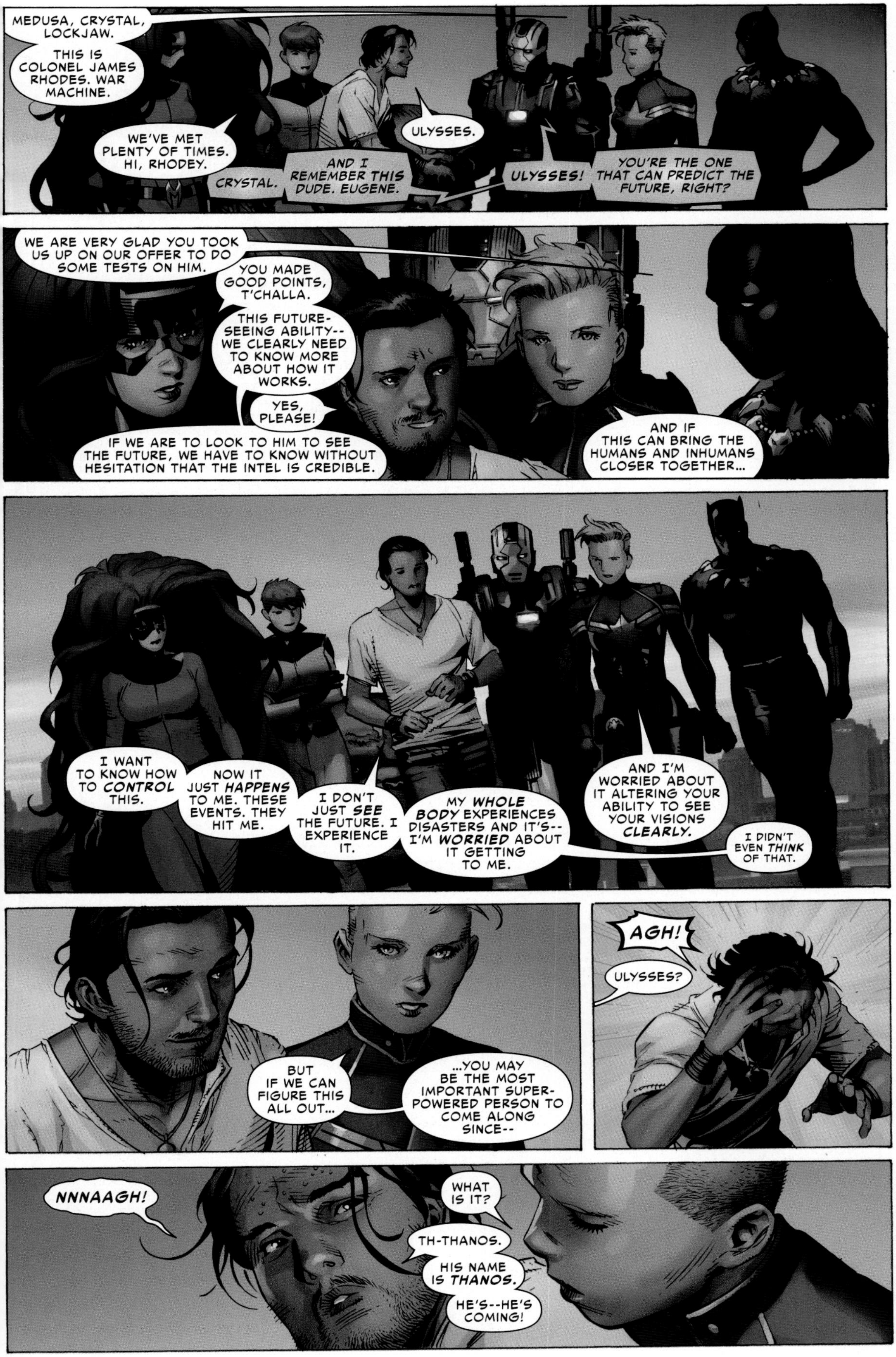
MEDUSA, CRYSTAL, LOCKJAW.
THIS IS COLONEL JAMES RHODES. WAR MACHINE.
WE'VE MET PLENTY OF TIMES. HI, RHODEY.
ULYSSES.
CRYSTAL.
AND I REMEMBER THIS DUDE. EUGENE.
ULYSSES!
YOU'RE THE ONE THAT CAN PREDICT THE FUTURE, RIGHT?
WE ARE VERY GLAD YOU TOOK US UP ON OUR OFFER TO DO SOME TESTS ON HIM.
YOU MADE GOOD POINTS, T'CHALLA.
THIS FUTURE-SEEING ABILITY-- WE CLEARLY NEED TO KNOW MORE ABOUT HOW IT WORKS.
YES, PLEASE!
IF WE ARE TO LOOK TO HIM TO SEE THE FUTURE, WE HAVE TO KNOW WITHOUT HESITATION THAT THE INTEL IS CREDIBLE.
AND IF THIS CAN BRING THE HUMANS AND INHUMANS CLOSER TOGETHER...
I WANT TO KNOW HOW TO CONTROL THIS.
NOW IT JUST HAPPENS TO ME. THESE EVENTS. THEY HIT ME.
I DON'T JUST SEE THE FUTURE. I EXPERIENCE IT.
MY WHOLE BODY EXPERIENCES DISASTERS AND IT'S-- I'M WORRIED ABOUT IT GETTING TO ME.
AND I'M WORRIED ABOUT IT ALTERING YOUR ABILITY TO SEE YOUR VISIONS CLEARLY.
I DIDN'T EVEN THINK OF THAT.
BUT IF WE CAN FIGURE THIS ALL OUT...
...YOU MAY BE THE MOST IMPORTANT SUPER-POWERED PERSON TO COME ALONG SINCE--
AGH!
ULYSSES?
NNNAAGH!
WHAT IS IT?
TH-THANOS.
HIS NAME IS THANOS.
HE'S--HE'S COMING!

PROJECT P.E.G.A.S.U.S.
MOUNT ATHENA, NEW YORK.

A SPECIAL INSTALLATION DESIGNED
TO INVESTIGATE UNEXPLAINABLE
OR ALIEN ENERGY SOURCES.

THE ENTIRE PROJECT IS CLEAR. ALL *"ITEMS OF POWER"* HAVE BEEN EVACUATED.

ALL PERSONNEL HAVE BEEN EVACUATED.

LIFE-MODEL DECOYS, SHE-HULK.

THEN WHO ARE ALL THESE--?

WE WANT HIM TO THINK EVERYTHING IS KOSHER.

NICE.

NOT BAD FOR THREE HOURS NOTICE.

HOW LONG DO WE WAIT?

IF THIS WORKS...

ANY MINUTE NOW...

CALL ME CRAZY, I ACTUALLY THINK IT--*HOLD ON!*

KRAKDOOM

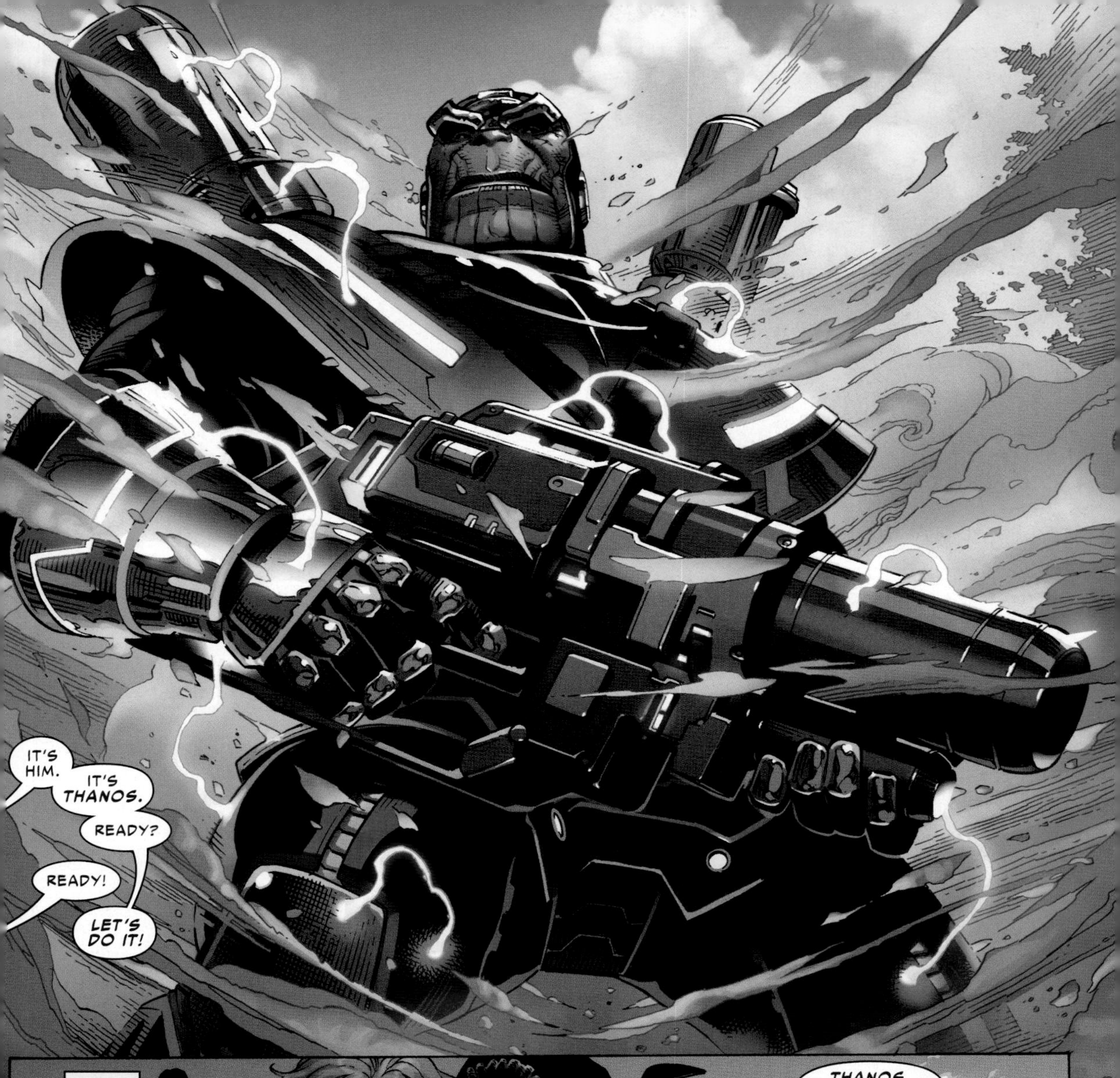

IT'S HIM.
IT'S THANOS.
READY?
READY!
LET'S DO IT!

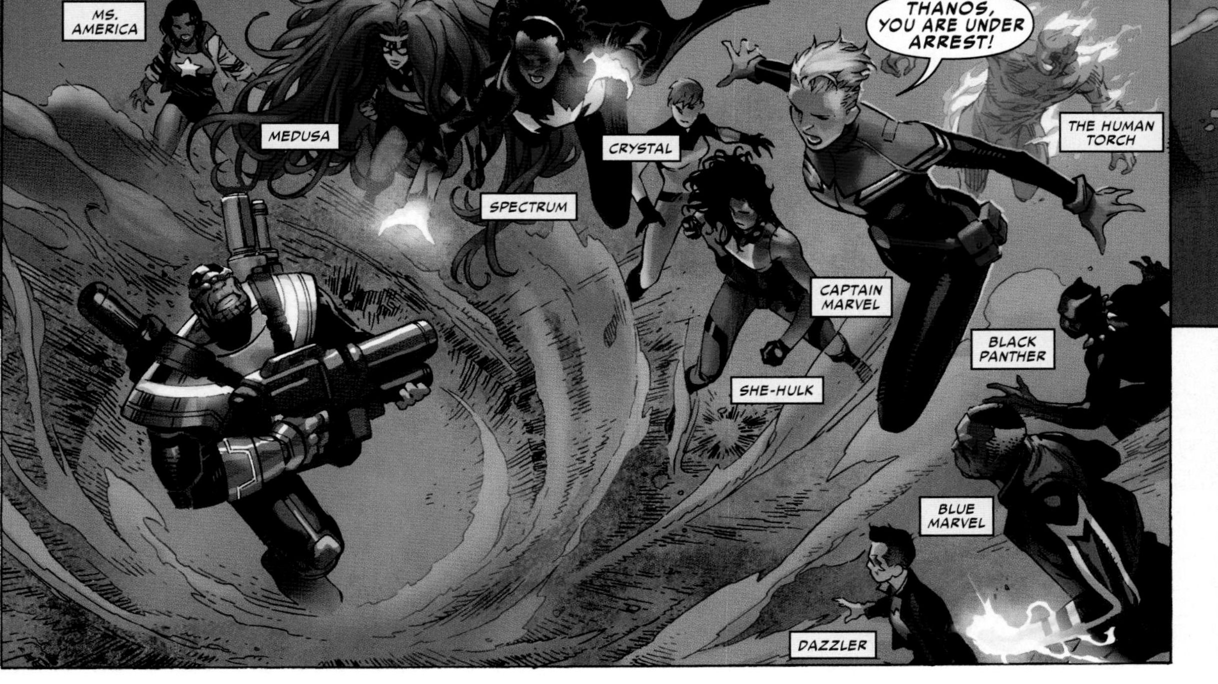

MS. AMERICA
MEDUSA
THANOS, YOU ARE UNDER ARREST!
CRYSTAL
THE HUMAN TORCH
SPECTRUM
CAPTAIN MARVEL
BLACK PANTHER
SHE-HULK
BLUE MARVEL
DAZZLER

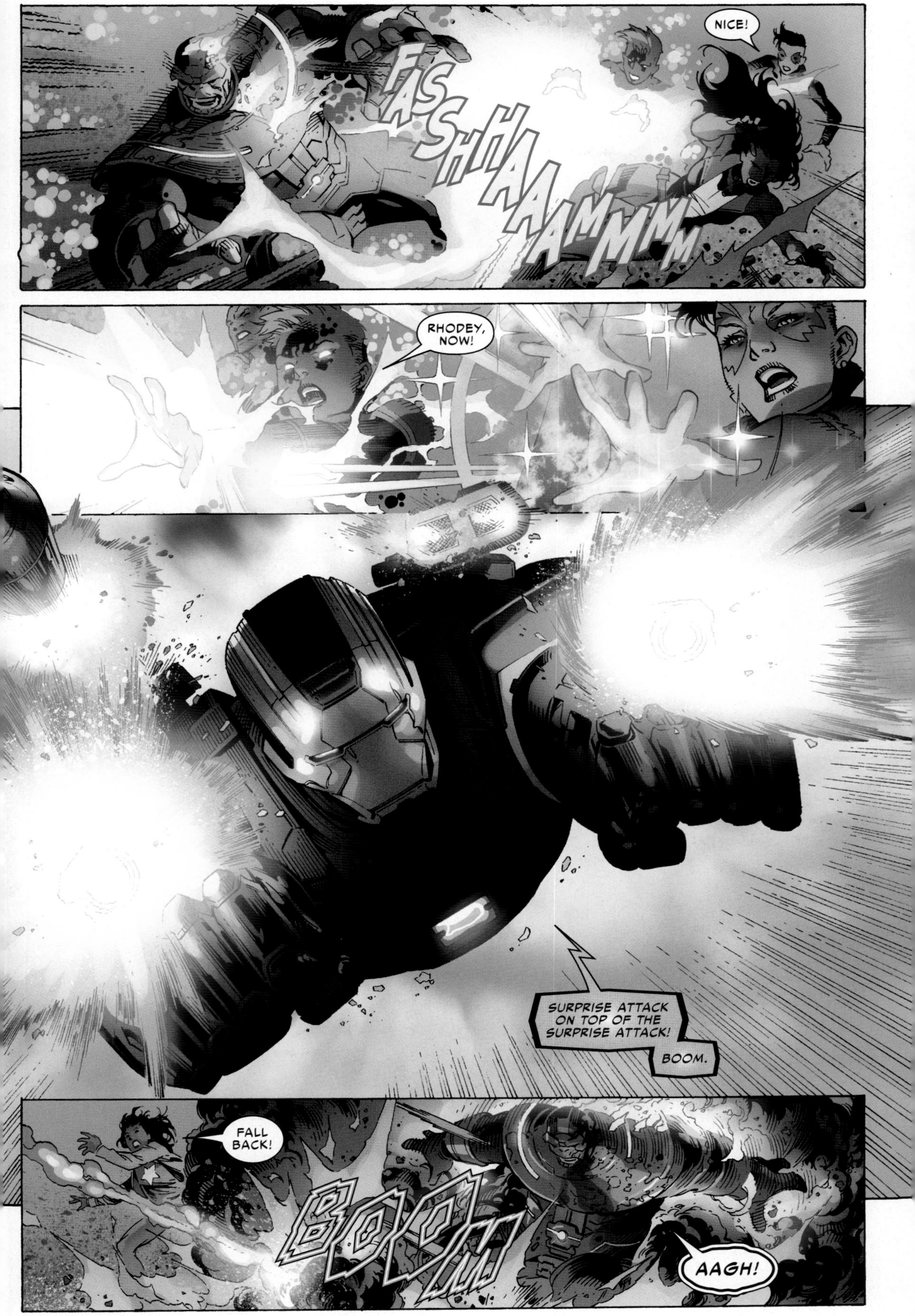
NICE!
FASSHHAAAMMMM
RHODEY, NOW!
SURPRISE ATTACK ON TOP OF THE SURPRISE ATTACK!
BOOM.
FALL BACK!
BOOM
AAGH!

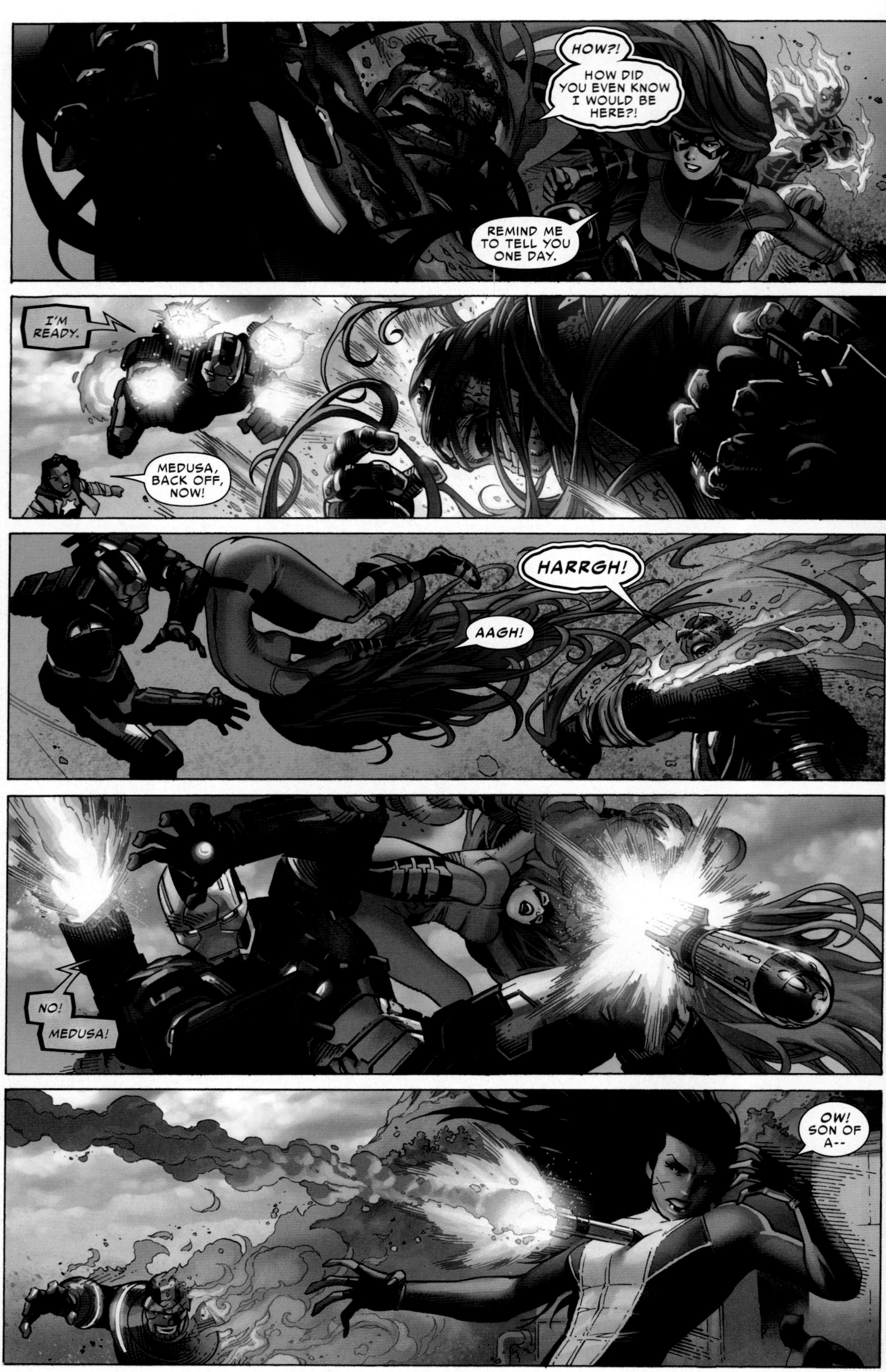
HOW?!
HOW DID YOU EVEN KNOW I WOULD BE HERE?!
REMIND ME TO TELL YOU ONE DAY.
I'M READY.
MEDUSA, BACK OFF, NOW!
HARRGH!
AAGH!
NO!
MEDUSA!
OW! SON OF A--

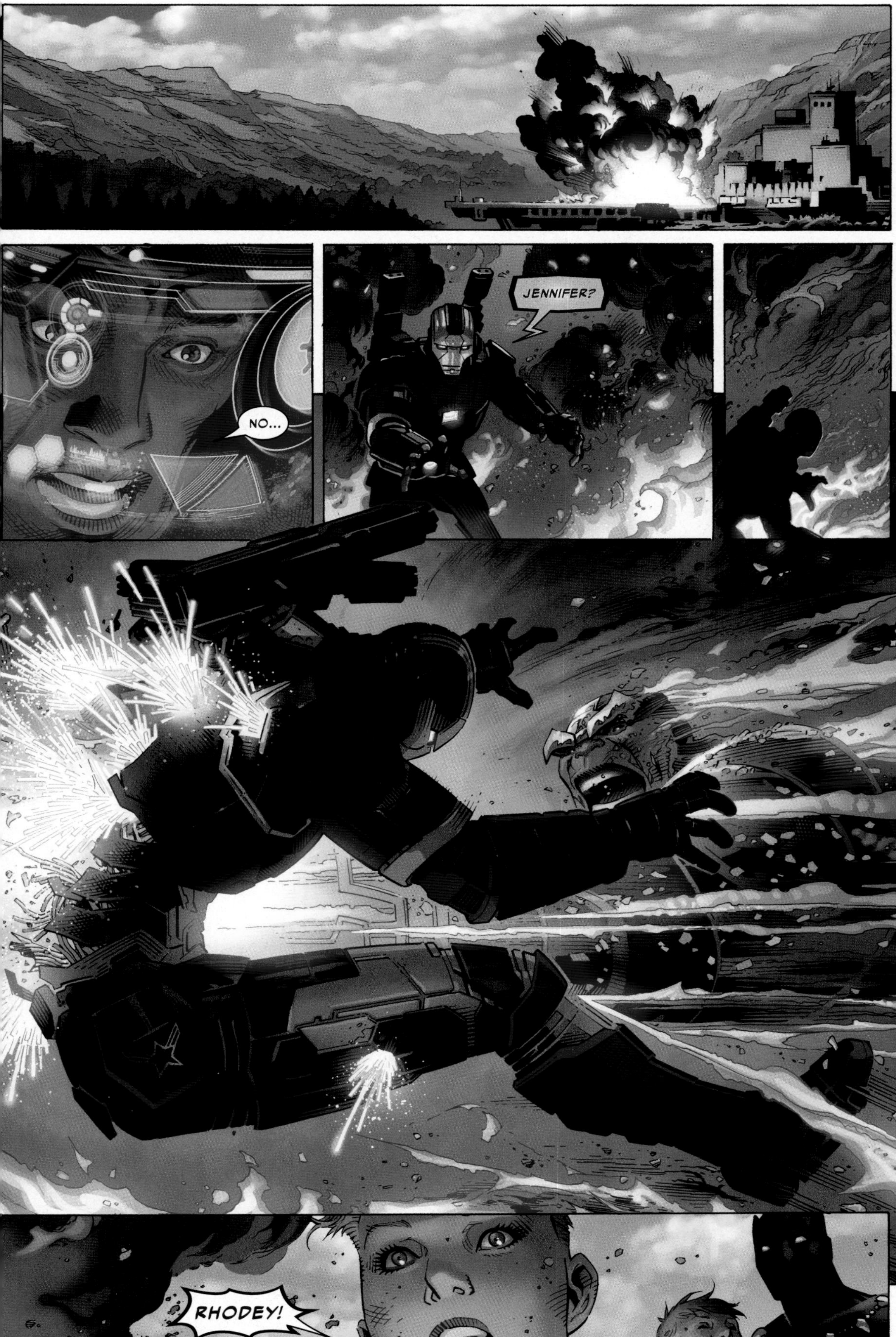
NO...
JENNIFER?
RHODEY!

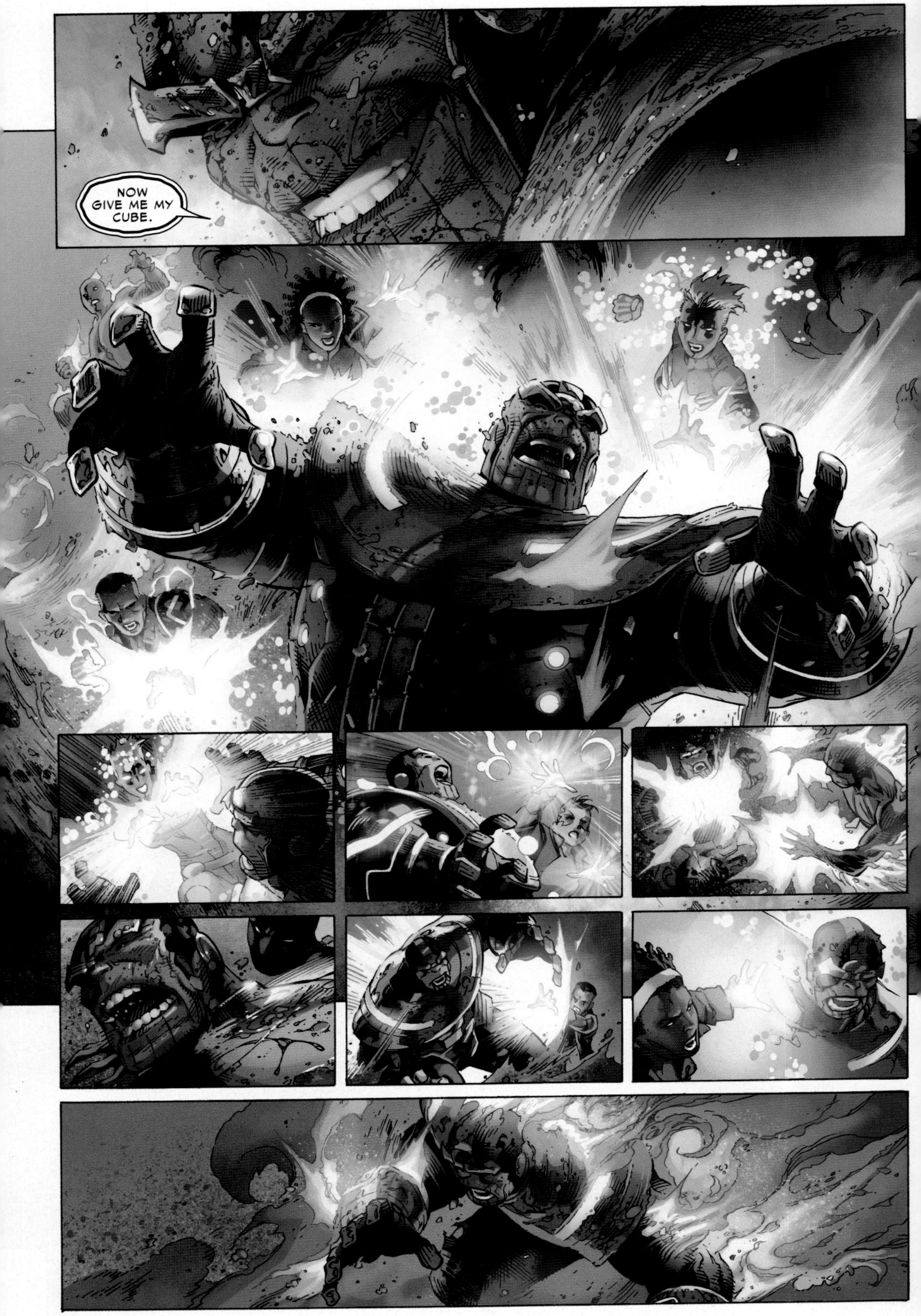
NOW GIVE ME MY CUBE.

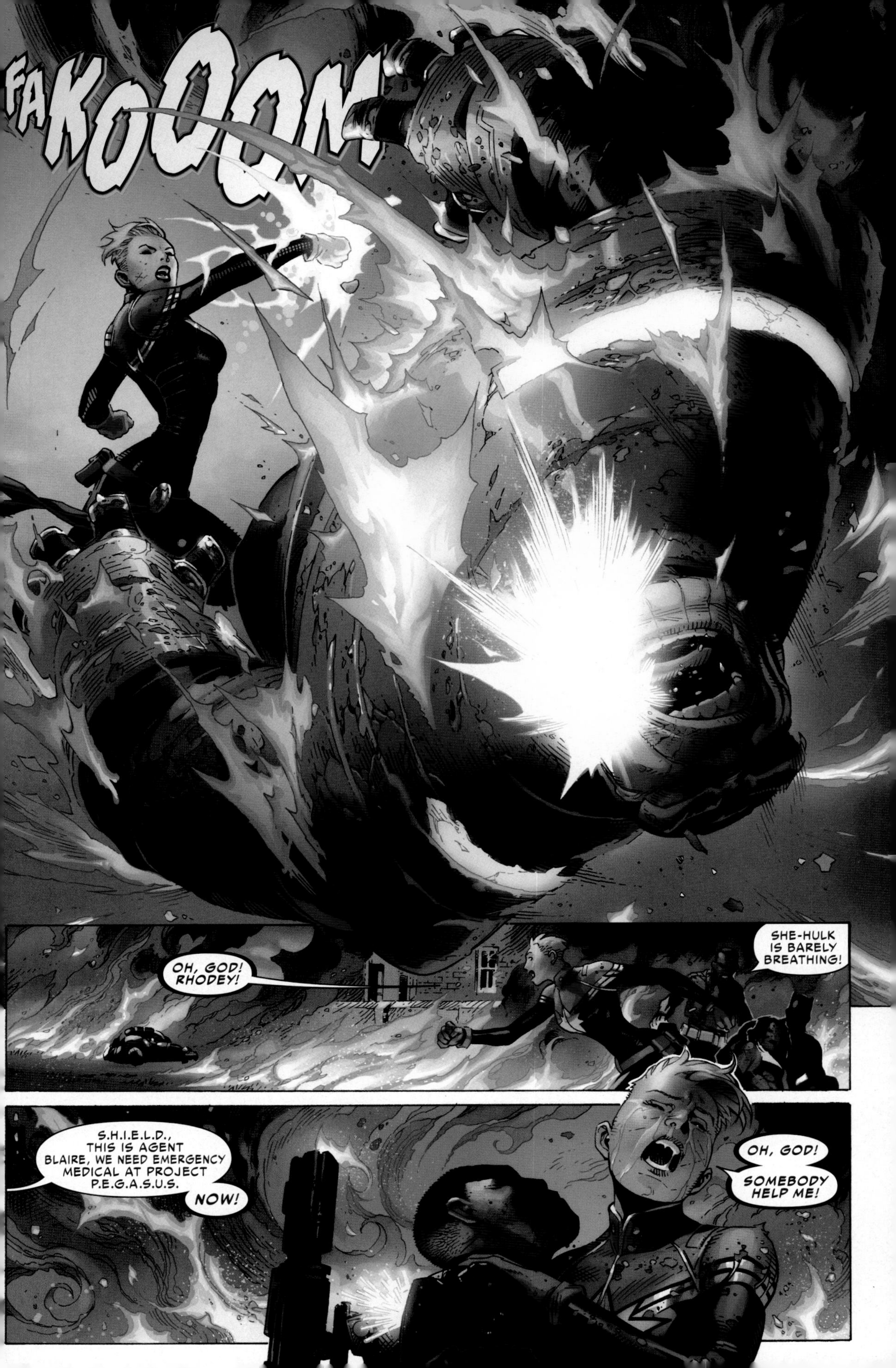
FAKOOOM
OH, GOD! RHODEY!
SHE-HULK IS BARELY BREATHING!
S.H.I.E.L.D., THIS IS AGENT BLAIRE, WE NEED EMERGENCY MEDICAL AT PROJECT P.E.G.A.S.U.S.
NOW!
OH, GOD!
SOMEBODY HELP ME!

CIVIL WAR II #1

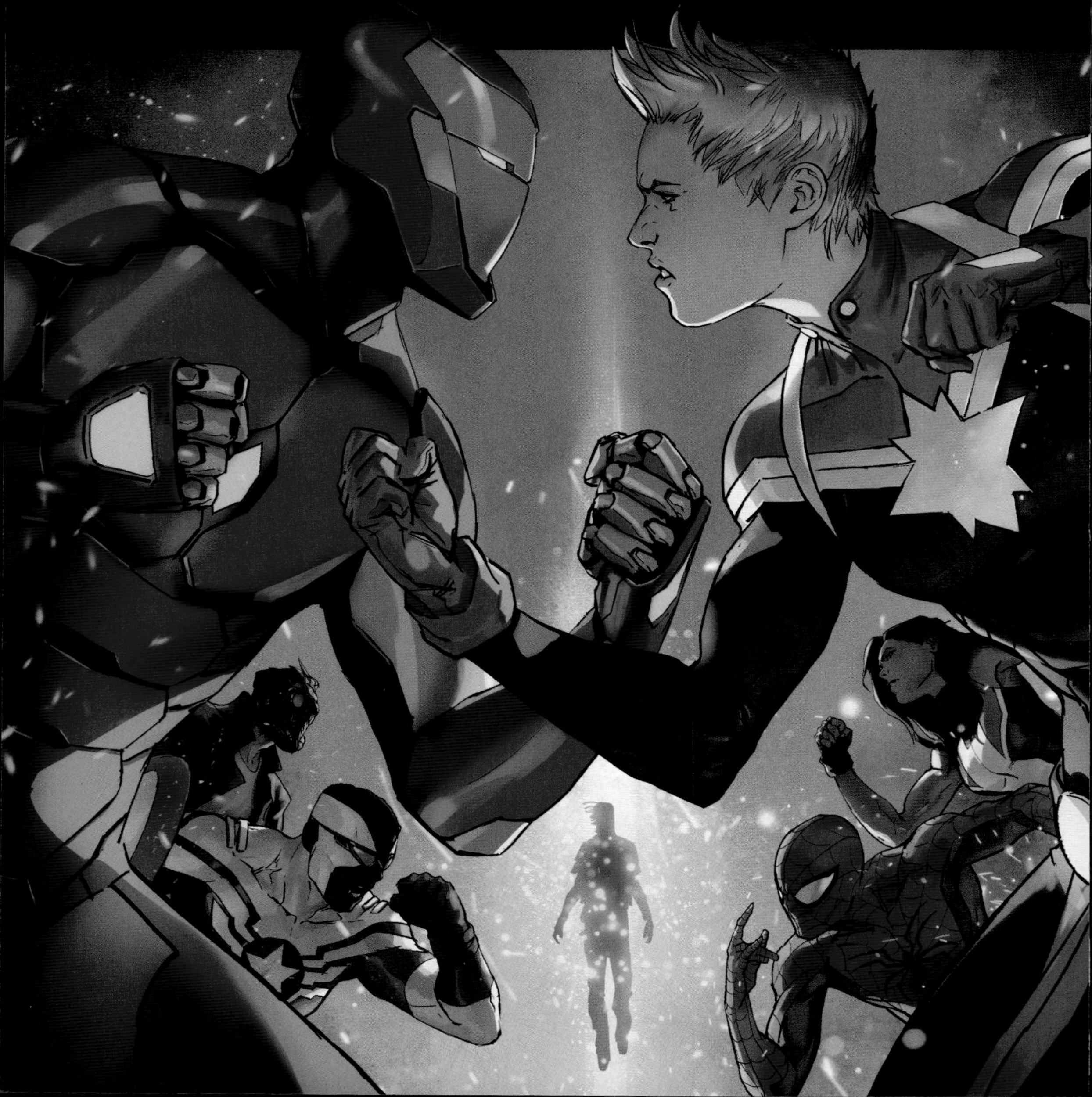

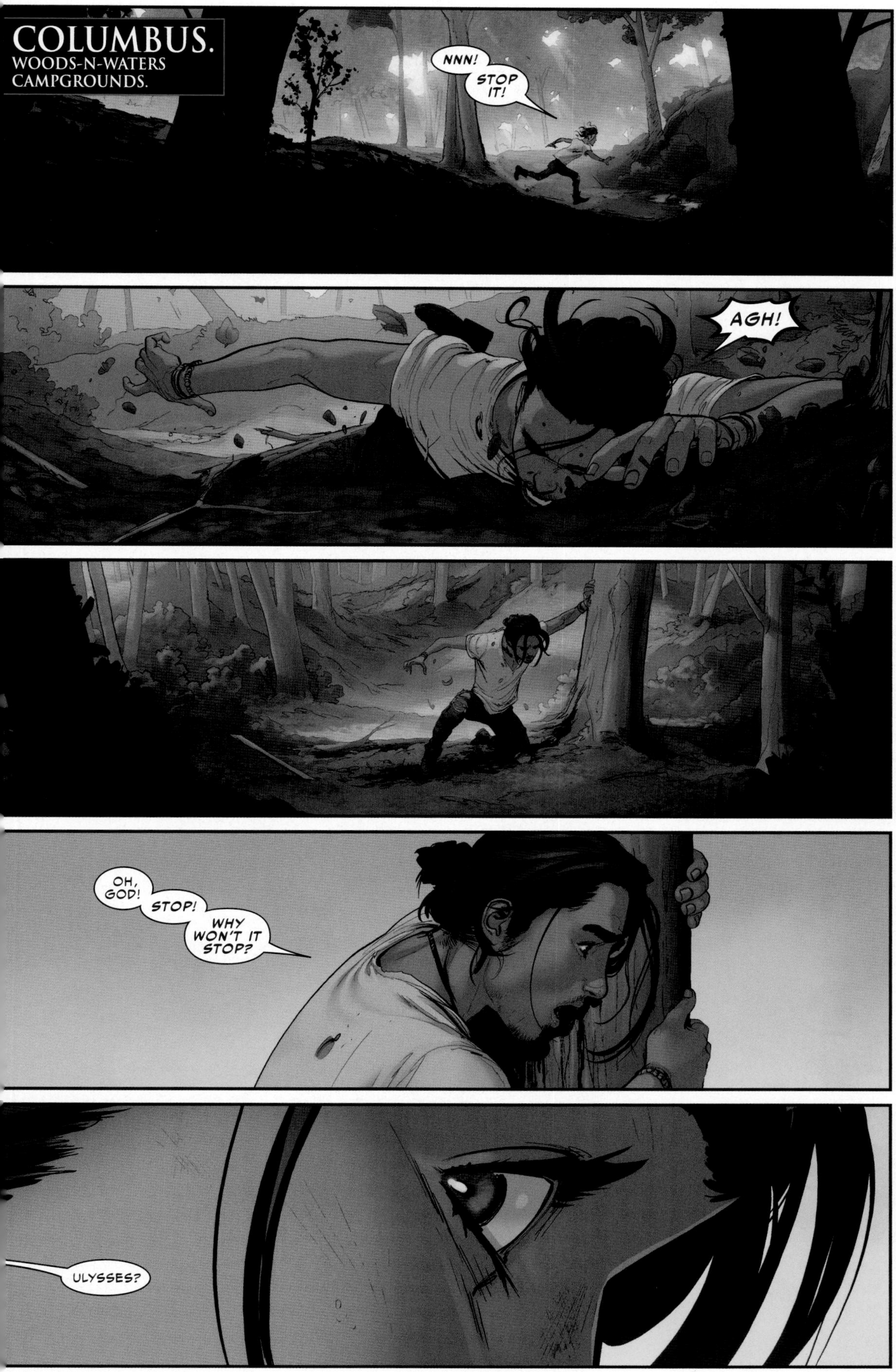
COLUMBUS.
WOODS-N-WATERS CAMPGROUNDS.
NNN!
STOP IT!
AGH!
OH, GOD!
STOP!
WHY WON'T IT STOP?
ULYSSES?

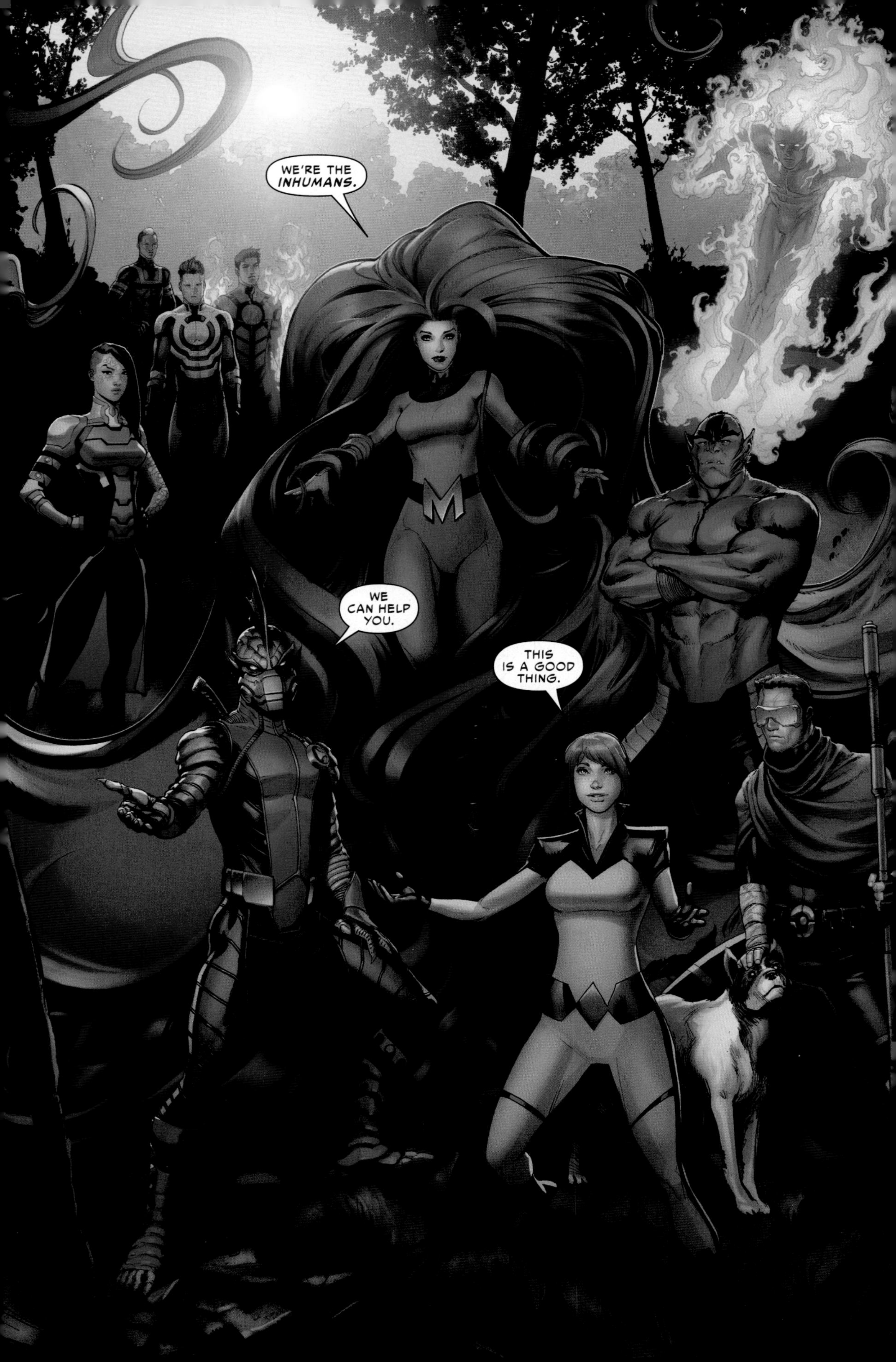
WE'RE THE *INHUMANS.*
WE CAN HELP YOU.
THIS IS A GOOD THING.

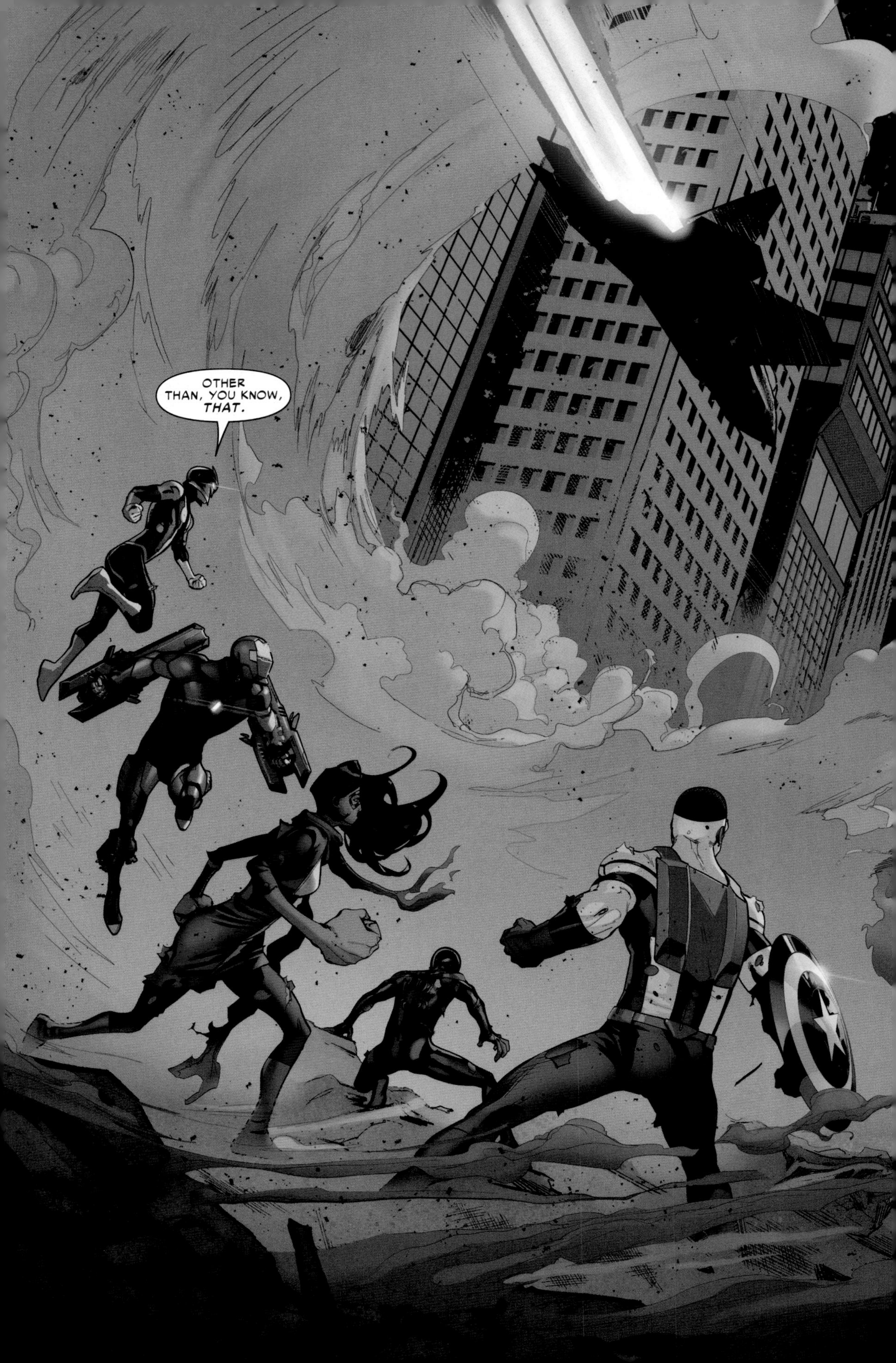
OTHER THAN, YOU KNOW, *THAT*.

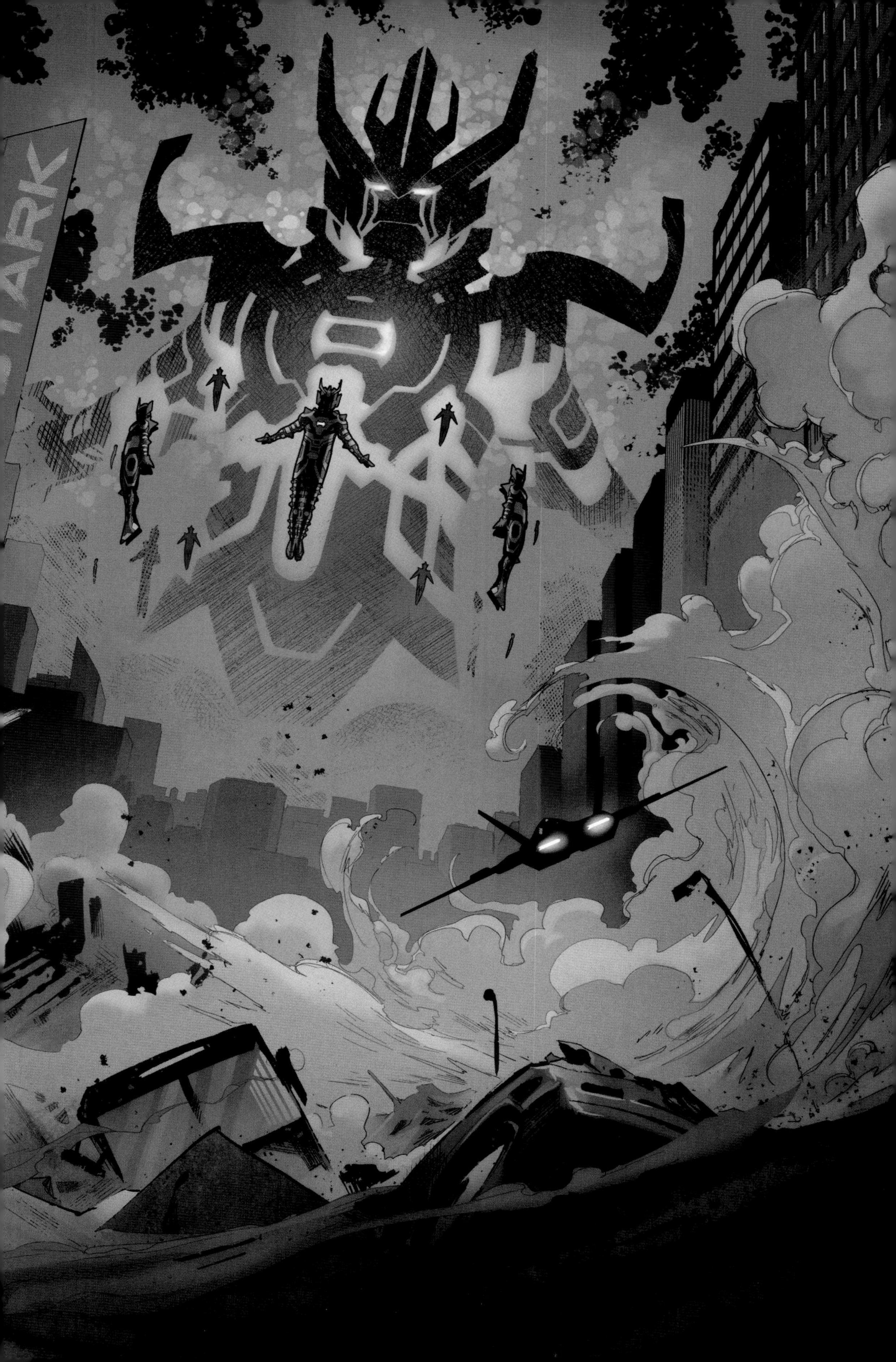
ARK

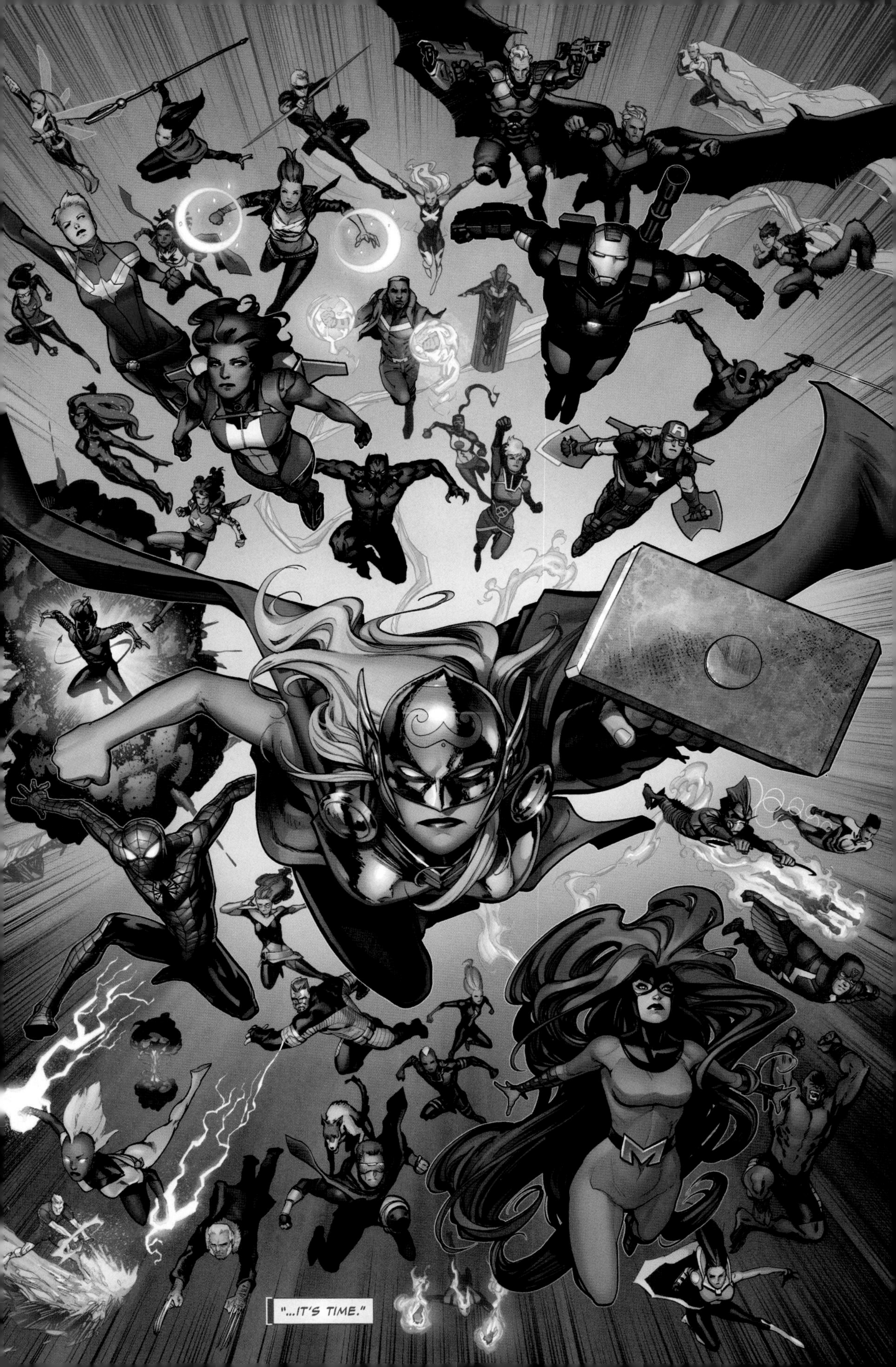
"...IT'S TIME."

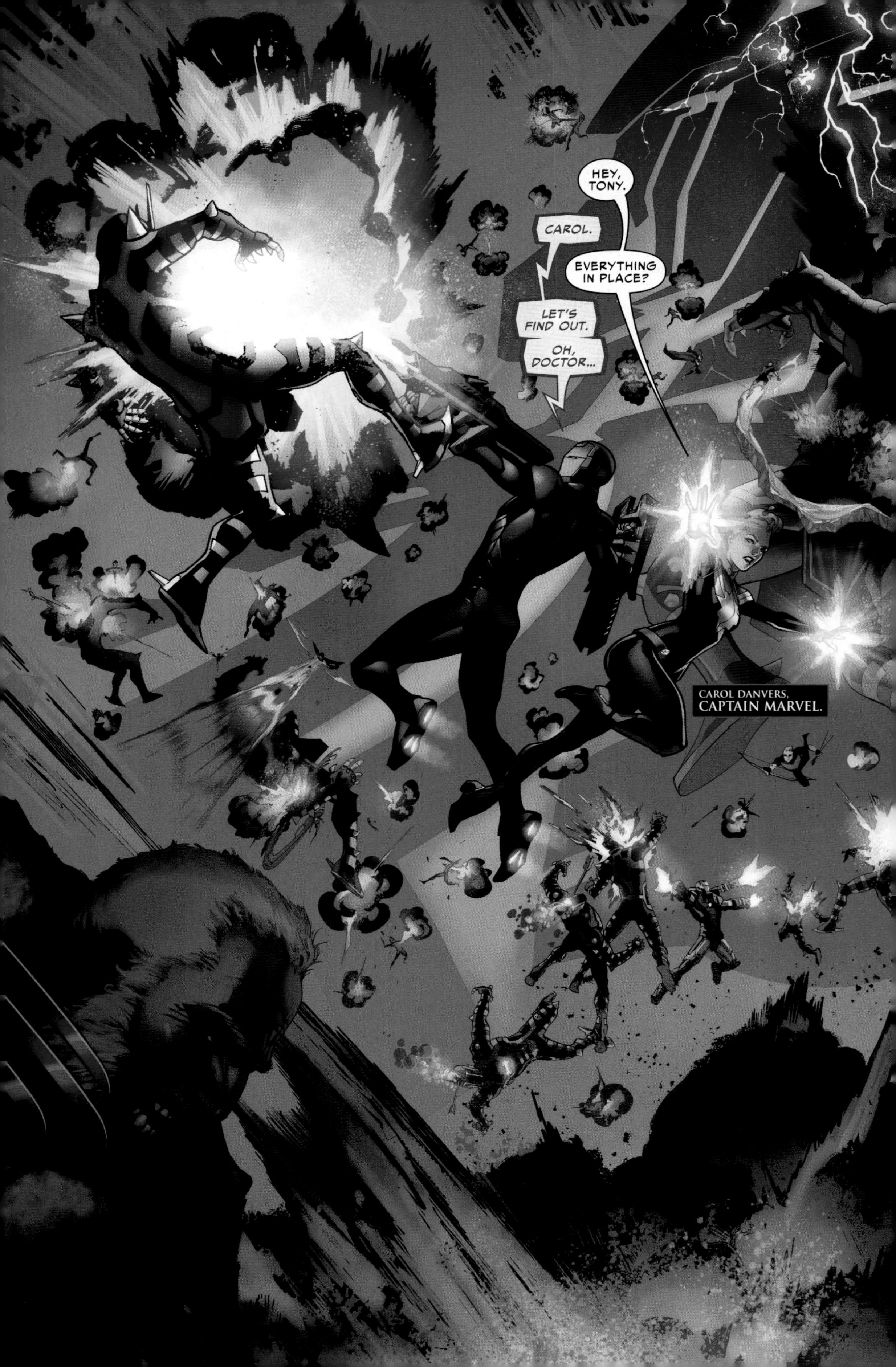
HEY, TONY.
CAROL.
EVERYTHING IN PLACE?
LET'S FIND OUT.
OH, DOCTOR...
CAROL DANVERS, CAPTAIN MARVEL.

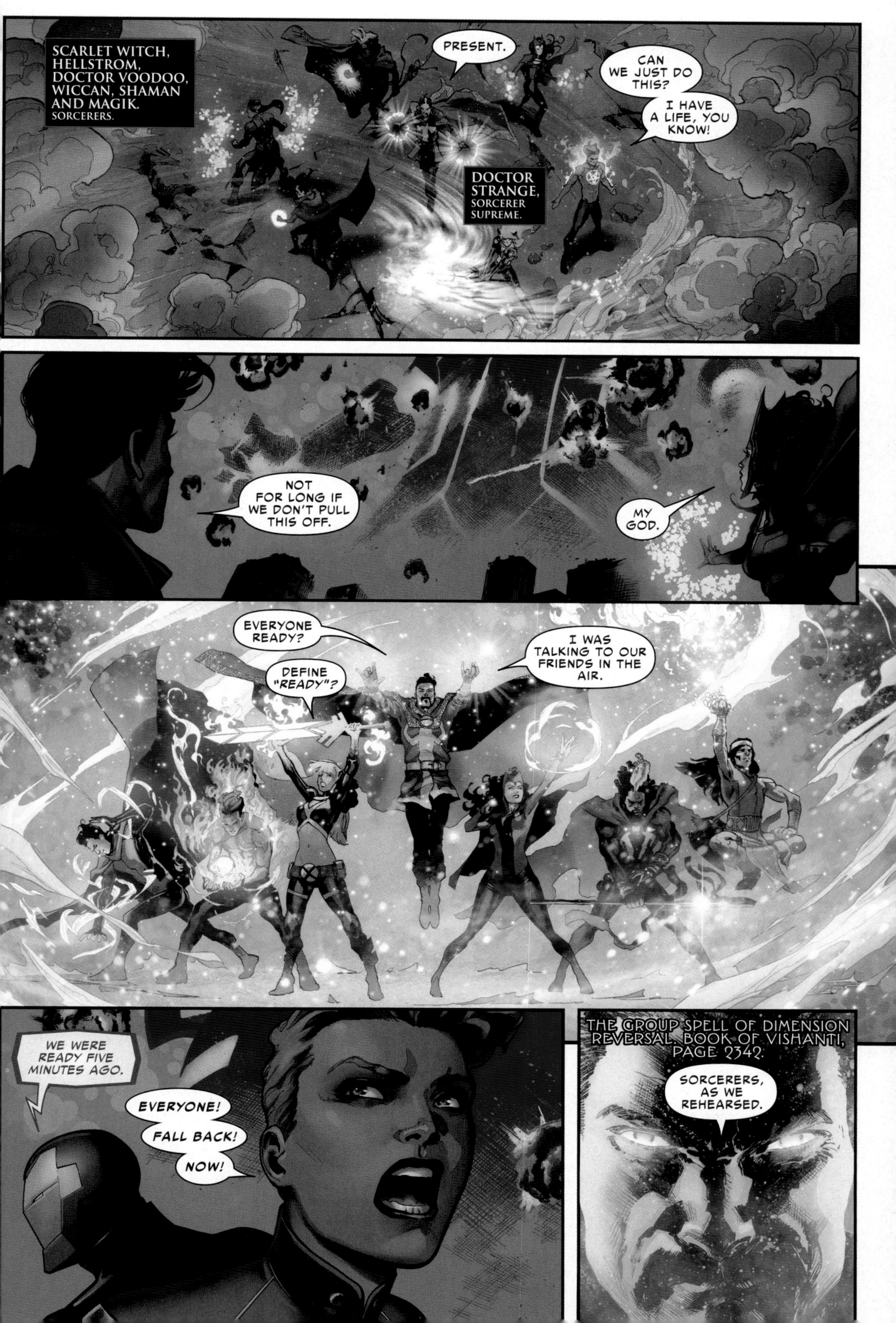
SCARLET WITCH, HELLSTROM, DOCTOR VOODOO, WICCAN, SHAMAN AND MAGIK. SORCERERS.
PRESENT.
CAN WE JUST DO THIS?
I HAVE A LIFE, YOU KNOW!
DOCTOR STRANGE, SORCERER SUPREME.
NOT FOR LONG IF WE DON'T PULL THIS OFF.
MY GOD.
EVERYONE READY?
DEFINE "READY"?
I WAS TALKING TO OUR FRIENDS IN THE AIR.
WE WERE READY FIVE MINUTES AGO.
EVERYONE!
FALL BACK!
NOW!
THE GROUP SPELL OF DIMENSION REVERSAL. BOOK OF VISHANTI, PAGE 2342.
SORCERERS, AS WE REHEARSED.

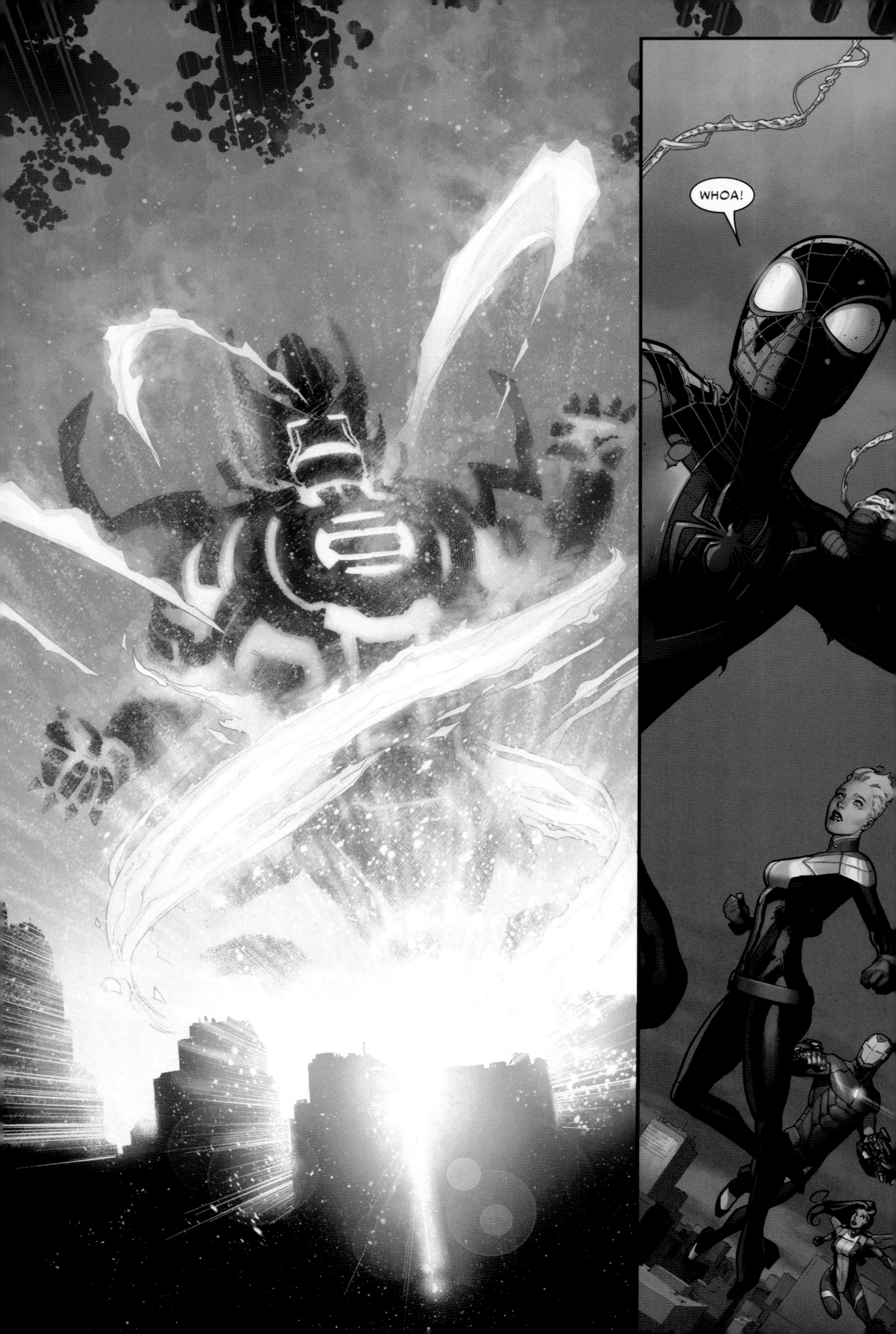
WHOA!

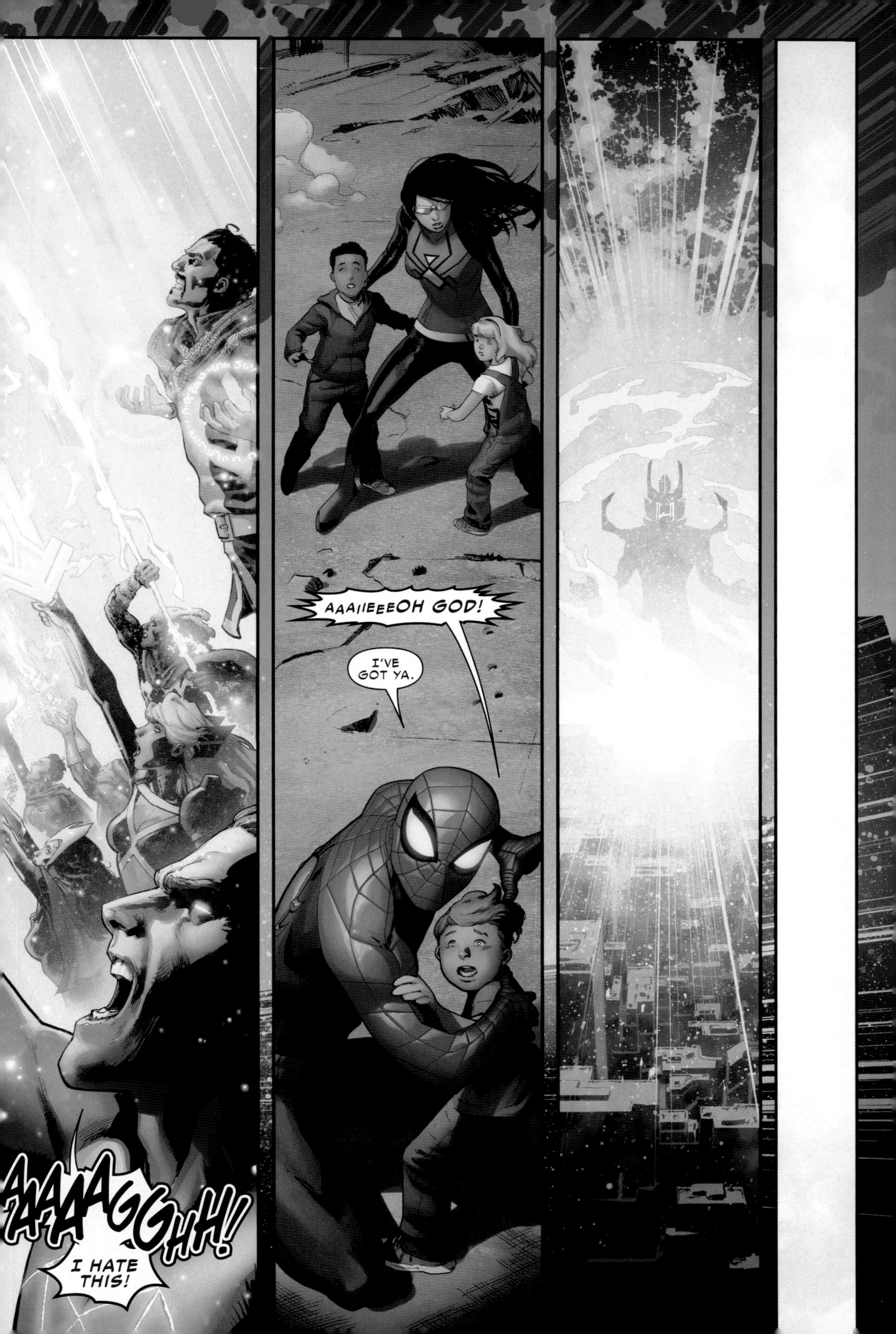
AAAAAGGHH!
I HATE THIS!
AAAIIEEEOH GOD!
I'VE GOT YA.

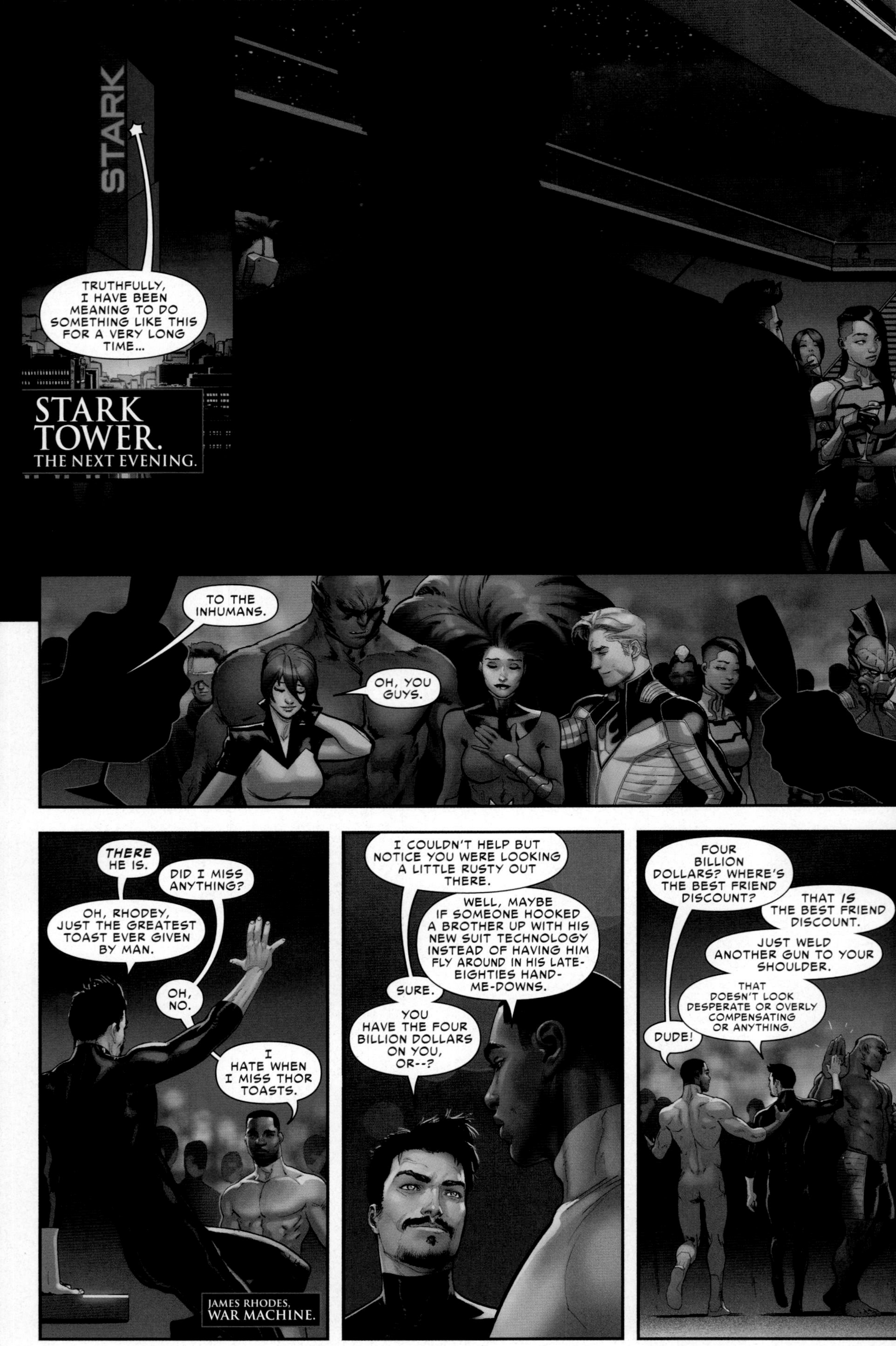
STARK
TRUTHFULLY, I HAVE BEEN MEANING TO DO SOMETHING LIKE THIS FOR A VERY LONG TIME...
STARK TOWER. THE NEXT EVENING.
TO THE INHUMANS.
OH, YOU GUYS.
THERE HE IS.
DID I MISS ANYTHING?
OH, RHODEY, JUST THE GREATEST TOAST EVER GIVEN BY MAN.
OH, NO.
I HATE WHEN I MISS THOR TOASTS.
JAMES RHODES, WAR MACHINE.
I COULDN'T HELP BUT NOTICE YOU WERE LOOKING A LITTLE RUSTY OUT THERE.
WELL, MAYBE IF SOMEONE HOOKED A BROTHER UP WITH HIS NEW SUIT TECHNOLOGY INSTEAD OF HAVING HIM FLY AROUND IN HIS LATE-EIGHTIES HAND-ME-DOWNS.
SURE.
YOU HAVE THE FOUR BILLION DOLLARS ON YOU, OR--?
FOUR BILLION DOLLARS? WHERE'S THE BEST FRIEND DISCOUNT?
THAT *IS* THE BEST FRIEND DISCOUNT.
JUST WELD ANOTHER GUN TO YOUR SHOULDER.
THAT DOESN'T LOOK DESPERATE OR OVERLY COMPENSATING OR ANYTHING.
DUDE!

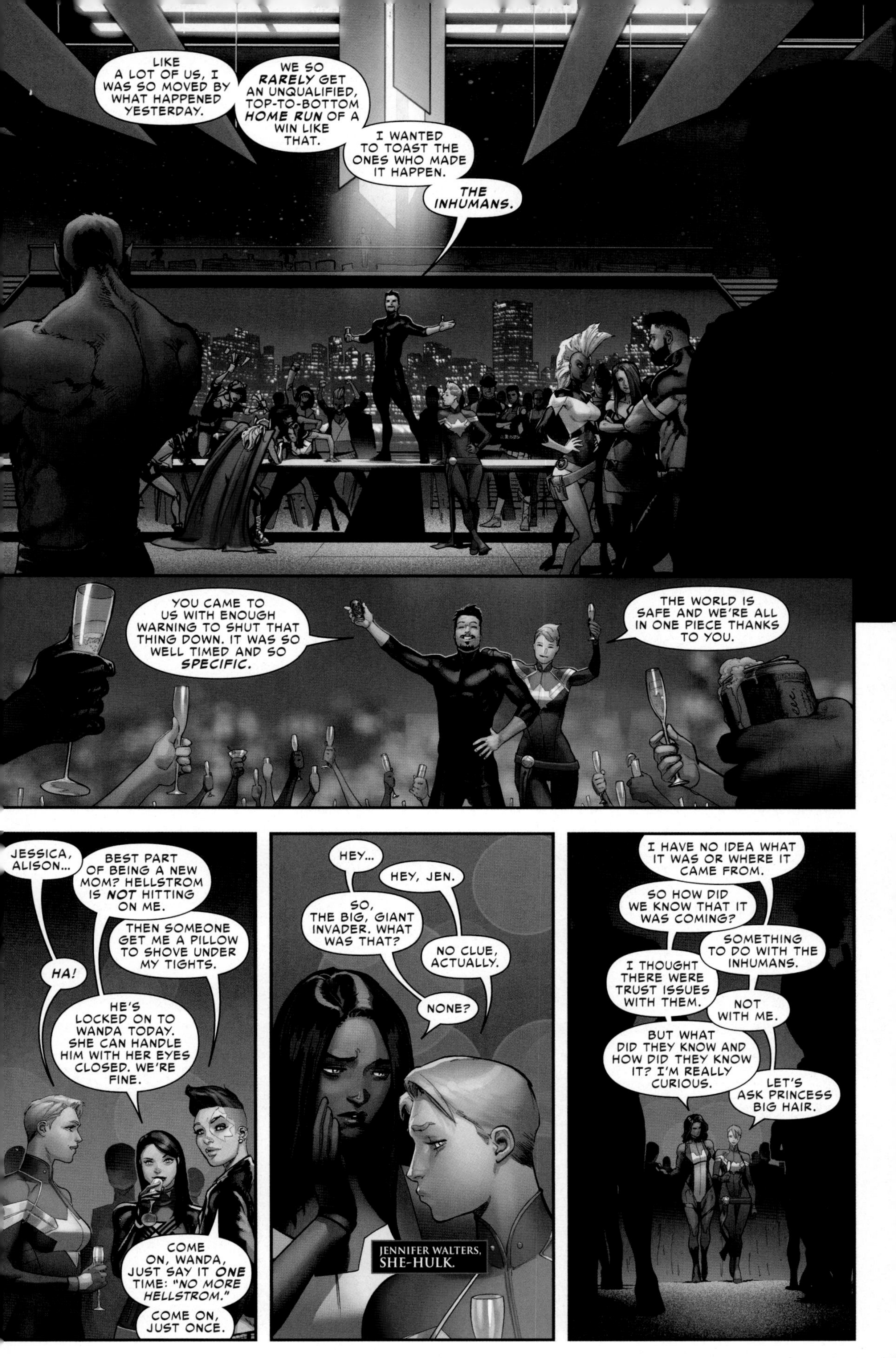
LIKE A LOT OF US, I WAS SO MOVED BY WHAT HAPPENED YESTERDAY.
WE SO RARELY GET AN UNQUALIFIED, TOP-TO-BOTTOM HOME RUN OF A WIN LIKE THAT.
I WANTED TO TOAST THE ONES WHO MADE IT HAPPEN.
THE INHUMANS.
YOU CAME TO US WITH ENOUGH WARNING TO SHUT THAT THING DOWN. IT WAS SO WELL TIMED AND SO SPECIFIC.
THE WORLD IS SAFE AND WE'RE ALL IN ONE PIECE THANKS TO YOU.
JESSICA, ALISON...
BEST PART OF BEING A NEW MOM? HELLSTROM IS NOT HITTING ON ME.
THEN SOMEONE GET ME A PILLOW TO SHOVE UNDER MY TIGHTS.
HA!
HE'S LOCKED ON TO WANDA TODAY. SHE CAN HANDLE HIM WITH HER EYES CLOSED. WE'RE FINE.
COME ON, WANDA, JUST SAY IT ONE TIME: "NO MORE HELLSTROM."
COME ON, JUST ONCE.
HEY...
HEY, JEN.
SO, THE BIG, GIANT INVADER. WHAT WAS THAT?
NO CLUE, ACTUALLY.
NONE?
JENNIFER WALTERS, SHE-HULK.
I HAVE NO IDEA WHAT IT WAS OR WHERE IT CAME FROM.
SO HOW DID WE KNOW THAT IT WAS COMING?
SOMETHING TO DO WITH THE INHUMANS.
I THOUGHT THERE WERE TRUST ISSUES WITH THEM.
NOT WITH ME.
BUT WHAT DID THEY KNOW AND HOW DID THEY KNOW IT? I'M REALLY CURIOUS.
LET'S ASK PRINCESS BIG HAIR.

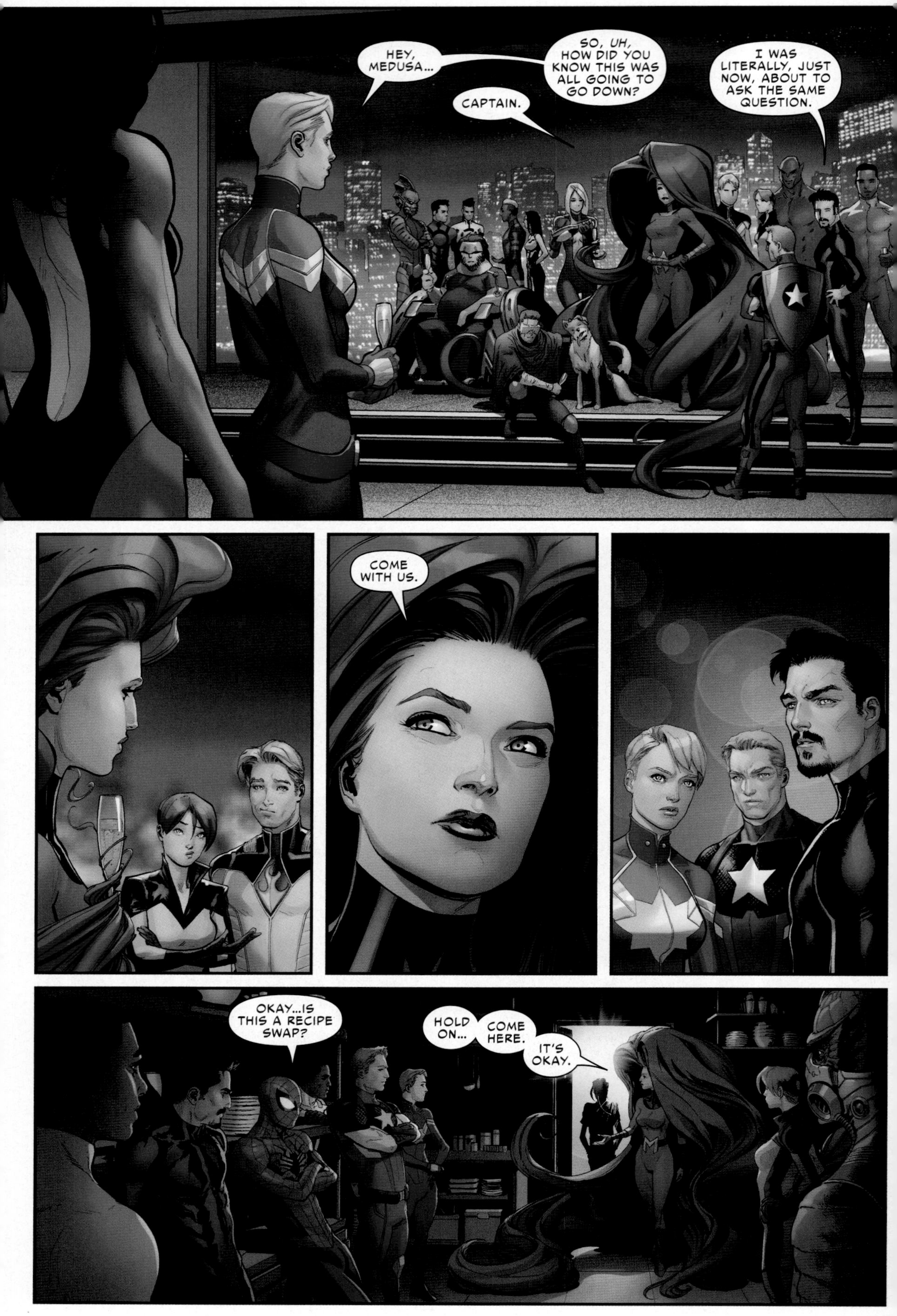
HEY, MEDUSA...
CAPTAIN.
SO, UH, HOW DID YOU KNOW THIS WAS ALL GOING TO GO DOWN?
I WAS LITERALLY, JUST NOW, ABOUT TO ASK THE SAME QUESTION.
COME WITH US.
OKAY...IS THIS A RECIPE SWAP?
HOLD ON...
COME HERE.
IT'S OKAY.

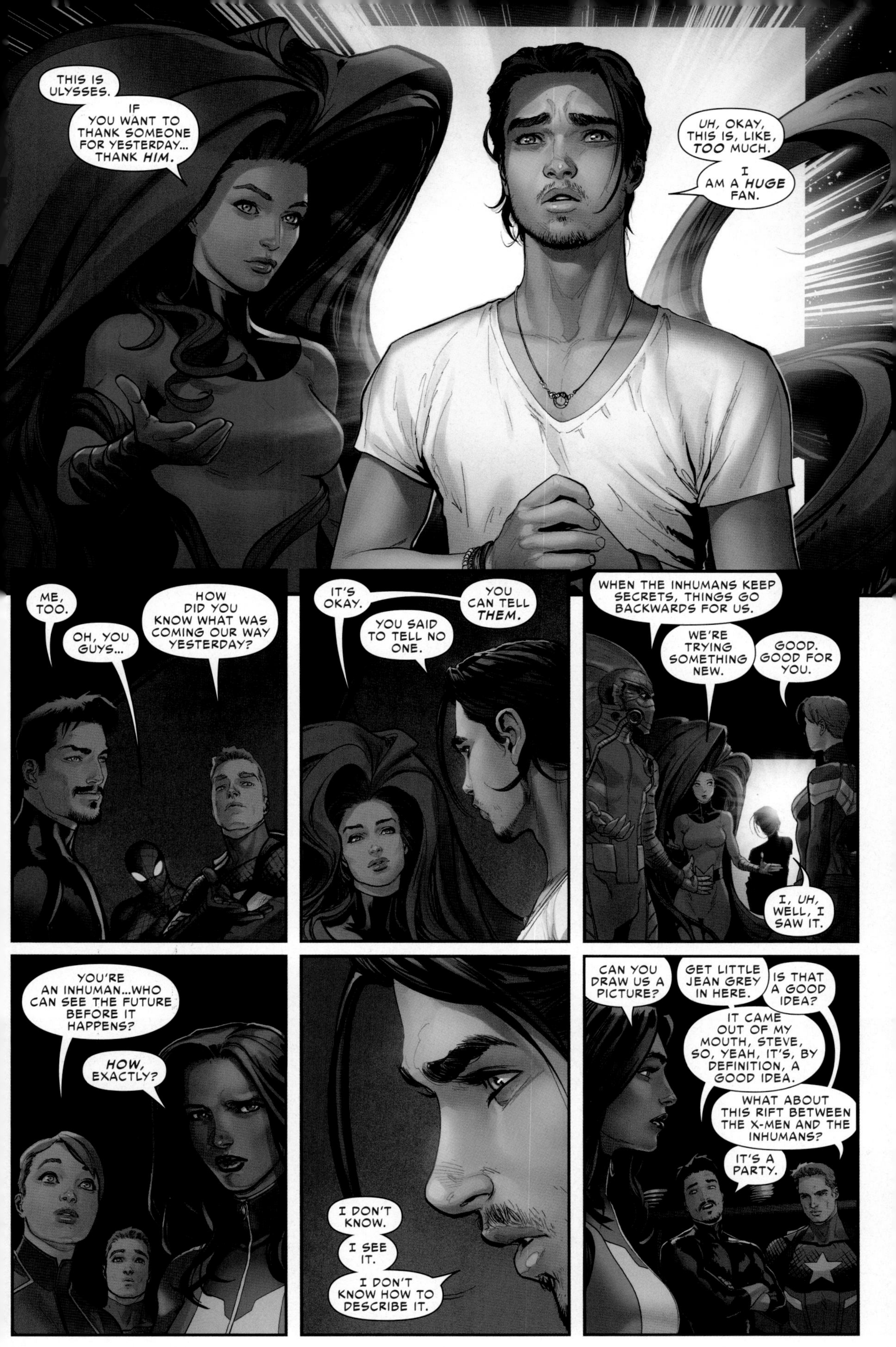
THIS IS ULYSSES.
IF YOU WANT TO THANK SOMEONE FOR YESTERDAY... THANK *HIM*.
UH, OKAY, THIS IS, LIKE, *TOO* MUCH.
I AM A *HUGE* FAN.
ME, TOO.
OH, YOU GUYS...
HOW DID YOU KNOW WHAT WAS COMING OUR WAY YESTERDAY?
IT'S OKAY.
YOU CAN TELL *THEM*.
YOU SAID TO TELL NO ONE.
WHEN THE INHUMANS KEEP SECRETS, THINGS GO BACKWARDS FOR US.
WE'RE TRYING SOMETHING NEW.
GOOD. GOOD FOR YOU.
I, UH, WELL, I SAW IT.
YOU'RE AN INHUMAN...WHO CAN SEE THE FUTURE BEFORE IT HAPPENS?
HOW, EXACTLY?
I DON'T KNOW.
I SEE IT.
I DON'T KNOW HOW TO DESCRIBE IT.
CAN YOU DRAW US A PICTURE?
GET LITTLE JEAN GREY IN HERE.
IS THAT A GOOD IDEA?
IT CAME OUT OF MY MOUTH, STEVE, SO, YEAH, IT'S, BY DEFINITION, A GOOD IDEA.
WHAT ABOUT THIS RIFT BETWEEN THE X-MEN AND THE INHUMANS?
IT'S A PARTY.

HI. I'M JEAN GREY.

I'M ONE OF THE X-MEN. I'M A PSYCHIC.

IS THIS REALLY NECESSARY?

LET'S SAY: YES.

RESPECTFULLY.

UH...

WHAT I'M GOING TO DO IS CREATE A LIMITED MIND HIVE BETWEEN *YOU* AND EVERYONE ELSE IN THIS KITCHEN.

THAT MEANS YOU CAN ACTUALLY *SHOW* THEM WHAT YOU SEE AND WHAT YOU DO...

...BUT YOU WON'T SHOW THEM EVERYTHING. YOU WON'T SHOW EVERY WEIRD THOUGHT YOU HAVE IN YOUR HEAD.

UH...

UM--

I DON'T HAVE ANY WEIRD THOUGHTS IN MY HEAD.

EVERYBODY DOES.

YOU SHOULD SEE WHAT SHE-HULK IS THINKING ABOUT RIGHT NOW.

HEY.

NOT COOL.

WHAT DO I DO?

JUST RELAX.

AND TELL US YOUR STORY.

AND I'LL SHOW THEM WHAT YOU SEE WHEN YOU SEE WHAT YOU SEE...

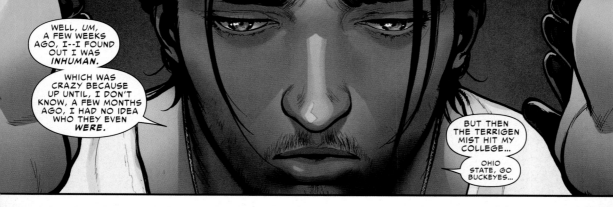

WELL, UM, A FEW WEEKS AGO, I--I FOUND OUT I WAS *INHUMAN*.

WHICH WAS CRAZY BECAUSE UP UNTIL, I DON'T KNOW, A FEW MONTHS AGO, I HAD NO IDEA WHO THEY EVEN *WERE*.

BUT THEN THE TERRIGEN MIST HIT MY COLLEGE...

OHIO STATE, GO BUCKEYES...

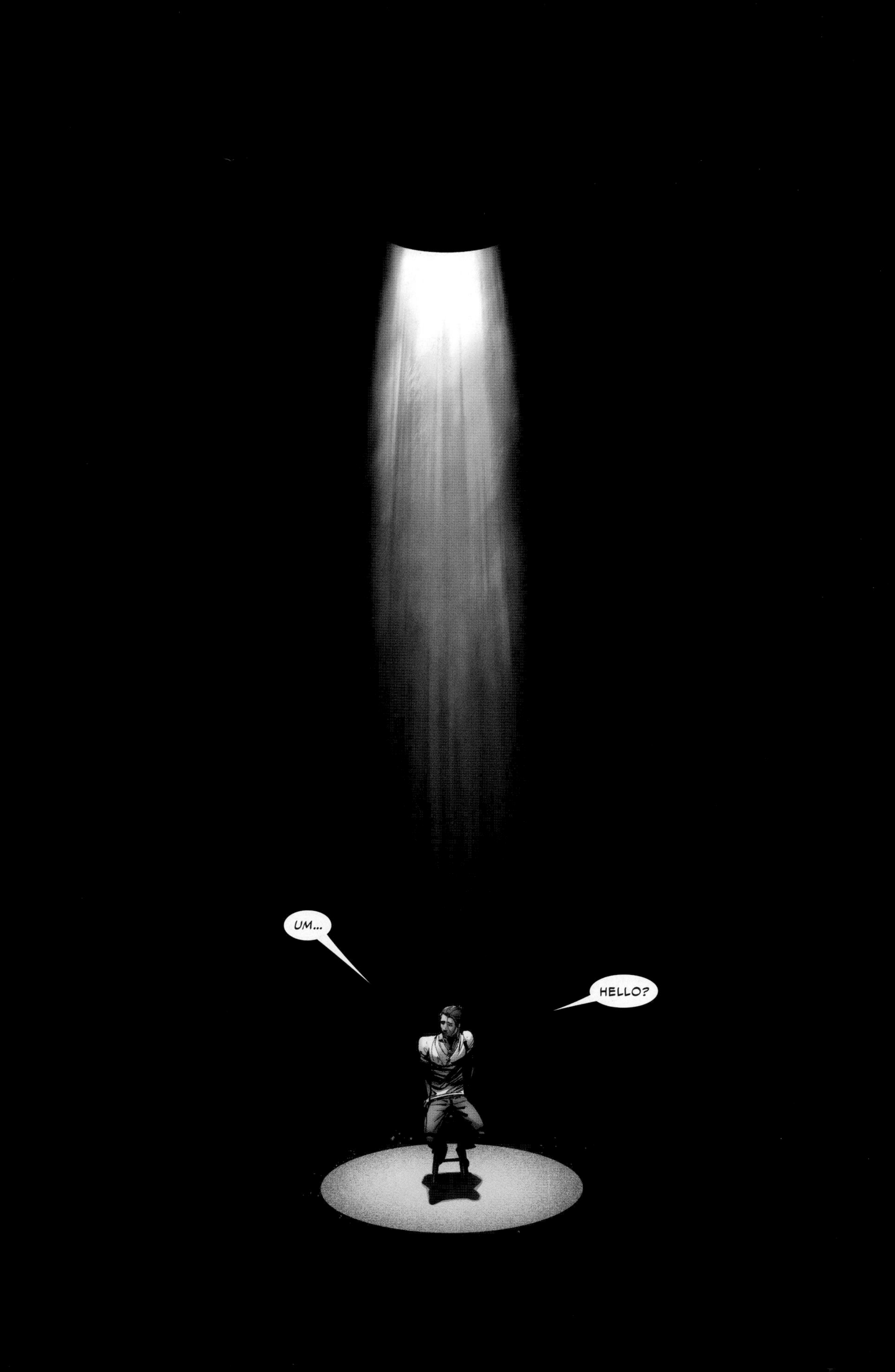
UM...
HELLO?

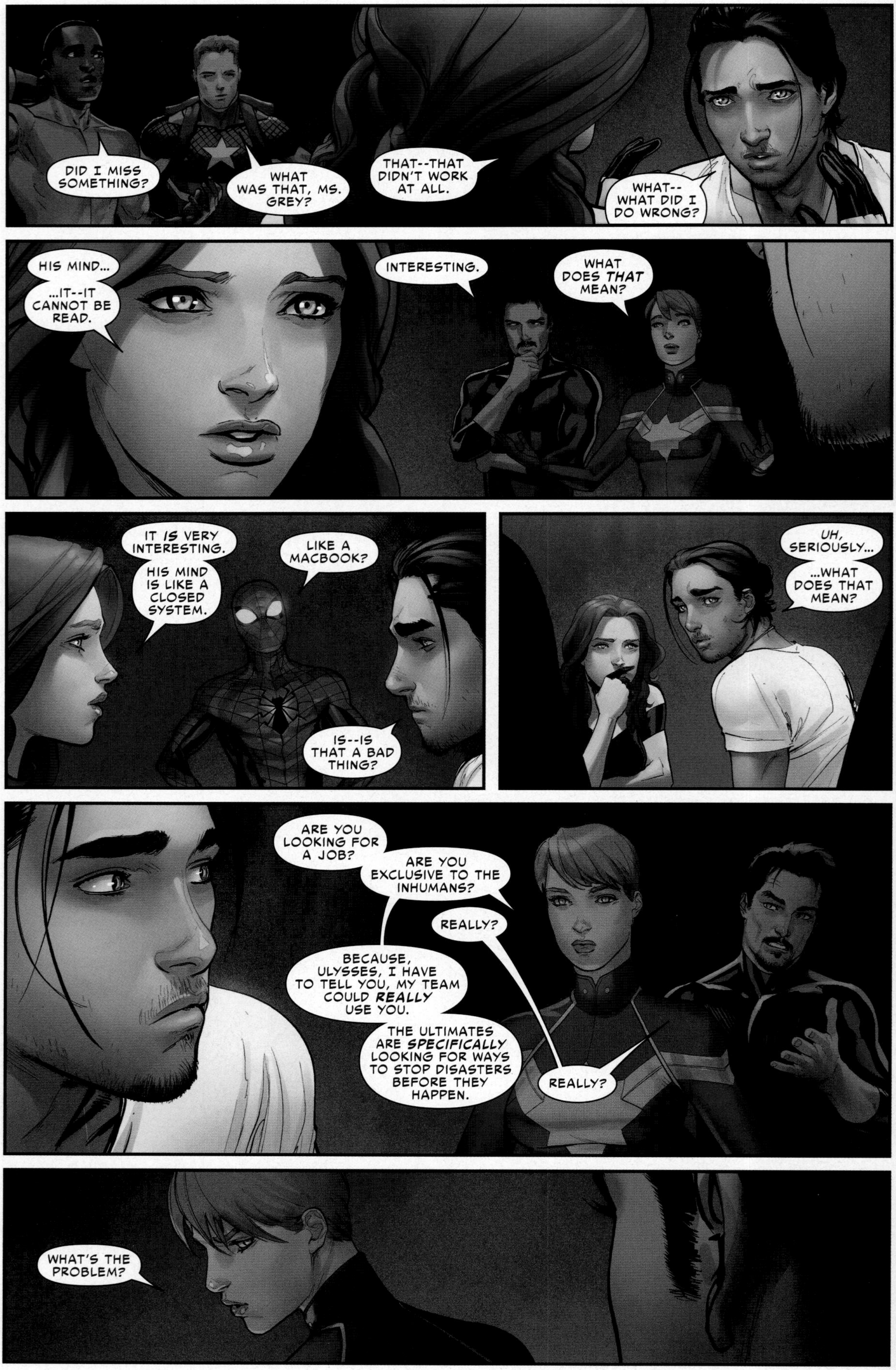
DID I MISS SOMETHING?
WHAT WAS THAT, MS. GREY?
THAT--THAT DIDN'T WORK AT ALL.
WHAT-- WHAT DID I DO WRONG?
HIS MIND...
...IT--IT CANNOT BE READ.
INTERESTING.
WHAT DOES *THAT* MEAN?
IT *IS* VERY INTERESTING.
HIS MIND IS LIKE A CLOSED SYSTEM.
LIKE A MACBOOK?
IS--IS THAT A BAD THING?
UH, SERIOUSLY...
...WHAT DOES THAT MEAN?
ARE YOU LOOKING FOR A JOB?
ARE YOU EXCLUSIVE TO THE INHUMANS?
REALLY?
BECAUSE, ULYSSES, I HAVE TO TELL YOU, MY TEAM COULD *REALLY* USE YOU.
THE ULTIMATES ARE *SPECIFICALLY* LOOKING FOR WAYS TO STOP DISASTERS BEFORE THEY HAPPEN.
REALLY?
WHAT'S THE PROBLEM?

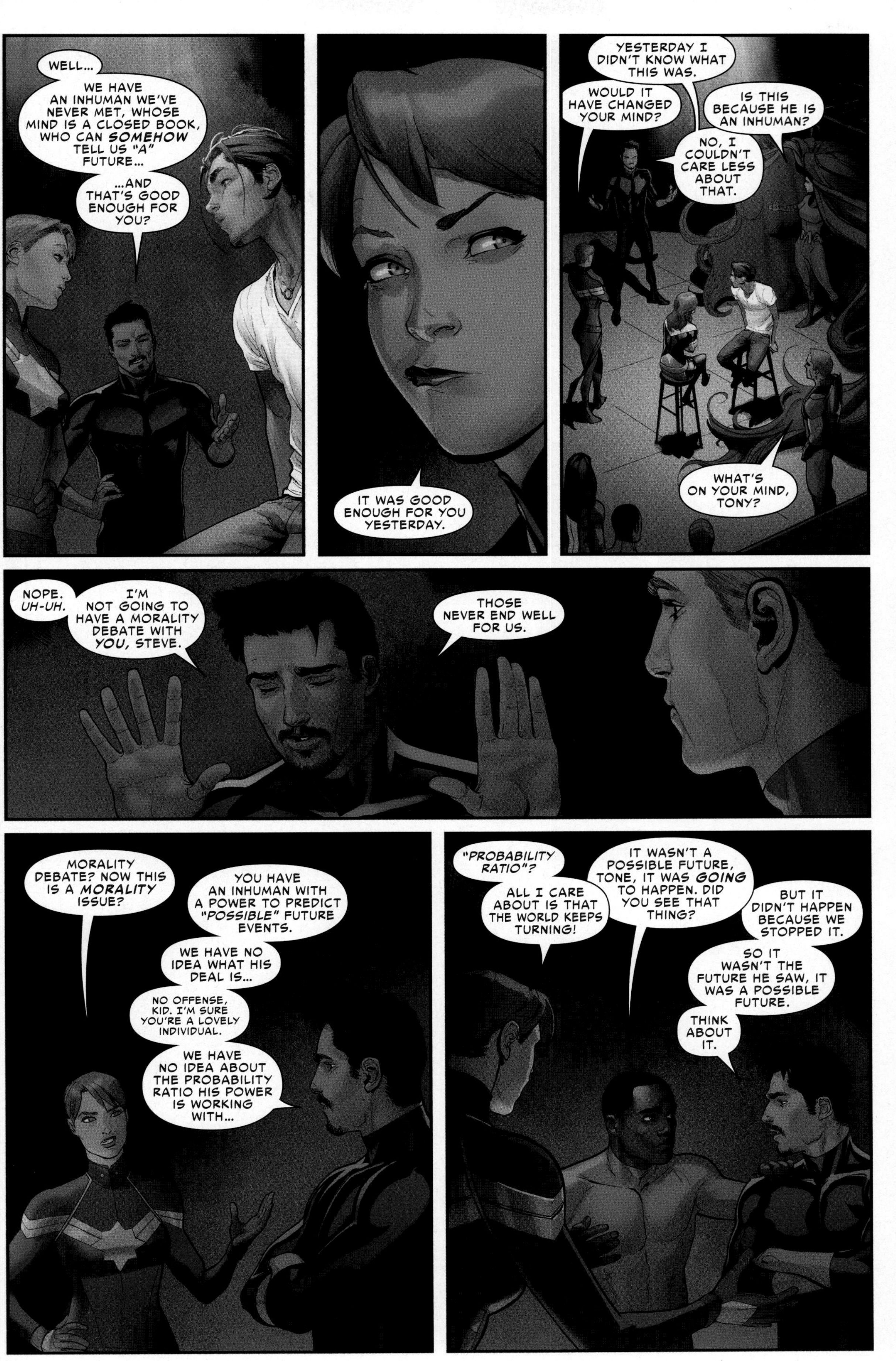
WELL...
WE HAVE AN INHUMAN WE'VE NEVER MET, WHOSE MIND IS A CLOSED BOOK, WHO CAN SOMEHOW TELL US "A" FUTURE...
...AND THAT'S GOOD ENOUGH FOR YOU?
IT WAS GOOD ENOUGH FOR YOU YESTERDAY.
YESTERDAY I DIDN'T KNOW WHAT THIS WAS.
WOULD IT HAVE CHANGED YOUR MIND?
IS THIS BECAUSE HE IS AN INHUMAN?
NO, I COULDN'T CARE LESS ABOUT THAT.
WHAT'S ON YOUR MIND, TONY?
NOPE. UH-UH.
I'M NOT GOING TO HAVE A MORALITY DEBATE WITH YOU, STEVE.
THOSE NEVER END WELL FOR US.
MORALITY DEBATE? NOW THIS IS A MORALITY ISSUE?
YOU HAVE AN INHUMAN WITH A POWER TO PREDICT "POSSIBLE" FUTURE EVENTS.
WE HAVE NO IDEA WHAT HIS DEAL IS...
NO OFFENSE, KID. I'M SURE YOU'RE A LOVELY INDIVIDUAL.
WE HAVE NO IDEA ABOUT THE PROBABILITY RATIO HIS POWER IS WORKING WITH...
"PROBABILITY RATIO"?
ALL I CARE ABOUT IS THAT THE WORLD KEEPS TURNING!
IT WASN'T A POSSIBLE FUTURE, TONE, IT WAS GOING TO HAPPEN. DID YOU SEE THAT THING?
BUT IT DIDN'T HAPPEN BECAUSE WE STOPPED IT.
SO IT WASN'T THE FUTURE HE SAW, IT WAS A POSSIBLE FUTURE.
THINK ABOUT IT.

IF EVERYONE'S ALIVE AT THE END OF THE DAY...

...IT WAS THE RIGHT THING TO DO.

TELL US YOUR STORY, KID...

...TELL US MORE ABOUT YOUR--HOW YOU GOT YOUR POWERS...

WELL, UM, OKAY. A FEW WEEKS AGO, I--I FOUND OUT I WAS INHUMAN.

GREAT.

SO, YOU ALL PROBABLY KNOW MORE ABOUT ALL THAT THAN I DO, BUT THIS TERRIGEN MIST CRAWLS AROUND THE PLANET AND TURNS ANYONE WHO HAS SOME INHUMAN DNA IN THEM INTO INHUMANS.

SURE, SURE...

AND I WAS ONE OF "THE LUCKY ONES."

AND I HAD NO IDEA WHAT WAS DIFFERENT ABOUT ME.

I LOOKED OKAY. I MEAN, THE SAME...

AND THEN--

--THEN IT HAPPENED.

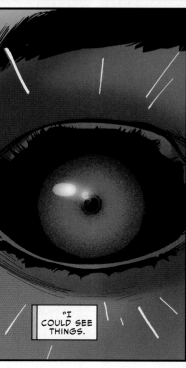

"I COULD SEE THINGS."

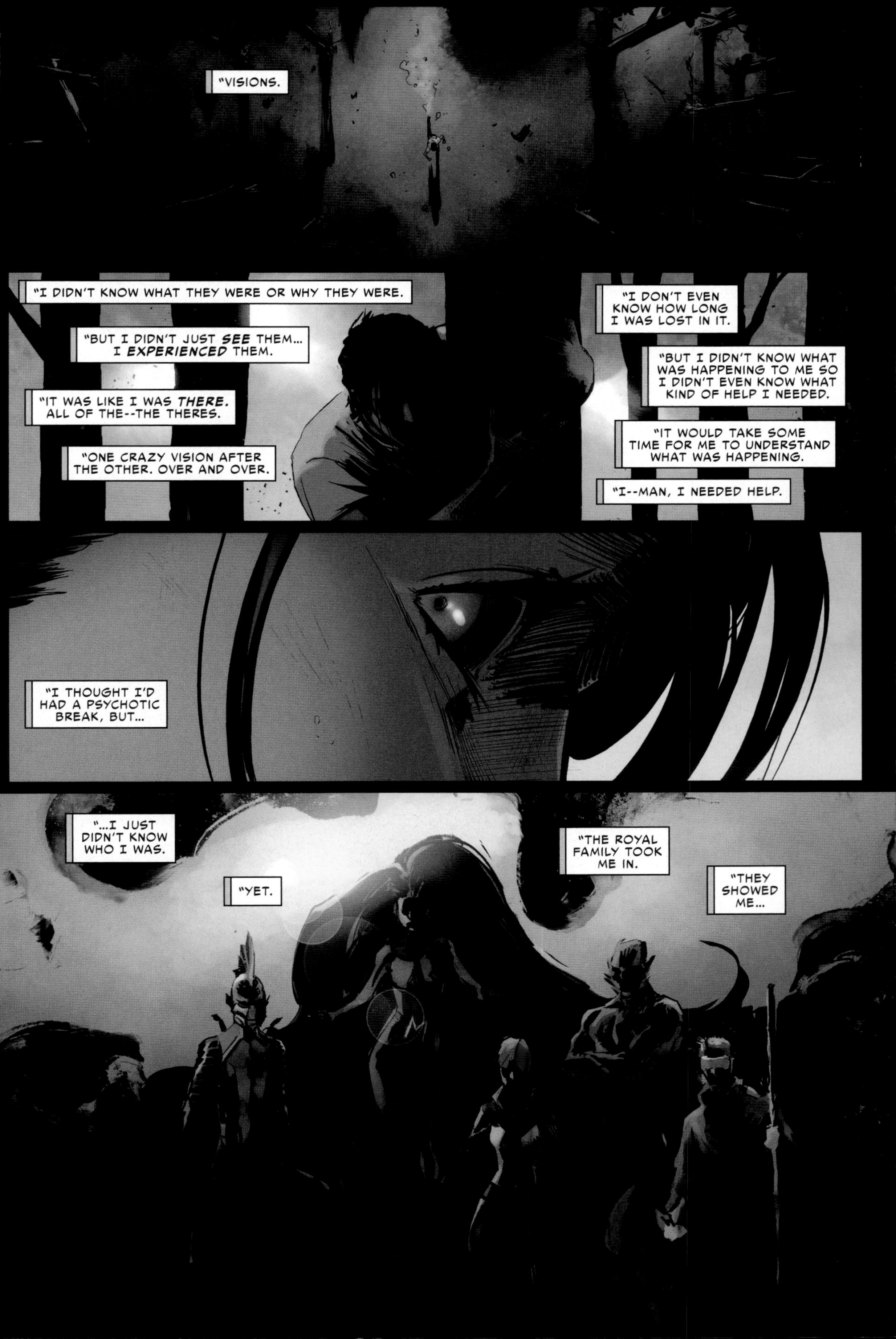
"VISIONS.
"I DIDN'T KNOW WHAT THEY WERE OR WHY THEY WERE.
"BUT I DIDN'T JUST *SEE* THEM... I *EXPERIENCED* THEM.
"IT WAS LIKE I WAS *THERE.* ALL OF THE--THE THERES.
"ONE CRAZY VISION AFTER THE OTHER. OVER AND OVER.
"I DON'T EVEN KNOW HOW LONG I WAS LOST IN IT.
"BUT I DIDN'T KNOW WHAT WAS HAPPENING TO ME SO I DIDN'T EVEN KNOW WHAT KIND OF HELP I NEEDED.
"IT WOULD TAKE SOME TIME FOR ME TO UNDERSTAND WHAT WAS HAPPENING.
"I--MAN, I NEEDED HELP.
"I THOUGHT I'D HAD A PSYCHOTIC BREAK, BUT...
"...I JUST DIDN'T KNOW WHO I WAS.
"YET.
"THE ROYAL FAMILY TOOK ME IN.
"THEY SHOWED ME...

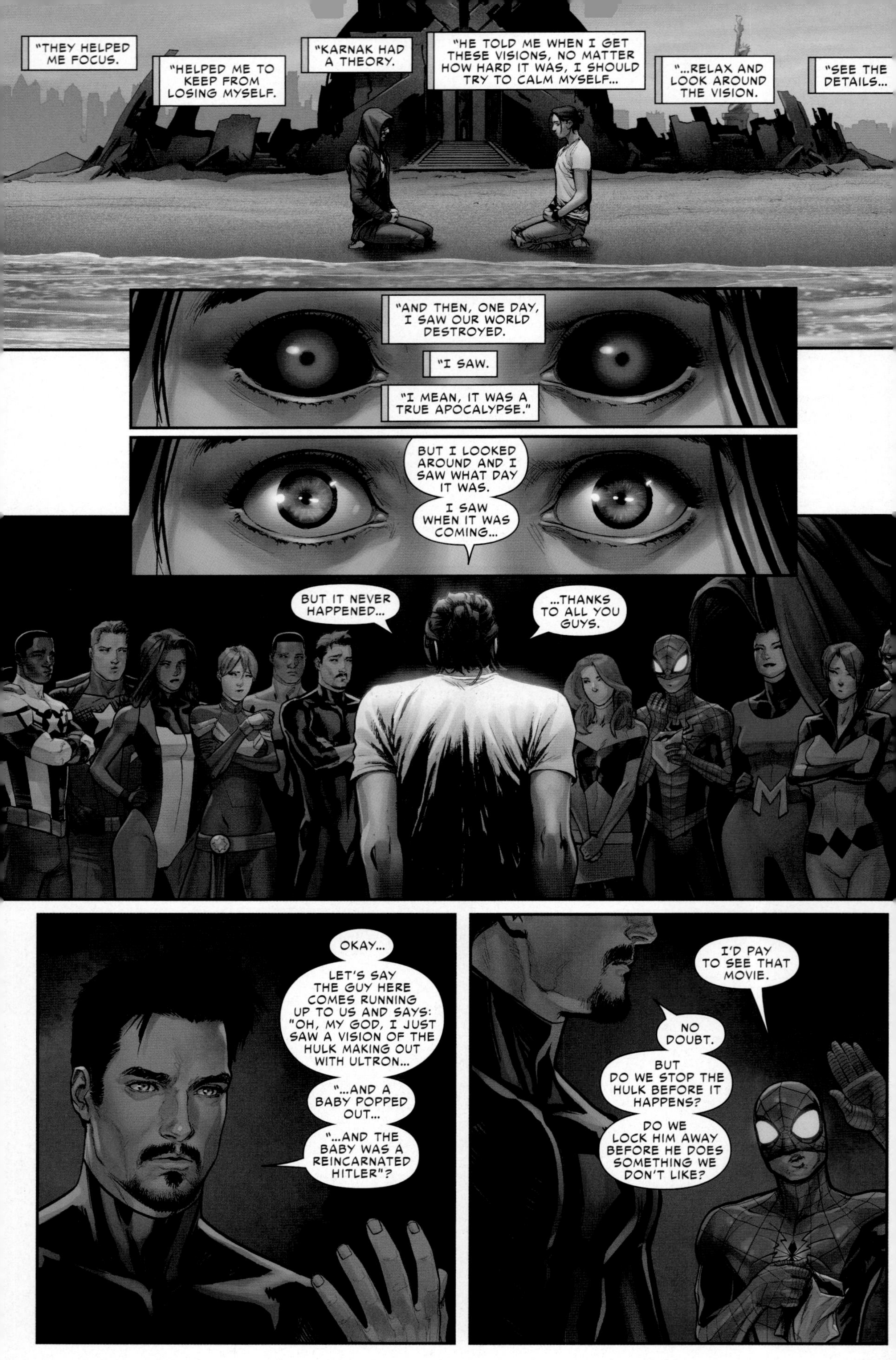
"THEY HELPED ME FOCUS.
"HELPED ME TO KEEP FROM LOSING MYSELF.
"KARNAK HAD A THEORY.
"HE TOLD ME WHEN I GET THESE VISIONS, NO MATTER HOW HARD IT WAS, I SHOULD TRY TO CALM MYSELF...
"...RELAX AND LOOK AROUND THE VISION.
"SEE THE DETAILS...
"AND THEN, ONE DAY, I SAW OUR WORLD DESTROYED.
"I SAW.
"I MEAN, IT WAS A TRUE APOCALYPSE."
BUT I LOOKED AROUND AND I SAW WHAT DAY IT WAS.
I SAW WHEN IT WAS COMING...
BUT IT NEVER HAPPENED...
...THANKS TO ALL YOU GUYS.
OKAY...
LET'S SAY THE GUY HERE COMES RUNNING UP TO US AND SAYS: "OH, MY GOD, I JUST SAW A VISION OF THE HULK MAKING OUT WITH ULTRON...
"...AND A BABY POPPED OUT...
"...AND THE BABY WAS A REINCARNATED HITLER"?
I'D PAY TO SEE THAT MOVIE.
NO DOUBT.
BUT DO WE STOP THE HULK BEFORE IT HAPPENS?
DO WE LOCK HIM AWAY BEFORE HE DOES SOMETHING WE DON'T LIKE?

AGAIN, YESTERDAY WAS YESTERDAY, EASY CALL...

THE BIG COSMIC MONSTER DOESN'T INVADE? NO HARM, NO FOUL.

BUT WHAT IF THE NEXT ONE ISN'T SO EASY?

WHAT IF THE NEXT ONE IS...ONE OF US?

WHAT IF ULYSSES TELLS US *YOU* ARE A DANGER TO OUR FUTURE?

DO WE STOP YOU BEFORE YOU DO YOUR VOODOO THAT YOU'RE GOING TO DO, EVEN THOUGH MAYBE YOU DIDN'T EVEN KNOW YOU WERE GOING TO DO IT?

DEPENDS.

ON WHAT?

I THOUGHT YOU WERE "A FUTURIST"!

I AM. TO MY CORE.

I WORSHIP AT ITS *FEET*.

THAT MEANS I *RESPECT* THE FUTURE. I *BELIEVE* IN THE FUTURE.

I'M SAYING: MAYBE WE SHOULD BE *VERY* CAREFUL ABOUT WHAT OUR NEW BUDDY ULYSSES HERE TELLS US AND WHAT WE DO ABOUT IT.

BUT I'M GLAD YOU'RE ALL HERE, AND ENJOY THE PARTY.

WEREN'T WE JUST HIGH-FIVING EACH OTHER TEN MINUTES AGO ABOUT SAVING THE PLANET?

I AM *STUNNED* BY THAT MAN. AGAIN.

THANK YOU FOR YOUR SERVICE, INHUMANS.

WE WON'T FORGET IT.

WOW. TONY STARK.

YEAH, IT'S EXCITING.

THEN YOU GET OVER IT.

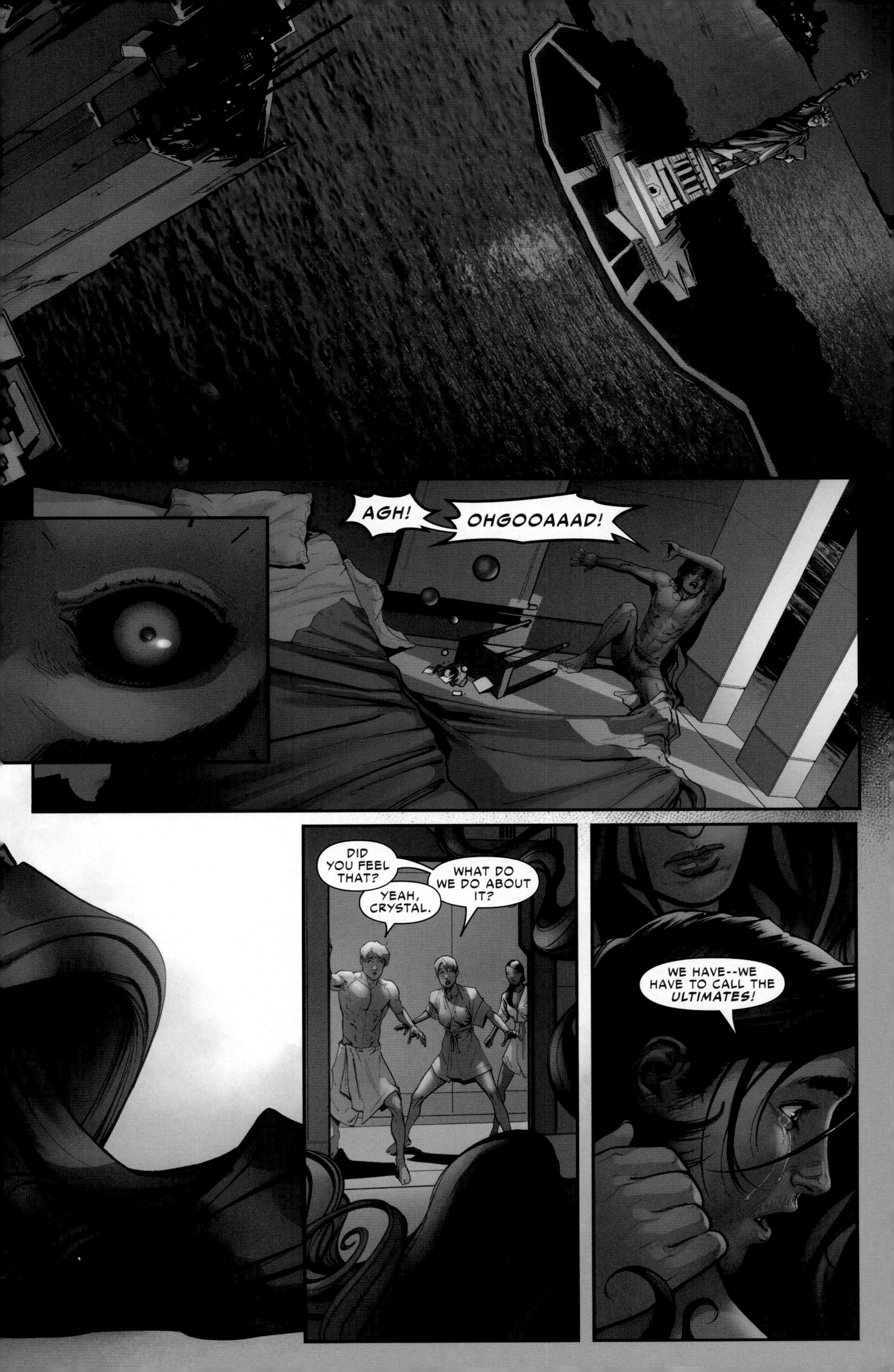
AGH!
OHGOOAAAD!
DID YOU FEEL THAT?
YEAH, CRYSTAL.
WHAT DO WE DO ABOUT IT?
WE HAVE--WE HAVE TO CALL THE *ULTIMATES!*

COME ON, FRIDAY, WHERE IS IT?

YOU TOLD ME NOT TO TELL YOU.

THAT WAS TWO HOURS AGO.

NO. PLEASE.

YOU WANTED PROOF THAT THE NEW ARMOR STEALTH MODE IS FAR SUPERIOR TO THE LAST ONE.

THIS IS THE PROOF.

UGH! I HATE YOU!

I AM YOU. YOU PROGRAMMED ME.

JUST BECAUSE I PROGRAMMED YOU DOESN'T MEAN--

TONY.

HELLO, MISS WATSON.

WHAT DID I DO WRONG NOW?

WHAT?

IT'S RHODEY.

HE'S HERE?

HE'S GONE.

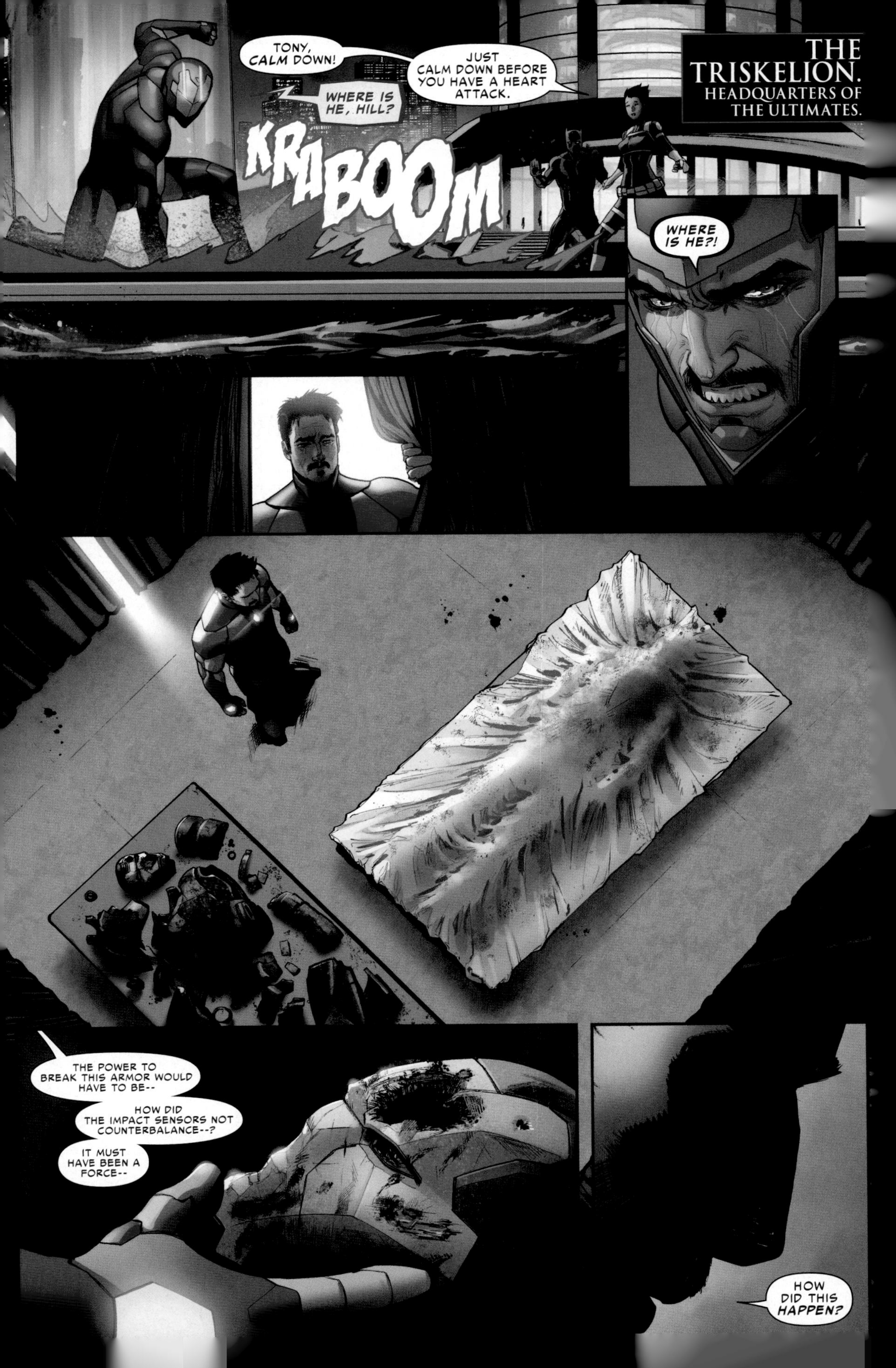
THE TRISKELION.
HEADQUARTERS OF THE ULTIMATES.
TONY, CALM DOWN!
WHERE IS HE, HILL?
JUST CALM DOWN BEFORE YOU HAVE A HEART ATTACK.
KRABOOM
WHERE IS HE?!
THE POWER TO BREAK THIS ARMOR WOULD HAVE TO BE--
HOW DID THE IMPACT SENSORS NOT COUNTERBALANCE--?
IT MUST HAVE BEEN A FORCE--
HOW DID THIS HAPPEN?

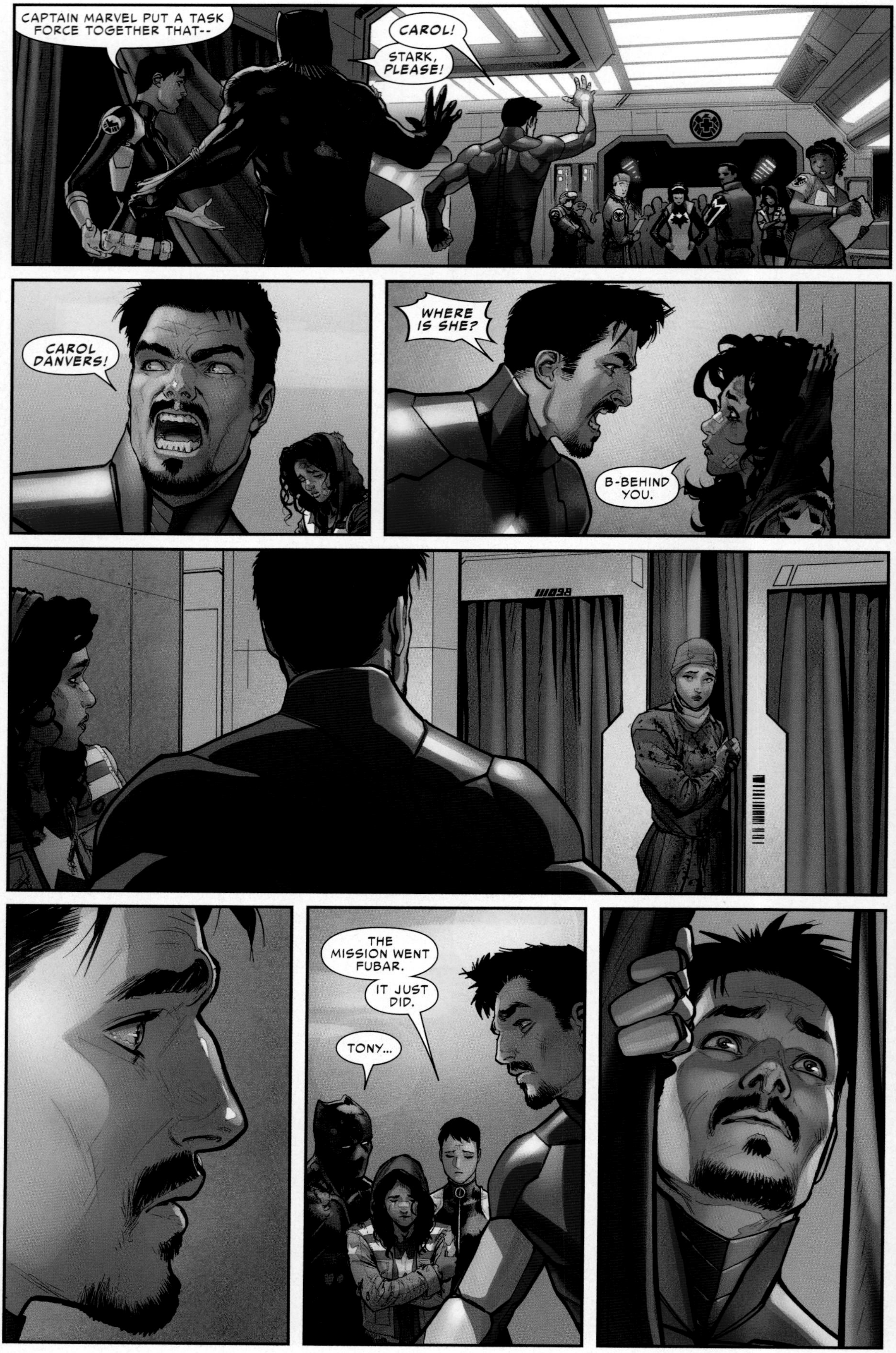
CAPTAIN MARVEL PUT A TASK FORCE TOGETHER THAT--
CAROL!
STARK, PLEASE!
CAROL DANVERS!
WHERE IS SHE?
B-BEHIND YOU.
THE MISSION WENT FUBAR.
IT JUST DID.
TONY...

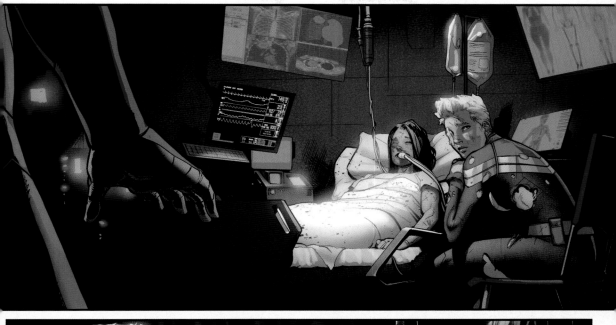

IS SHE-HULK--? IS--IS SHE--?

SHE'S ALIVE.

BUT THEY'RE NOT SURE IF SHE'LL EVER WAKE UP.

OR IF SHE WILL EVER *WALK* AGAIN.

HER BIOLOGY IS SO SPECIFIC. SO UNIQUE.

THEY JUST DON'T KNOW. THEY NEED A GAMMA SPECIALIST. WE NEED BRUCE BANNER.

WHAT HAPPENED?

THANOS.

THANOS WAS BACK ON EARTH?

HE--HE ATTACKED YOU?

NOT EXACTLY.

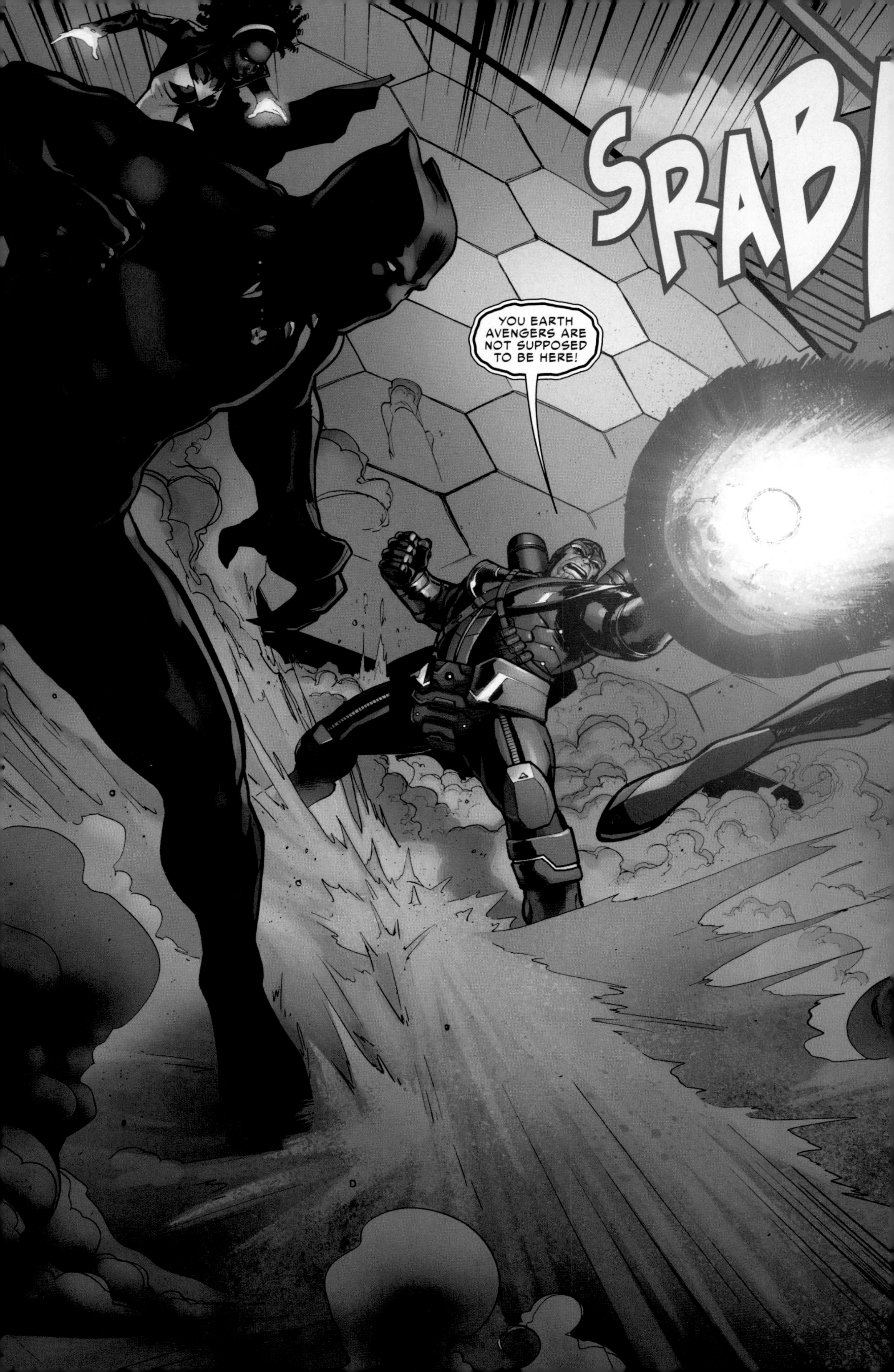
SRAB
YOU EARTH AVENGERS ARE NOT SUPPOSED TO BE HERE!

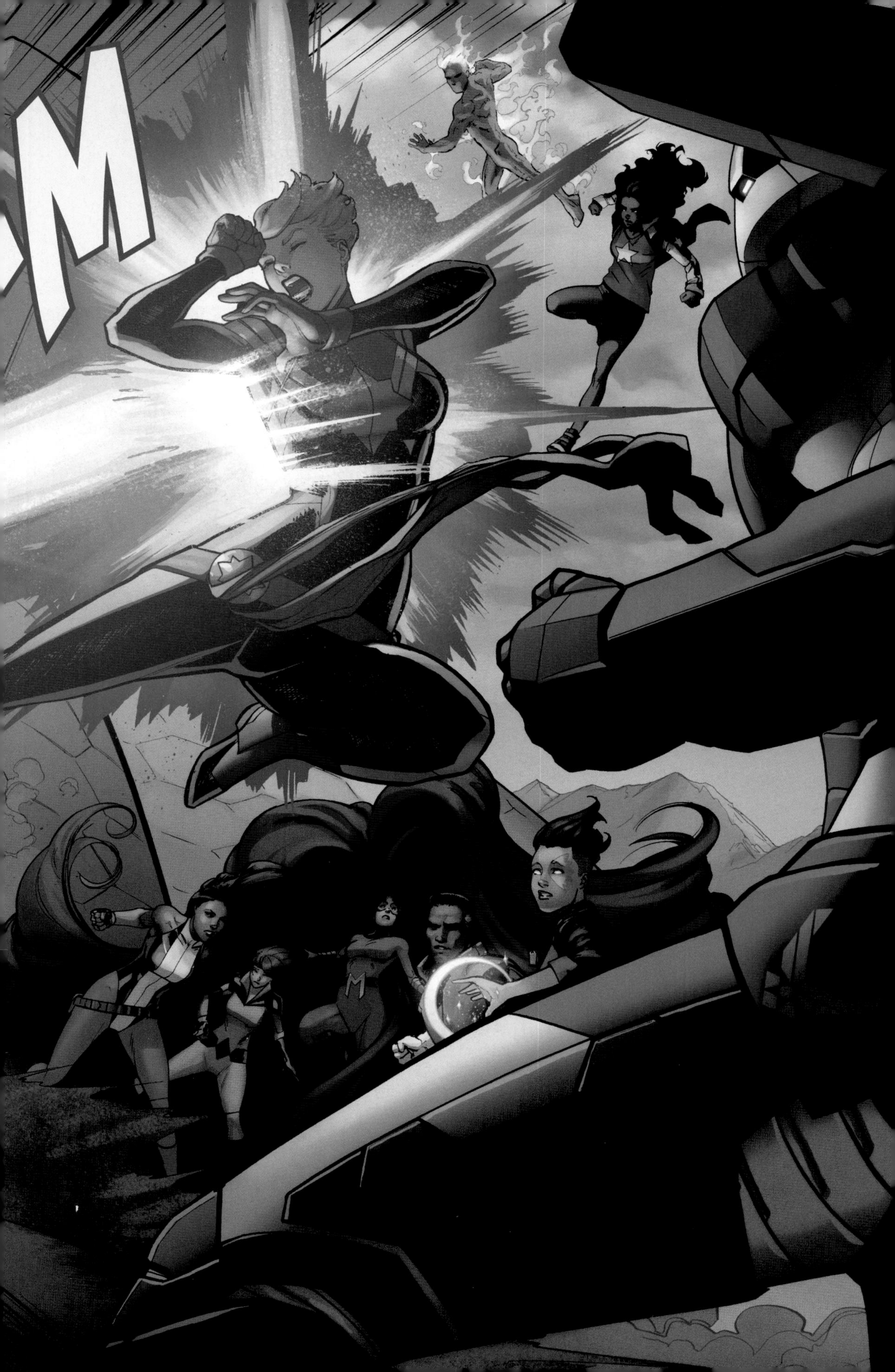
M

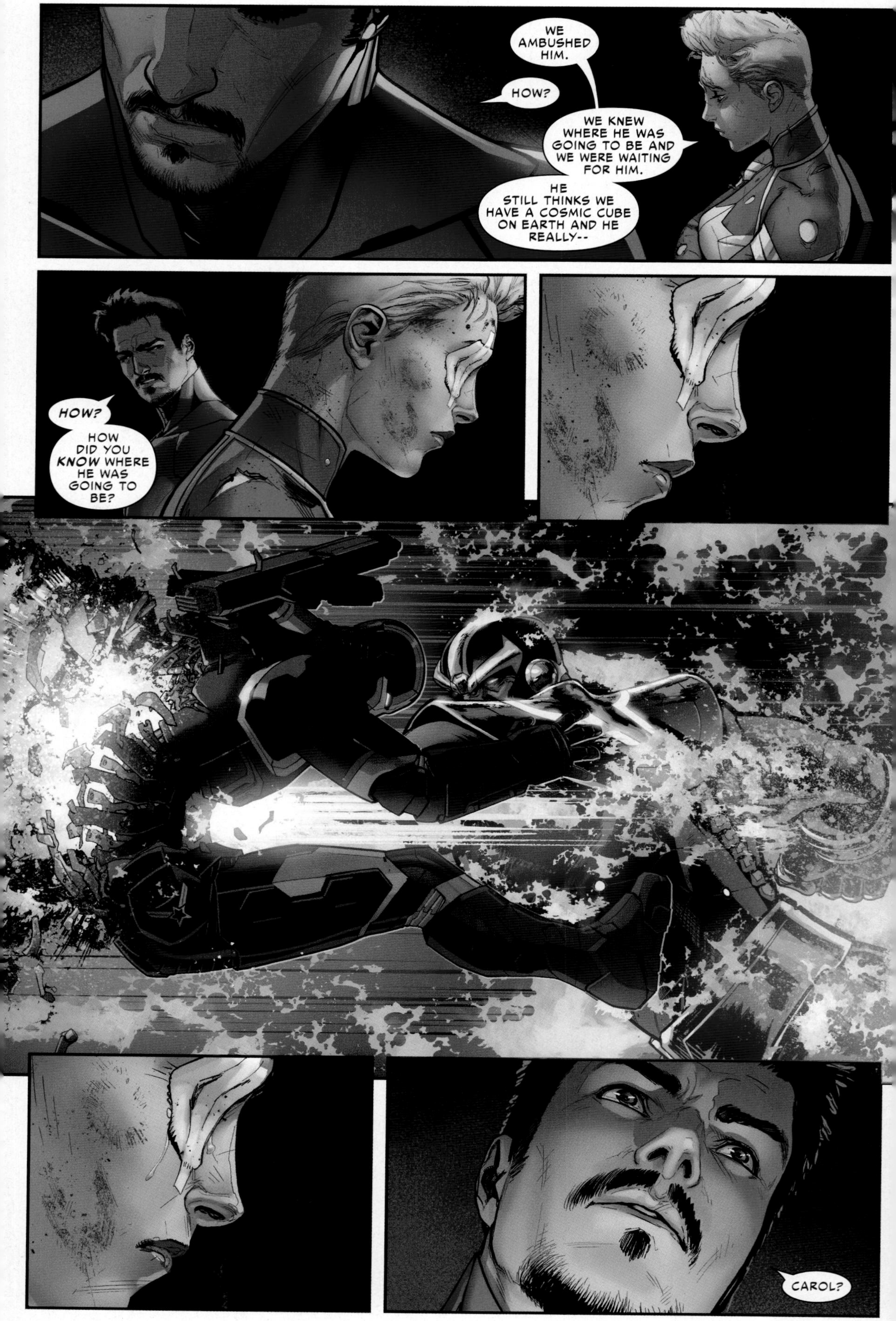
WE AMBUSHED HIM.
HOW?
WE KNEW WHERE HE WAS GOING TO BE AND WE WERE WAITING FOR HIM.
HE STILL THINKS WE HAVE A COSMIC CUBE ON EARTH AND HE REALLY--
HOW?
HOW DID YOU KNOW WHERE HE WAS GOING TO BE?
CAROL?

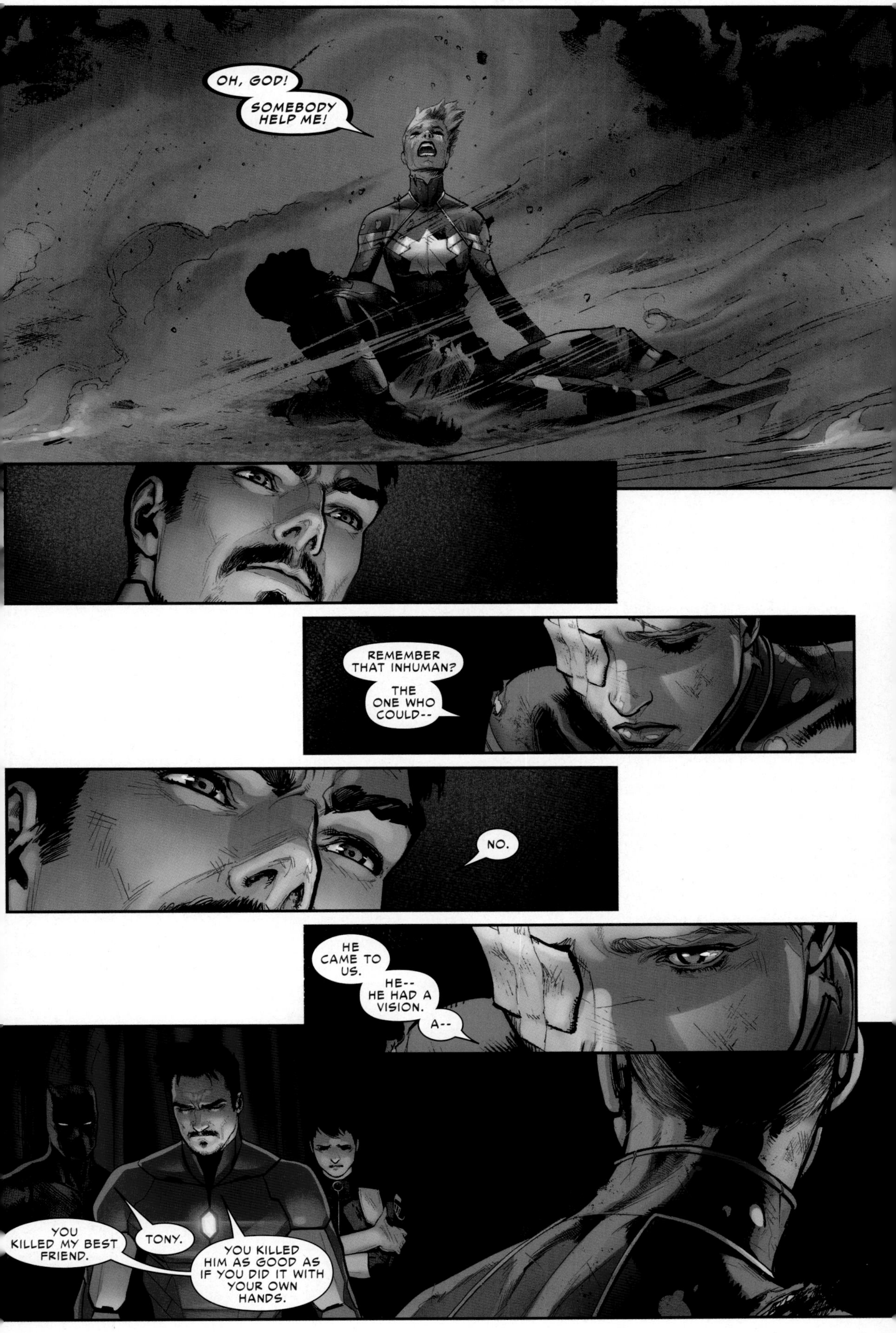
OH, GOD!
SOMEBODY HELP ME!
REMEMBER THAT INHUMAN?
THE ONE WHO COULD--
NO.
HE CAME TO US.
HE-- HE HAD A VISION.
A--
YOU KILLED MY BEST FRIEND.
TONY.
YOU KILLED HIM AS GOOD AS IF YOU DID IT WITH YOUR OWN HANDS.

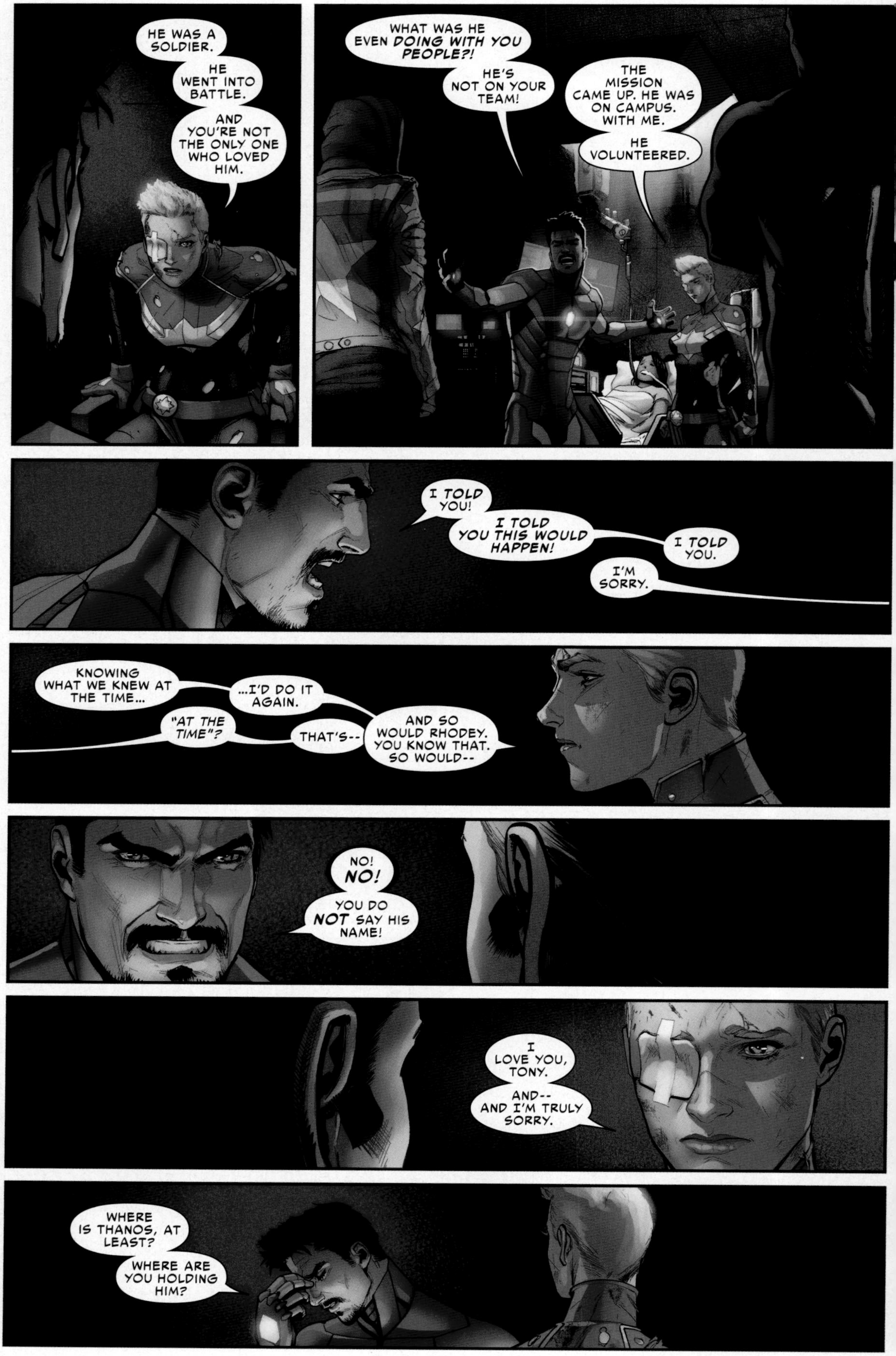
HE WAS A SOLDIER.
HE WENT INTO BATTLE.
AND YOU'RE NOT THE ONLY ONE WHO LOVED HIM.
WHAT WAS HE EVEN *DOING WITH YOU PEOPLE?!*
HE'S NOT ON YOUR TEAM!
THE MISSION CAME UP. HE WAS ON CAMPUS. WITH ME.
HE VOLUNTEERED.
I *TOLD* YOU!
I TOLD YOU THIS WOULD HAPPEN!
I *TOLD* YOU.
I'M SORRY.
KNOWING WHAT WE KNEW AT THE TIME...
...I'D DO IT AGAIN.
"AT THE TIME"?
THAT'S--
AND SO WOULD RHODEY. YOU KNOW THAT. SO WOULD--
NO! ***NO!***
YOU DO ***NOT*** SAY HIS NAME!
I LOVE YOU, TONY.
AND-- AND I'M TRULY SORRY.
WHERE IS THANOS, AT LEAST?
WHERE ARE YOU HOLDING HIM?

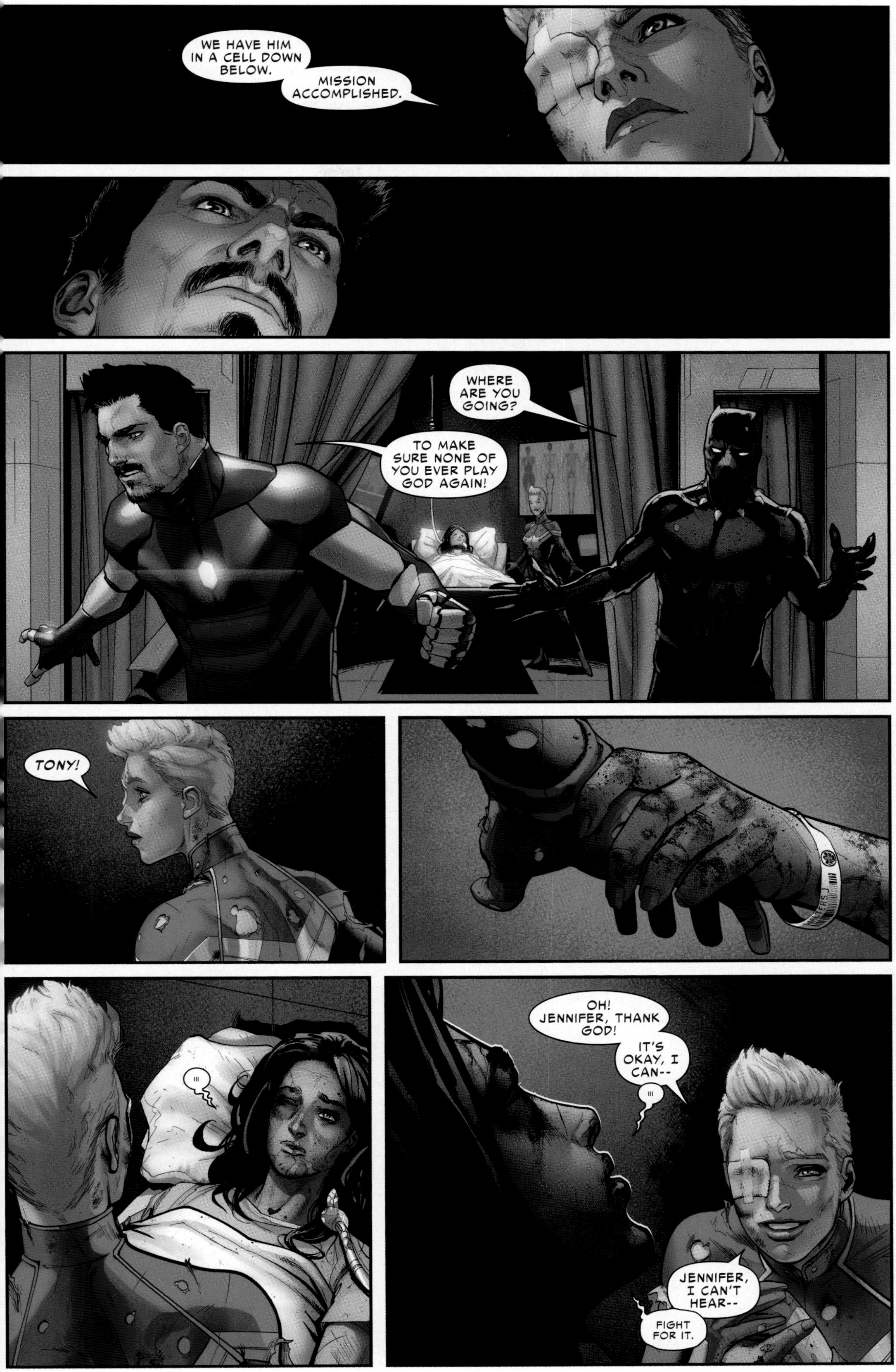
WE HAVE HIM IN A CELL DOWN BELOW.
MISSION ACCOMPLISHED.
WHERE ARE YOU GOING?
TO MAKE SURE NONE OF YOU EVER PLAY GOD AGAIN!
TONY!
OH! JENNIFER, THANK GOD!
IT'S OKAY, I CAN--
JENNIFER, I CAN'T HEAR--
FIGHT FOR IT.

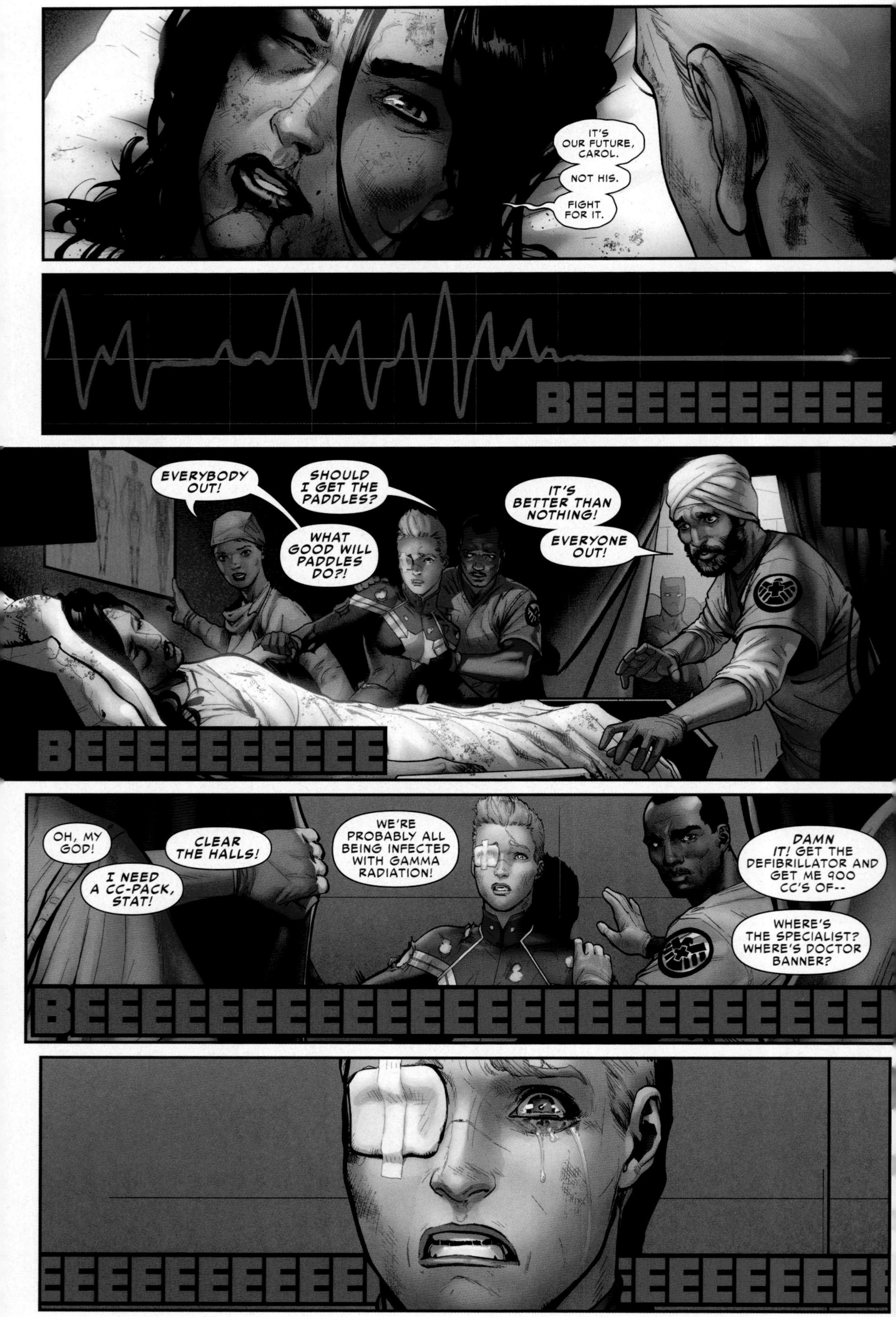
IT'S OUR FUTURE, CAROL.
NOT HIS.
FIGHT FOR IT.
BEEEEEEEEEE
EVERYBODY OUT!
SHOULD I GET THE PADDLES?
WHAT GOOD WILL PADDLES DO?!
IT'S BETTER THAN NOTHING!
EVERYONE OUT!
BEEEEEEEEEE
OH, MY GOD!
I NEED A CC-PACK, STAT!
CLEAR THE HALLS!
WE'RE PROBABLY ALL BEING INFECTED WITH GAMMA RADIATION!
DAMN IT! GET THE DEFIBRILLATOR AND GET ME 900 CC'S OF--
WHERE'S THE SPECIALIST? WHERE'S DOCTOR BANNER?
BEEEEEEEEEEEEEEEEEEEEEEEEE
EEEEEEEEEE
EEEEEEEEEE

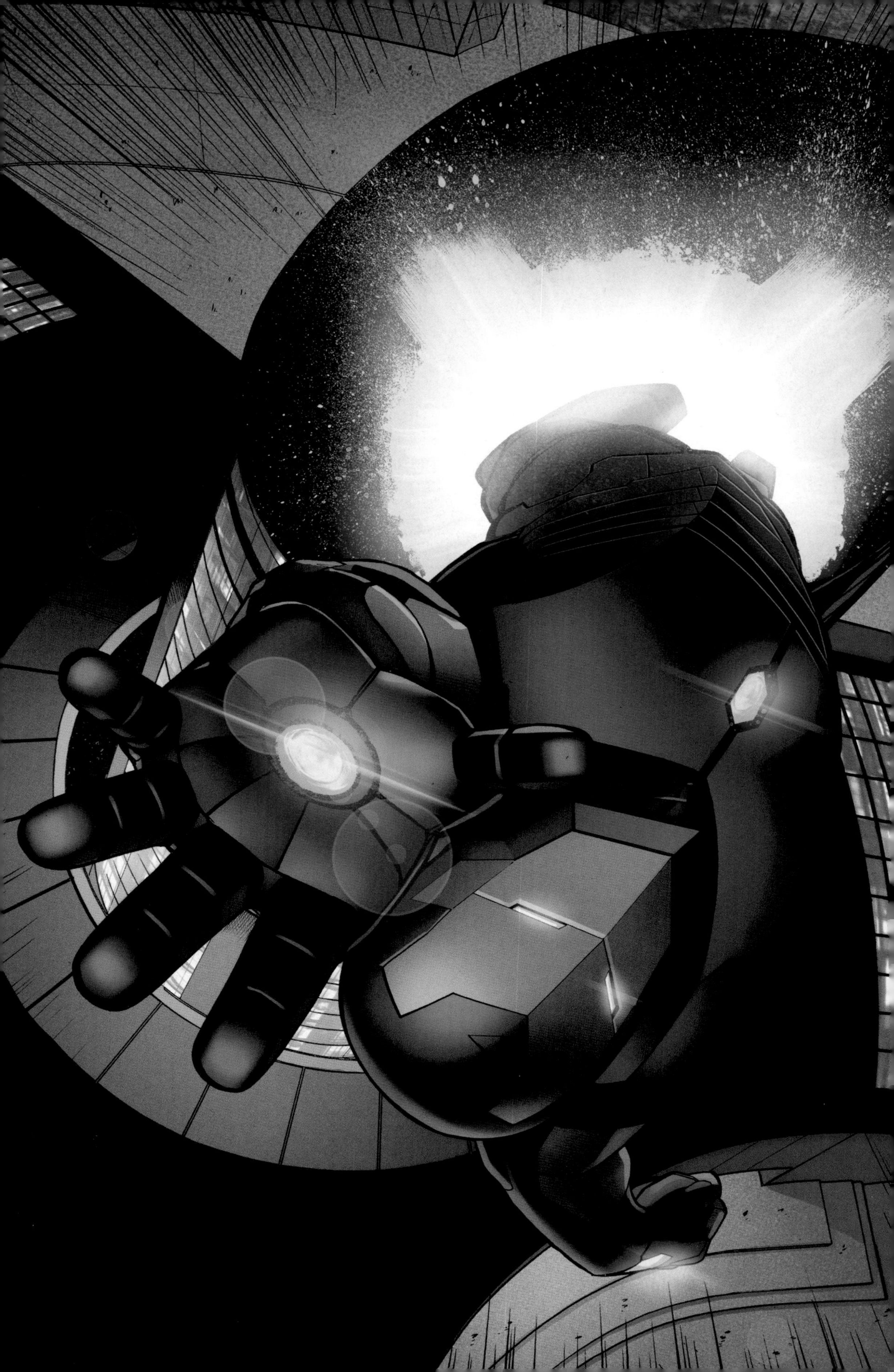

CIVIL WAR II #2

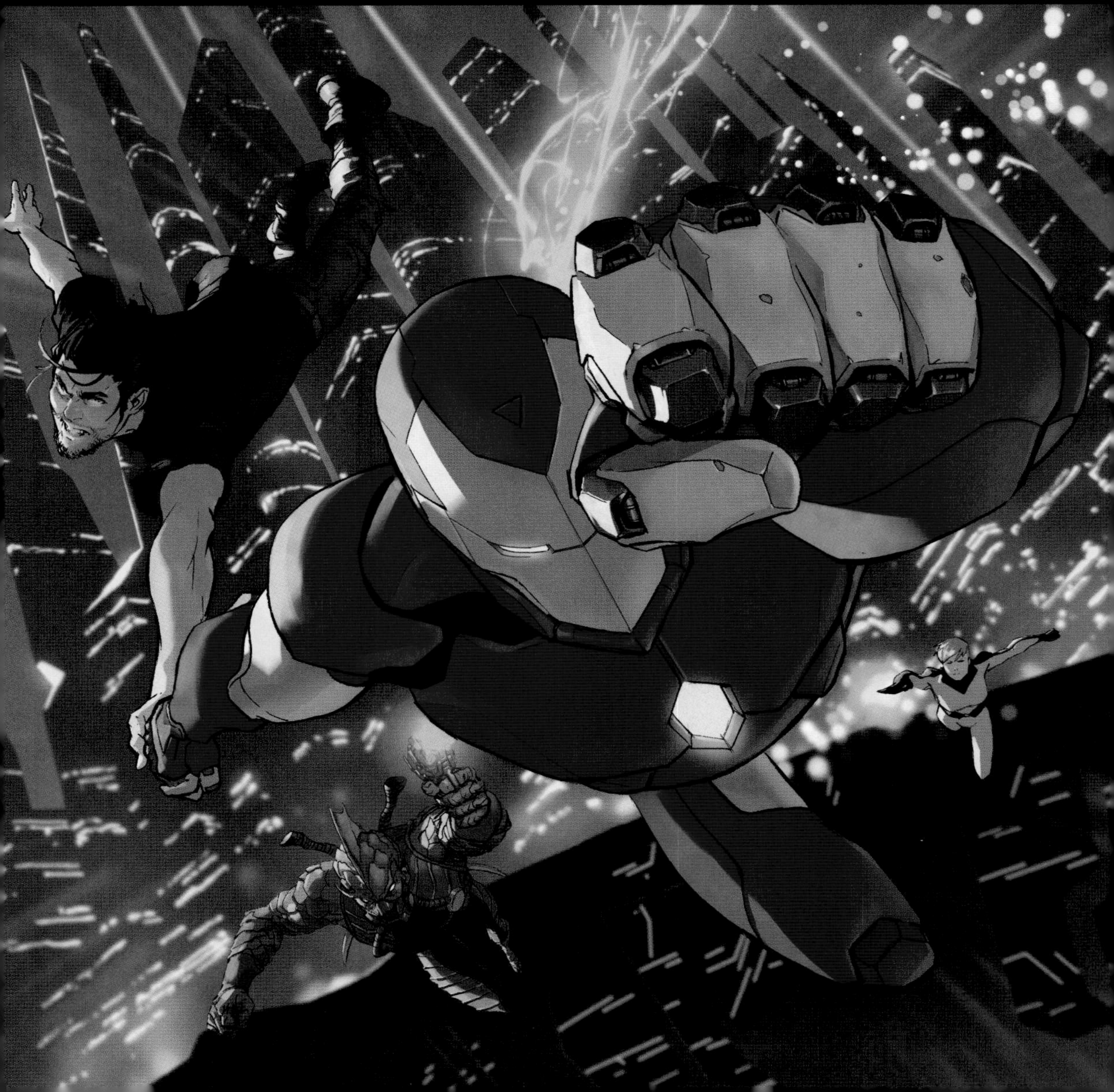

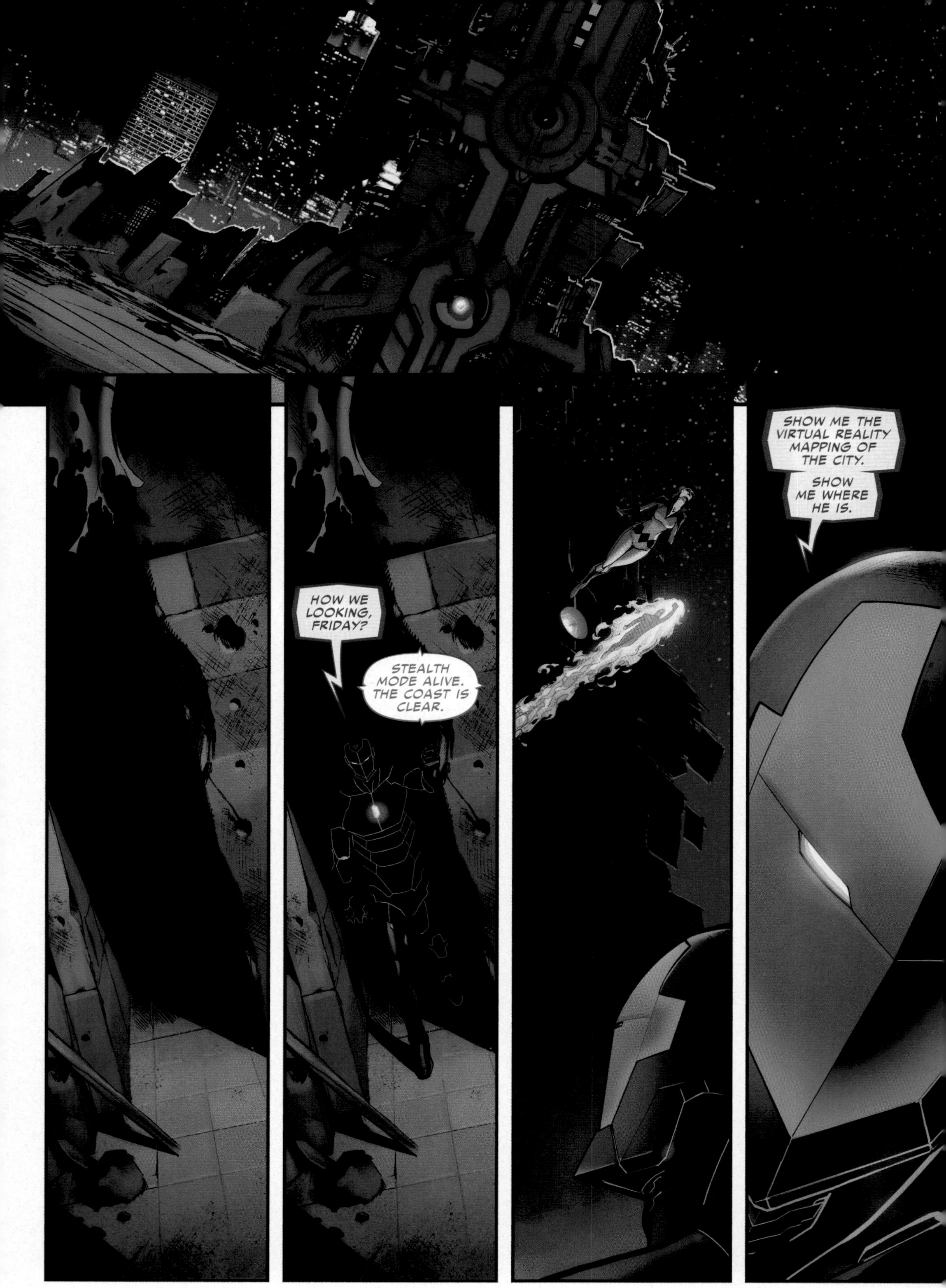
HOW WE LOOKING, FRIDAY?
STEALTH MODE ALIVE. THE COAST IS CLEAR.
SHOW ME THE VIRTUAL REALITY MAPPING OF THE CITY.
SHOW ME WHERE HE IS.

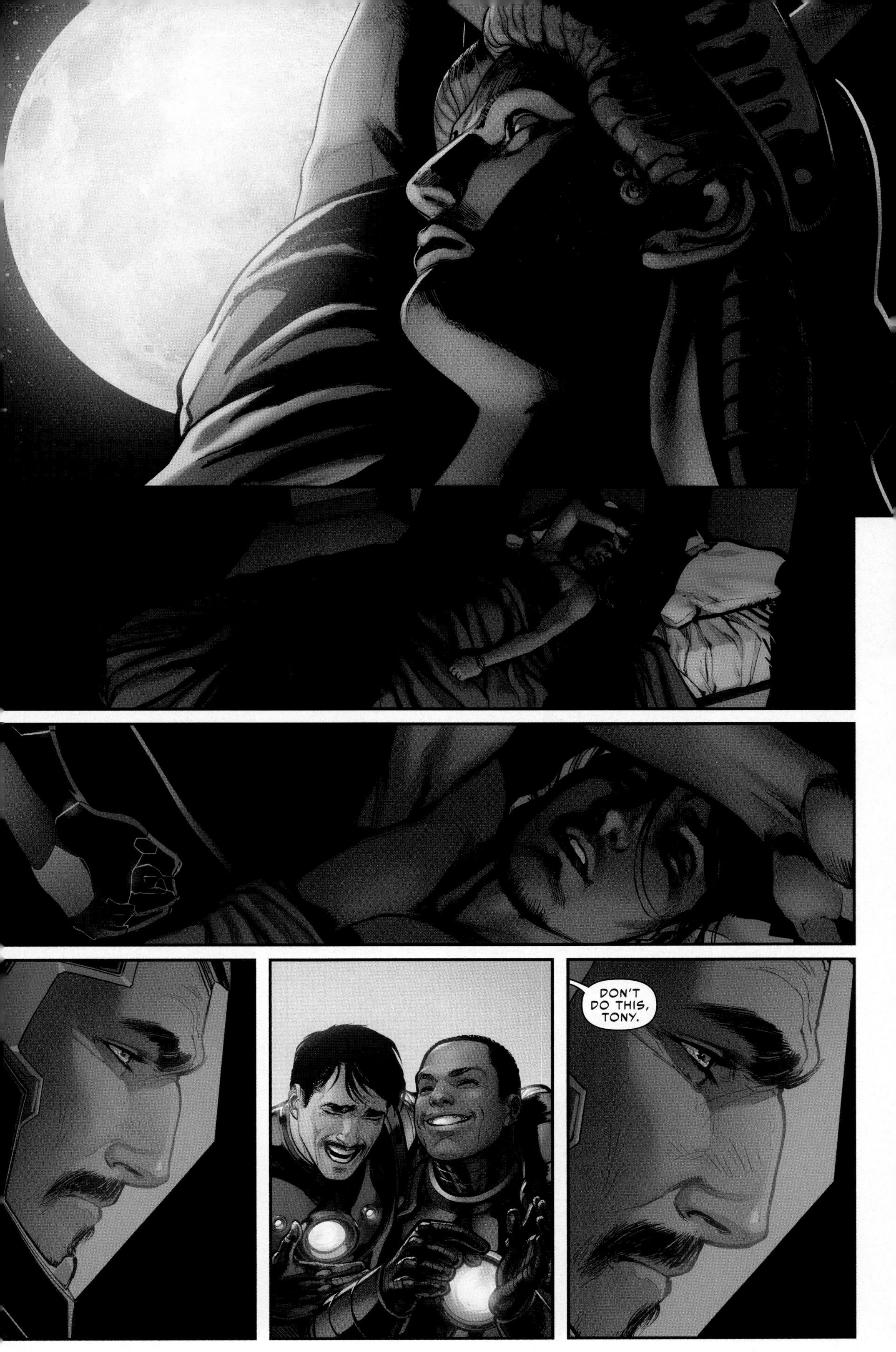
DON'T DO THIS, TONY.

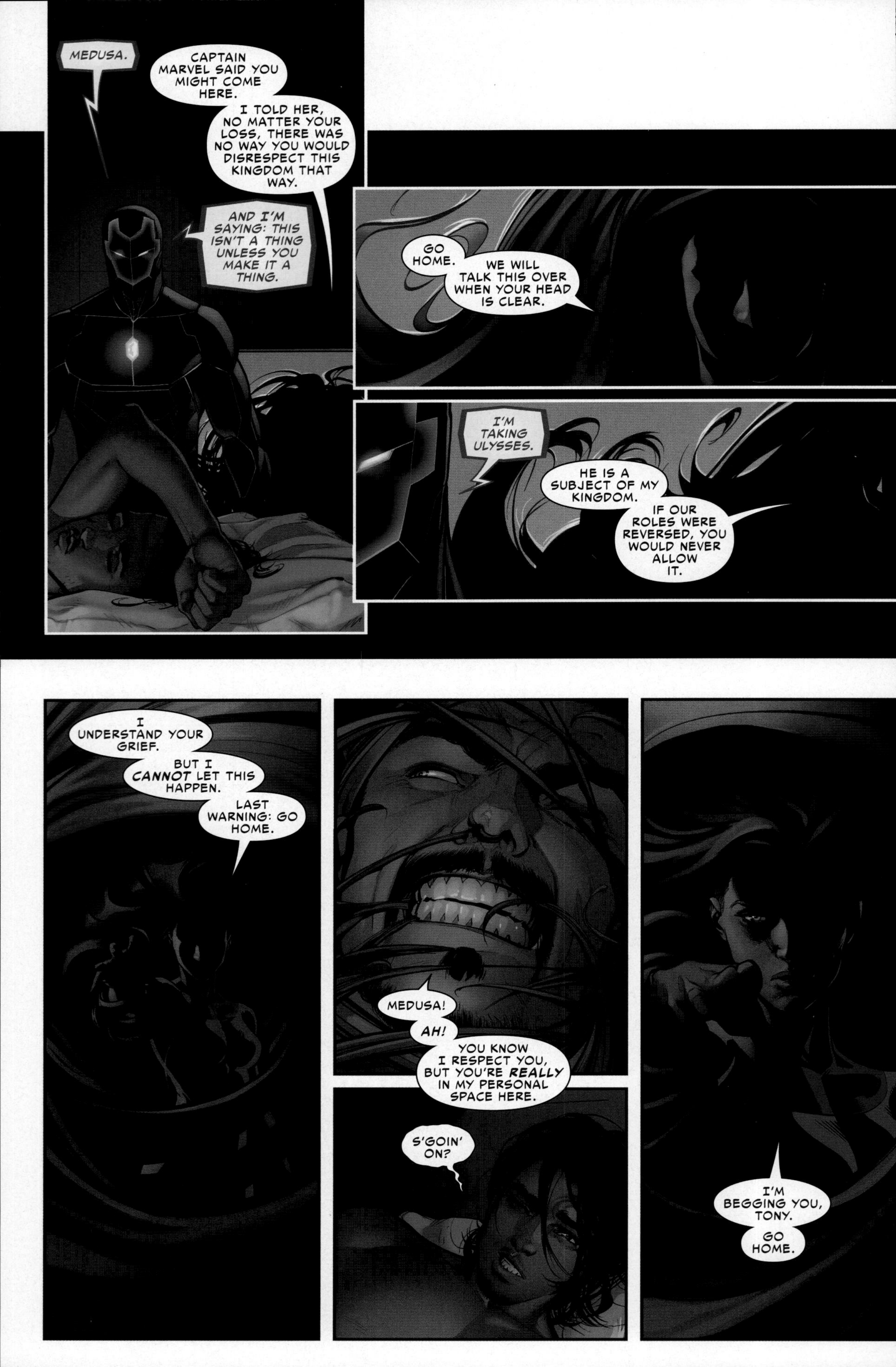
MEDUSA.
CAPTAIN MARVEL SAID YOU MIGHT COME HERE.
I TOLD HER, NO MATTER YOUR LOSS, THERE WAS NO WAY YOU WOULD DISRESPECT THIS KINGDOM THAT WAY.
AND I'M SAYING: THIS ISN'T A THING UNLESS YOU MAKE IT A THING.
GO HOME.
WE WILL TALK THIS OVER WHEN YOUR HEAD IS CLEAR.
I'M TAKING ULYSSES.
HE IS A SUBJECT OF MY KINGDOM.
IF OUR ROLES WERE REVERSED, YOU WOULD NEVER ALLOW IT.
I UNDERSTAND YOUR GRIEF.
BUT I *CANNOT* LET THIS HAPPEN.
LAST WARNING: GO HOME.
MEDUSA!
AH!
YOU KNOW I RESPECT YOU, BUT YOU'RE *REALLY* IN MY PERSONAL SPACE HERE.
S'GOIN' ON?
I'M BEGGING YOU, TONY.
GO HOME.

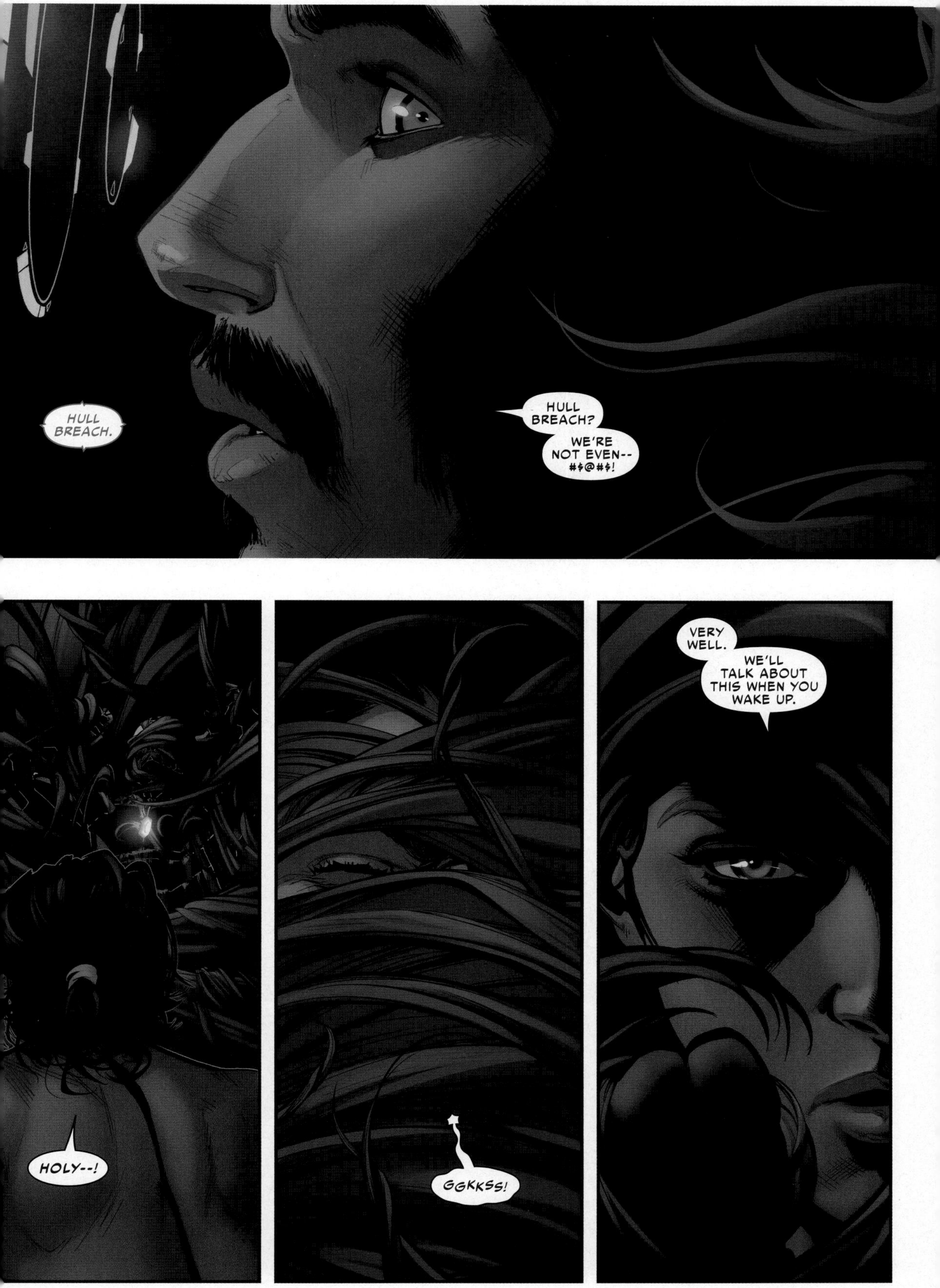
HULL BREACH.
HULL BREACH?
WE'RE NOT EVEN-- #$@#$!
HOLY--!
GGKKSS!
VERY WELL.
WE'LL TALK ABOUT THIS WHEN YOU WAKE UP.

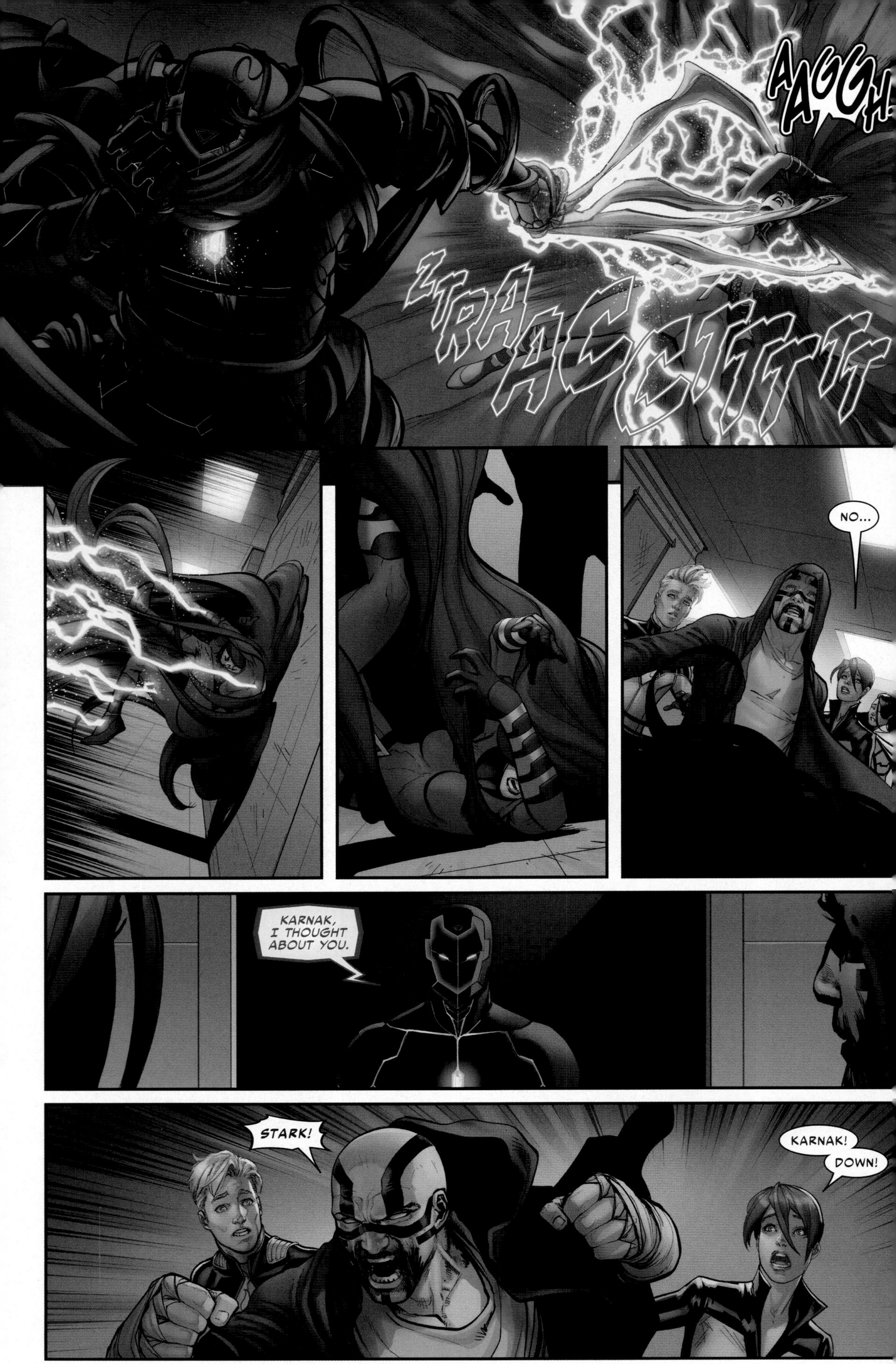
AAGGH!
ZTRAACKTTTT
NO...
KARNAK, I THOUGHT ABOUT YOU.
STARK!
KARNAK! DOWN!

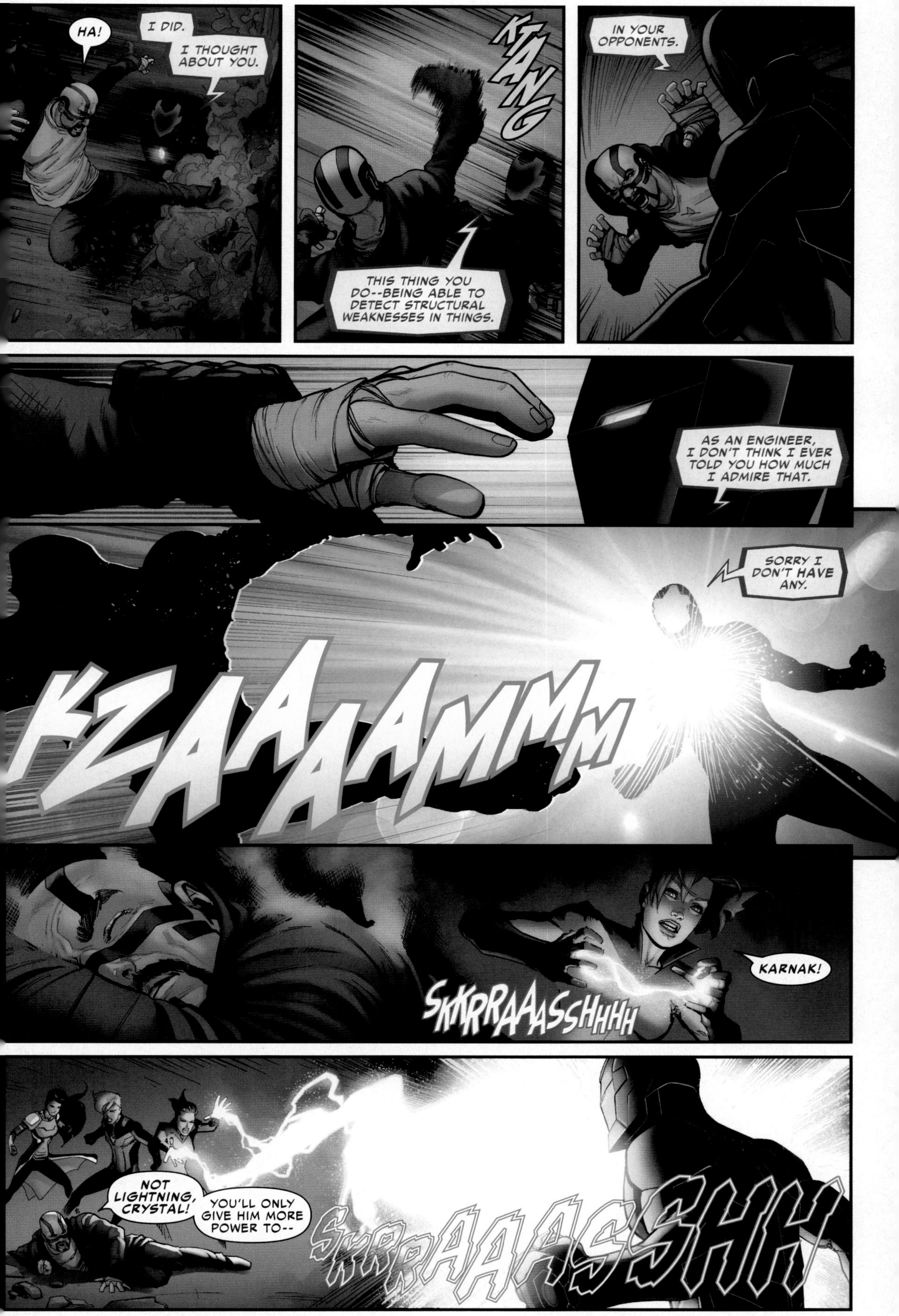
HA!
I DID.
I THOUGHT ABOUT YOU.
KLANG
THIS THING YOU DO--BEING ABLE TO DETECT STRUCTURAL WEAKNESSES IN THINGS.
IN YOUR OPPONENTS.
AS AN ENGINEER, I DON'T THINK I EVER TOLD YOU HOW MUCH I ADMIRE THAT.
SORRY I DON'T HAVE ANY.
KZAAAAMMM
KARNAK!
SKKRRAAASSHHHH
NOT LIGHTNING, CRYSTAL!
YOU'LL ONLY GIVE HIM MORE POWER TO--
SKRRAAAASSHH

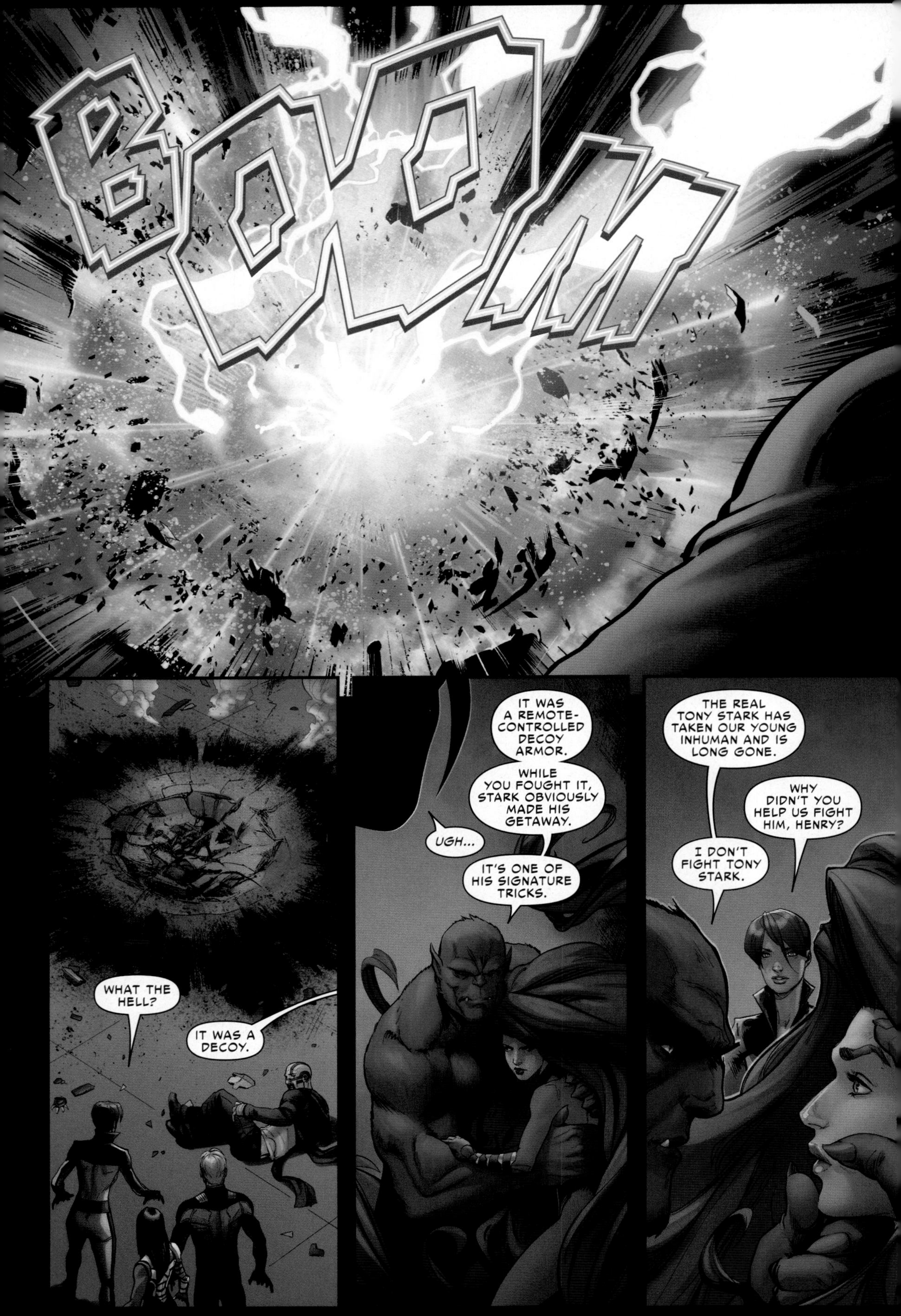
BOOOM
WHAT THE HELL?
IT WAS A DECOY.
UGH...
IT WAS A REMOTE-CONTROLLED DECOY ARMOR.
WHILE YOU FOUGHT IT, STARK OBVIOUSLY MADE HIS GETAWAY.
IT'S ONE OF HIS SIGNATURE TRICKS.
THE REAL TONY STARK HAS TAKEN OUR YOUNG INHUMAN AND IS LONG GONE.
WHY DIDN'T YOU HELP US FIGHT HIM, HENRY?
I DON'T FIGHT TONY STARK.

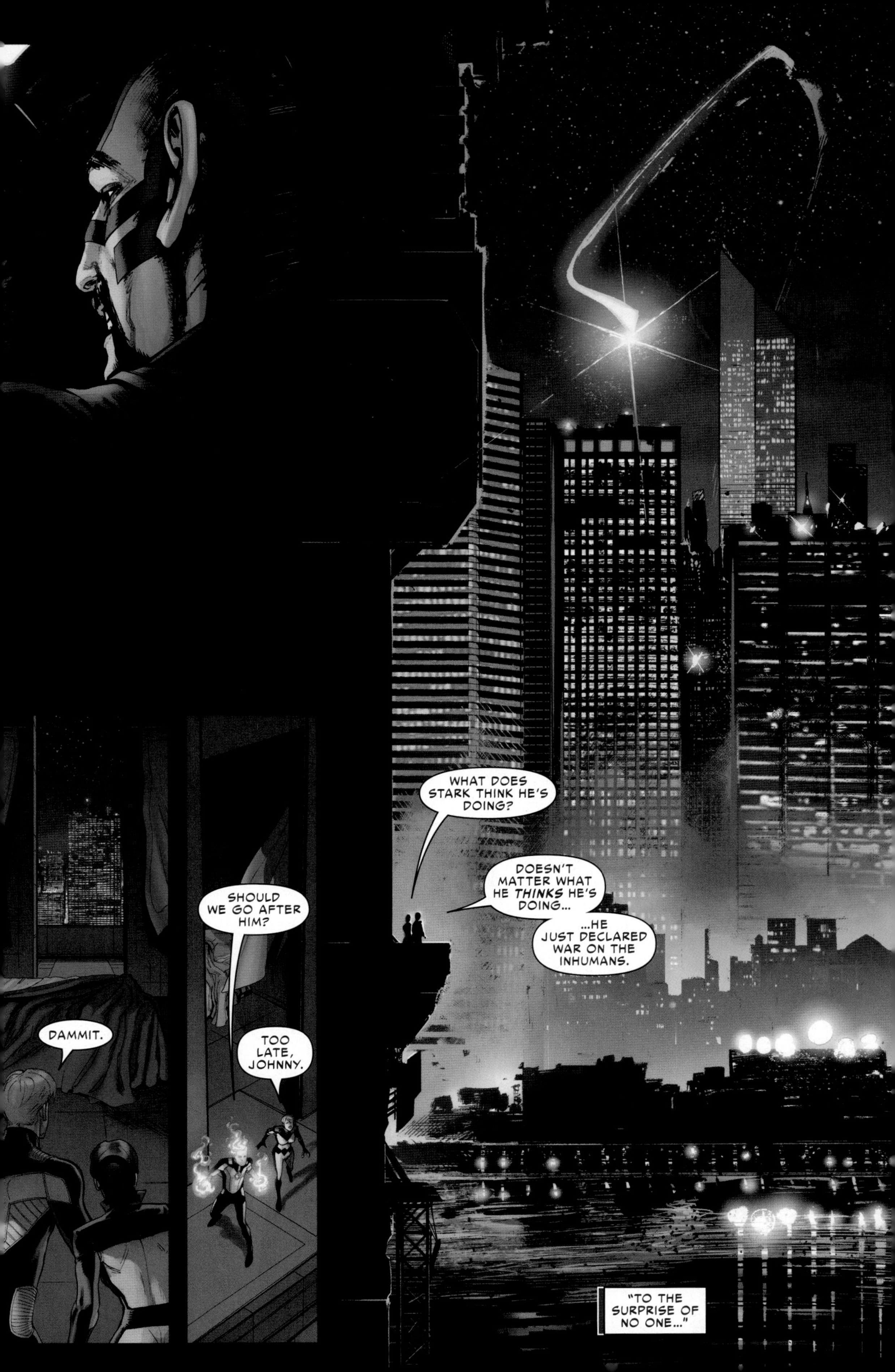
DAMMIT.
SHOULD WE GO AFTER HIM?
TOO LATE, JOHNNY.
WHAT DOES STARK THINK HE'S DOING?
DOESN'T MATTER WHAT HE *THINKS* HE'S DOING...
...HE JUST DECLARED WAR ON THE INHUMANS.
"TO THE SURPRISE OF NO ONE..."

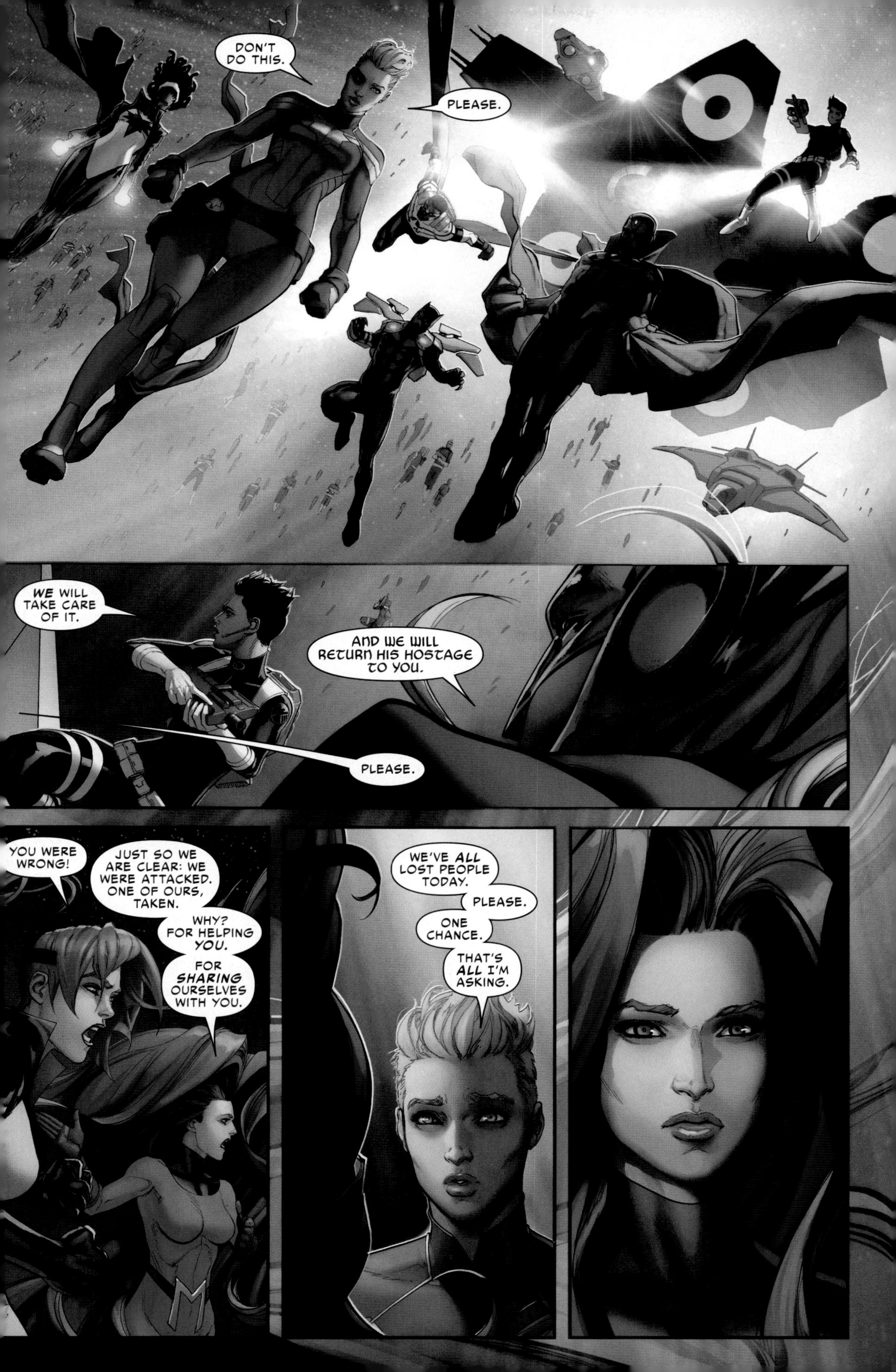
DON'T DO THIS.
PLEASE.
WE WILL TAKE CARE OF IT.
AND WE WILL RETURN HIS HOSTAGE TO YOU.
PLEASE.
YOU WERE WRONG!
JUST SO WE ARE CLEAR: WE WERE ATTACKED. ONE OF OURS, TAKEN.
WHY? FOR HELPING YOU.
FOR SHARING OURSELVES WITH YOU.
WE'VE ALL LOST PEOPLE TODAY.
PLEASE.
ONE CHANCE.
THAT'S ALL I'M ASKING.

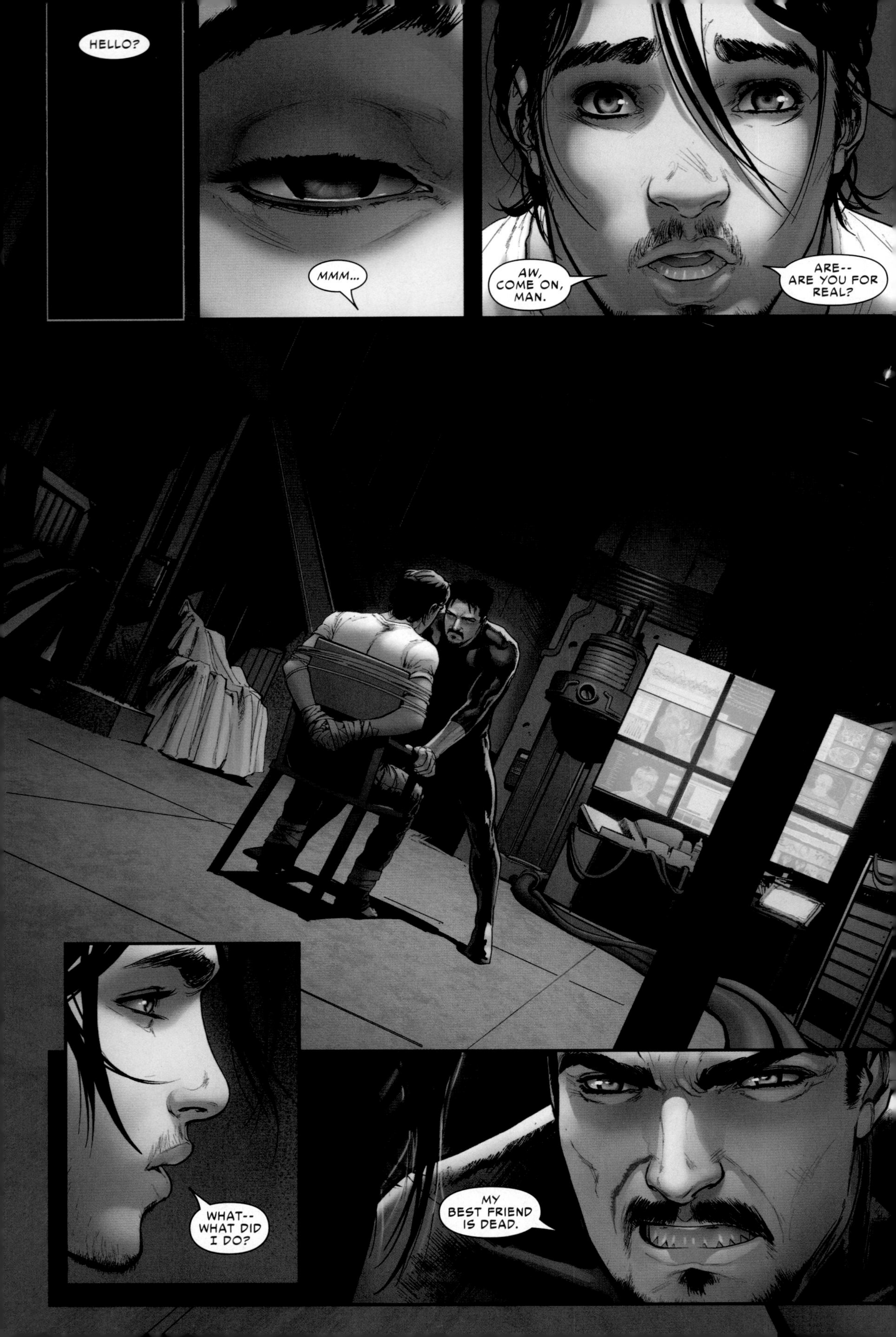
HELLO?
MMM...
AW, COME ON, MAN.
ARE-- ARE YOU FOR REAL?
WHAT-- WHAT DID I DO?
MY BEST FRIEND IS DEAD.

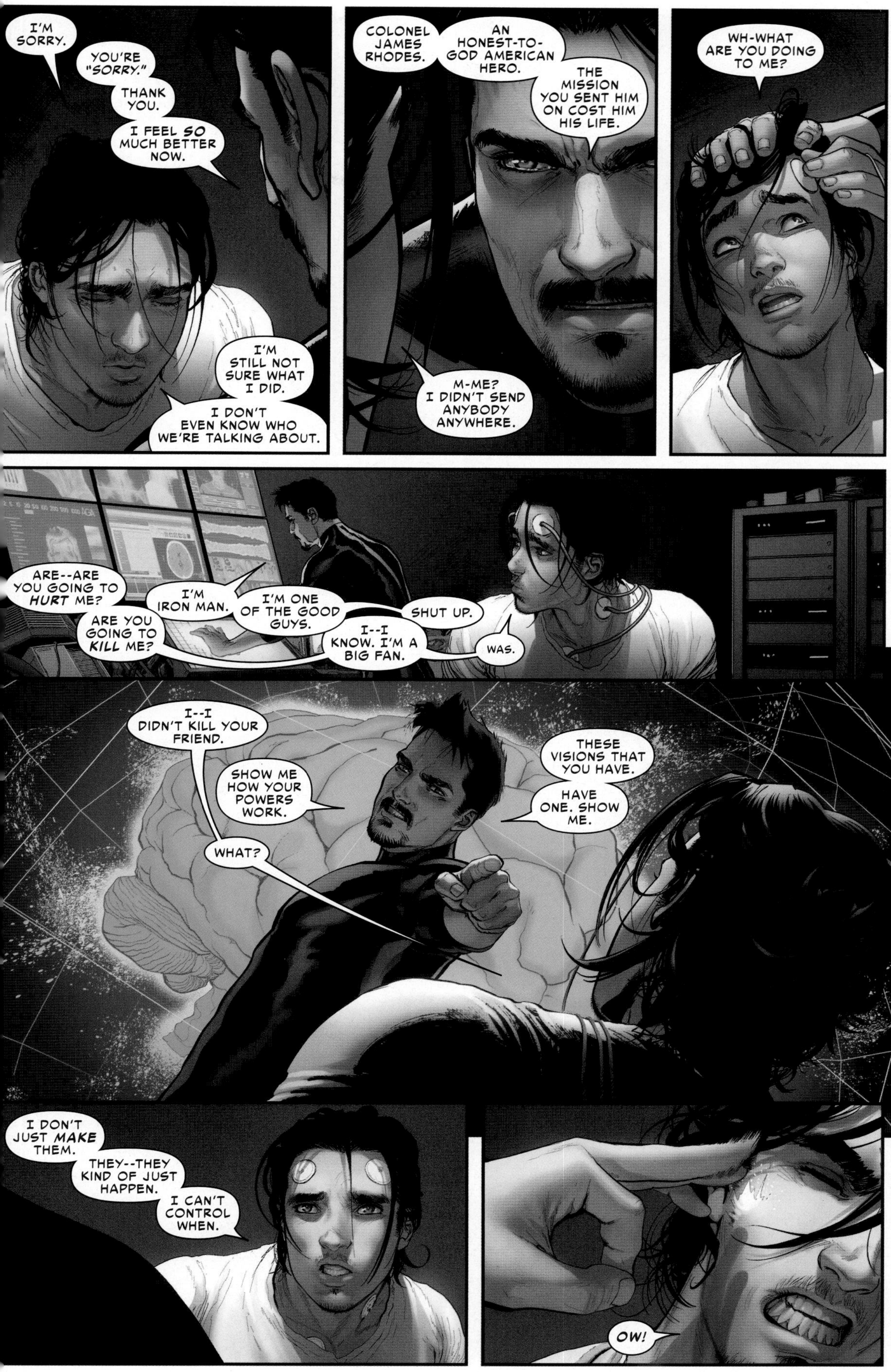

I'M SORRY.
YOU'RE "SORRY."
THANK YOU.
I FEEL *SO* MUCH BETTER NOW.
I'M STILL NOT SURE WHAT I DID.
I DON'T EVEN KNOW WHO WE'RE TALKING ABOUT.
COLONEL JAMES RHODES.
AN HONEST-TO-GOD AMERICAN HERO.
THE MISSION YOU SENT HIM ON COST HIM HIS LIFE.
M-ME? I DIDN'T SEND ANYBODY ANYWHERE.
WH-WHAT ARE YOU DOING TO ME?
ARE--ARE YOU GOING TO *HURT* ME?
ARE YOU GOING TO *KILL* ME?
I'M IRON MAN.
I'M ONE OF THE GOOD GUYS.
I--I KNOW. I'M A BIG FAN.
SHUT UP.
WAS.
I--I DIDN'T KILL YOUR FRIEND.
SHOW ME HOW YOUR POWERS WORK.
WHAT?
THESE VISIONS THAT YOU HAVE.
HAVE ONE. SHOW ME.
I DON'T JUST *MAKE* THEM.
THEY--THEY KIND OF JUST HAPPEN.
I CAN'T CONTROL WHEN.
OW!

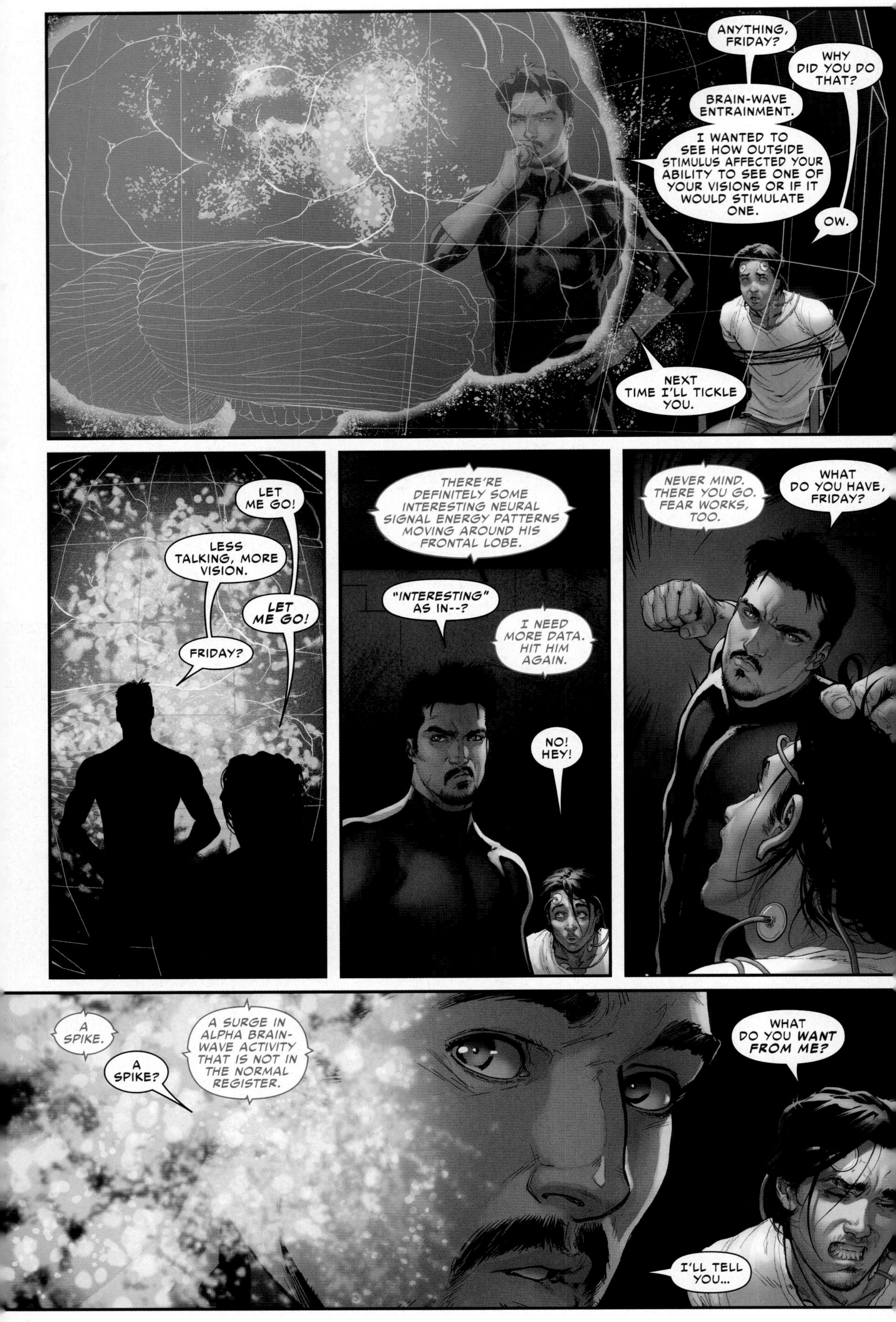
ANYTHING, FRIDAY?
BRAIN-WAVE ENTRAINMENT.
I WANTED TO SEE HOW OUTSIDE STIMULUS AFFECTED YOUR ABILITY TO SEE ONE OF YOUR VISIONS OR IF IT WOULD STIMULATE ONE.
WHY DID YOU DO THAT?
OW.
NEXT TIME I'LL TICKLE YOU.
LET ME GO!
LESS TALKING, MORE VISION.
LET ME GO!
FRIDAY?
THERE'RE DEFINITELY SOME INTERESTING NEURAL SIGNAL ENERGY PATTERNS MOVING AROUND HIS FRONTAL LOBE.
"INTERESTING" AS IN--?
I NEED MORE DATA. HIT HIM AGAIN.
NO! HEY!
NEVER MIND. THERE YOU GO. FEAR WORKS, TOO.
WHAT DO YOU HAVE, FRIDAY?
A SPIKE.
A SPIKE?
A SURGE IN ALPHA BRAIN-WAVE ACTIVITY THAT IS NOT IN THE NORMAL REGISTER.
WHAT DO YOU WANT FROM ME?
I'LL TELL YOU...

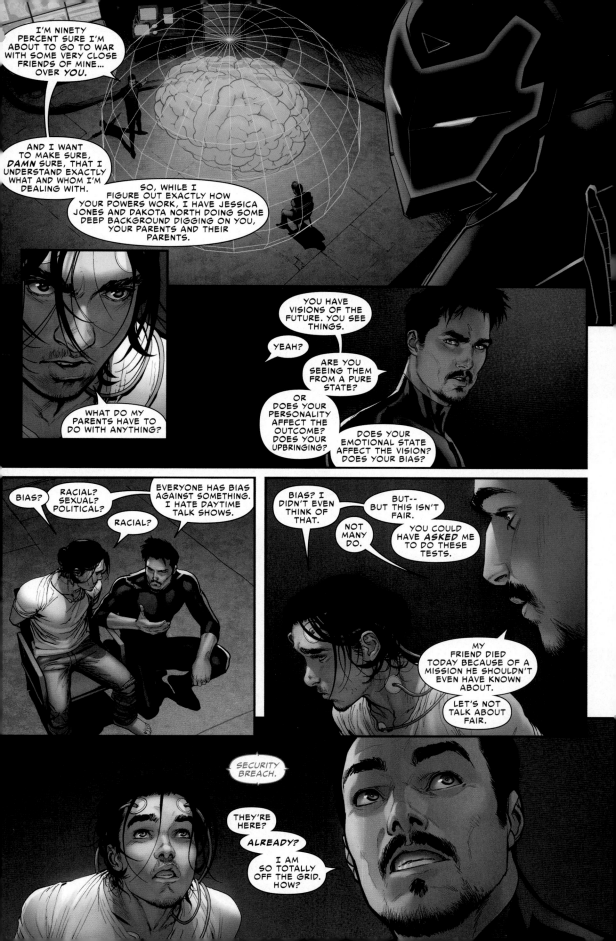

I'M NINETY PERCENT SURE I'M ABOUT TO GO TO WAR WITH SOME VERY CLOSE FRIENDS OF MINE... OVER *YOU.*

AND I WANT TO MAKE SURE, *DAMN* SURE, THAT I UNDERSTAND EXACTLY WHAT AND WHOM I'M DEALING WITH.

SO, WHILE I FIGURE OUT EXACTLY HOW YOUR POWERS WORK, I HAVE JESSICA JONES AND DAKOTA NORTH DOING SOME DEEP BACKGROUND DIGGING ON YOU, YOUR PARENTS AND THEIR PARENTS.

WHAT DO MY PARENTS HAVE TO DO WITH ANYTHING?

YOU HAVE VISIONS OF THE FUTURE. YOU SEE THINGS.

YEAH?

ARE YOU SEEING THEM FROM A PURE STATE?

OR DOES YOUR PERSONALITY AFFECT THE OUTCOME? DOES YOUR UPBRINGING?

DOES YOUR EMOTIONAL STATE AFFECT THE VISION? DOES YOUR BIAS?

BIAS?

RACIAL? SEXUAL? POLITICAL?

RACIAL?

EVERYONE HAS BIAS AGAINST SOMETHING. I HATE DAYTIME TALK SHOWS.

BIAS? I DIDN'T EVEN THINK OF THAT.

BUT-- BUT THIS ISN'T FAIR.

NOT MANY DO.

YOU COULD HAVE *ASKED* ME TO DO THESE TESTS.

MY FRIEND DIED TODAY BECAUSE OF A MISSION HE SHOULDN'T EVEN HAVE KNOWN ABOUT.

LET'S NOT TALK ABOUT FAIR.

SECURITY BREACH.

THEY'RE HERE?

ALREADY?

I AM SO TOTALLY OFF THE GRID. HOW?

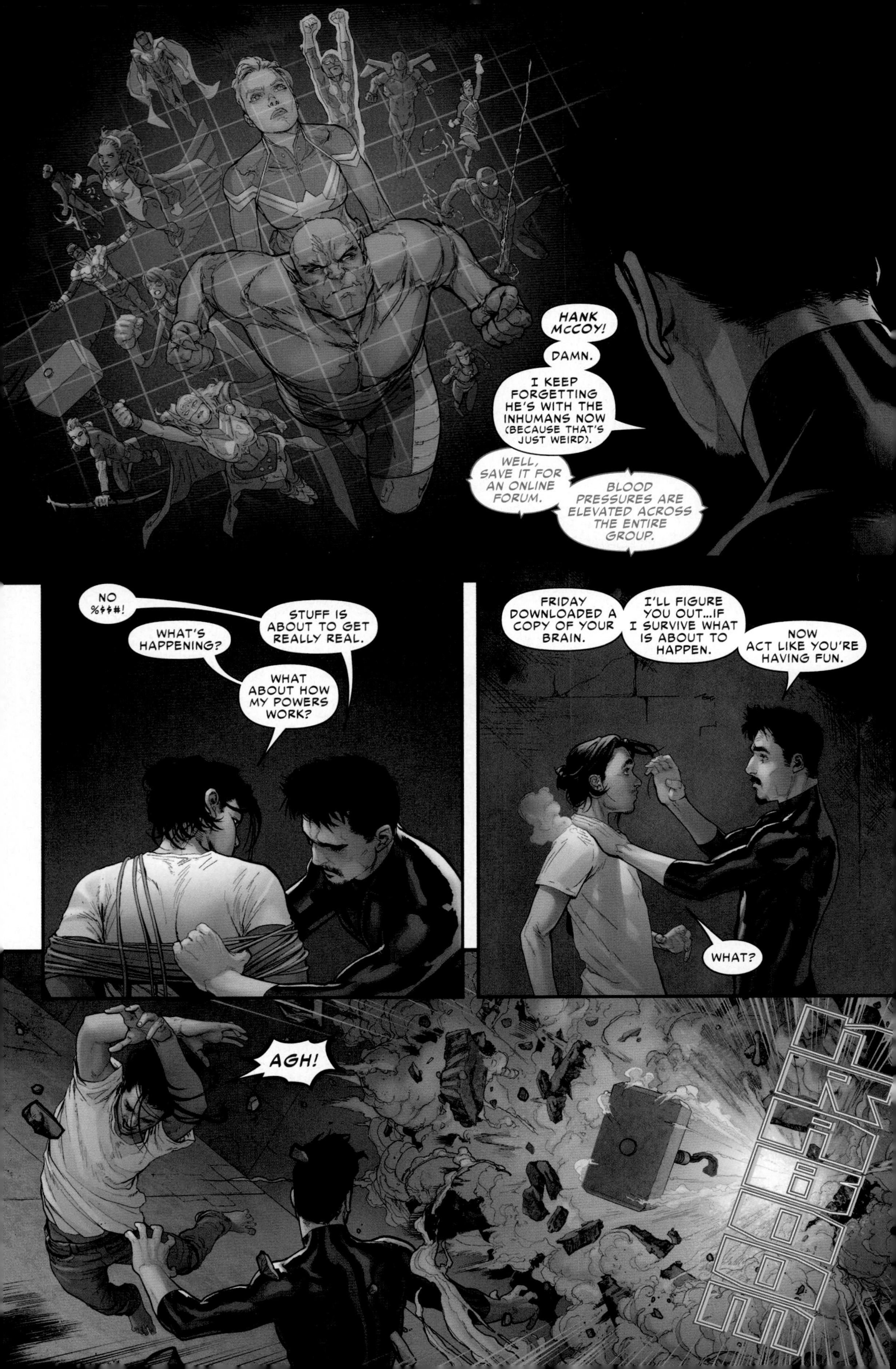
HANK McCOY!
DAMN.
I KEEP FORGETTING HE'S WITH THE INHUMANS NOW (BECAUSE THAT'S JUST WEIRD).
WELL, SAVE IT FOR AN ONLINE FORUM.
BLOOD PRESSURES ARE ELEVATED ACROSS THE ENTIRE GROUP.
NO %$$#!
STUFF IS ABOUT TO GET REALLY REAL.
WHAT'S HAPPENING?
WHAT ABOUT HOW MY POWERS WORK?
FRIDAY DOWNLOADED A COPY OF YOUR BRAIN.
I'LL FIGURE YOU OUT...IF I SURVIVE WHAT IS ABOUT TO HAPPEN.
NOW ACT LIKE YOU'RE HAVING FUN.
WHAT?
AGH!

TONY.

CAROL.

JUST IN TIME FOR PARCHEESI.

THAT *LINE* WAS PARCHEESI.

TRUE. BUT I'M IN MOURNING.

THEY'RE NOT ALL GOING TO BE WINNERS.

YOU CREATED QUITE AN INCIDENT.

NO, ACTUALLY, *YOU* DID.

I REACTED ACCORDINGLY.

WELL, NOW *WE* ARE. IN KIND.

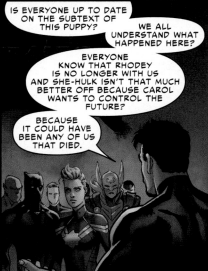

IS EVERYONE UP TO DATE ON THE SUBTEXT OF THIS PUPPY?

WE ALL UNDERSTAND WHAT HAPPENED HERE?

EVERYONE KNOW THAT RHODEY IS NO LONGER WITH US AND SHE-HULK ISN'T THAT MUCH BETTER OFF BECAUSE CAROL WANTS TO CONTROL THE FUTURE?

BECAUSE IT COULD HAVE BEEN ANY OF US THAT DIED.

IT COULD HAVE BEEN YOU, IT COULD HAVE BEEN YOU...

...AND I'M ACTUALLY *SHOCKED* THAT IT WASN'T YOU, CLINT.

TONY, YOU KIDNAPPED A KID FROM HIS HOME--

TORTURED HIM...

COME ON, I DIDN'T TORTURE HIM! LOOK.

A *LITTLE* BIT.

HE TORTURED ME.

TONY, I THINK YOU'RE HAVING A BIT OF A NERVOUS BREAKDOWN--

AND I WOULD LIKE TO HELP YOU.

OH!

IT'S NOT A *BIT* OF A NERVOUS BREAKDOWN...I AM HAVING A *COMPLETE AND TOTAL NERVOUS BREAKDOWN!*

TONY.

ALL DAY EVERY DAY WE FIGHT FOR THE FUTURE. WE FIGHT TO MAKE THE WORLD A BETTER PLACE.

DON'T START LECTURING ME TO COVER--

AND IF WE WIN OR LOSE, WE ARE ACCOUNTABLE FOR OUR ACTIONS.

TONY, STOP.

I THOUGHT WE *AGREED* ON THIS. I *THOUGHT--*

AAH--

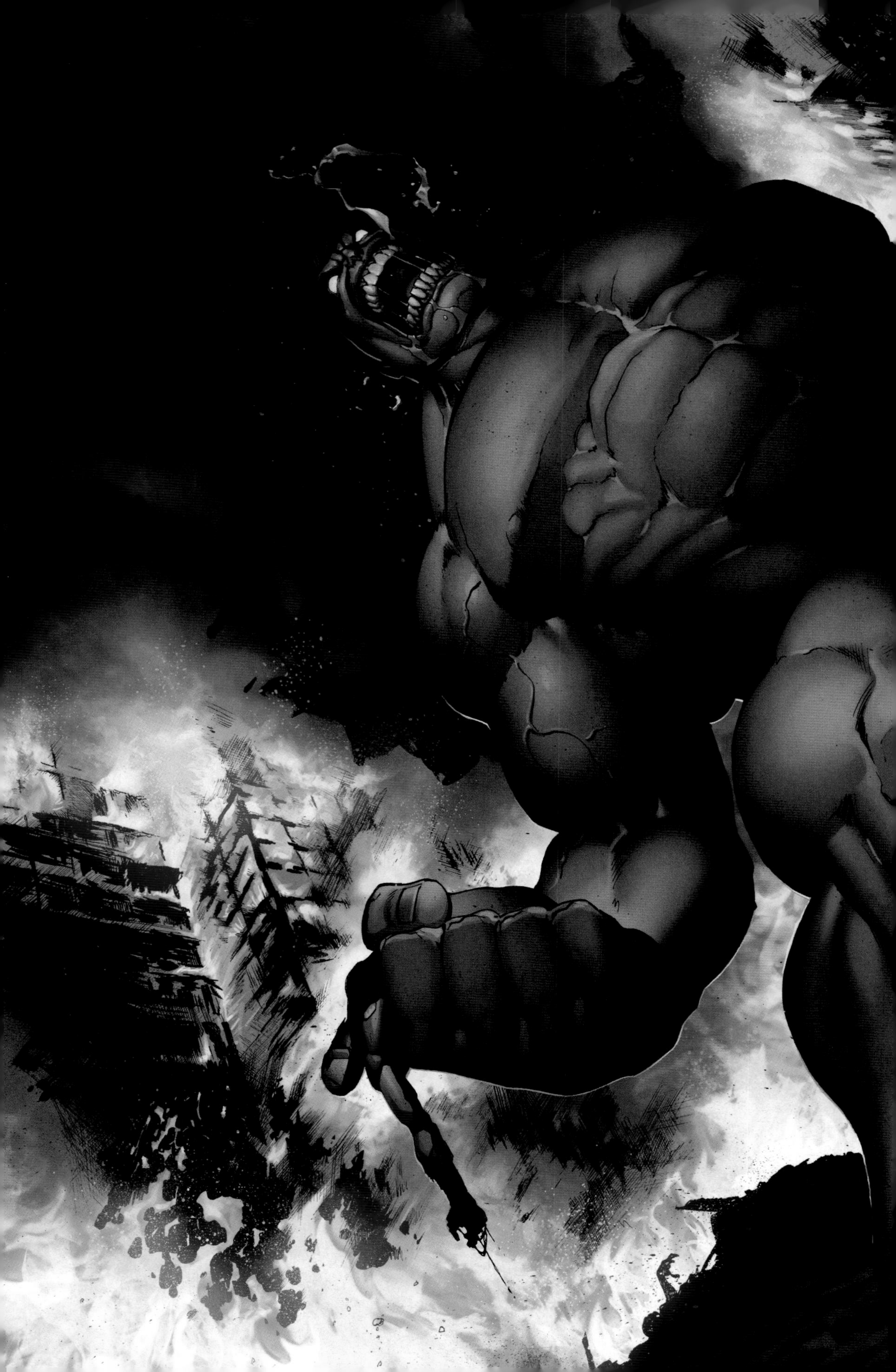

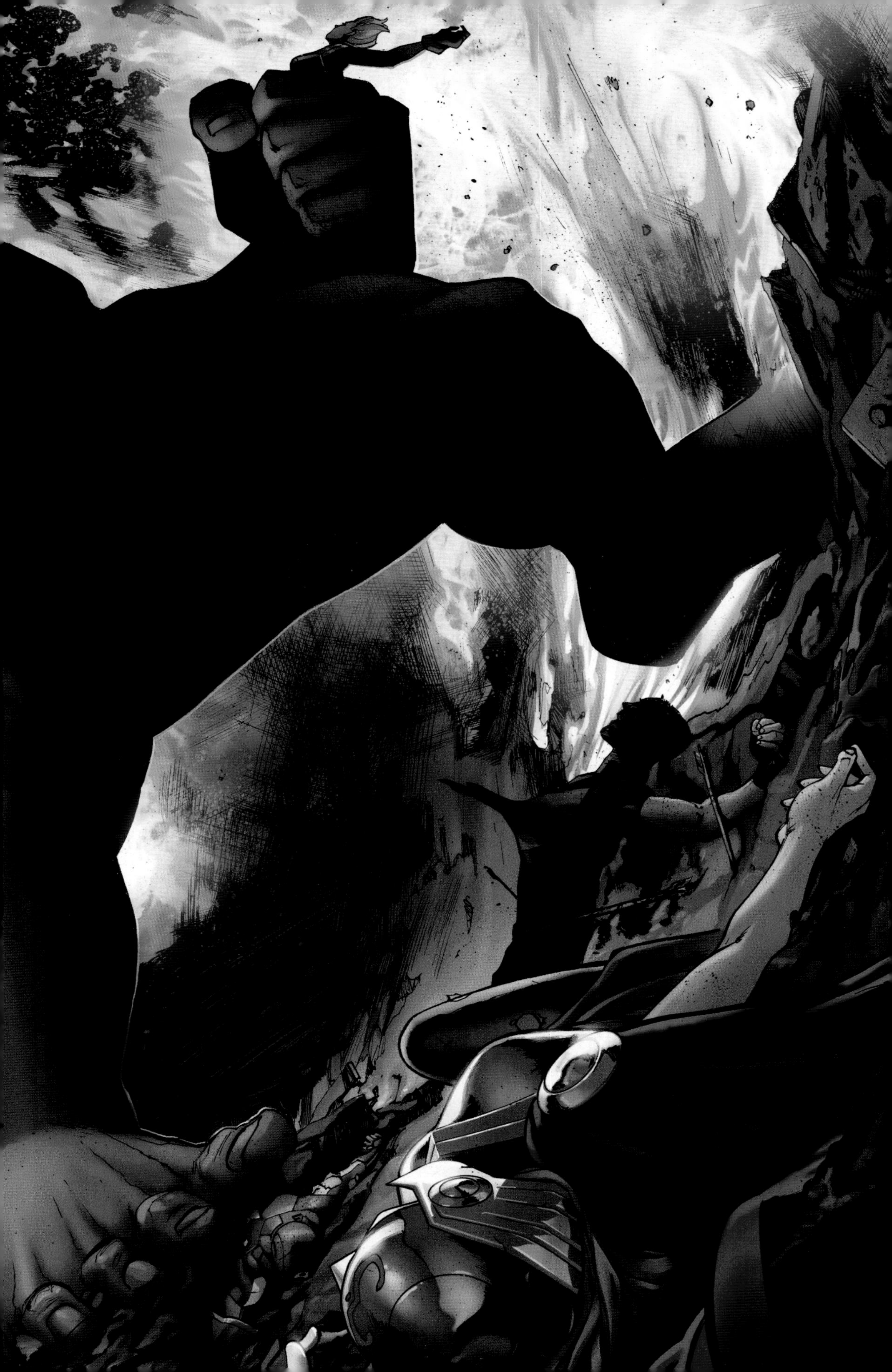

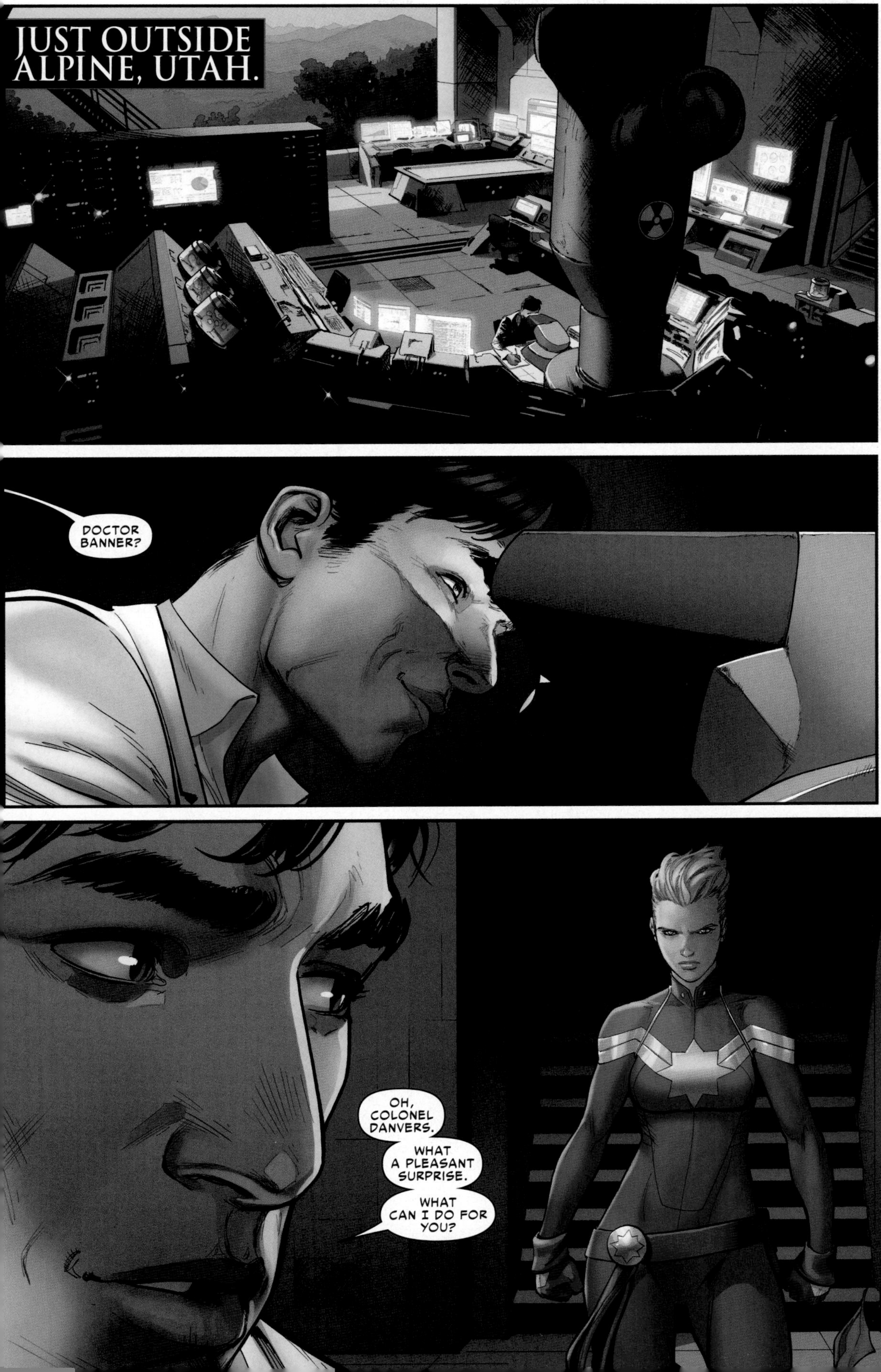
JUST OUTSIDE ALPINE, UTAH.
DOCTOR BANNER?
OH, COLONEL DANVERS.
WHAT A PLEASANT SURPRISE.
WHAT CAN I DO FOR YOU?

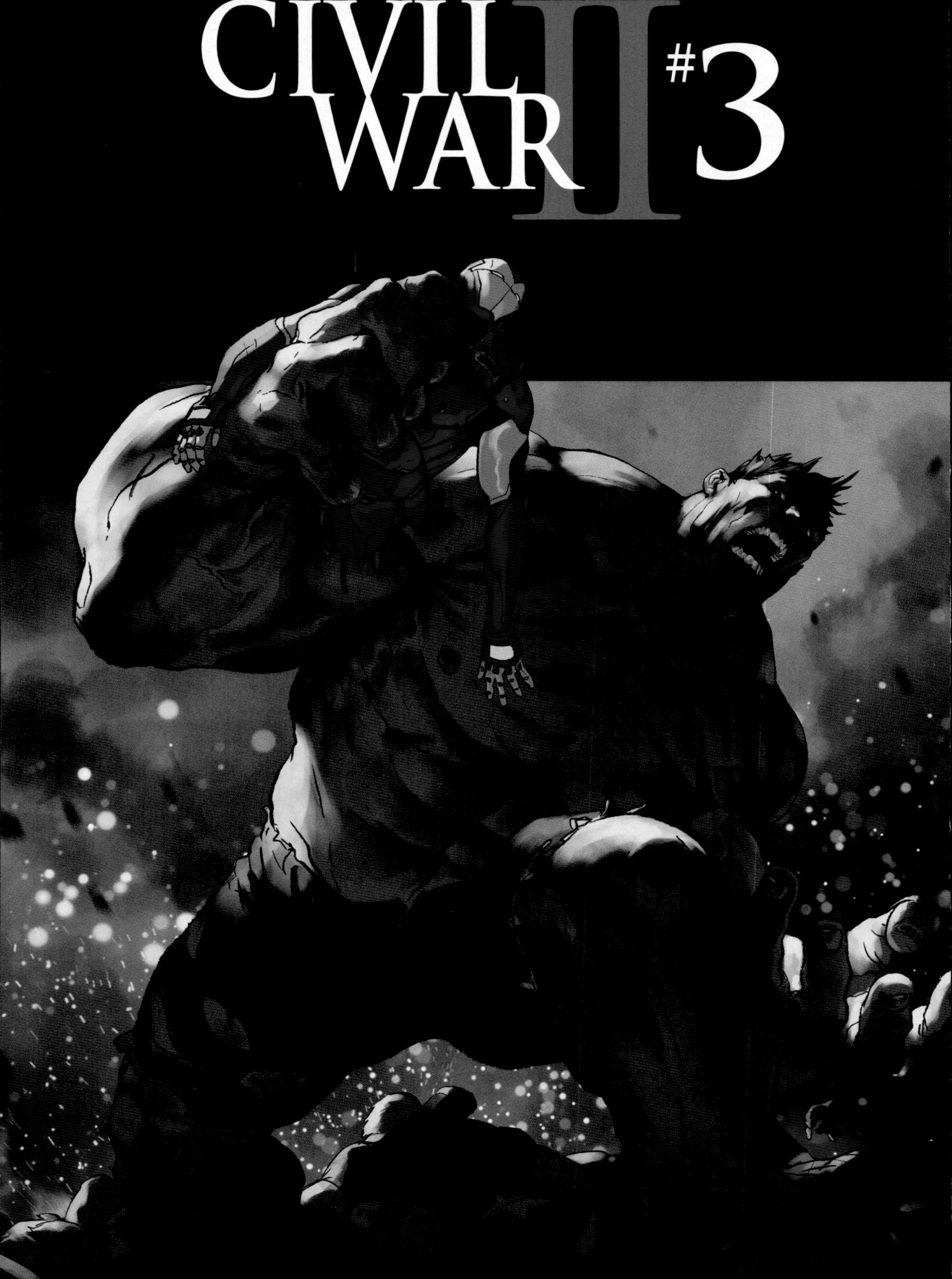
CIVIL WAR II
#3

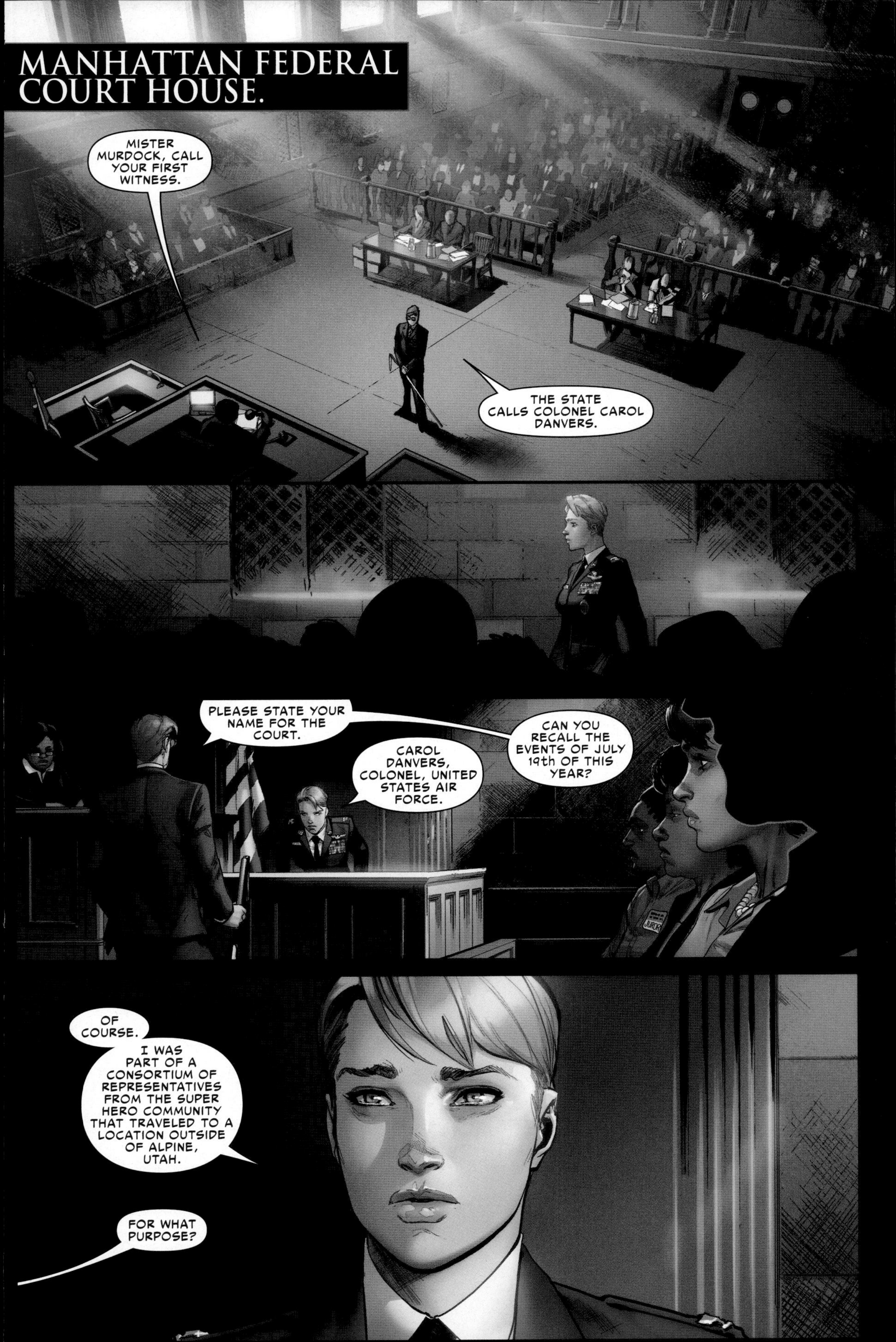
MANHATTAN FEDERAL COURT HOUSE.
MISTER MURDOCK, CALL YOUR FIRST WITNESS.
THE STATE CALLS COLONEL CAROL DANVERS.
PLEASE STATE YOUR NAME FOR THE COURT.
CAROL DANVERS, COLONEL, UNITED STATES AIR FORCE.
CAN YOU RECALL THE EVENTS OF JULY 19th OF THIS YEAR?
JUROR
OF COURSE.
I WAS PART OF A CONSORTIUM OF REPRESENTATIVES FROM THE SUPER HERO COMMUNITY THAT TRAVELED TO A LOCATION OUTSIDE OF ALPINE, UTAH.
FOR WHAT PURPOSE?

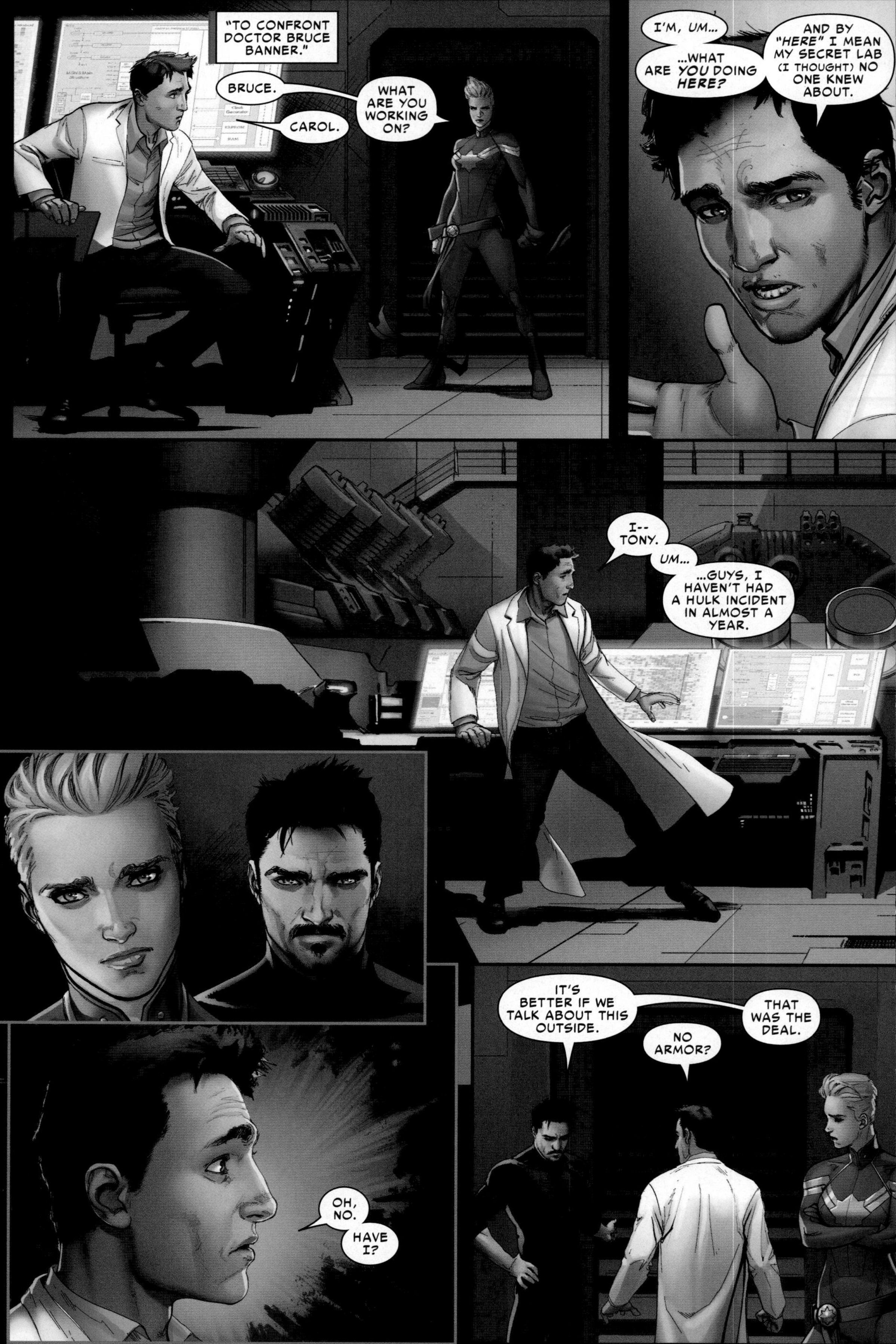
"TO CONFRONT DOCTOR BRUCE BANNER."
BRUCE.
CAROL.
WHAT ARE YOU WORKING ON?
I'M, UM...
...WHAT ARE YOU DOING HERE?
AND BY "HERE" I MEAN MY SECRET LAB (I THOUGHT) NO ONE KNEW ABOUT.
I-- TONY.
UM...
...GUYS, I HAVEN'T HAD A HULK INCIDENT IN ALMOST A YEAR.
OH, NO.
HAVE I?
IT'S BETTER IF WE TALK ABOUT THIS OUTSIDE.
NO ARMOR?
THAT WAS THE DEAL.

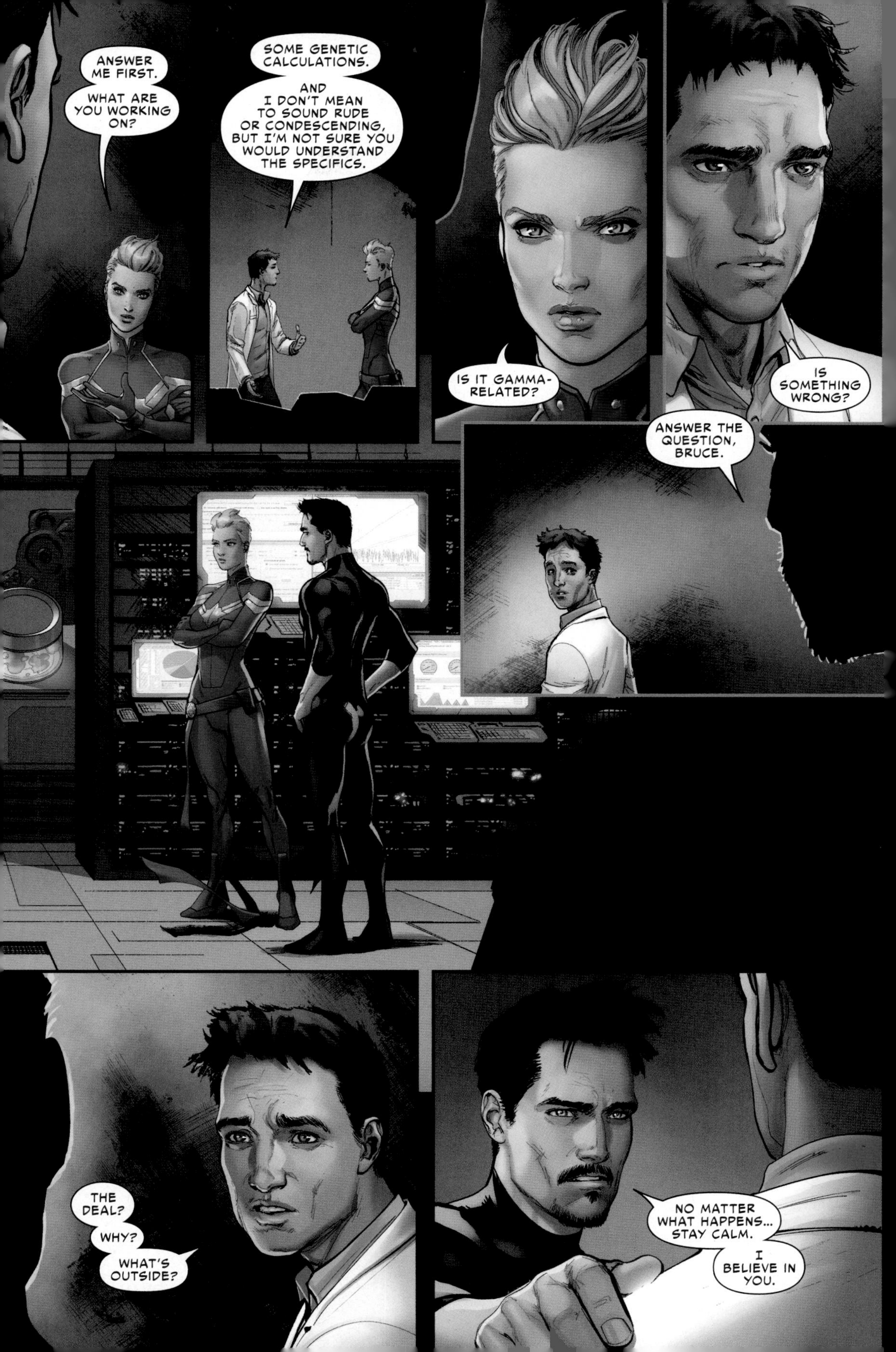
ANSWER ME FIRST.
WHAT ARE YOU WORKING ON?
SOME GENETIC CALCULATIONS.
AND I DON'T MEAN TO SOUND RUDE OR CONDESCENDING, BUT I'M NOT SURE YOU WOULD UNDERSTAND THE SPECIFICS.
IS IT GAMMA-RELATED?
IS SOMETHING WRONG?
ANSWER THE QUESTION, BRUCE.
THE DEAL?
WHY?
WHAT'S OUTSIDE?
NO MATTER WHAT HAPPENS... STAY CALM.
I BELIEVE IN YOU.

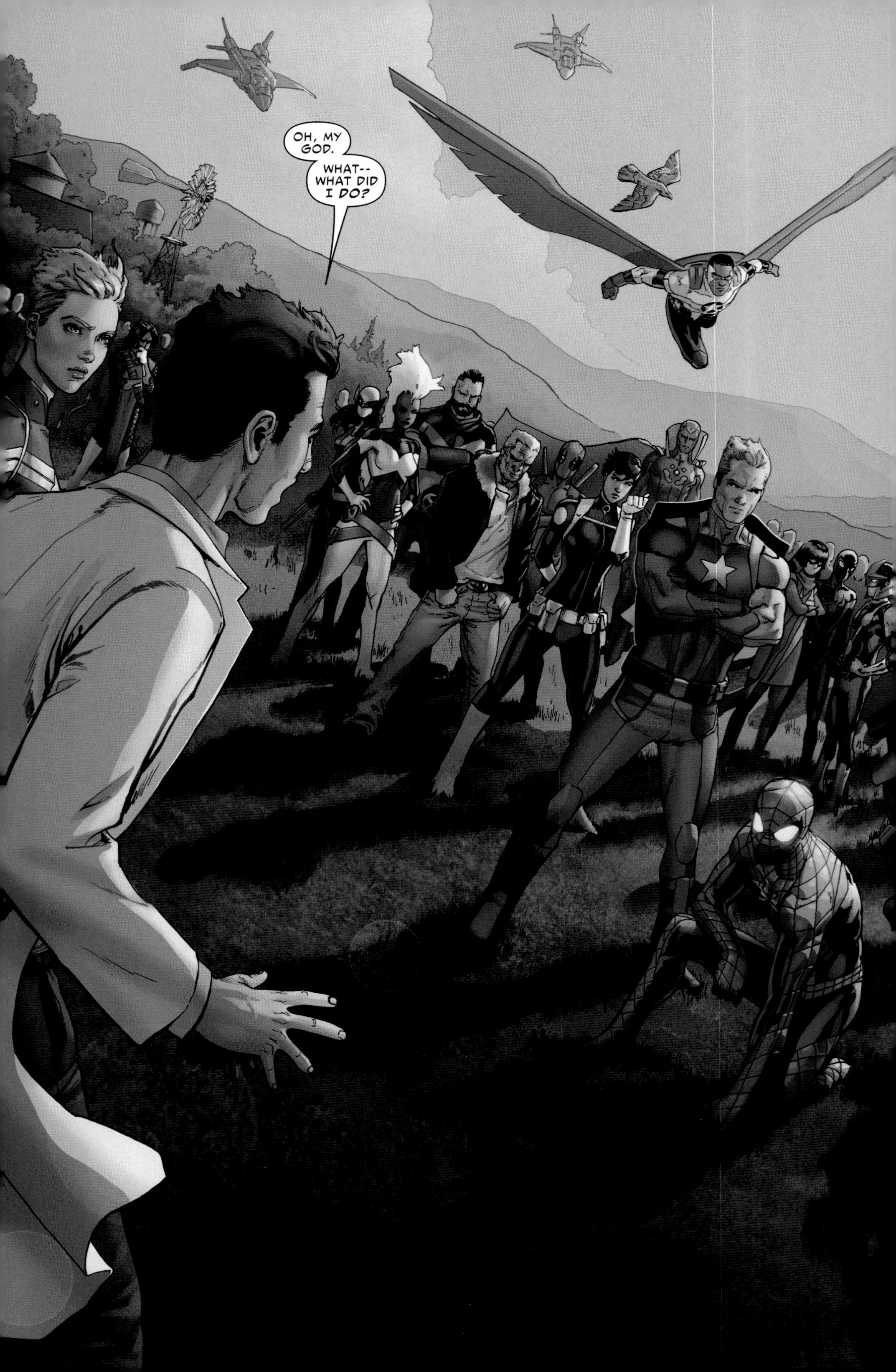
OH, MY GOD.
WHAT-- WHAT DID I DO?

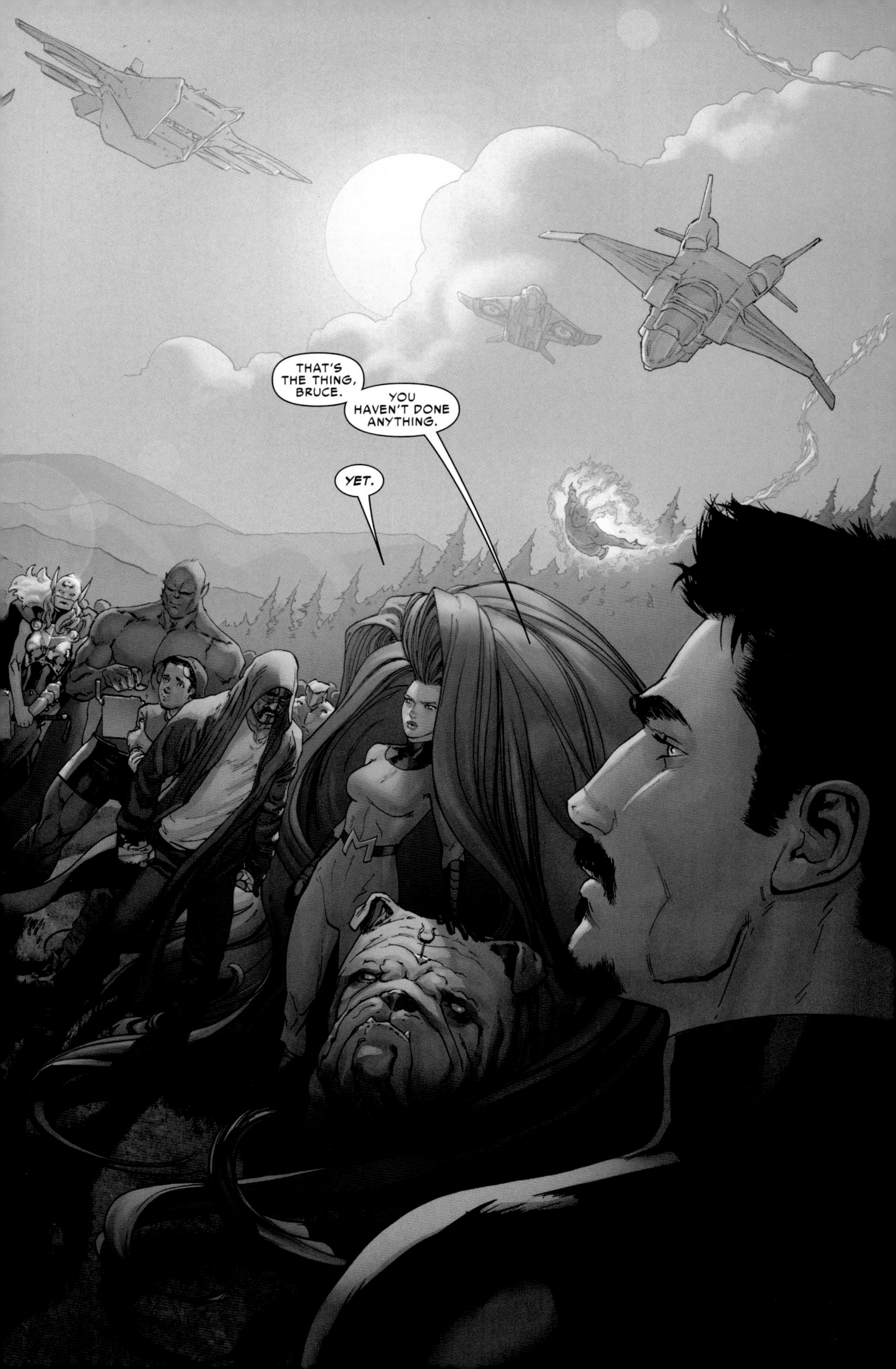
THAT'S THE THING, BRUCE.
YOU HAVEN'T DONE ANYTHING.
YET.

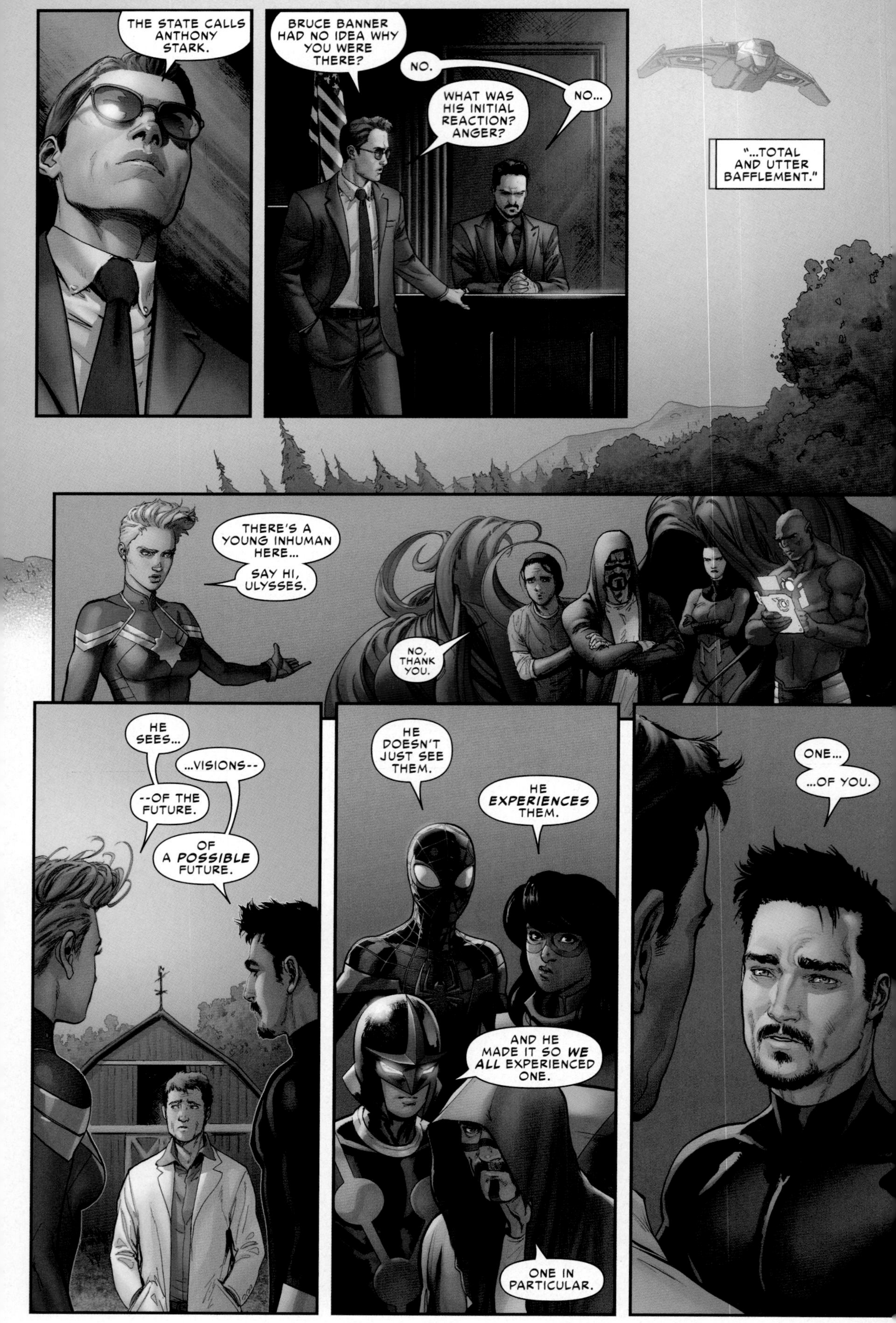
THE STATE CALLS ANTHONY STARK.
BRUCE BANNER HAD NO IDEA WHY YOU WERE THERE?
NO.
WHAT WAS HIS INITIAL REACTION? ANGER?
NO...
"...TOTAL AND UTTER BAFFLEMENT."
THERE'S A YOUNG INHUMAN HERE...
SAY HI, ULYSSES.
NO, THANK YOU.
HE SEES...
...VISIONS--
--OF THE FUTURE.
OF A *POSSIBLE* FUTURE.
HE DOESN'T JUST SEE THEM.
HE *EXPERIENCES* THEM.
AND HE MADE IT SO *WE ALL* EXPERIENCED ONE.
ONE IN PARTICULAR.
ONE...
...OF YOU.

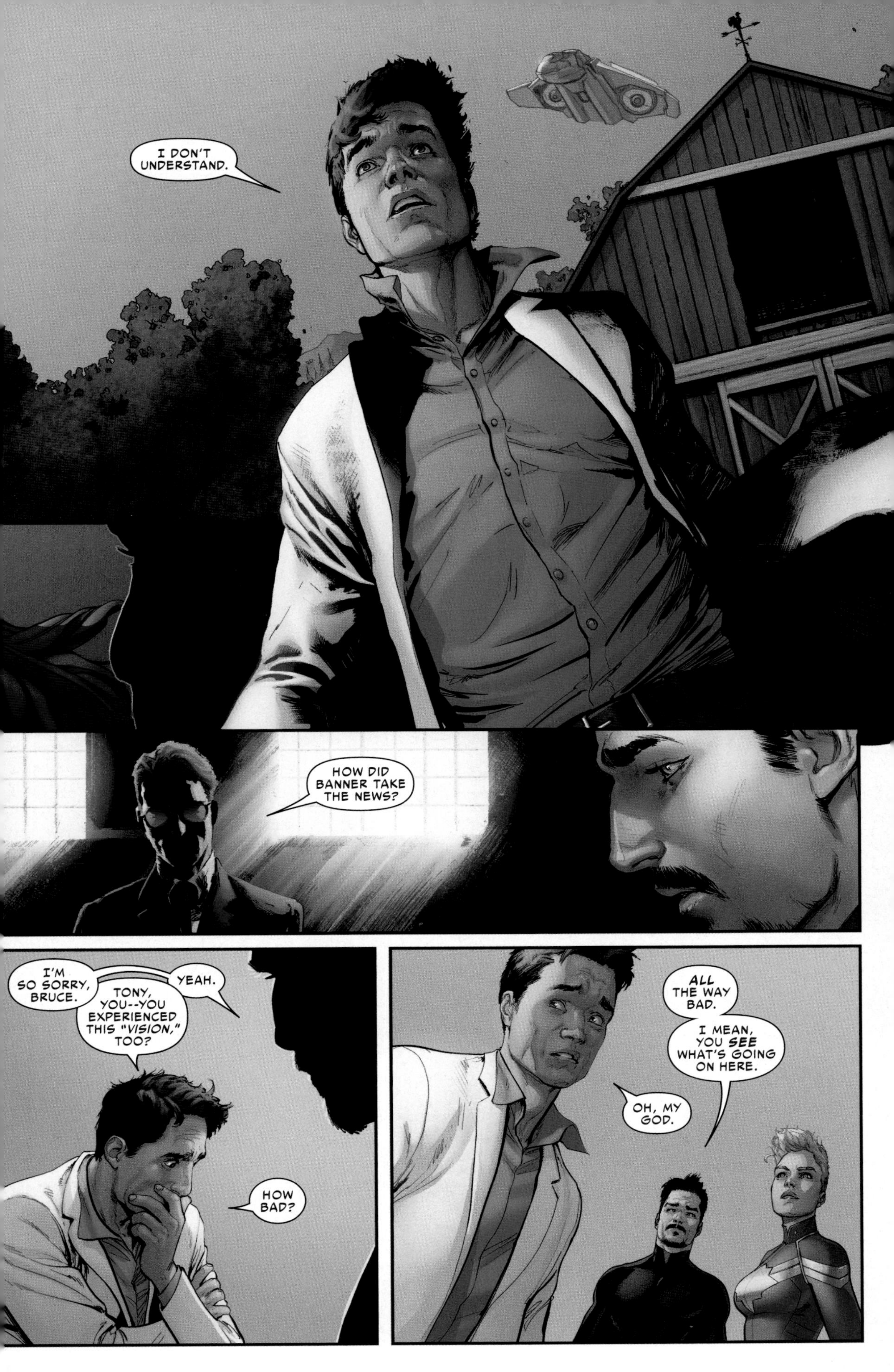
I DON'T UNDERSTAND.
HOW DID BANNER TAKE THE NEWS?
I'M SO SORRY, BRUCE.
YEAH.
TONY, YOU--YOU EXPERIENCED THIS "VISION," TOO?
HOW BAD?
ALL THE WAY BAD.
I MEAN, YOU SEE WHAT'S GOING ON HERE.
OH, MY GOD.

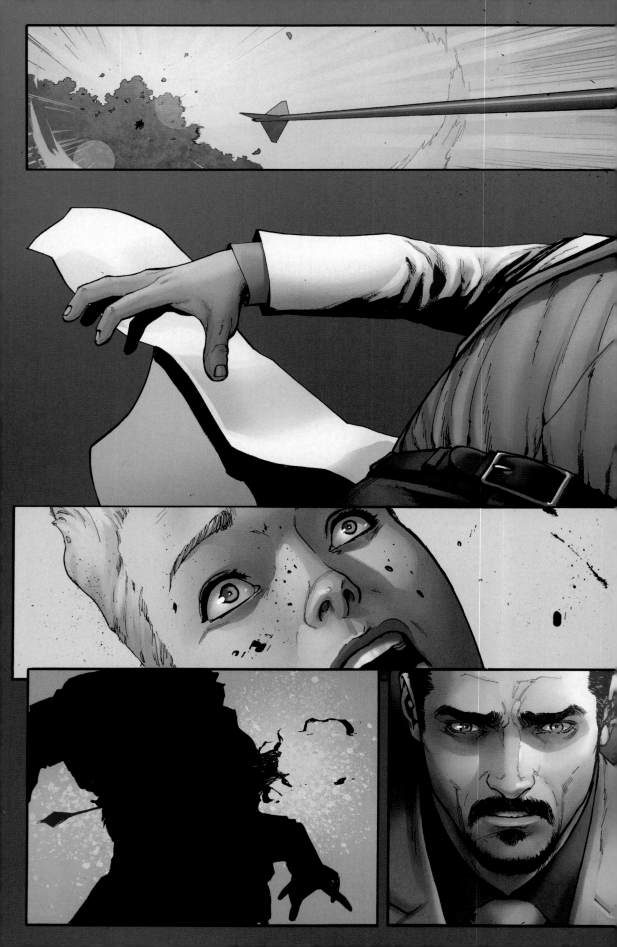

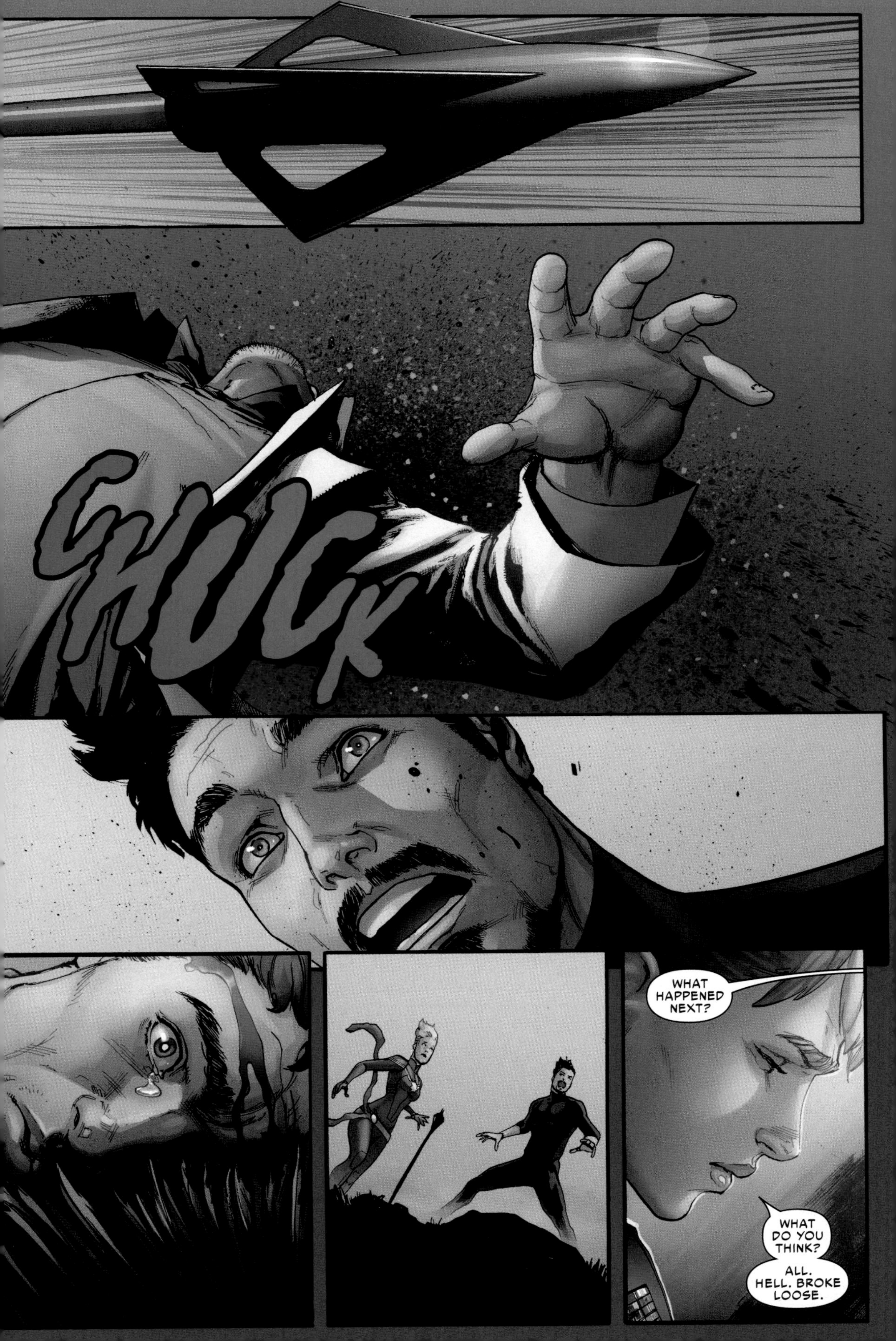
CHUCK
WHAT HAPPENED NEXT?
WHAT DO YOU THINK?
ALL. HELL. BROKE LOOSE.

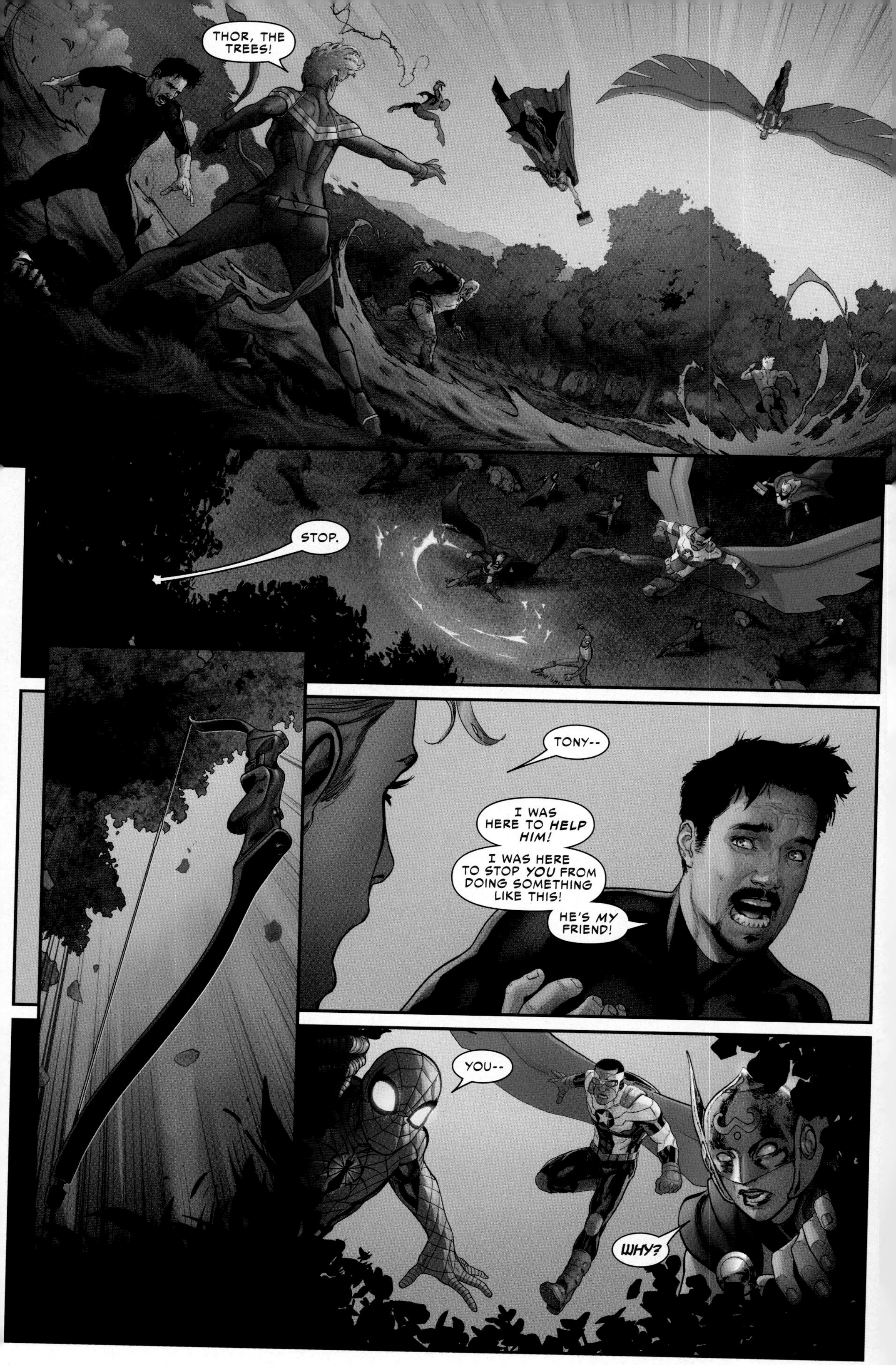
THOR, THE TREES!
STOP.
TONY--
I WAS HERE TO HELP HIM!
I WAS HERE TO STOP YOU FROM DOING SOMETHING LIKE THIS!
HE'S MY FRIEND!
YOU--
WHY?

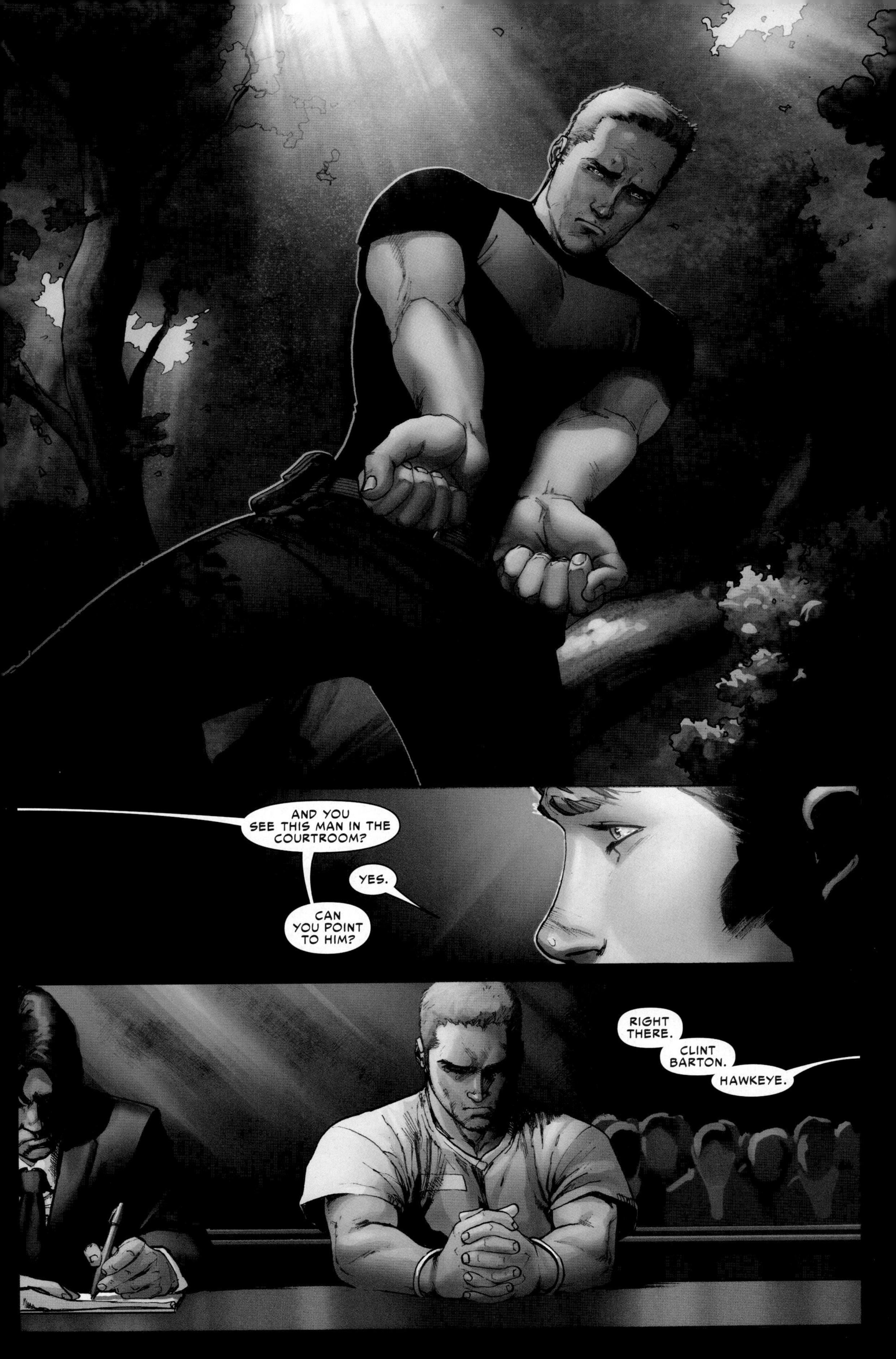
AND YOU SEE THIS MAN IN THE COURTROOM?
YES.
CAN YOU POINT TO HIM?
RIGHT THERE.
CLINT BARTON.
HAWKEYE.

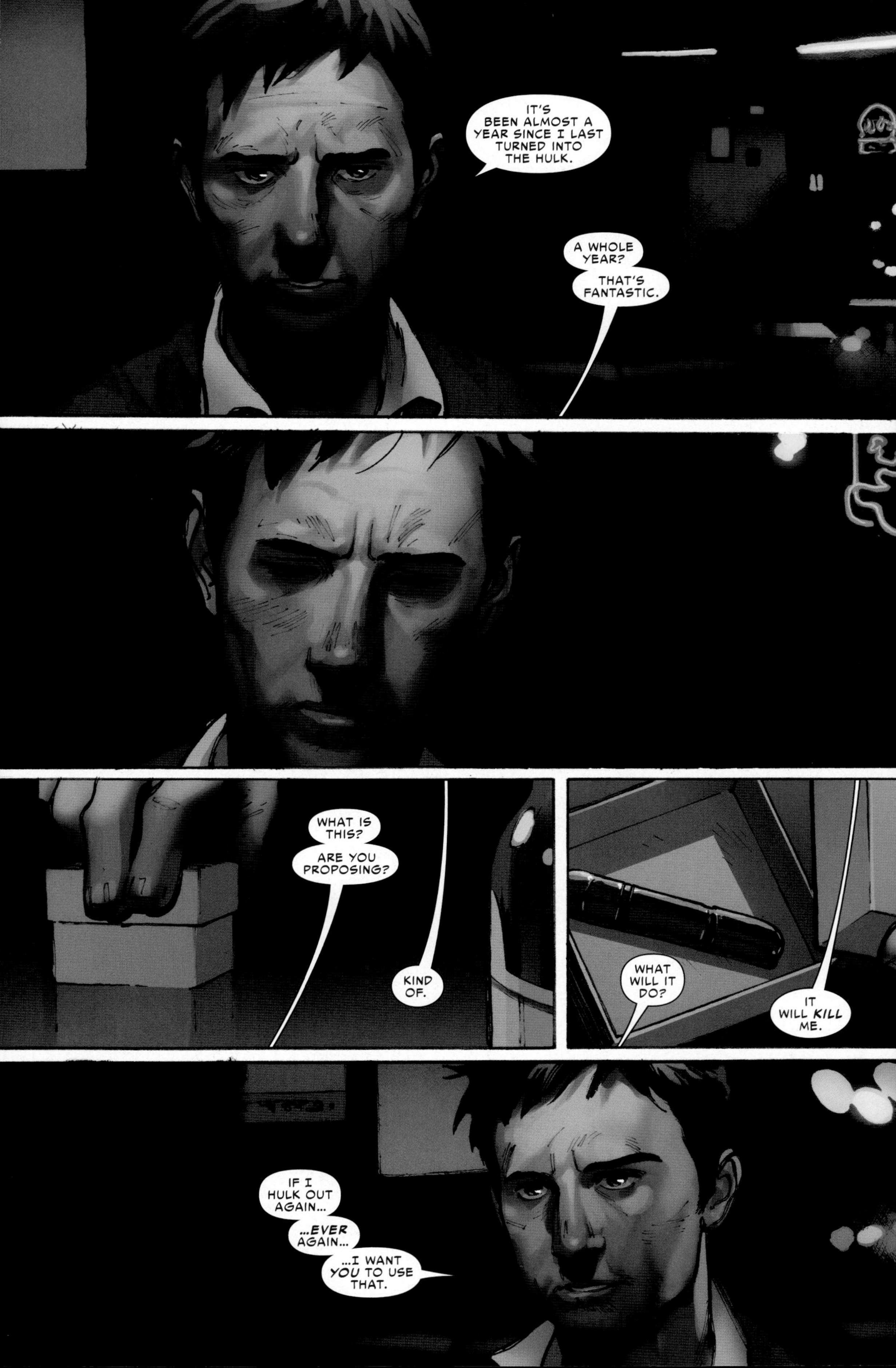
IT'S BEEN ALMOST A YEAR SINCE I LAST TURNED INTO THE HULK.
A WHOLE YEAR?
THAT'S FANTASTIC.
WHAT IS THIS?
ARE YOU PROPOSING?
KIND OF.
WHAT WILL IT DO?
IT WILL KILL ME.
IF I HULK OUT AGAIN...
...EVER AGAIN...
...I WANT YOU TO USE THAT.

I'M NOT GOING TO KILL YOU, BRUCE.
YES, YOU WILL, CLINT.
YOU'LL *HAVE* TO.
WHY ME?
BECAUSE YOU ARE ONE OF THE FEW PEOPLE I KNOW WHO, EVENTUALLY, WILL BE ABLE TO LIVE WITH THE CHOICE.
WELL, THAT'S WEIRDLY INSULTING.
IT'S NOT.
I PROMISE.
I'M TELLING YOU I TRUST YOU WITH MY LIFE.
IF IT'S BEEN ALMOST A WHOLE YEAR...
...MAYBE-- MAYBE IT'S ALL *BEHIND* YOU.
I DREAM AS HIM.
I DREAM RAGE.
I WAKE UP WITH THE TASTE OF BLOOD IN MY MOUTH.
I WAKE UP AND I'M NOT SURE IF IT HAPPENED OR NOT.
SOMETIMES I HAVE TO TURN ON THE NEWS TO MAKE SURE.
AND I KNOW, YOU KNOW, EVERYONE KNOWS...I MAY WAKE UP ONE DAY AND IT'S *NOT* A DREAM.
AND IF *THAT* HAPPENS...
...IT MEANS I HAVE TRIED EVERYTHING ELSE AND *NOTHING* ELSE WORKED.
I NEED YOU TO PROMISE ME YOU'LL STOP ME ONCE AND FOR ALL.

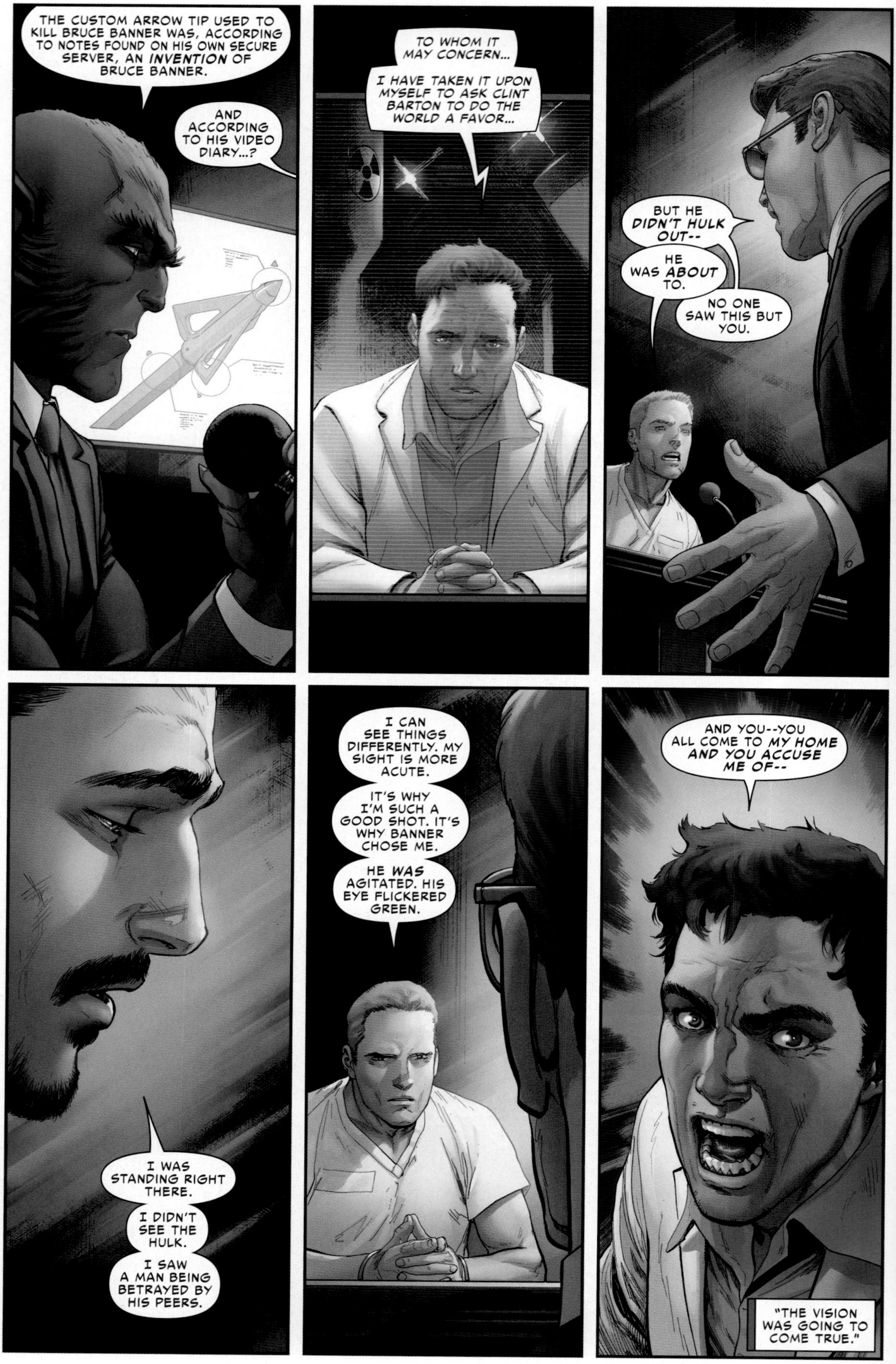
THE CUSTOM ARROW TIP USED TO KILL BRUCE BANNER WAS, ACCORDING TO NOTES FOUND ON HIS OWN SECURE SERVER, AN *INVENTION* OF BRUCE BANNER.
AND ACCORDING TO HIS VIDEO DIARY...?
TO WHOM IT MAY CONCERN...
I HAVE TAKEN IT UPON MYSELF TO ASK CLINT BARTON TO DO THE WORLD A FAVOR...
BUT HE *DIDN'T HULK OUT--*
HE WAS *ABOUT* TO.
NO ONE SAW THIS BUT YOU.
I WAS STANDING RIGHT THERE.
I DIDN'T SEE THE HULK.
I SAW A MAN BEING BETRAYED BY HIS PEERS.
I CAN SEE THINGS DIFFERENTLY. MY SIGHT IS MORE ACUTE.
IT'S WHY I'M SUCH A GOOD SHOT. IT'S WHY BANNER CHOSE ME.
HE *WAS* AGITATED. HIS EYE FLICKERED GREEN.
AND YOU--YOU ALL COME TO *MY HOME AND YOU ACCUSE ME OF--*
"THE VISION WAS GOING TO COME TRUE."

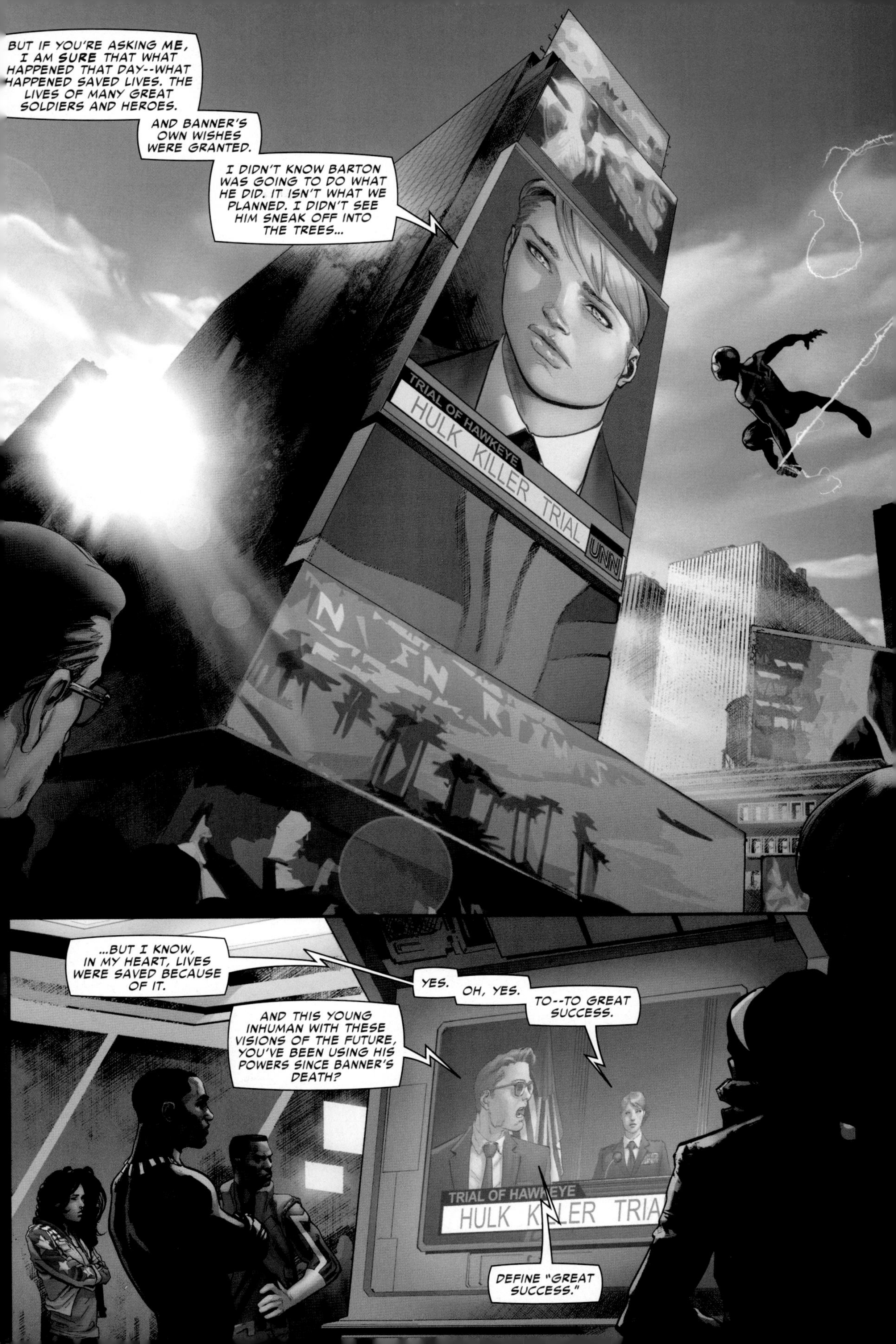
BUT IF YOU'RE ASKING ME, I AM SURE THAT WHAT HAPPENED THAT DAY--WHAT HAPPENED SAVED LIVES. THE LIVES OF MANY GREAT SOLDIERS AND HEROES.
AND BANNER'S OWN WISHES WERE GRANTED.
I DIDN'T KNOW BARTON WAS GOING TO DO WHAT HE DID. IT ISN'T WHAT WE PLANNED. I DIDN'T SEE HIM SNEAK OFF INTO THE TREES...
TRIAL OF HAWKEYE
HULK KILLER TRIAL
UNN
...BUT I KNOW, IN MY HEART, LIVES WERE SAVED BECAUSE OF IT.
YES.
OH, YES.
TO--TO GREAT SUCCESS.
AND THIS YOUNG INHUMAN WITH THESE VISIONS OF THE FUTURE, YOU'VE BEEN USING HIS POWERS SINCE BANNER'S DEATH?
TRIAL OF HAWKEYE
HULK K LER TRIA
DEFINE "GREAT SUCCESS."

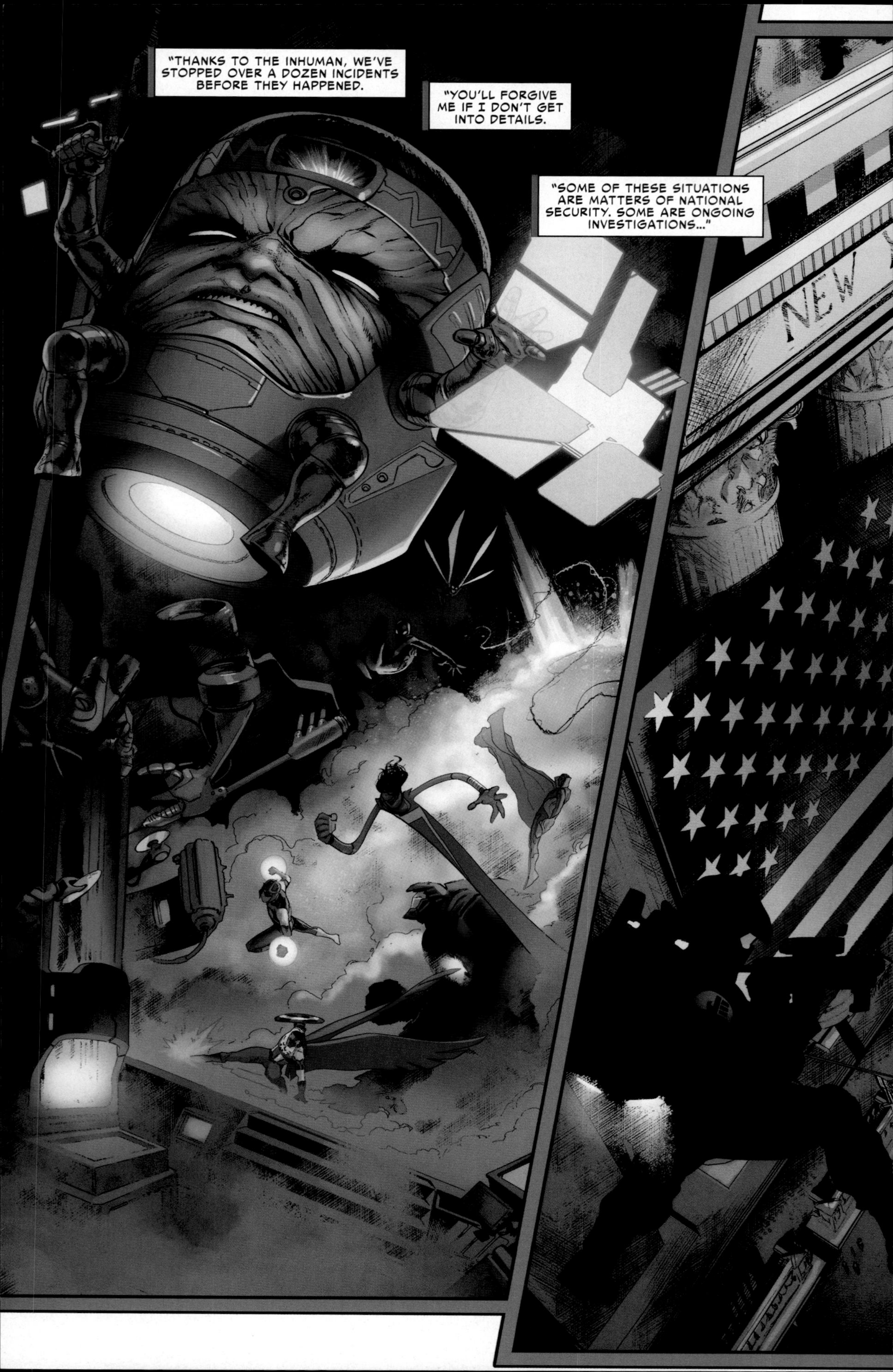
"THANKS TO THE INHUMAN, WE'VE STOPPED OVER A DOZEN INCIDENTS BEFORE THEY HAPPENED.
"YOU'LL FORGIVE ME IF I DON'T GET INTO DETAILS.
"SOME OF THESE SITUATIONS ARE MATTERS OF NATIONAL SECURITY. SOME ARE ONGOING INVESTIGATIONS..."
NEW

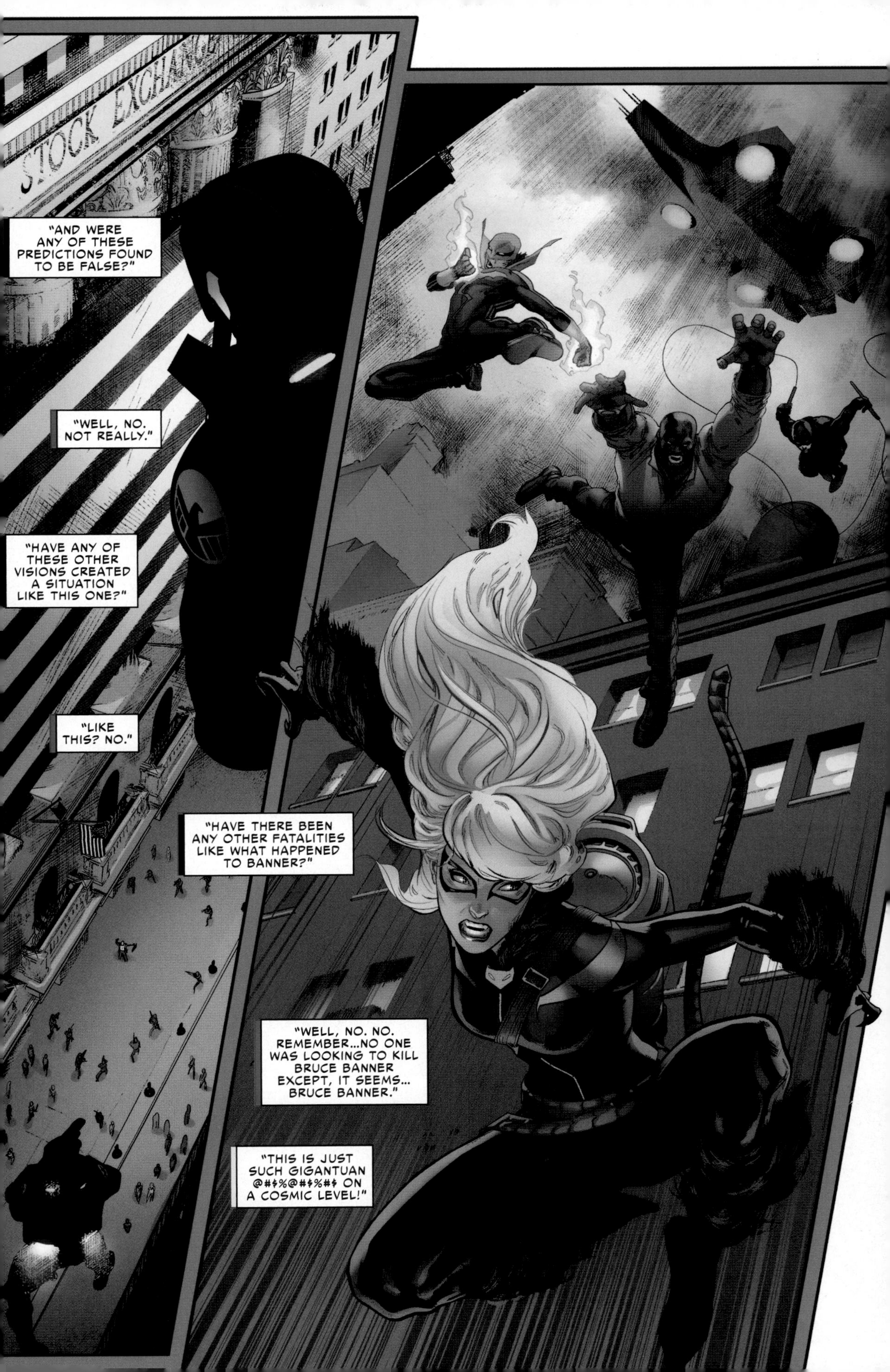
STOCK EXCHANGE
"AND WERE ANY OF THESE PREDICTIONS FOUND TO BE FALSE?"
"WELL, NO. NOT REALLY."
"HAVE ANY OF THESE OTHER VISIONS CREATED A SITUATION LIKE THIS ONE?"
"LIKE THIS? NO."
"HAVE THERE BEEN ANY OTHER FATALITIES LIKE WHAT HAPPENED TO BANNER?"
"WELL, NO. NO. REMEMBER...NO ONE WAS LOOKING TO KILL BRUCE BANNER EXCEPT, IT SEEMS... BRUCE BANNER."
"THIS IS JUST SUCH GIGANTUAN @#$%@#$%#$ ON A COSMIC LEVEL!"

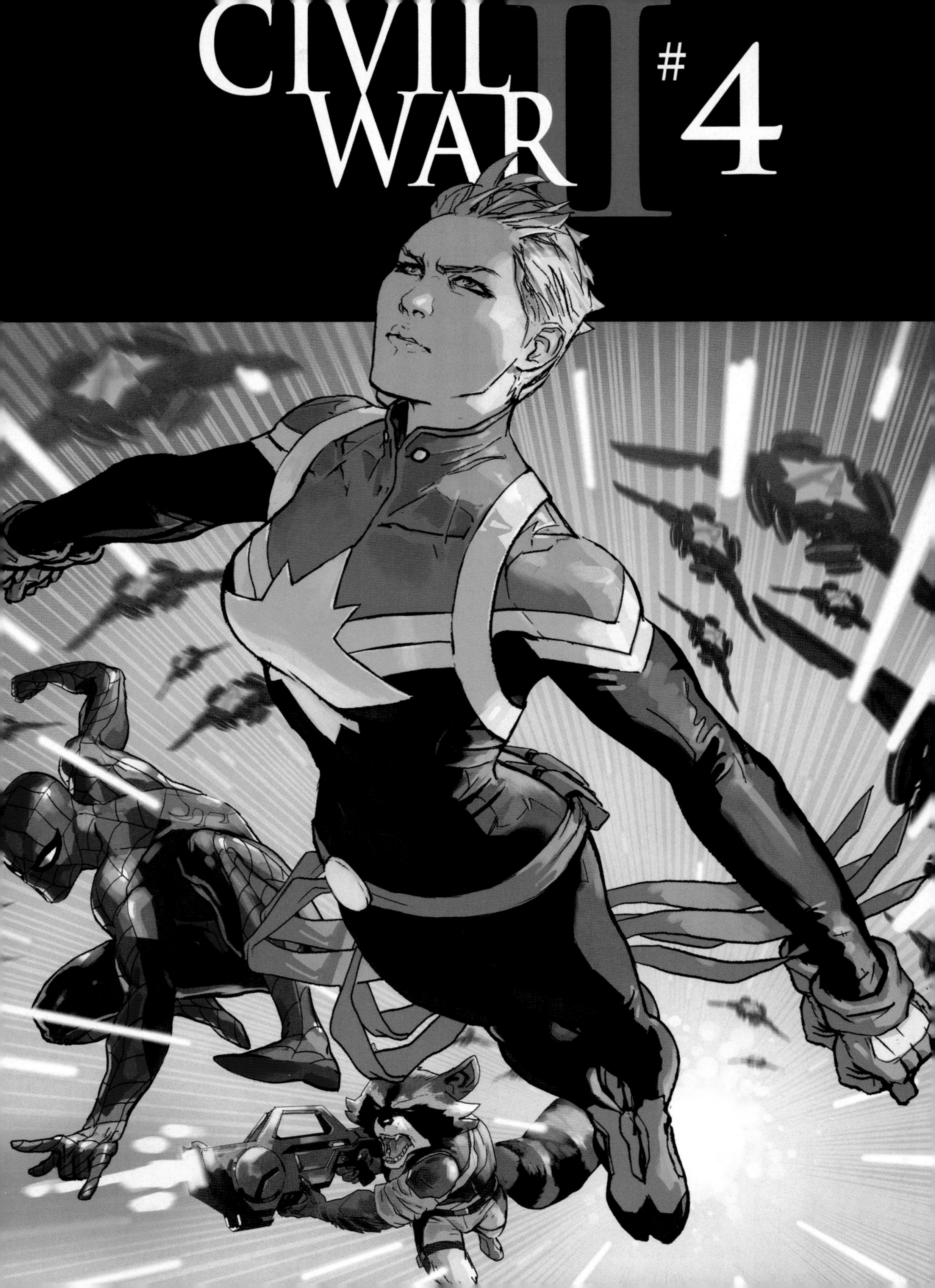
CIVIL WAR II
#4

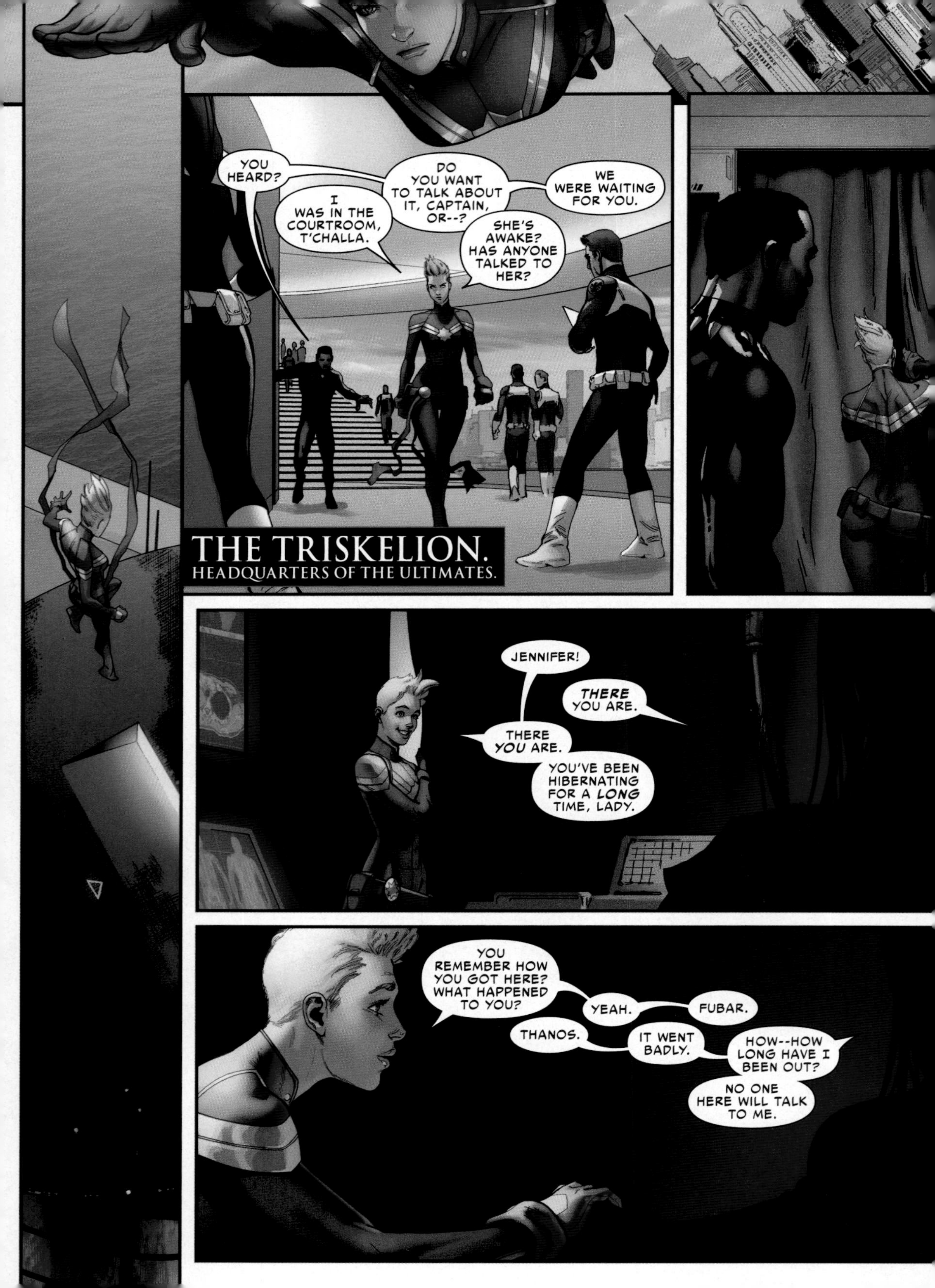
YOU HEARD?
DO YOU WANT TO TALK ABOUT IT, CAPTAIN, OR--?
WE WERE WAITING FOR YOU.
I WAS IN THE COURTROOM, T'CHALLA.
SHE'S AWAKE? HAS ANYONE TALKED TO HER?
THE TRISKELION.
HEADQUARTERS OF THE ULTIMATES.
JENNIFER!
THERE YOU ARE.
THERE YOU ARE.
YOU'VE BEEN HIBERNATING FOR A LONG TIME, LADY.
YOU REMEMBER HOW YOU GOT HERE? WHAT HAPPENED TO YOU?
YEAH.
FUBAR.
THANOS.
IT WENT BADLY.
HOW--HOW LONG HAVE I BEEN OUT?
NO ONE HERE WILL TALK TO ME.

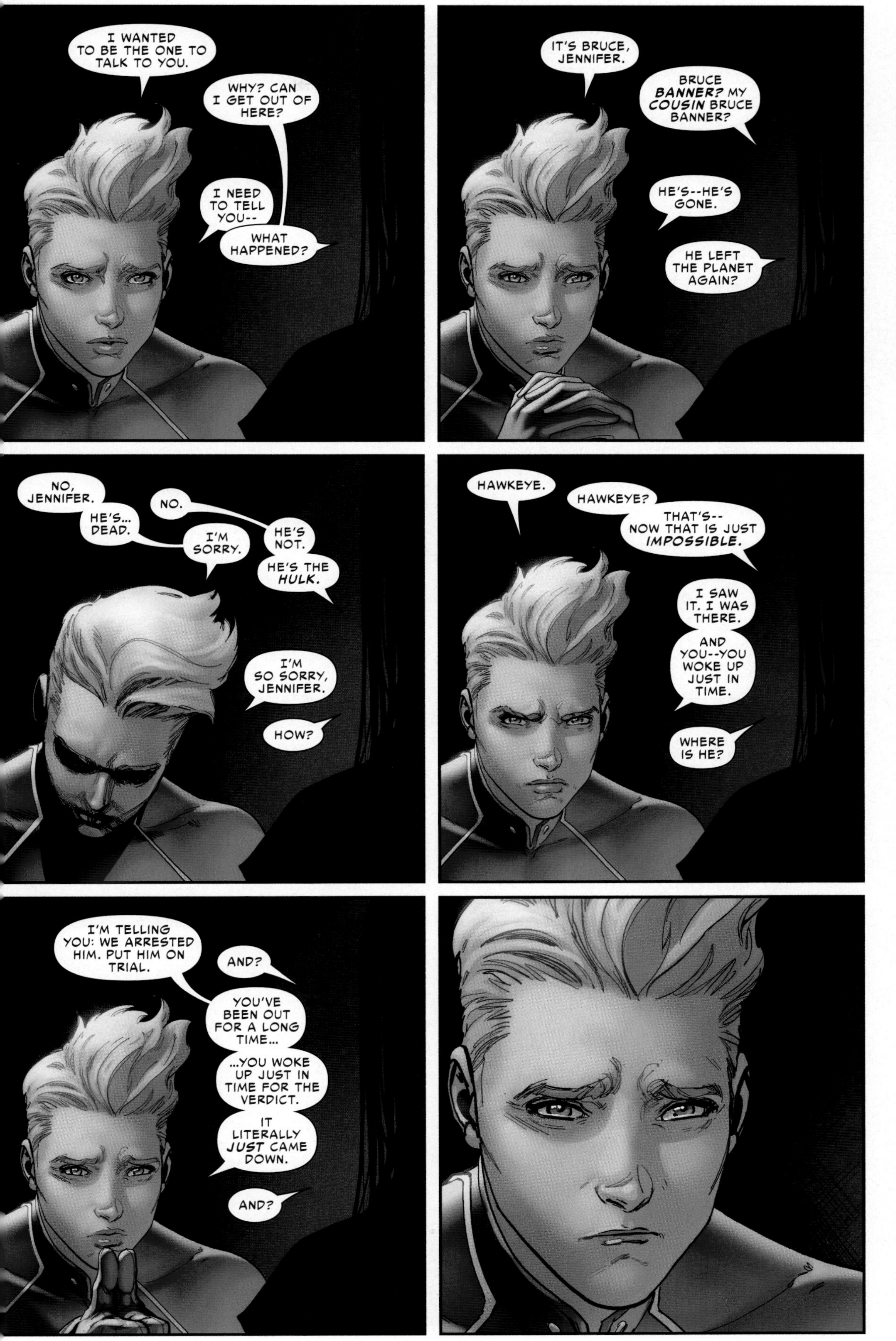
I WANTED TO BE THE ONE TO TALK TO YOU.
WHY? CAN I GET OUT OF HERE?
I NEED TO TELL YOU--
WHAT HAPPENED?
IT'S BRUCE, JENNIFER.
BRUCE BANNER? MY COUSIN BRUCE BANNER?
HE'S--HE'S GONE.
HE LEFT THE PLANET AGAIN?
NO, JENNIFER.
HE'S... DEAD.
NO.
I'M SORRY.
HE'S NOT.
HE'S THE HULK.
I'M SO SORRY, JENNIFER.
HOW?
HAWKEYE.
HAWKEYE?
THAT'S-- NOW THAT IS JUST IMPOSSIBLE.
I SAW IT. I WAS THERE.
AND YOU--YOU WOKE UP JUST IN TIME.
WHERE IS HE?
I'M TELLING YOU: WE ARRESTED HIM. PUT HIM ON TRIAL.
AND?
YOU'VE BEEN OUT FOR A LONG TIME...
...YOU WOKE UP JUST IN TIME FOR THE VERDICT.
IT LITERALLY JUST CAME DOWN.
AND?

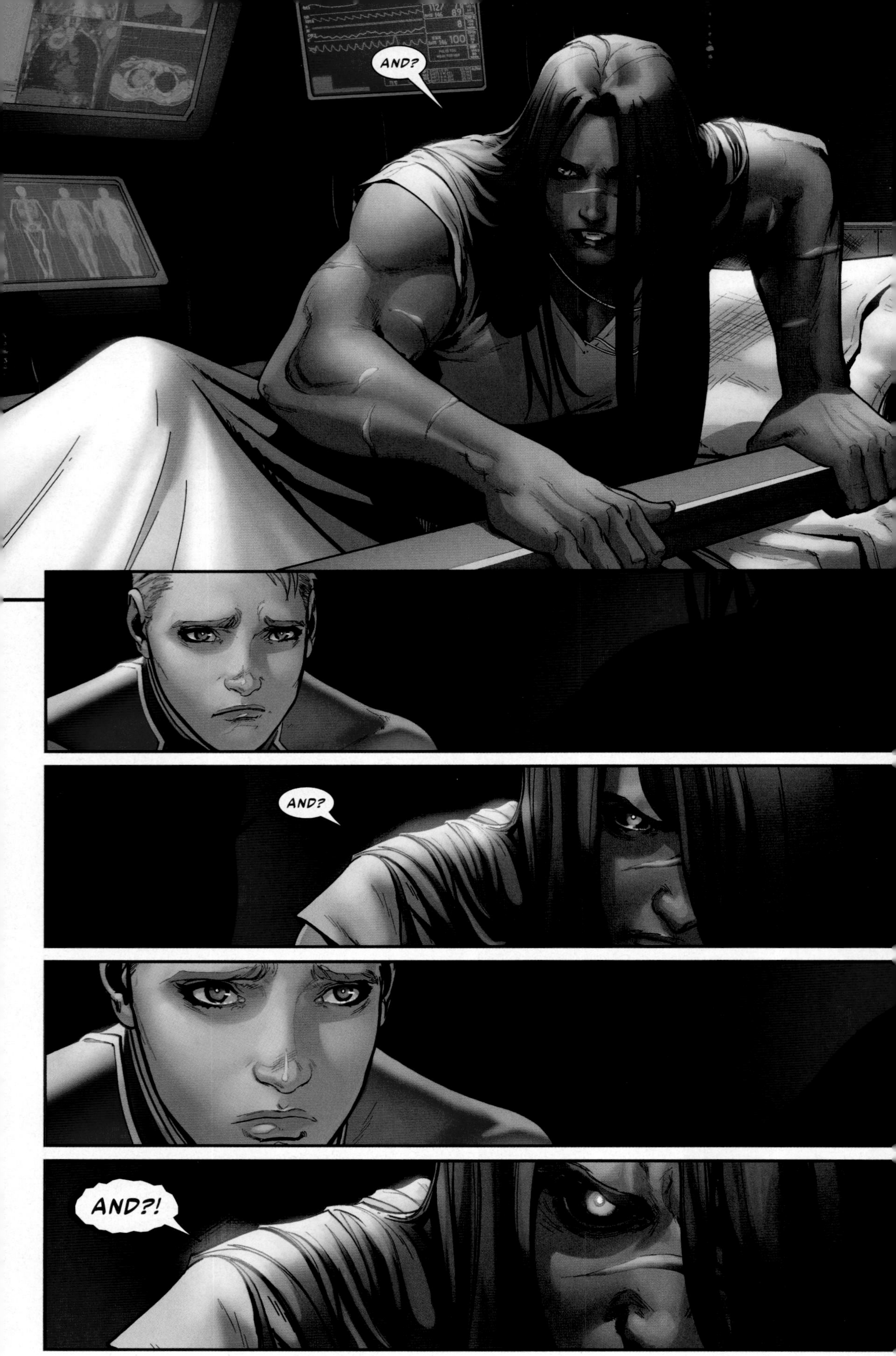
AND?
AND?
AND?!

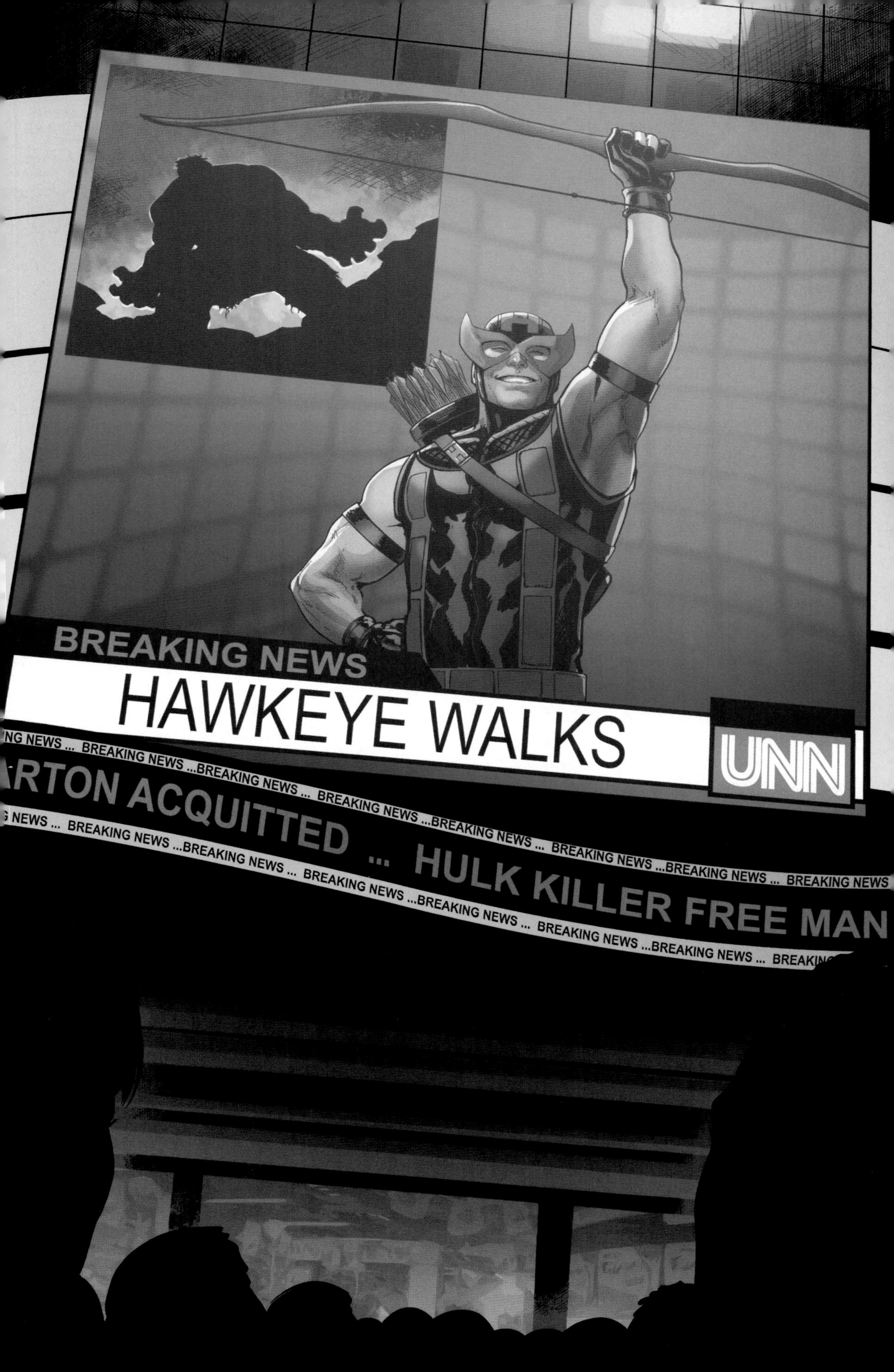
BREAKING NEWS
HAWKEYE WALKS
UNN
NG NEWS ... BREAKING NEWS ...BREAKING NEWS ... BREAKING NEWS ...BREAKING NEWS ... BREAKING NEWS ...BREAKING NEWS ... BREAKING NEWS
ARTON ACQUITTED ... HULK KILLER FREE MAN
G NEWS ... BREAKING NEWS ...BREAKING NEWS ... BREAKING NEWS ...BREAKING NEWS ... BREAKING NEWS ...BREAKING NEWS ... BREAKIN

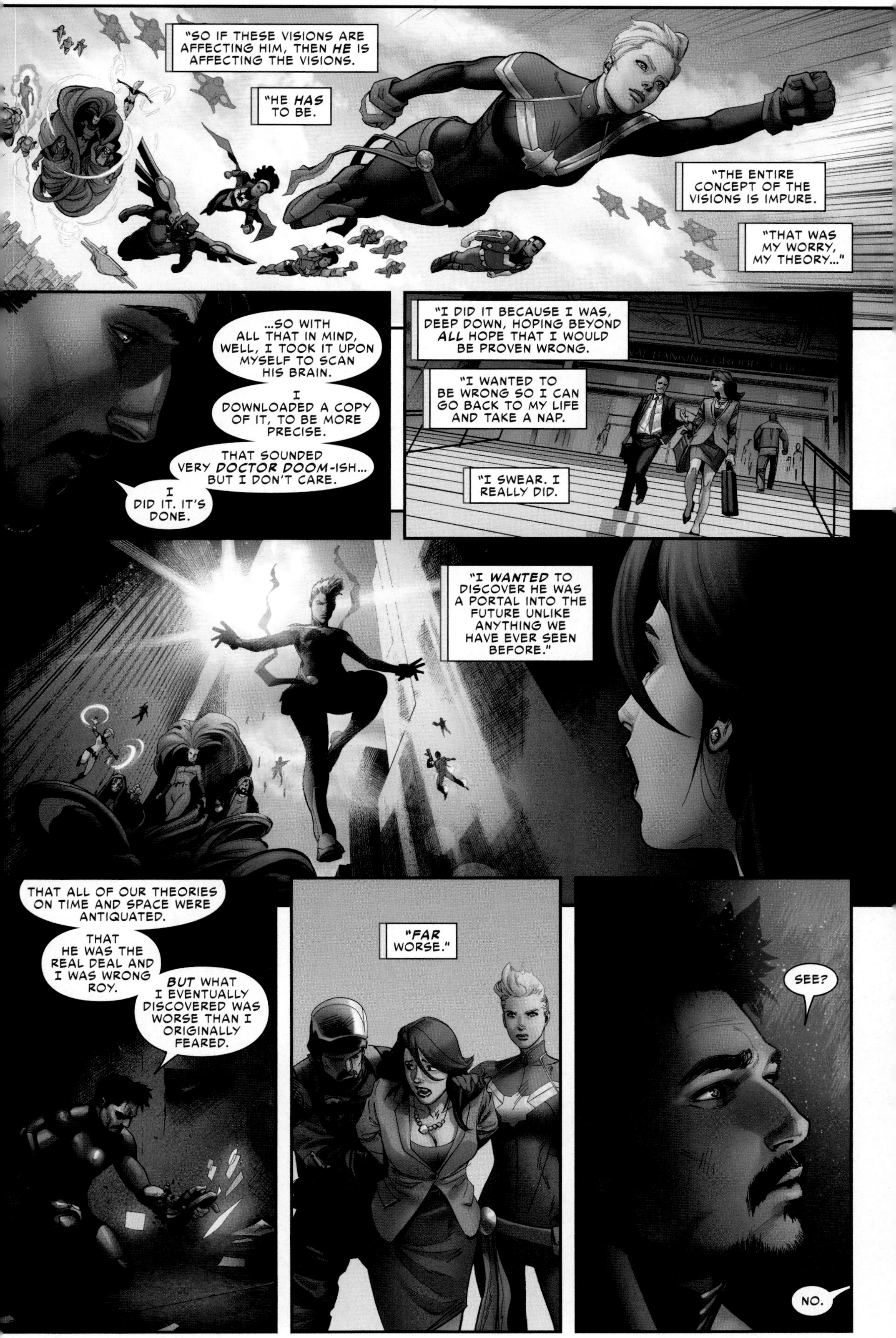
"SO IF THESE VISIONS ARE AFFECTING HIM, THEN *HE* IS AFFECTING THE VISIONS.
"HE *HAS* TO BE.
"THE ENTIRE CONCEPT OF THE VISIONS IS IMPURE.
"THAT WAS MY WORRY, MY THEORY..."
...SO WITH ALL THAT IN MIND, WELL, I TOOK IT UPON MYSELF TO SCAN HIS BRAIN.
I DOWNLOADED A COPY OF IT, TO BE MORE PRECISE.
THAT SOUNDED VERY *DOCTOR DOOM*-ISH... BUT I DON'T CARE.
I DID IT. IT'S DONE.
"I DID IT BECAUSE I WAS, DEEP DOWN, HOPING BEYOND *ALL* HOPE THAT I WOULD BE PROVEN WRONG.
"I WANTED TO BE WRONG SO I CAN GO BACK TO MY LIFE AND TAKE A NAP.
"I SWEAR. I REALLY DID.
"I *WANTED* TO DISCOVER HE WAS A PORTAL INTO THE FUTURE UNLIKE ANYTHING WE HAVE EVER SEEN BEFORE."
THAT ALL OF OUR THEORIES ON TIME AND SPACE WERE ANTIQUATED.
THAT HE WAS THE REAL DEAL AND I WAS WRONG ROY.
BUT WHAT I EVENTUALLY DISCOVERED WAS WORSE THAN I ORIGINALLY FEARED.
"*FAR* WORSE."
SEE?
NO.

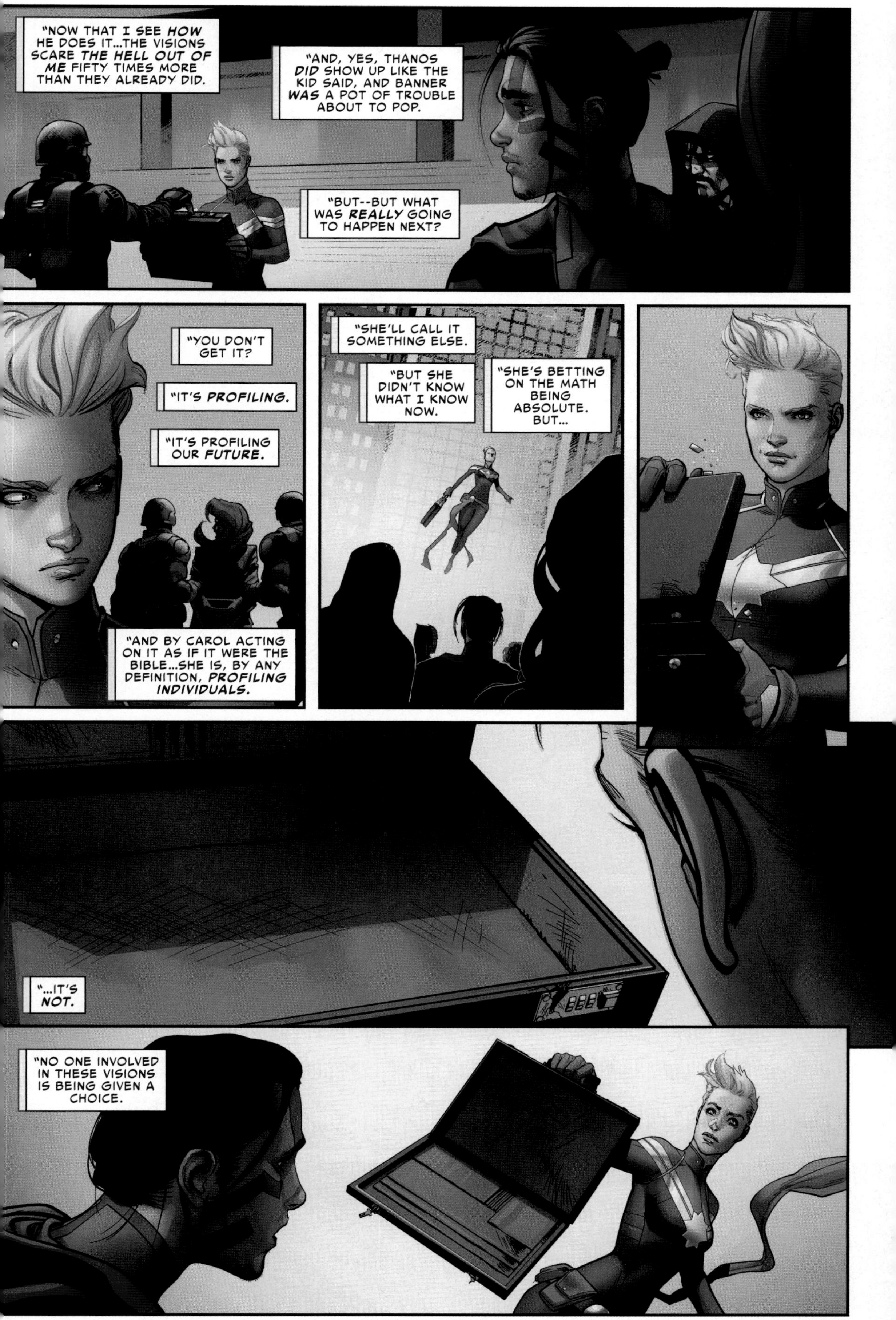
"NOW THAT I SEE HOW HE DOES IT...THE VISIONS SCARE THE HELL OUT OF ME FIFTY TIMES MORE THAN THEY ALREADY DID.
"AND, YES, THANOS DID SHOW UP LIKE THE KID SAID, AND BANNER WAS A POT OF TROUBLE ABOUT TO POP.
"BUT--BUT WHAT WAS REALLY GOING TO HAPPEN NEXT?
"YOU DON'T GET IT?
"IT'S PROFILING.
"IT'S PROFILING OUR FUTURE.
"AND BY CAROL ACTING ON IT AS IF IT WERE THE BIBLE...SHE IS, BY ANY DEFINITION, PROFILING INDIVIDUALS.
"SHE'LL CALL IT SOMETHING ELSE.
"BUT SHE DIDN'T KNOW WHAT I KNOW NOW.
"SHE'S BETTING ON THE MATH BEING ABSOLUTE. BUT...
"...IT'S NOT.
"NO ONE INVOLVED IN THESE VISIONS IS BEING GIVEN A CHOICE.

"I'M SAYING *FREE WILL* IS BEING ELIMINATED FROM THE PROCESS OF CHOICE.

"I'M SAYING IF YOU ALLOW THIS KID'S POWER TO HAVE THE FINAL SAY--NO ONE IN HIS VISIONS HAS ACCOUNTABILITY FOR THEMSELVES.

"AND WITHOUT PERSONAL ACCOUNTABILITY, WHAT ARE WE?"

AND IF WE'RE OFFICIALLY IN THE WORLD OF ALGORITHMS AND PROBABILITY...

...WHAT *ARE* THE ODDS OF THESE VISIONS BEING TRUE AND PURE AND RIGHT?

AND NOW, SINCE THE HULK, THE KID'S VISIONS ARE GOING WIDER AND BECOMING MORE POWERFUL...

...NOW *OTHERS* CAN SEE AND EXPERIENCE THEM, TOO.

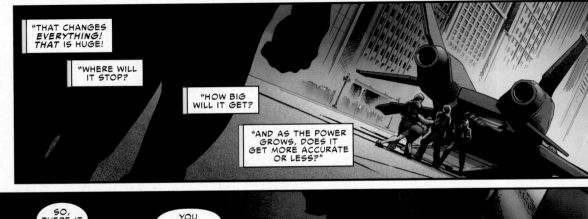

"THAT CHANGES *EVERYTHING!* THAT IS HUGE!

"WHERE WILL IT STOP?

"HOW BIG WILL IT GET?

"AND AS THE POWER GROWS, DOES IT GET MORE ACCURATE OR LESS?"

SO, THERE IT IS...

YOU TELL ME...YOU TELL ME I'M CRAZY.

YOU TELL ME I'M WRONG.

YOU TELL ME AND I SWEAR I'LL GIVE UP.

IF YOU TELL ME TO STOP... I WILL.

BECAUSE, I'VE LEARNED, FINALLY, AFTER *ALL* THESE YEARS...

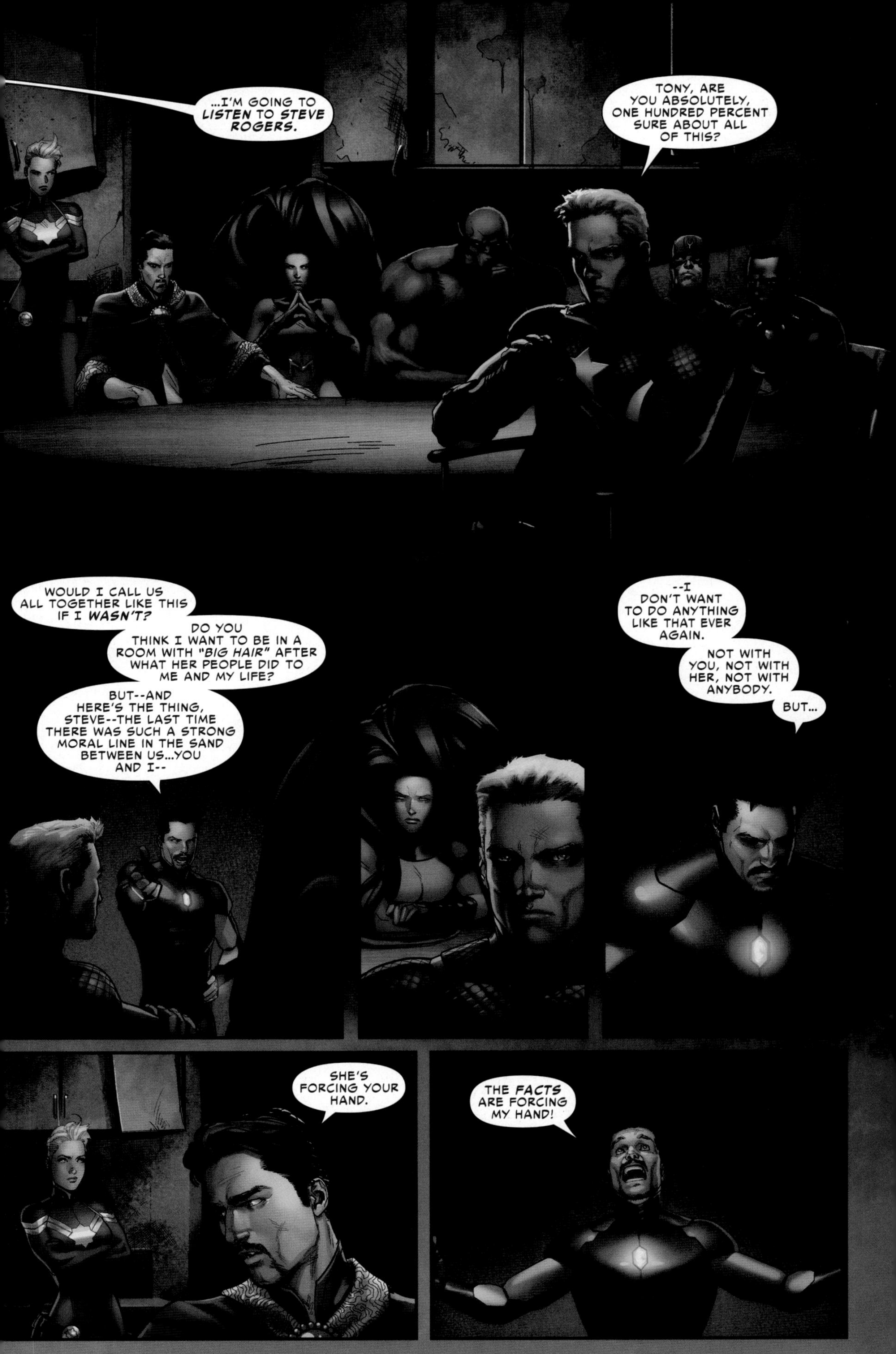
...I'M GOING TO LISTEN TO STEVE ROGERS.
TONY, ARE YOU ABSOLUTELY, ONE HUNDRED PERCENT SURE ABOUT ALL OF THIS?
WOULD I CALL US ALL TOGETHER LIKE THIS IF I WASN'T?
DO YOU THINK I WANT TO BE IN A ROOM WITH "BIG HAIR" AFTER WHAT HER PEOPLE DID TO ME AND MY LIFE?
BUT--AND HERE'S THE THING, STEVE--THE LAST TIME THERE WAS SUCH A STRONG MORAL LINE IN THE SAND BETWEEN US...YOU AND I--
--I DON'T WANT TO DO ANYTHING LIKE THAT EVER AGAIN.
NOT WITH YOU, NOT WITH HER, NOT WITH ANYBODY.
BUT...
SHE'S FORCING YOUR HAND.
THE FACTS ARE FORCING MY HAND!

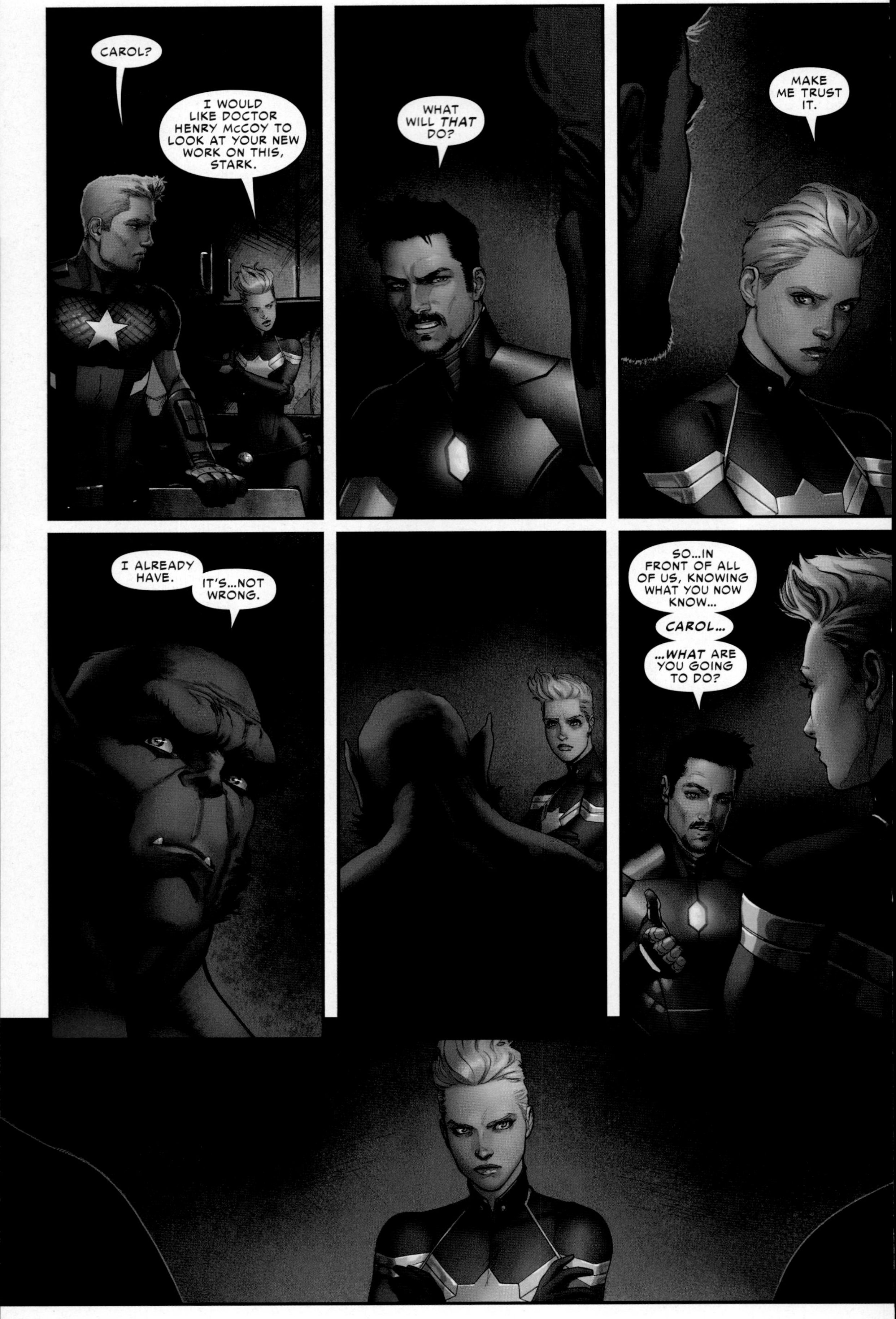
CAROL?
I WOULD LIKE DOCTOR HENRY McCOY TO LOOK AT YOUR NEW WORK ON THIS, STARK.
WHAT WILL *THAT* DO?
MAKE ME TRUST IT.
I ALREADY HAVE.
IT'S...NOT WRONG.
SO...IN FRONT OF ALL OF US, KNOWING WHAT YOU NOW KNOW...
CAROL...
...*WHAT* ARE YOU GOING TO DO?

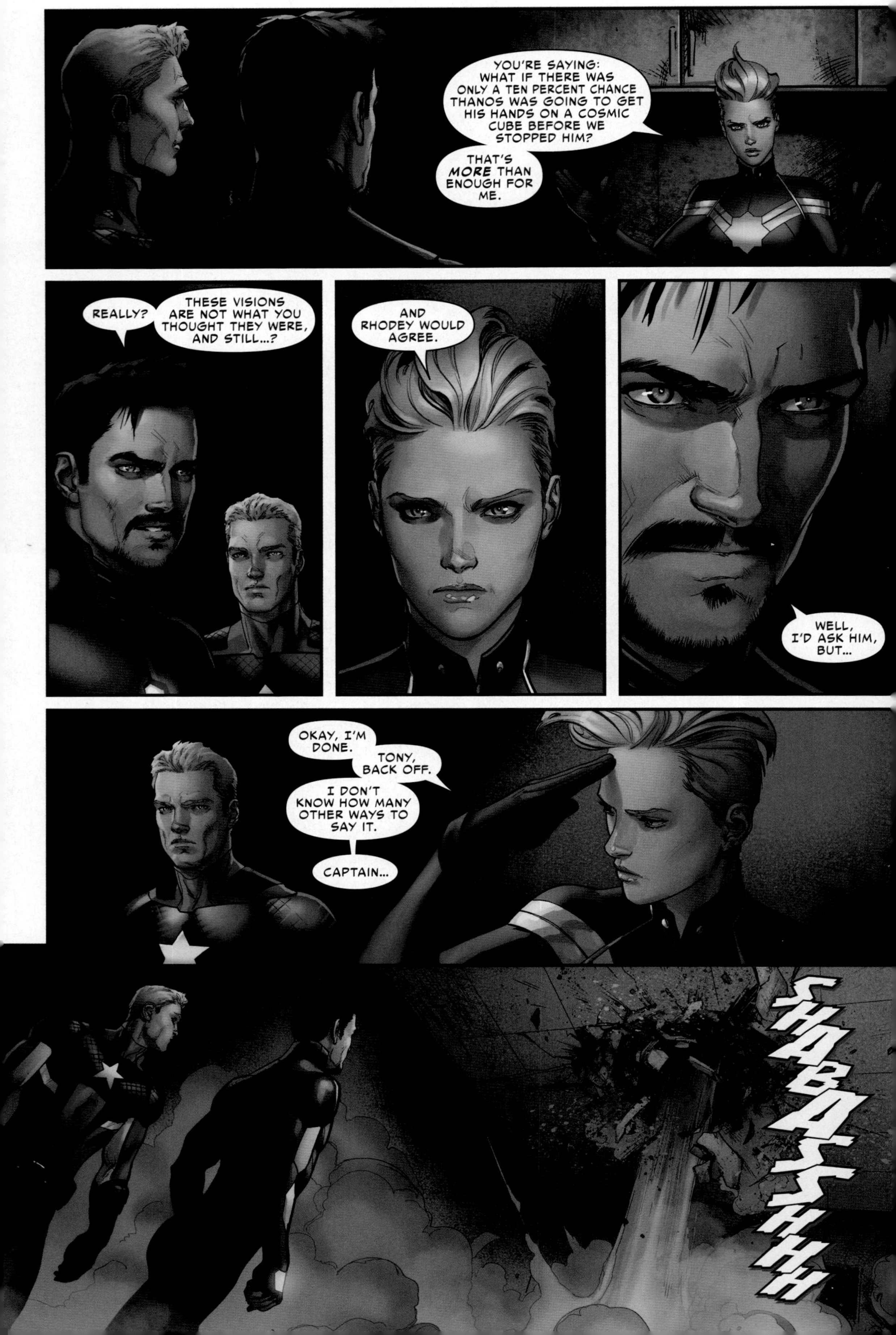
YOU'RE SAYING: WHAT IF THERE WAS ONLY A TEN PERCENT CHANCE THANOS WAS GOING TO GET HIS HANDS ON A COSMIC CUBE BEFORE WE STOPPED HIM?
THAT'S MORE THAN ENOUGH FOR ME.
REALLY?
THESE VISIONS ARE NOT WHAT YOU THOUGHT THEY WERE, AND STILL...?
AND RHODEY WOULD AGREE.
WELL, I'D ASK HIM, BUT...
OKAY, I'M DONE.
TONY, BACK OFF.
I DON'T KNOW HOW MANY OTHER WAYS TO SAY IT.
CAPTAIN...
SHBASHHH

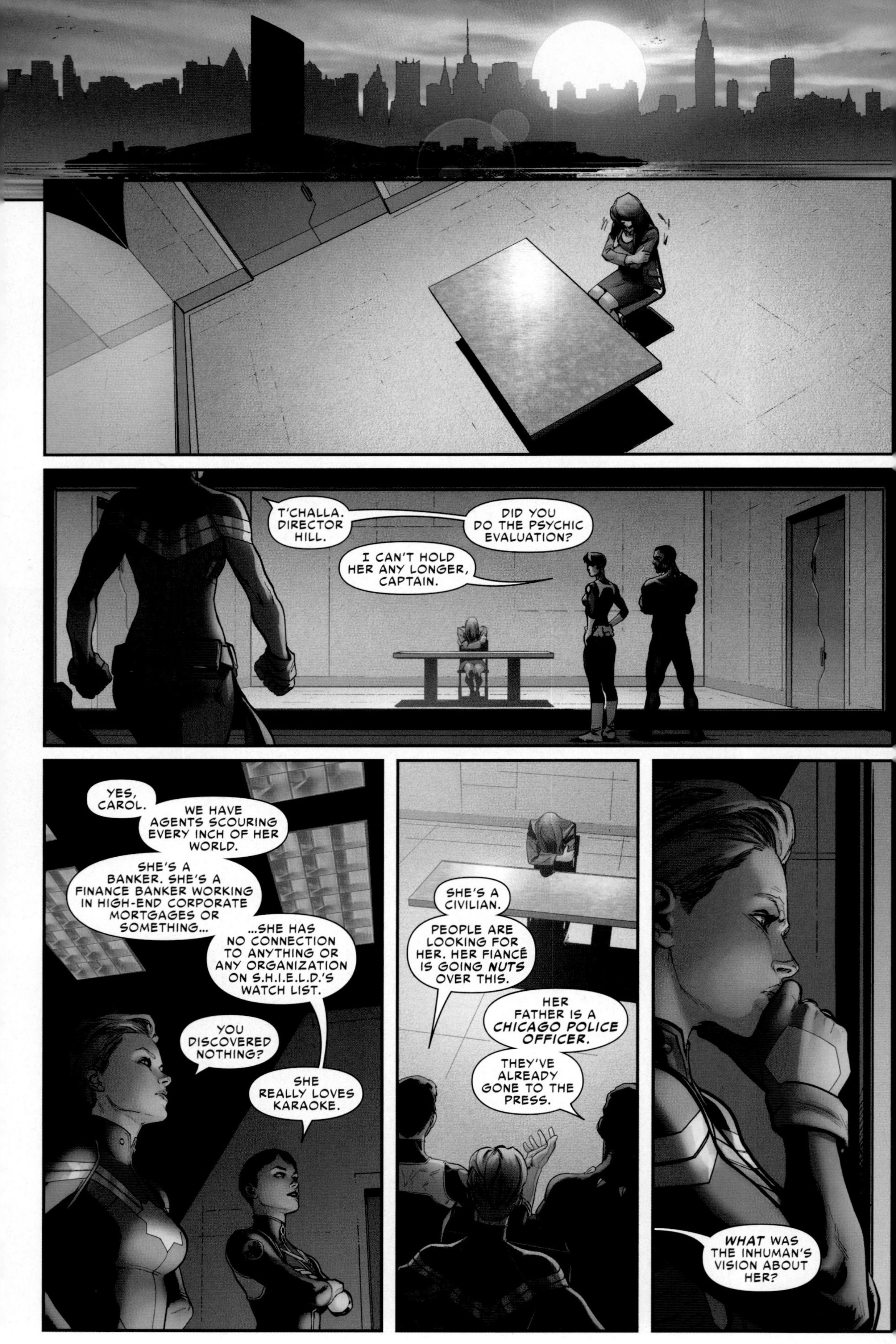
T'CHALLA. DIRECTOR HILL.
DID YOU DO THE PSYCHIC EVALUATION?
I CAN'T HOLD HER ANY LONGER, CAPTAIN.
YES, CAROL.
WE HAVE AGENTS SCOURING EVERY INCH OF HER WORLD.
SHE'S A BANKER. SHE'S A FINANCE BANKER WORKING IN HIGH-END CORPORATE MORTGAGES OR SOMETHING...
...SHE HAS NO CONNECTION TO ANYTHING OR ANY ORGANIZATION ON S.H.I.E.L.D.'S WATCH LIST.
YOU DISCOVERED NOTHING?
SHE REALLY LOVES KARAOKE.
SHE'S A CIVILIAN.
PEOPLE ARE LOOKING FOR HER. HER FIANCÉ IS GOING NUTS OVER THIS.
HER FATHER IS A CHICAGO POLICE OFFICER.
THEY'VE ALREADY GONE TO THE PRESS.
WHAT WAS THE INHUMAN'S VISION ABOUT HER?

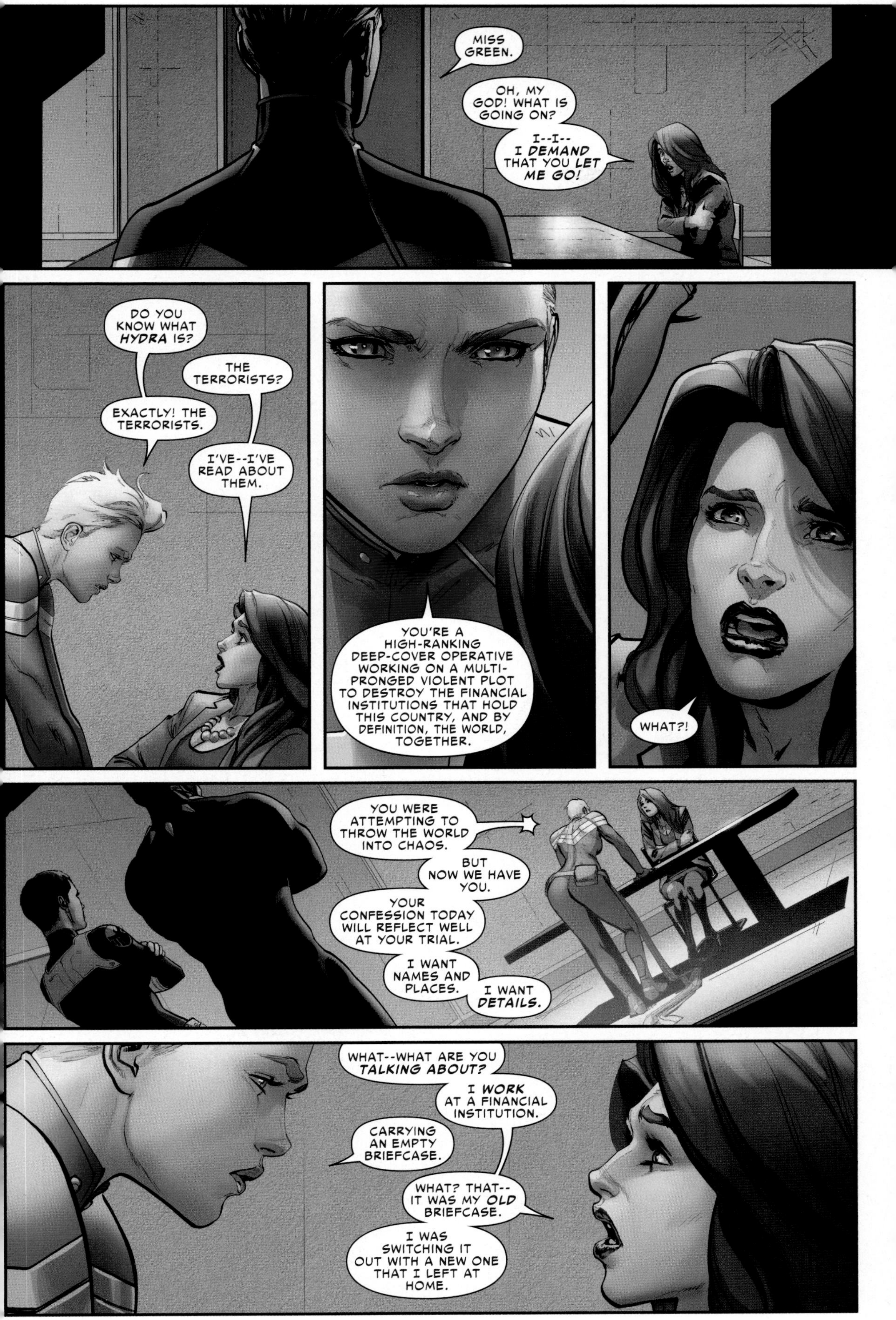
MISS GREEN.
OH, MY GOD! WHAT IS GOING ON?
I--I-- I DEMAND THAT YOU LET ME GO!
DO YOU KNOW WHAT HYDRA IS?
THE TERRORISTS?
EXACTLY! THE TERRORISTS.
I'VE--I'VE READ ABOUT THEM.
YOU'RE A HIGH-RANKING DEEP-COVER OPERATIVE WORKING ON A MULTI-PRONGED VIOLENT PLOT TO DESTROY THE FINANCIAL INSTITUTIONS THAT HOLD THIS COUNTRY, AND BY DEFINITION, THE WORLD, TOGETHER.
WHAT?!
YOU WERE ATTEMPTING TO THROW THE WORLD INTO CHAOS.
BUT NOW WE HAVE YOU.
YOUR CONFESSION TODAY WILL REFLECT WELL AT YOUR TRIAL.
I WANT NAMES AND PLACES.
I WANT DETAILS.
WHAT--WHAT ARE YOU TALKING ABOUT?
I WORK AT A FINANCIAL INSTITUTION.
CARRYING AN EMPTY BRIEFCASE.
WHAT? THAT-- IT WAS MY OLD BRIEFCASE.
I WAS SWITCHING IT OUT WITH A NEW ONE THAT I LEFT AT HOME.

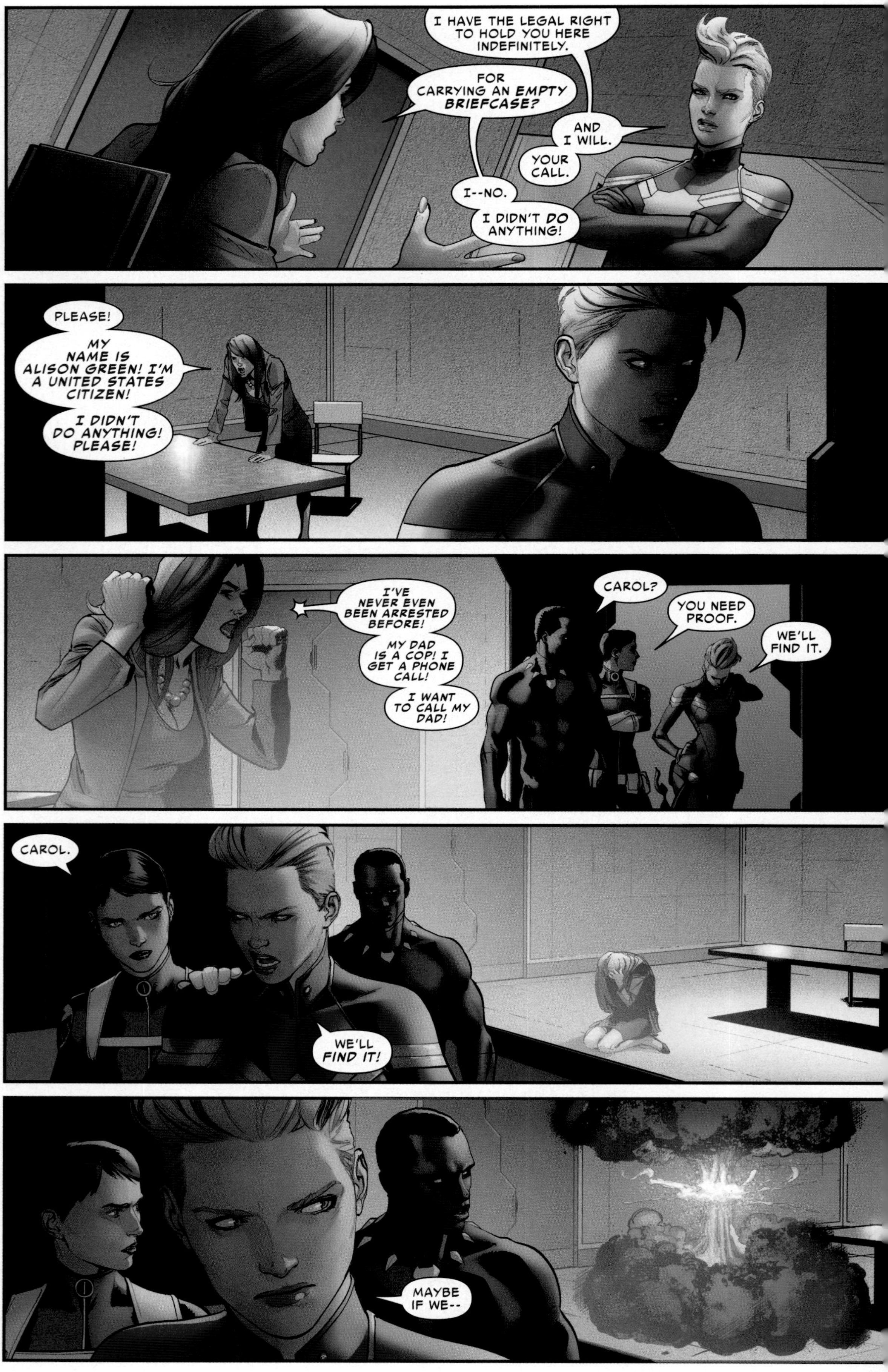
I HAVE THE LEGAL RIGHT TO HOLD YOU HERE INDEFINITELY.
FOR CARRYING AN EMPTY BRIEFCASE?
AND I WILL.
YOUR CALL.
I--NO.
I DIDN'T DO ANYTHING!
PLEASE!
MY NAME IS ALISON GREEN! I'M A UNITED STATES CITIZEN!
I DIDN'T DO ANYTHING! PLEASE!
I'VE NEVER EVEN BEEN ARRESTED BEFORE!
MY DAD IS A COP! I GET A PHONE CALL!
I WANT TO CALL MY DAD!
CAROL?
YOU NEED PROOF.
WE'LL FIND IT.
CAROL.
WE'LL FIND IT!
MAYBE IF WE--

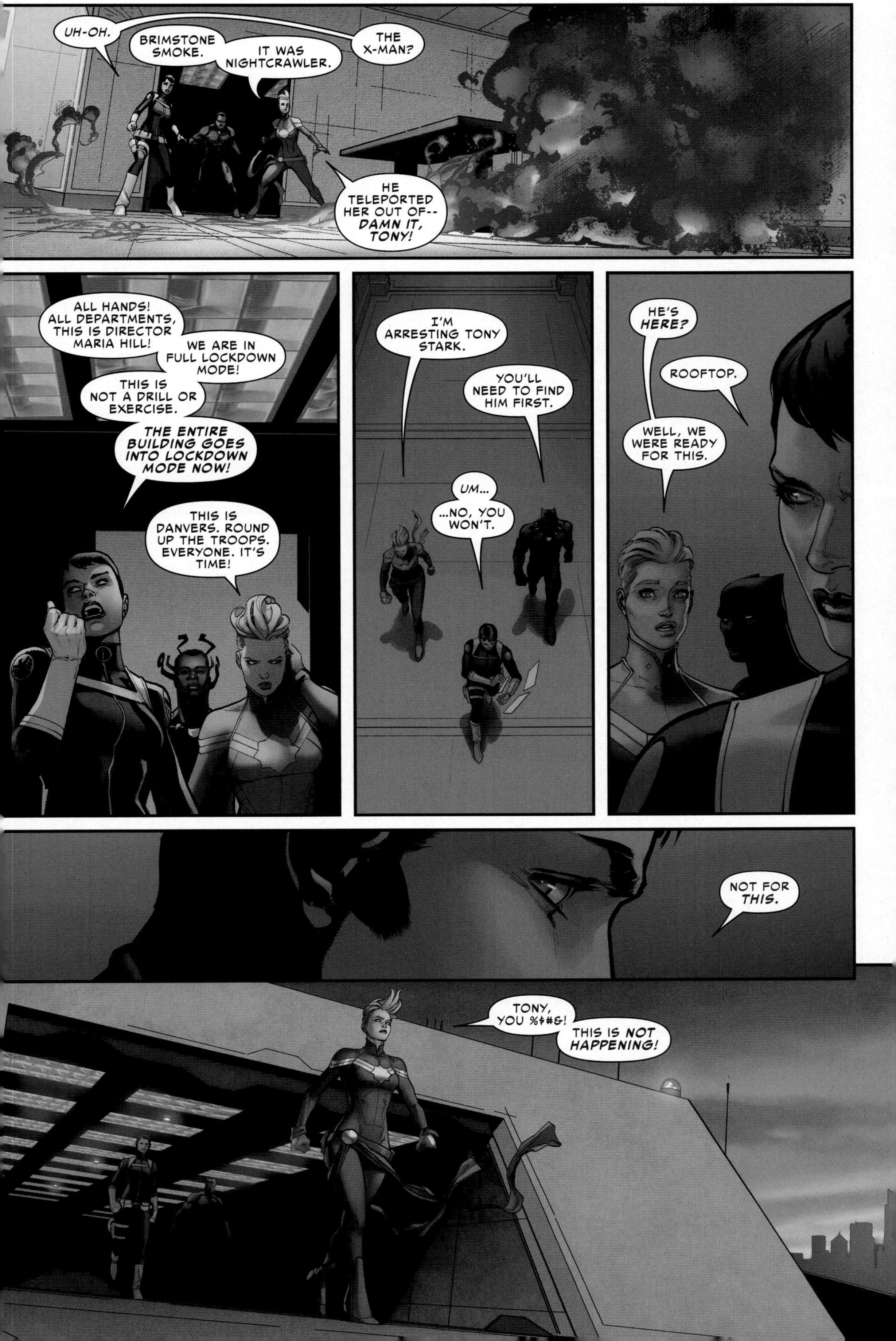
UH-OH.
BRIMSTONE SMOKE.
THE X-MAN?
IT WAS NIGHTCRAWLER.
HE TELEPORTED HER OUT OF-- DAMN IT, TONY!
ALL HANDS! ALL DEPARTMENTS, THIS IS DIRECTOR MARIA HILL!
WE ARE IN FULL LOCKDOWN MODE!
THIS IS NOT A DRILL OR EXERCISE.
THE ENTIRE BUILDING GOES INTO LOCKDOWN MODE NOW!
THIS IS DANVERS. ROUND UP THE TROOPS. EVERYONE. IT'S TIME!
I'M ARRESTING TONY STARK.
YOU'LL NEED TO FIND HIM FIRST.
UM...
...NO, YOU WON'T.
HE'S HERE?
ROOFTOP.
WELL, WE WERE READY FOR THIS.
NOT FOR THIS.
TONY, YOU %$#&!
THIS IS NOT HAPPENING!

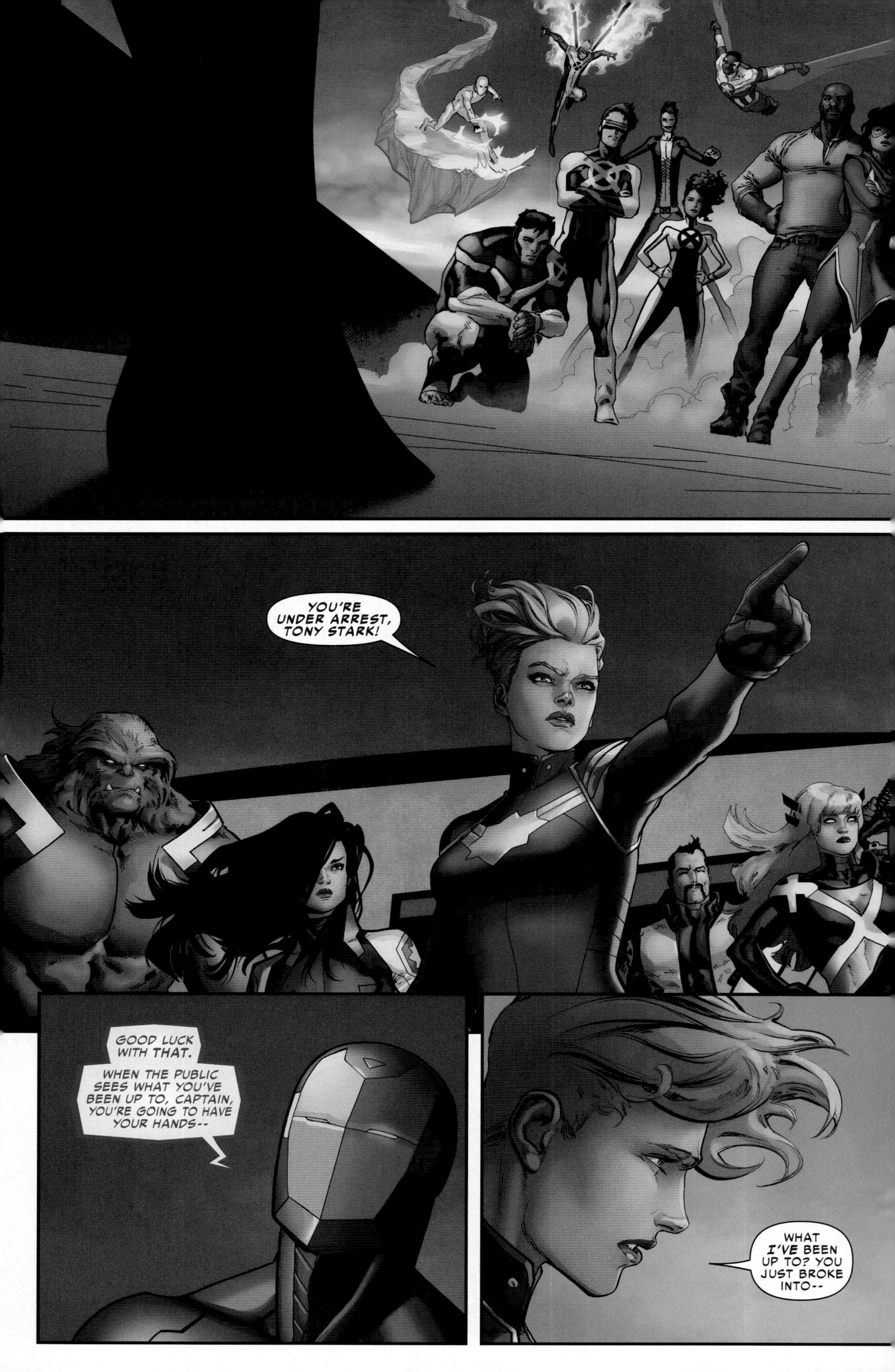
YOU'RE UNDER ARREST, TONY STARK!
GOOD LUCK WITH THAT.
WHEN THE PUBLIC SEES WHAT YOU'VE BEEN UP TO, CAPTAIN, YOU'RE GOING TO HAVE YOUR HANDS--
WHAT I'VE BEEN UP TO? YOU JUST BROKE INTO--

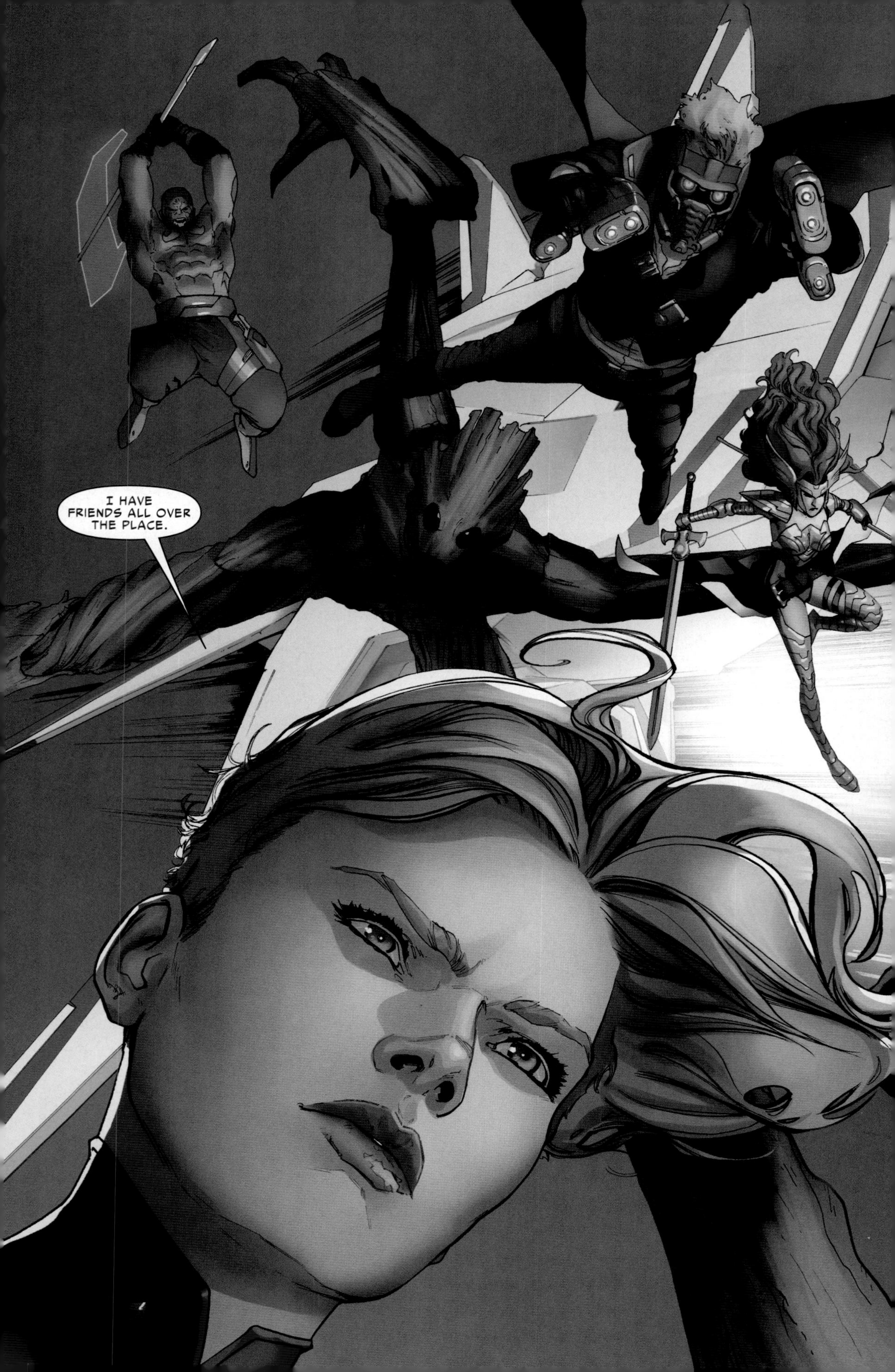
I HAVE FRIENDS ALL OVER THE PLACE.

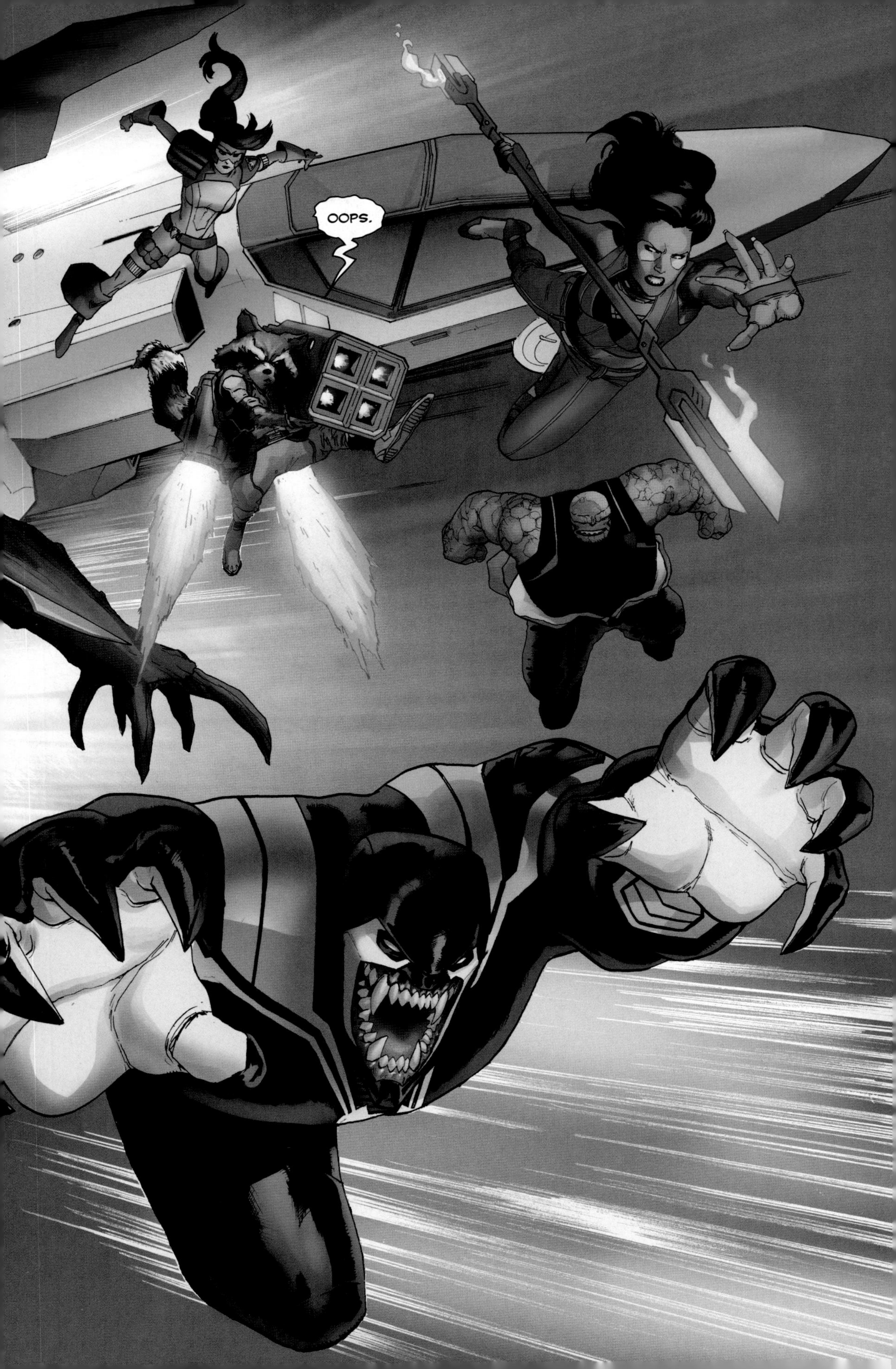
OOPS.

CIVIL WAR II #5

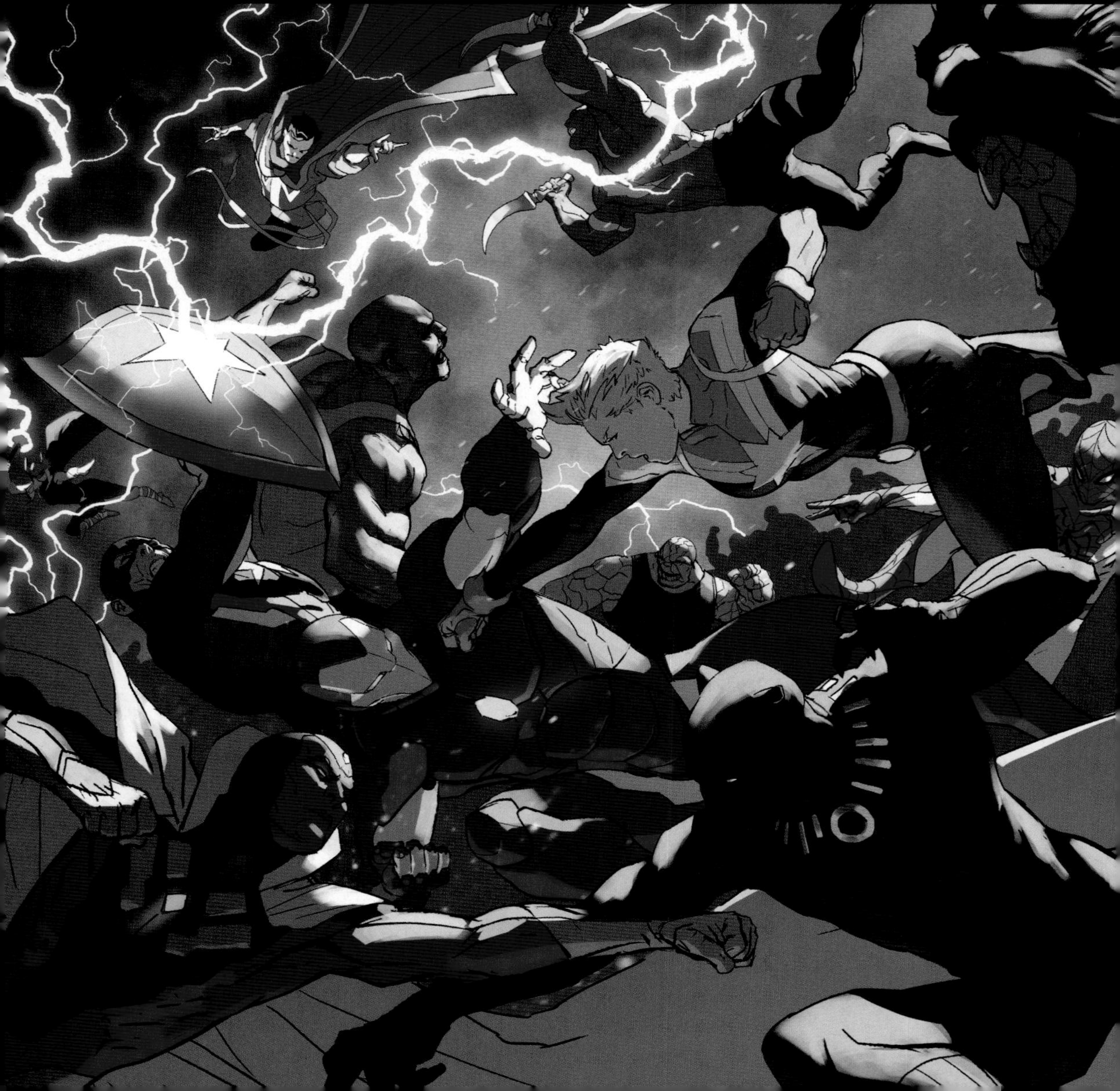

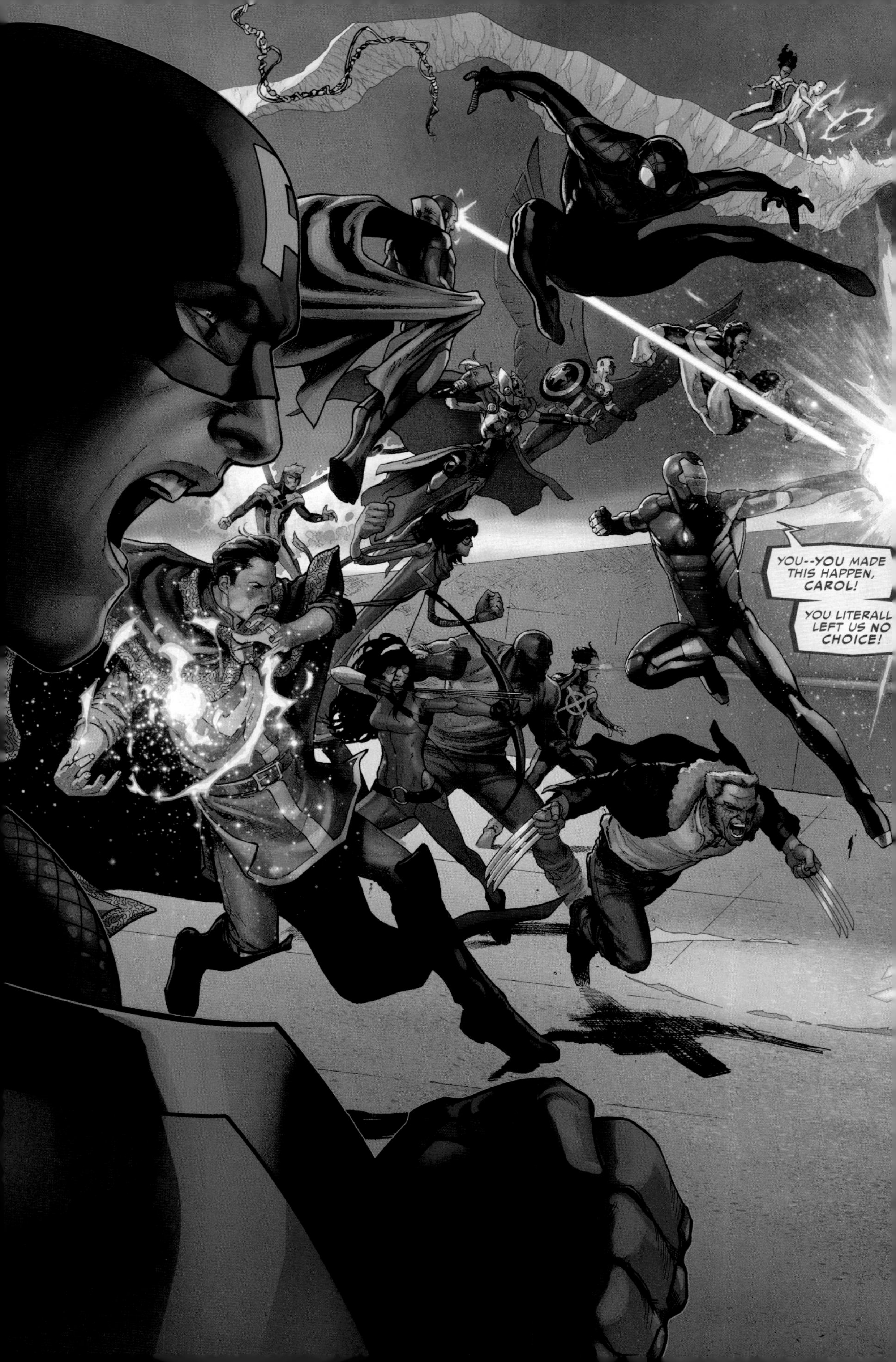
YOU--YOU MADE THIS HAPPEN, CAROL!
YOU LITERALL LEFT US NO CHOICE!

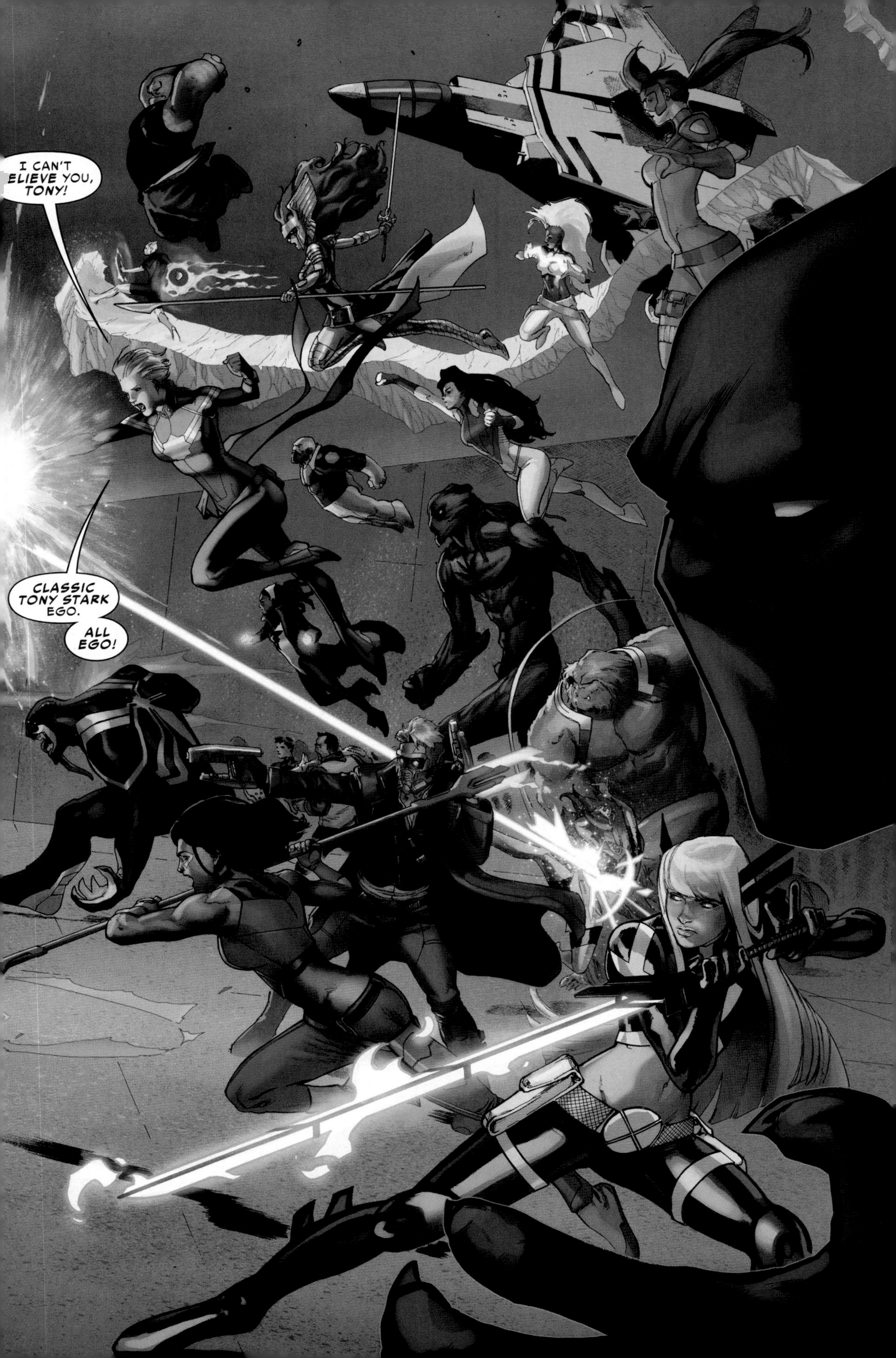
I CAN'T ELIEVE YOU, TONY!
CLASSIC TONY STARK EGO.
ALL EGO!

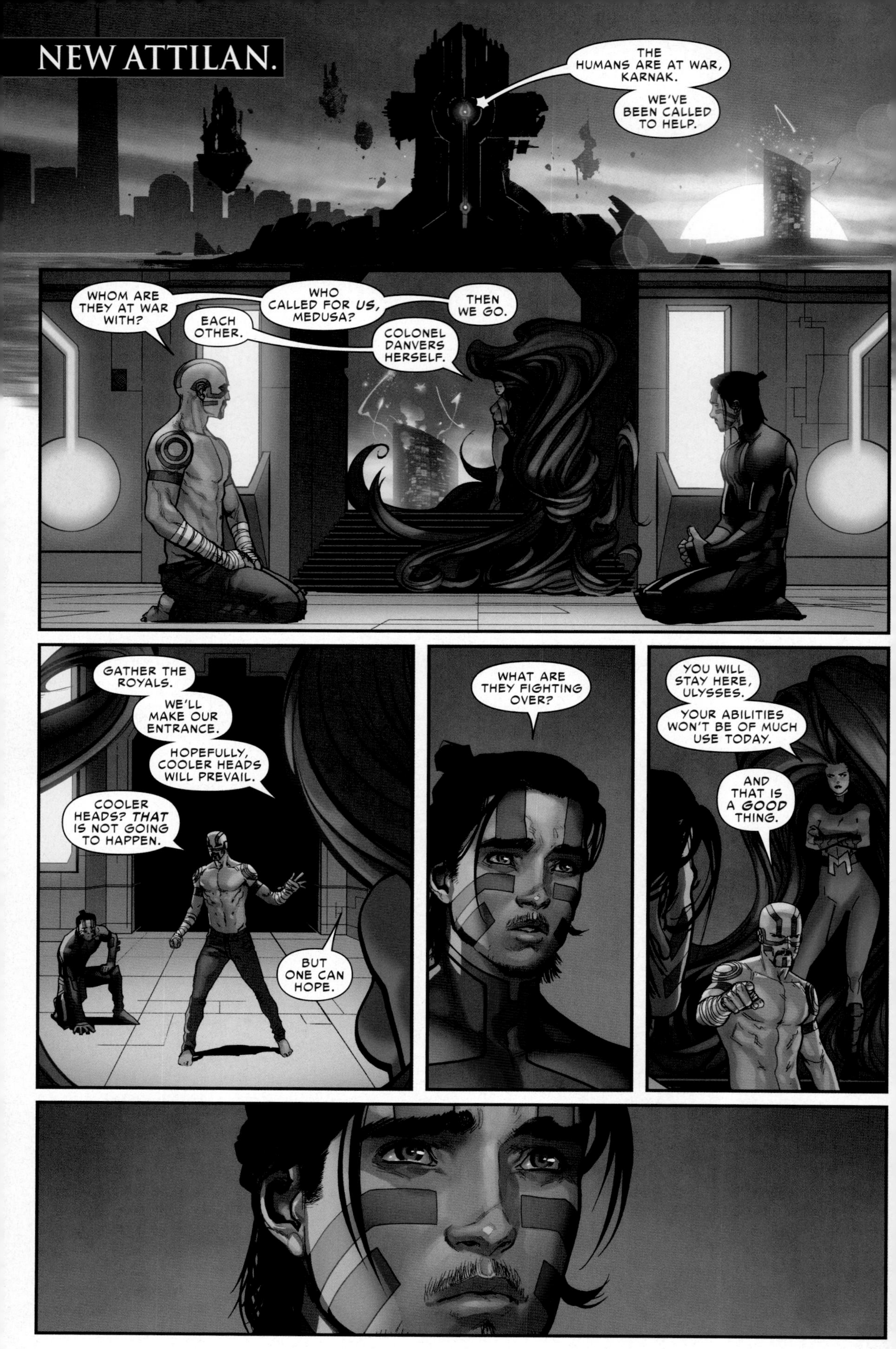
NEW ATTILAN.
THE HUMANS ARE AT WAR, KARNAK.
WE'VE BEEN CALLED TO HELP.
WHOM ARE THEY AT WAR WITH?
WHO CALLED FOR *US*, MEDUSA?
THEN WE GO.
EACH OTHER.
COLONEL DANVERS HERSELF.
GATHER THE ROYALS.
WE'LL MAKE OUR ENTRANCE.
HOPEFULLY, COOLER HEADS WILL PREVAIL.
COOLER HEADS? *THAT* IS NOT GOING TO HAPPEN.
BUT ONE CAN HOPE.
WHAT ARE THEY FIGHTING OVER?
YOU WILL STAY HERE, ULYSSES.
YOUR ABILITIES WON'T BE OF MUCH USE TODAY.
AND THAT IS A *GOOD* THING.

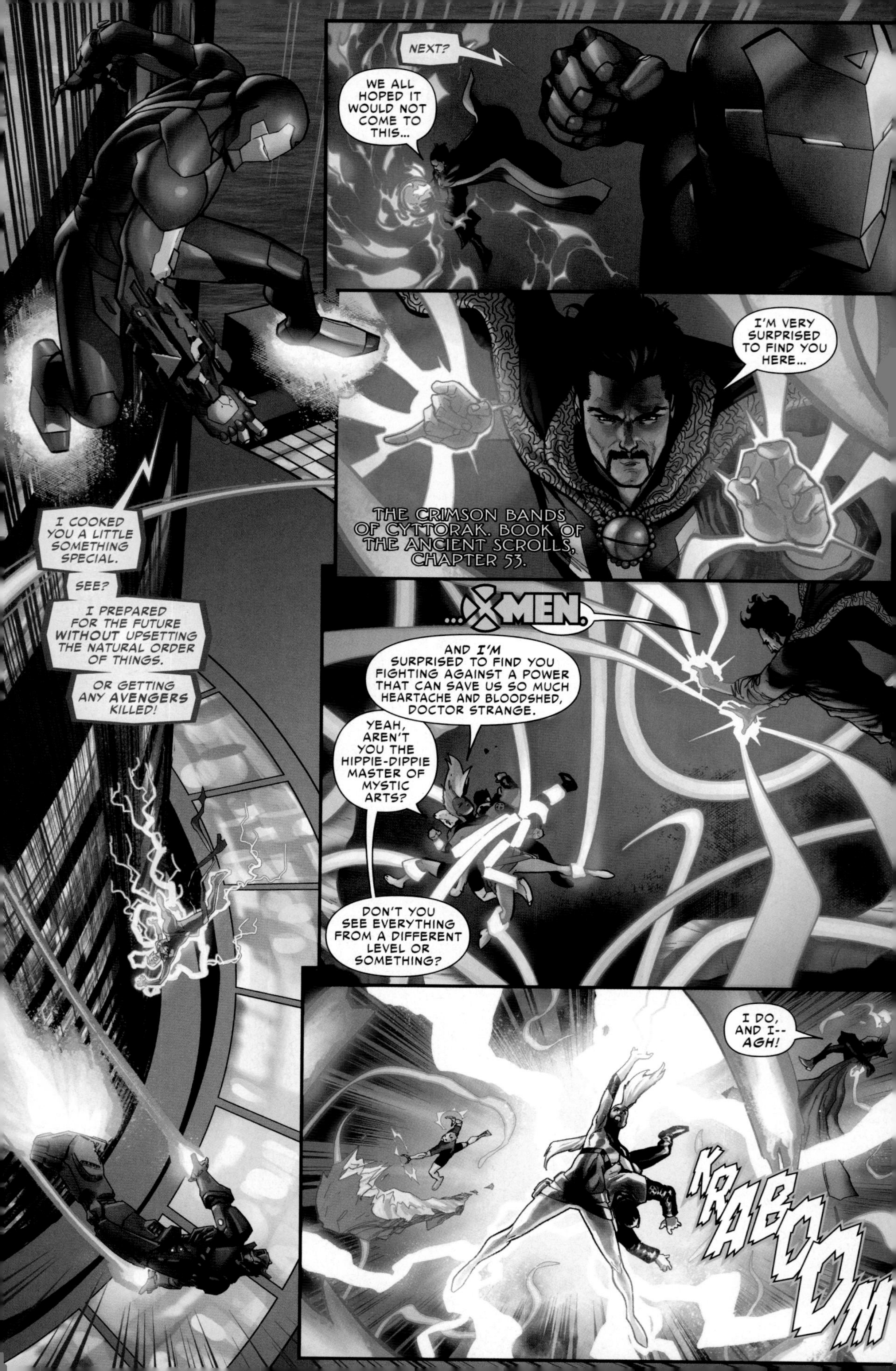
NEXT?
WE ALL HOPED IT WOULD NOT COME TO THIS...
I'M VERY SURPRISED TO FIND YOU HERE...
THE CRIMSON BANDS OF CYTTORAK. BOOK OF THE ANCIENT SCROLLS, CHAPTER 53.
I COOKED YOU A LITTLE SOMETHING SPECIAL.
SEE?
I PREPARED FOR THE FUTURE WITHOUT UPSETTING THE NATURAL ORDER OF THINGS.
OR GETTING ANY AVENGERS KILLED!
...X-MEN.
AND I'M SURPRISED TO FIND YOU FIGHTING AGAINST A POWER THAT CAN SAVE US SO MUCH HEARTACHE AND BLOODSHED, DOCTOR STRANGE.
YEAH, AREN'T YOU THE HIPPIE-DIPPIE MASTER OF MYSTIC ARTS?
DON'T YOU SEE EVERYTHING FROM A DIFFERENT LEVEL OR SOMETHING?
I DO, AND I-- AGH!
KRABOOM

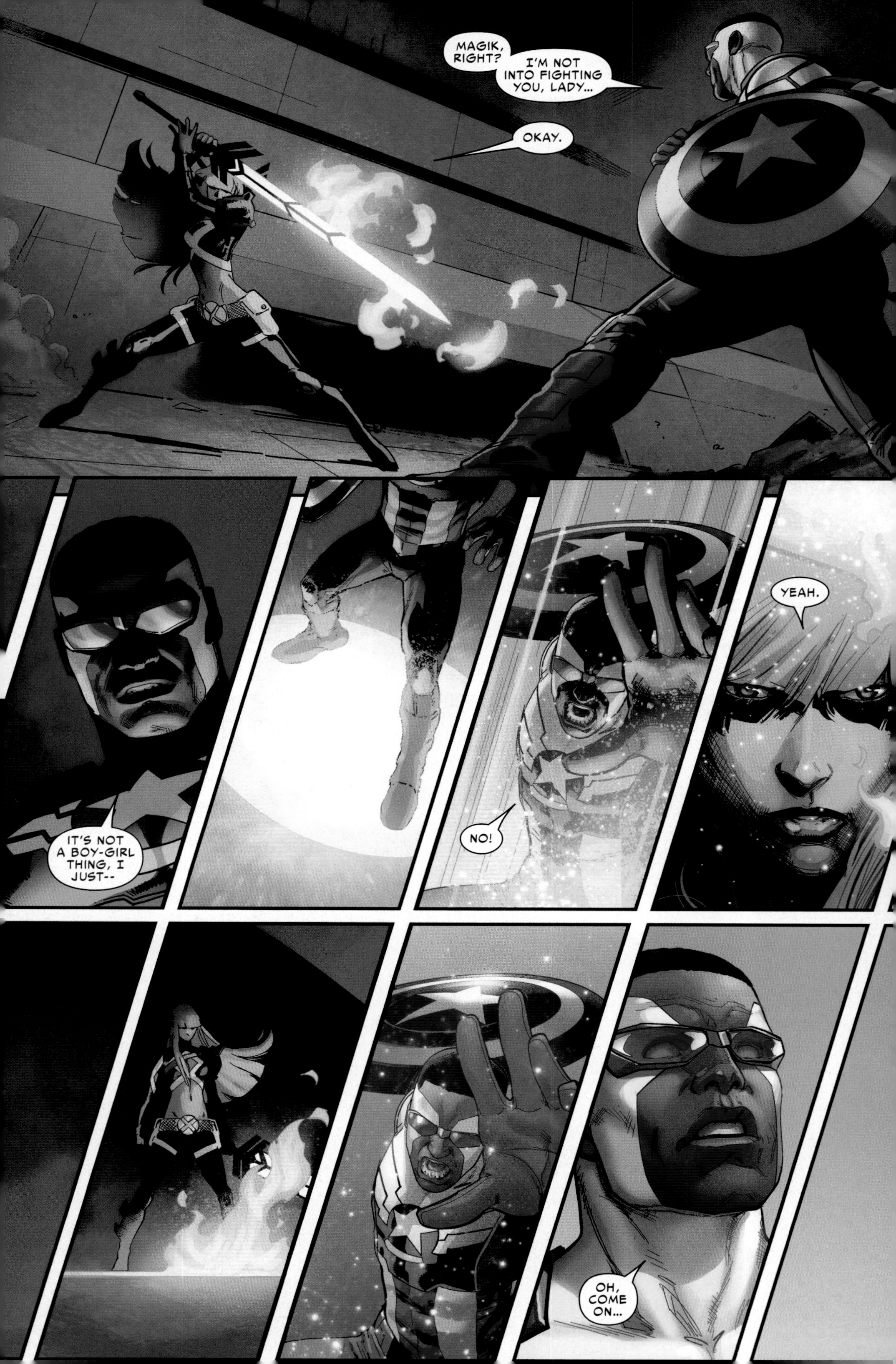
MAGIK, RIGHT?
I'M NOT INTO FIGHTING YOU, LADY...
OKAY.
IT'S NOT A BOY-GIRL THING, I JUST--
NO!
YEAH.
OH, COME ON...

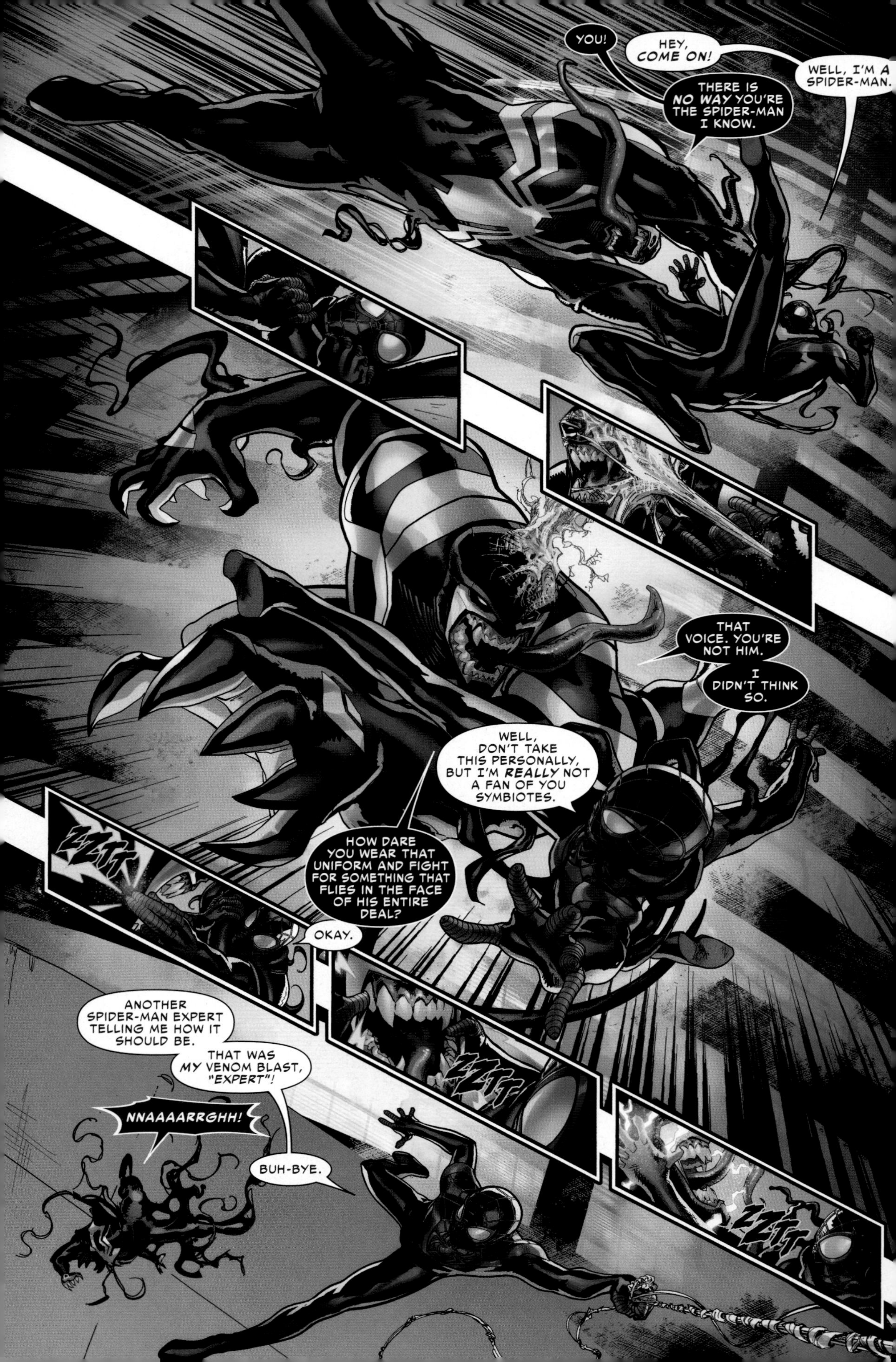
YOU!
HEY, COME ON!
WELL, I'M A SPIDER-MAN.
THERE IS NO WAY YOU'RE THE SPIDER-MAN I KNOW.
THAT VOICE. YOU'RE NOT HIM.
I DIDN'T THINK SO.
WELL, DON'T TAKE THIS PERSONALLY, BUT I'M REALLY NOT A FAN OF YOU SYMBIOTES.
HOW DARE YOU WEAR THAT UNIFORM AND FIGHT FOR SOMETHING THAT FLIES IN THE FACE OF HIS ENTIRE DEAL?
ZZZTT
OKAY.
ZZZTT
ANOTHER SPIDER-MAN EXPERT TELLING ME HOW IT SHOULD BE.
THAT WAS MY VENOM BLAST, "EXPERT"!
NNAAAARRGHH!
BUH-BYE.
ZZZTT

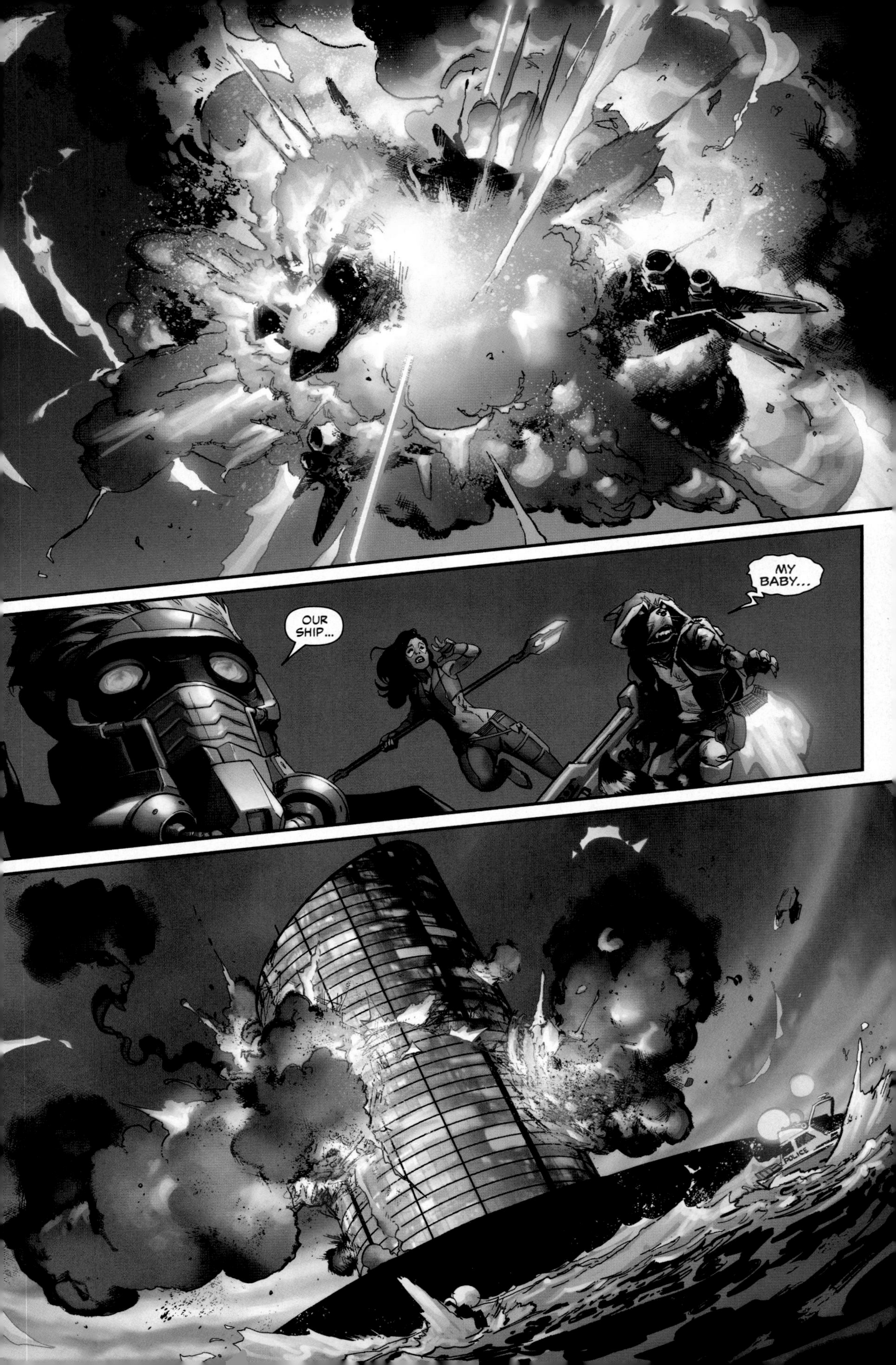
OUR SHIP...
MY BABY...
POLICE

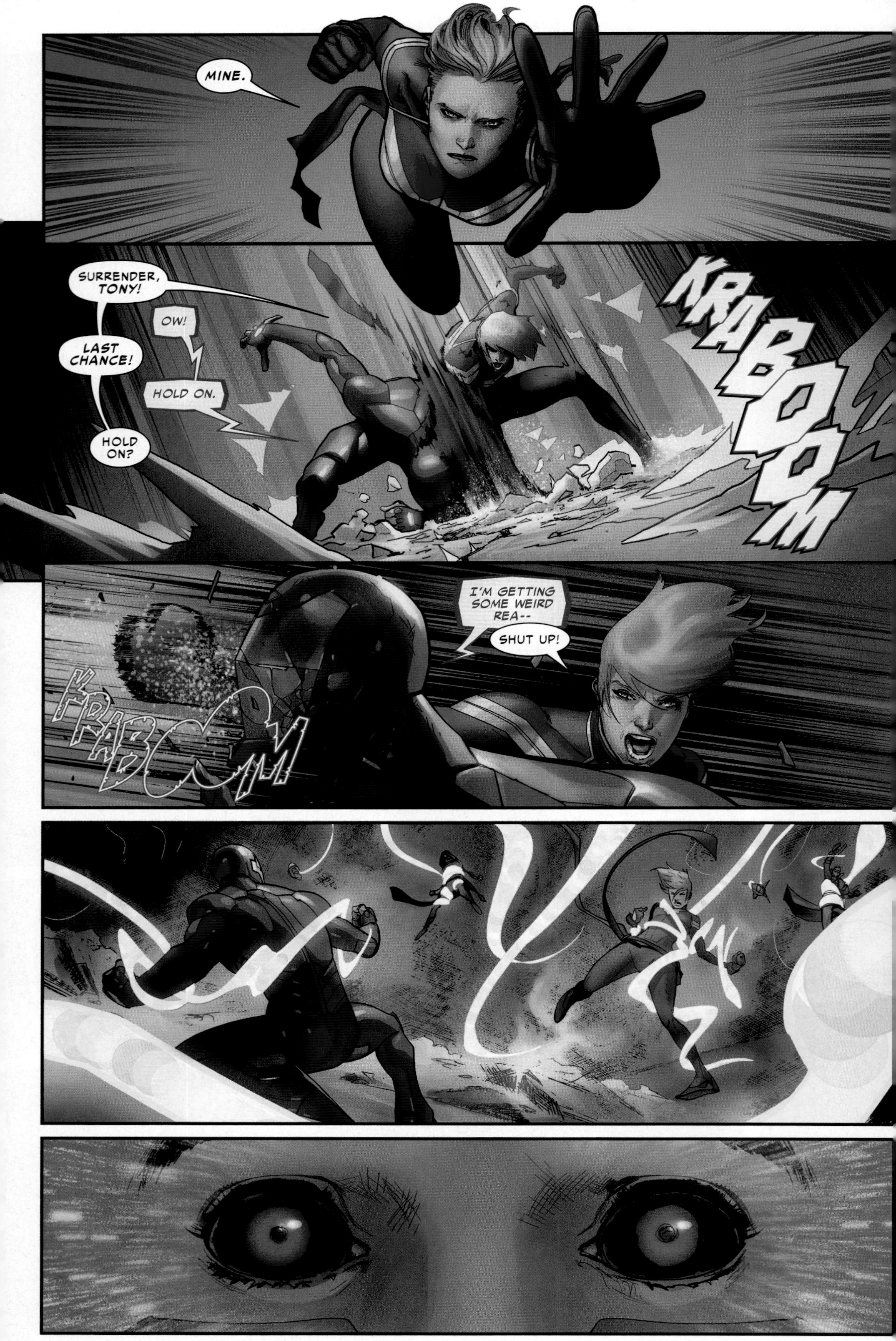
MINE.
SURRENDER, TONY!
OW!
LAST CHANCE!
HOLD ON.
HOLD ON?
KRABOOM
I'M GETTING SOME WEIRD REA--
SHUT UP!
KRABOOM

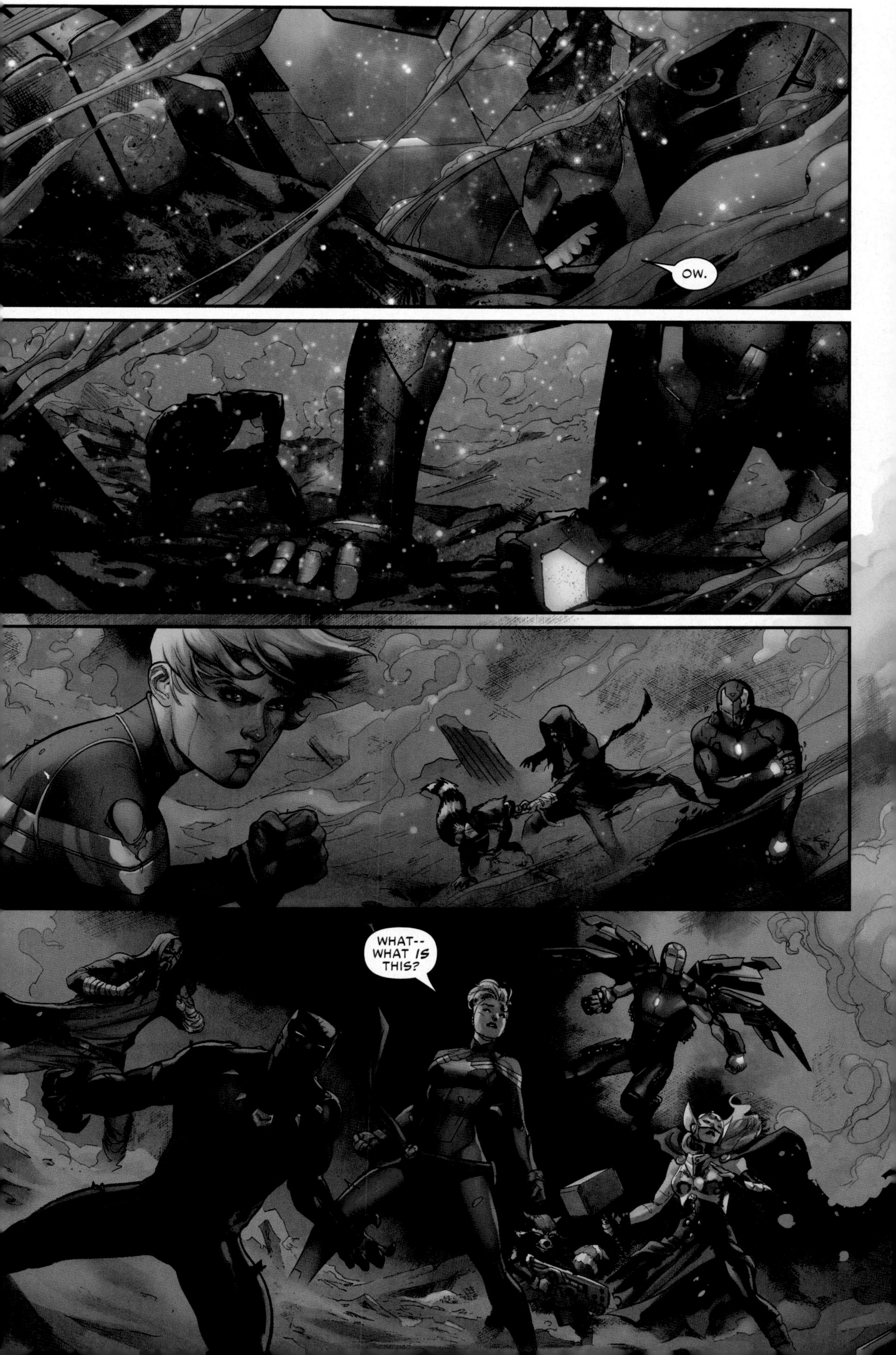
OW.
WHAT-- WHAT IS THIS?

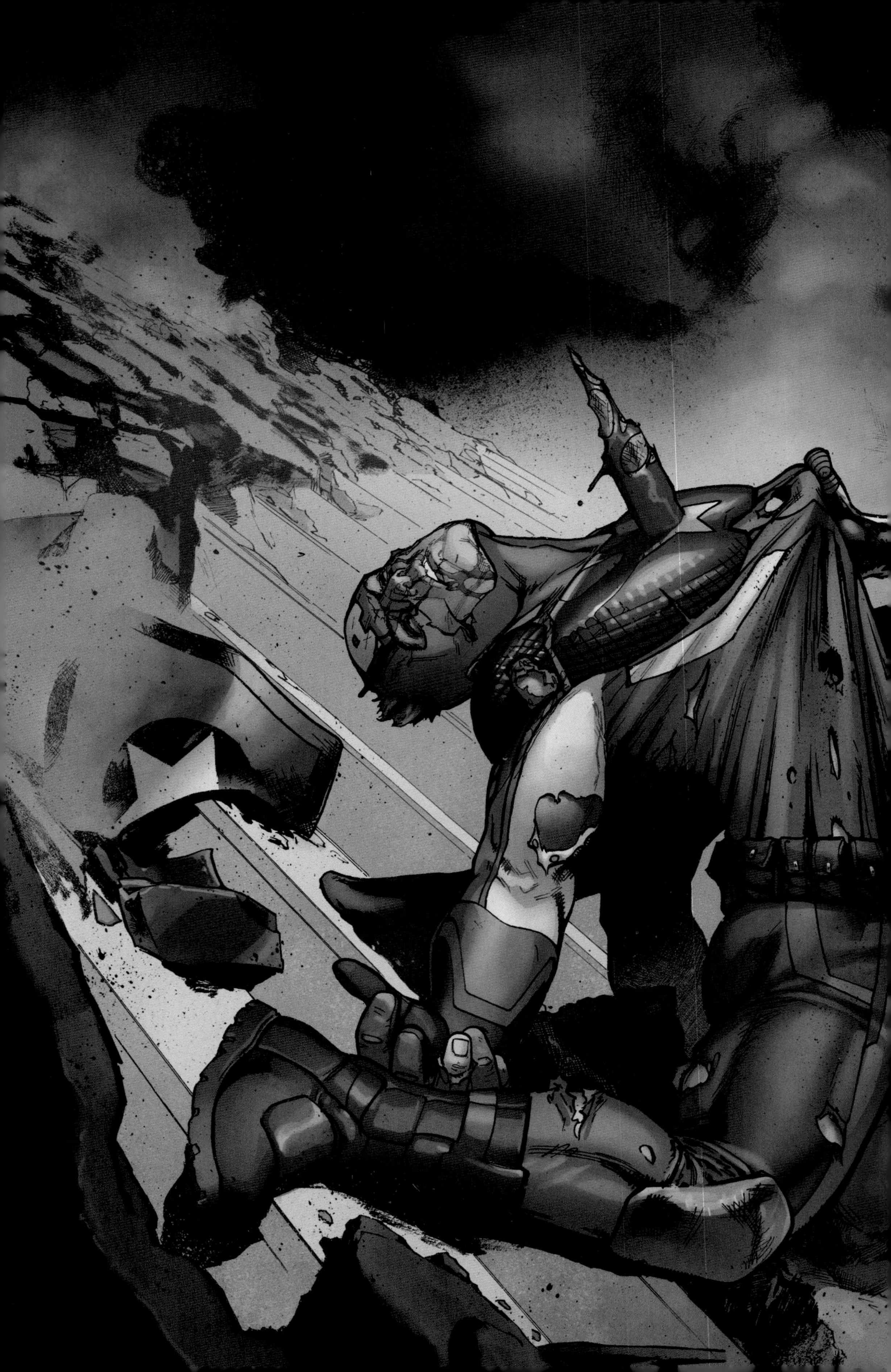

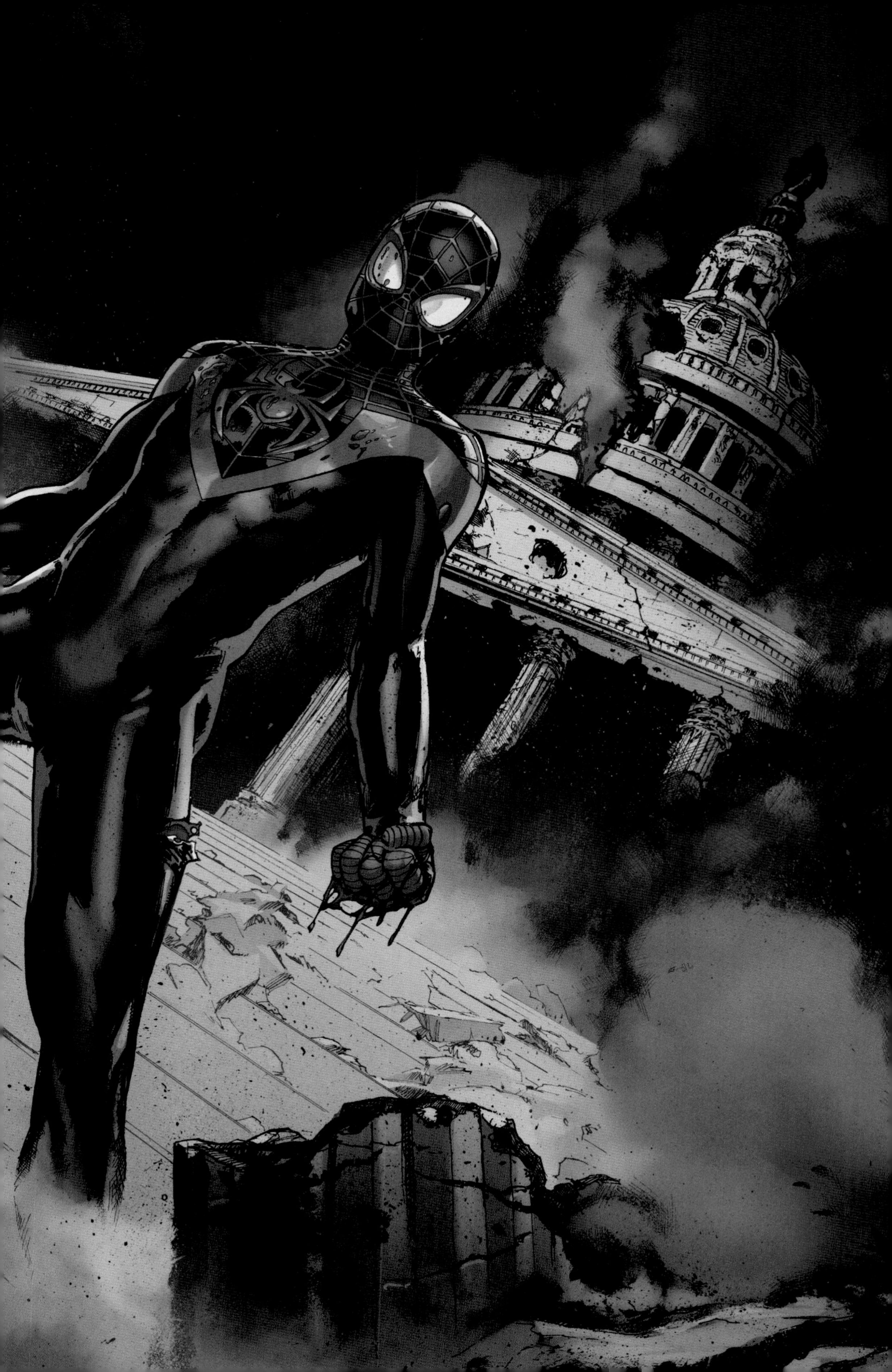

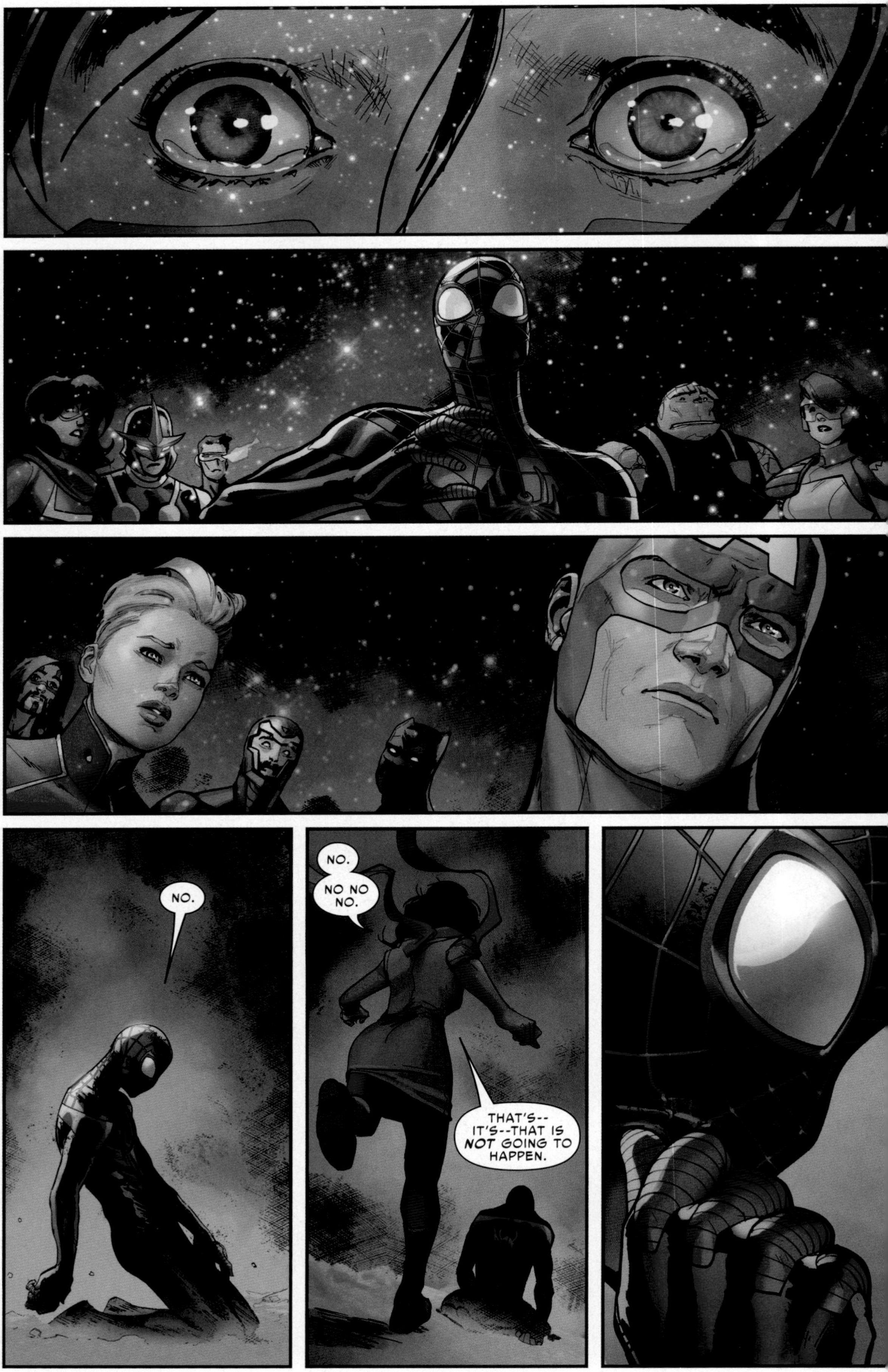
NO.
NO.
NO NO NO.
THAT'S-- IT'S--THAT IS NOT GOING TO HAPPEN.

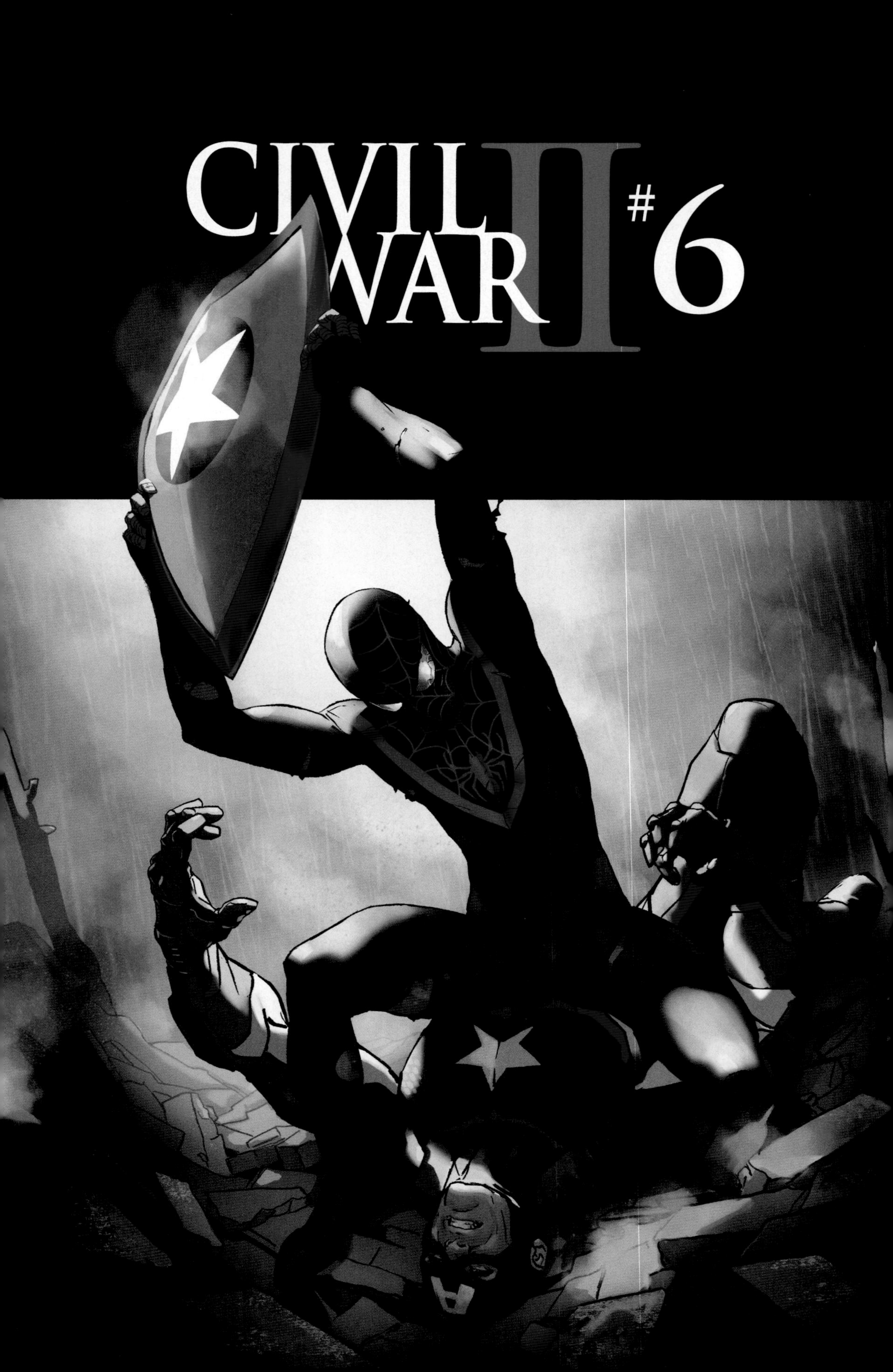
CIVIL WAR II
#6

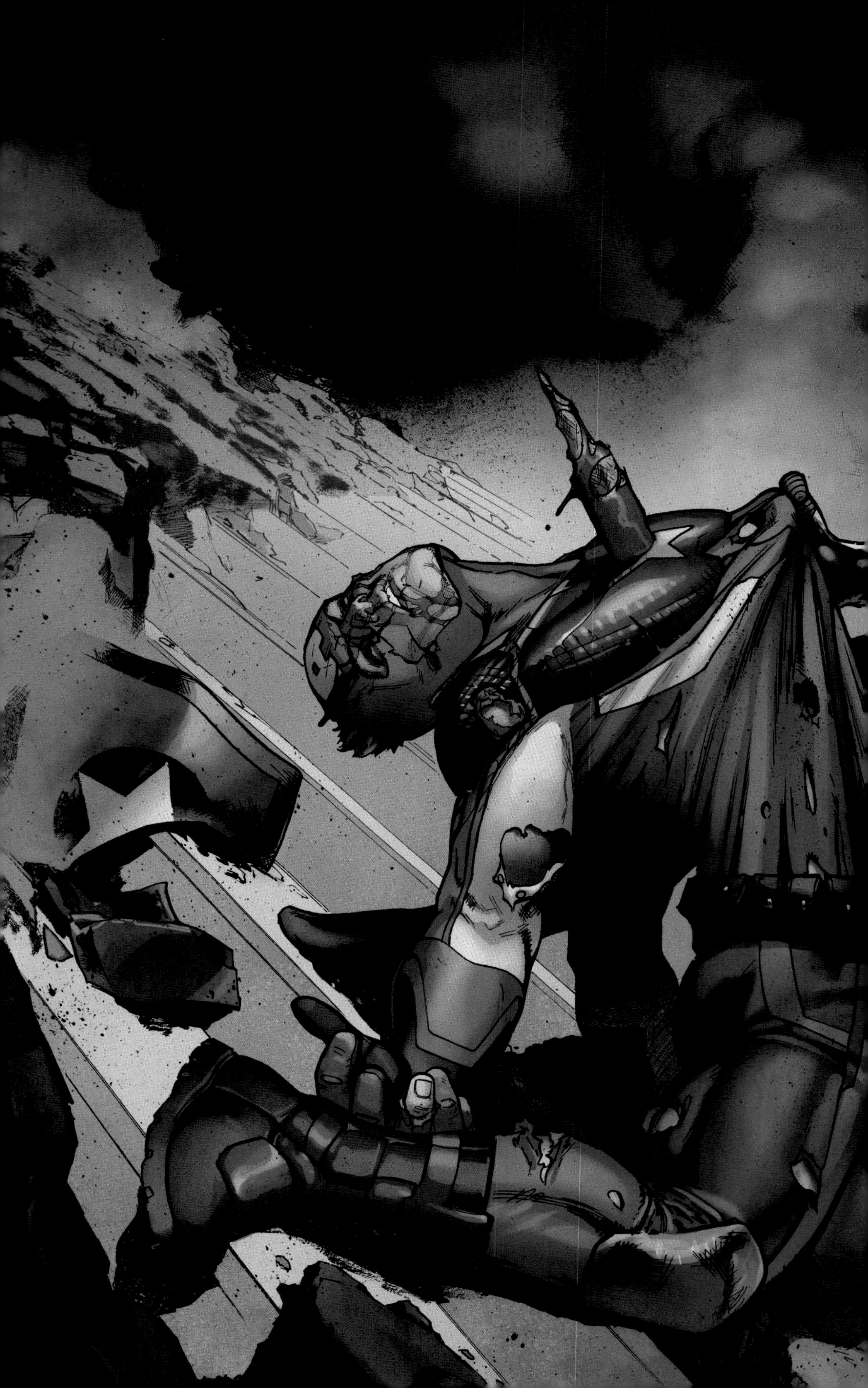

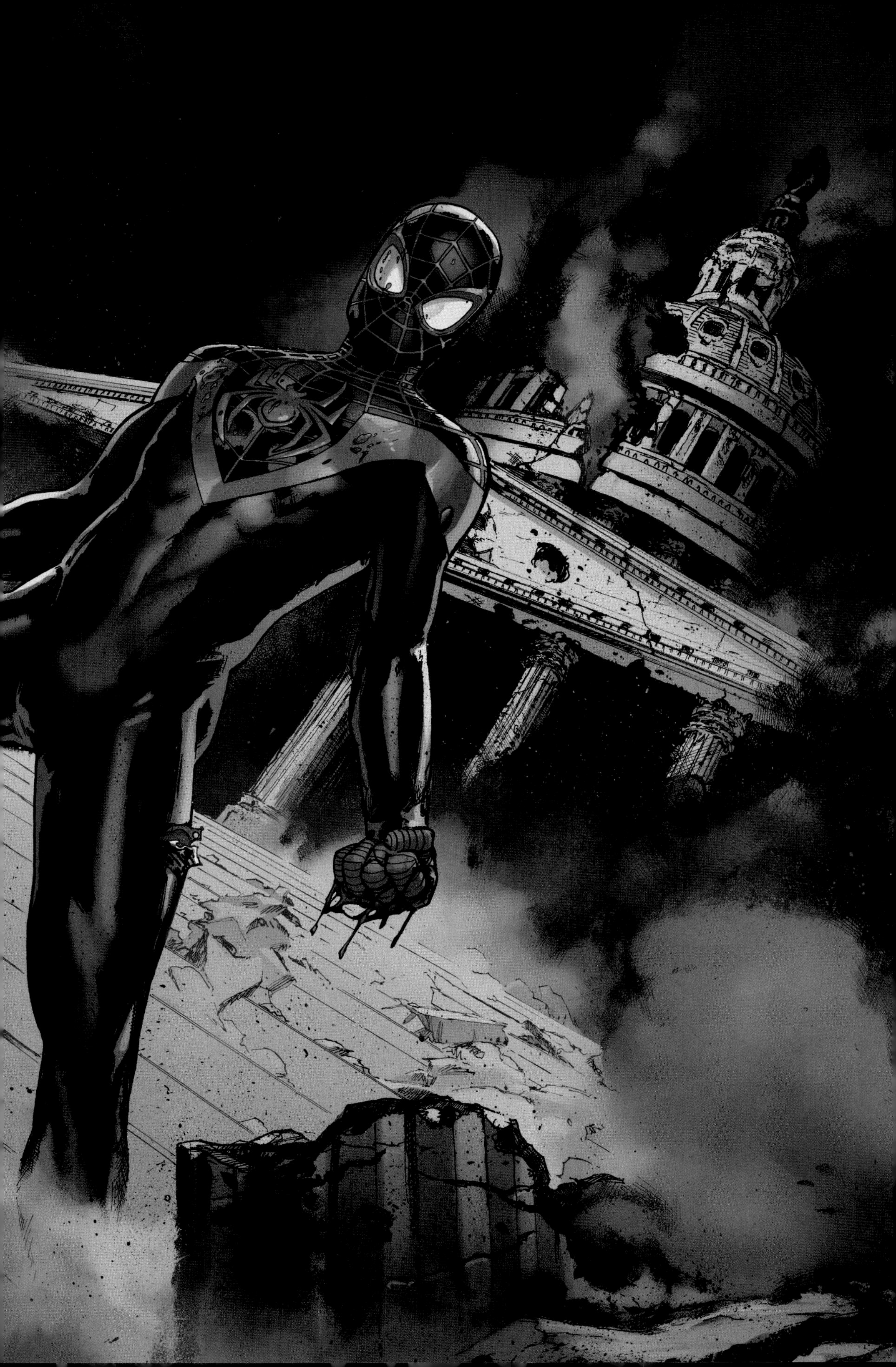

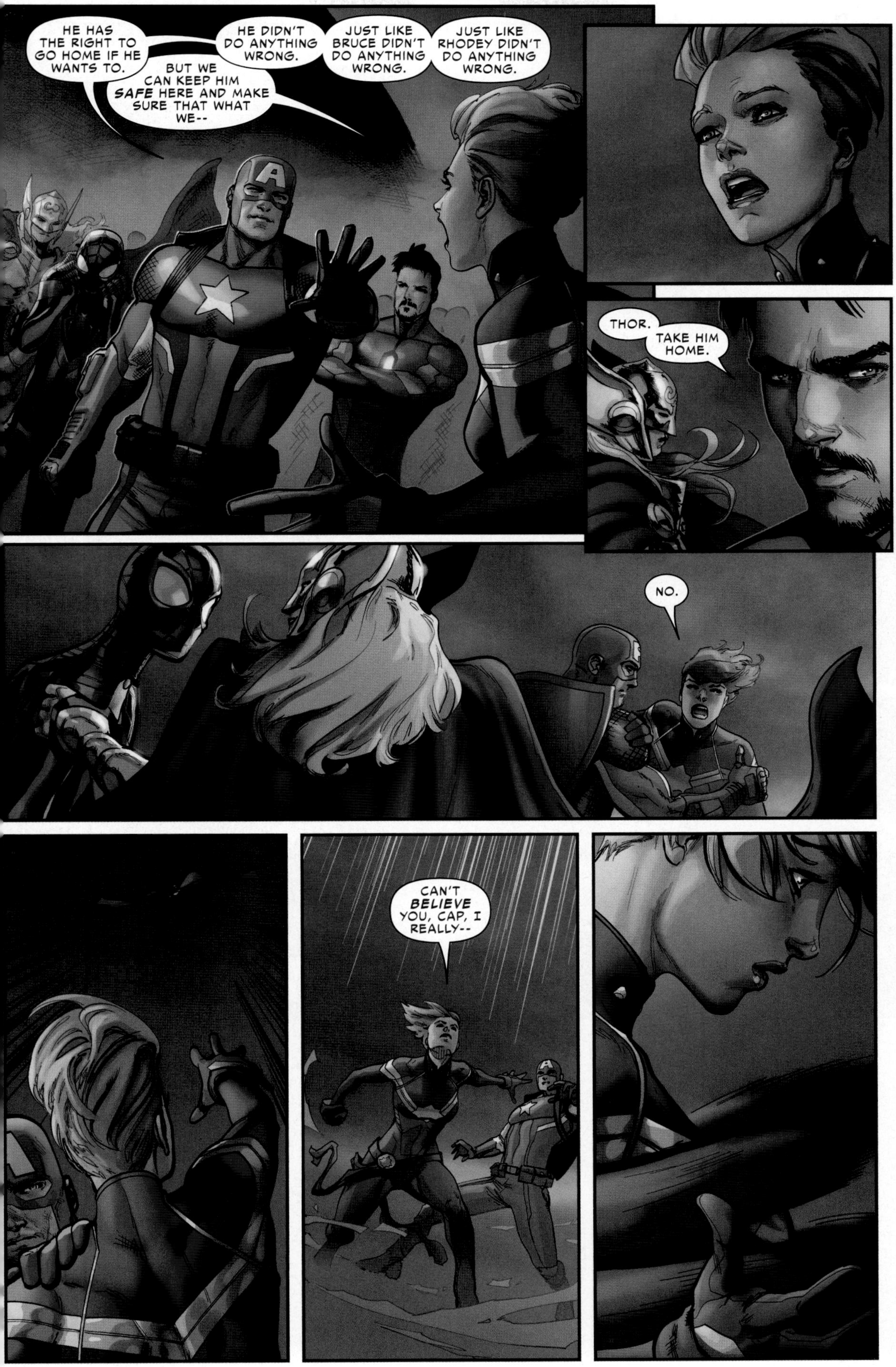
HE HAS THE RIGHT TO GO HOME IF HE WANTS TO.
BUT WE CAN KEEP HIM SAFE HERE AND MAKE SURE THAT WHAT WE--
HE DIDN'T DO ANYTHING WRONG.
JUST LIKE BRUCE DIDN'T DO ANYTHING WRONG.
JUST LIKE RHODEY DIDN'T DO ANYTHING WRONG.
THOR.
TAKE HIM HOME.
NO.
CAN'T BELIEVE YOU, CAP, I REALLY--

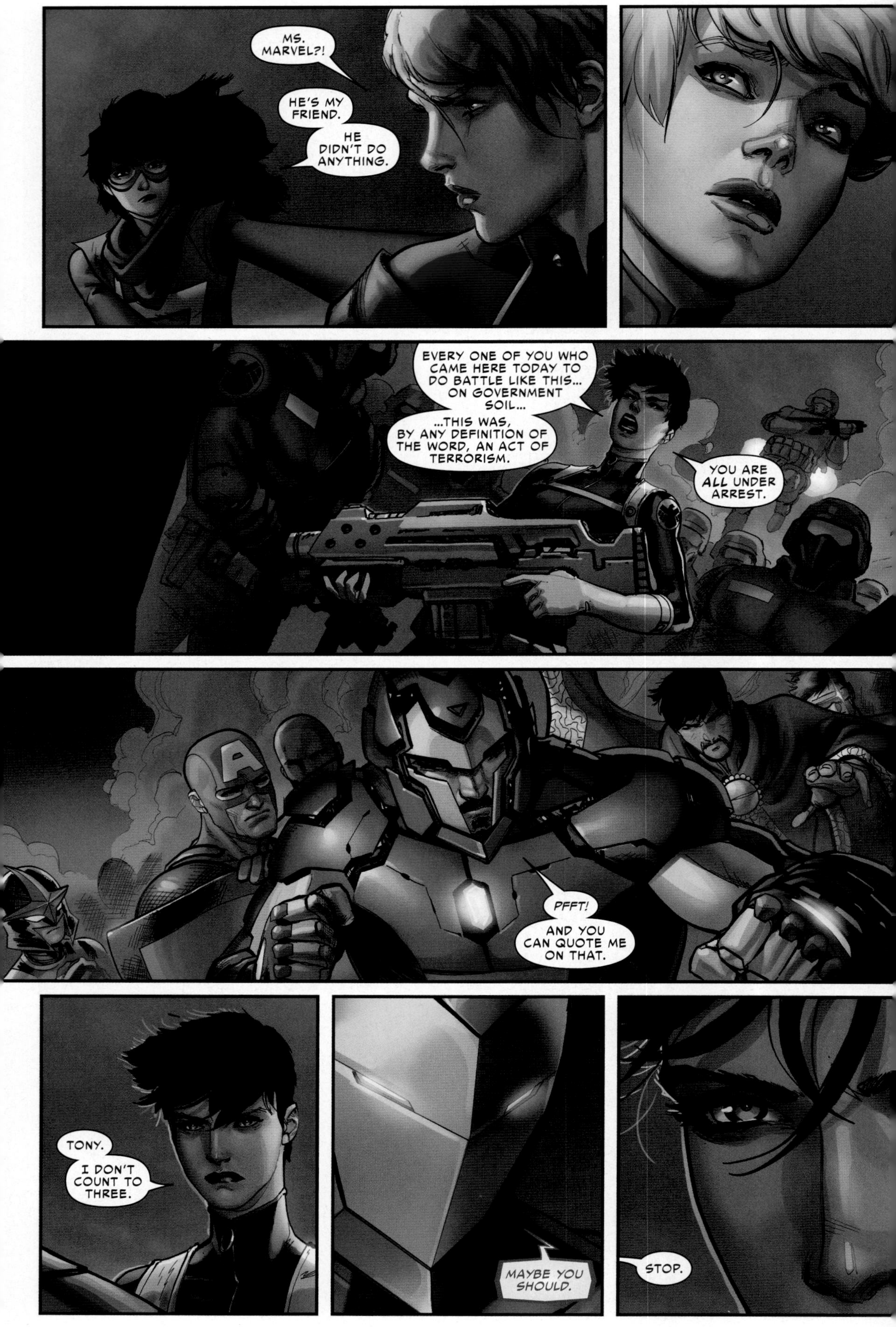
MS. MARVEL?!
HE'S MY FRIEND.
HE DIDN'T DO ANYTHING.
EVERY ONE OF YOU WHO CAME HERE TODAY TO DO BATTLE LIKE THIS... ON GOVERNMENT SOIL...
...THIS WAS, BY ANY DEFINITION OF THE WORD, AN ACT OF TERRORISM.
YOU ARE ALL UNDER ARREST.
PFFT!
AND YOU CAN QUOTE ME ON THAT.
TONY.
I DON'T COUNT TO THREE.
MAYBE YOU SHOULD.
STOP.

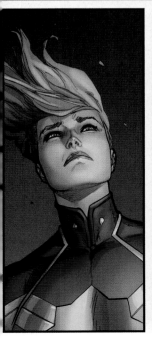

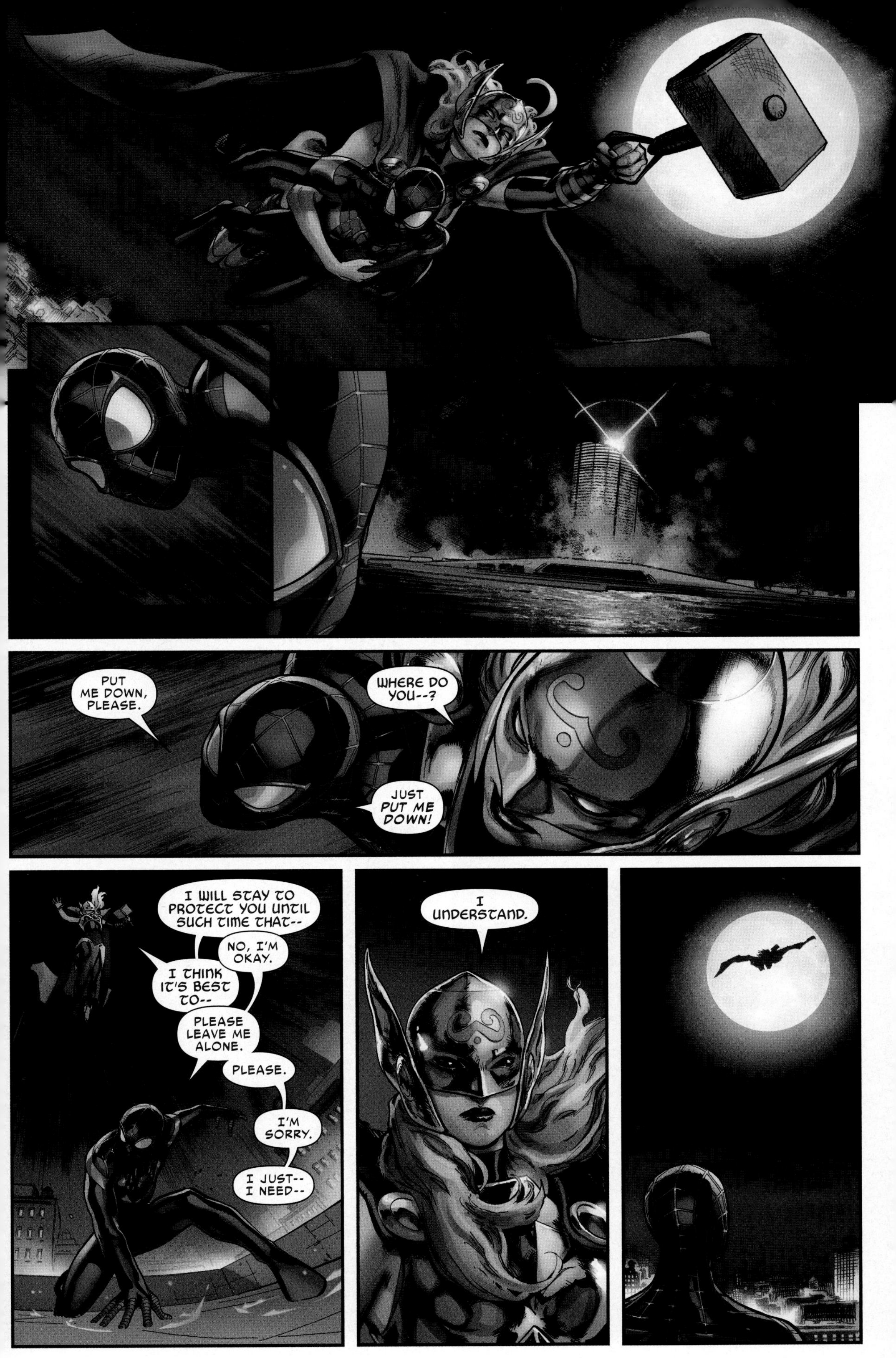
PUT ME DOWN, PLEASE.
WHERE DO YOU--?
JUST PUT ME DOWN!
I WILL STAY TO PROTECT YOU UNTIL SUCH TIME THAT--
NO, I'M OKAY.
I THINK IT'S BEST TO--
PLEASE LEAVE ME ALONE.
PLEASE.
I'M SORRY.
I JUST-- I NEED--
I UNDERSTAND.

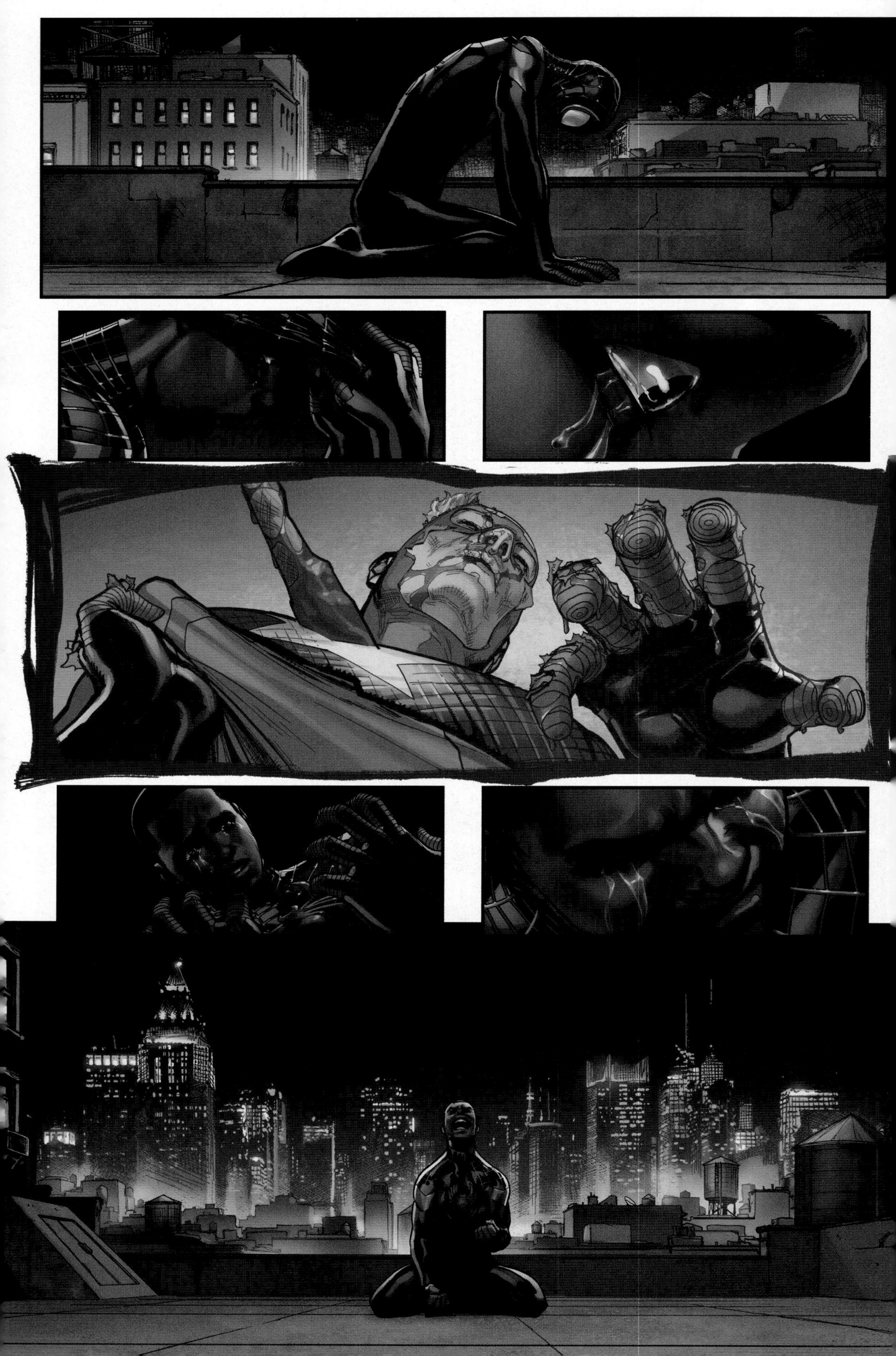

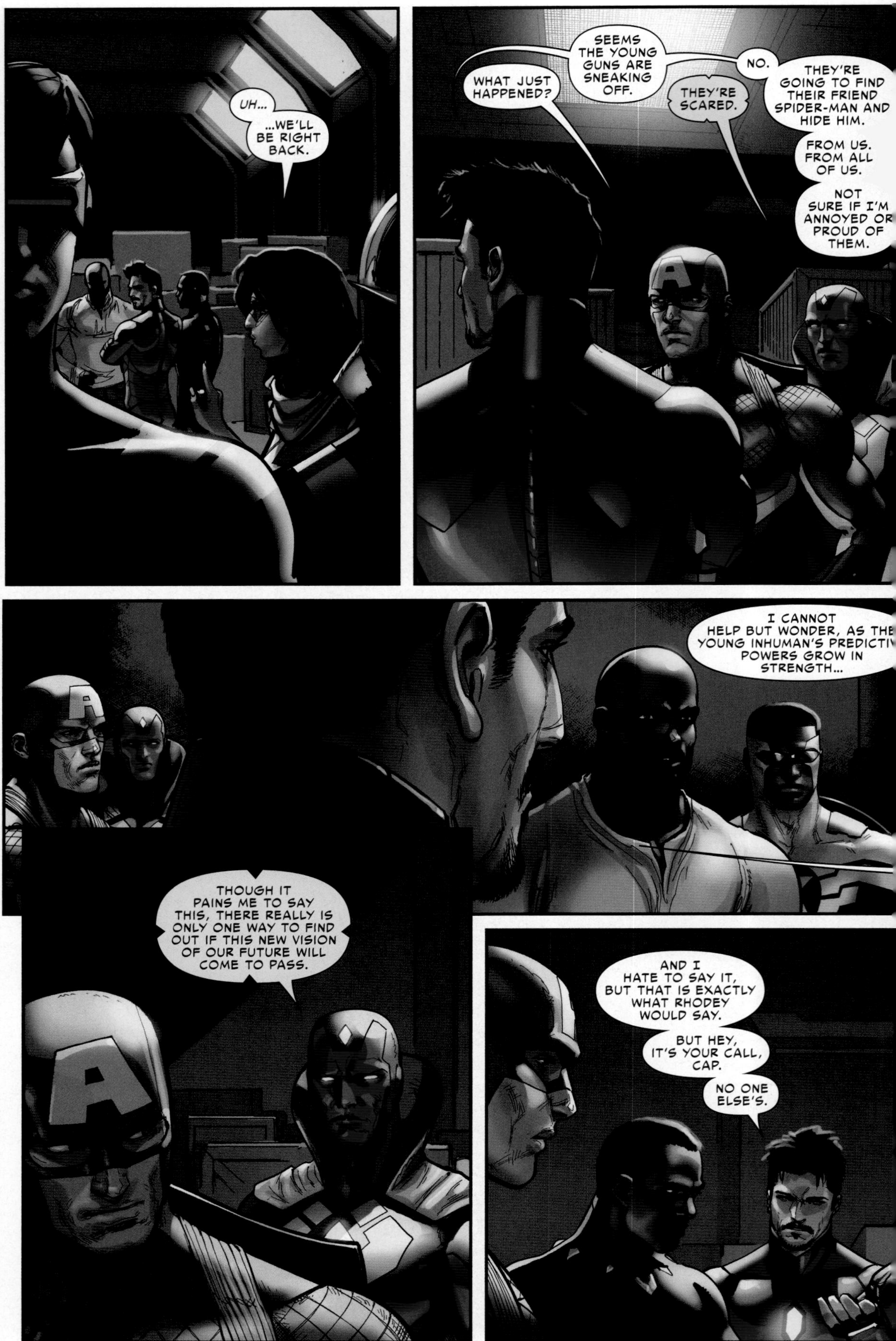
UH...
...WE'LL BE RIGHT BACK.
WHAT JUST HAPPENED?
SEEMS THE YOUNG GUNS ARE SNEAKING OFF.
THEY'RE SCARED.
NO.
THEY'RE GOING TO FIND THEIR FRIEND SPIDER-MAN AND HIDE HIM.
FROM US. FROM ALL OF US.
NOT SURE IF I'M ANNOYED OR PROUD OF THEM.
I CANNOT HELP BUT WONDER, AS THE YOUNG INHUMAN'S PREDICTIVE POWERS GROW IN STRENGTH...
THOUGH IT PAINS ME TO SAY THIS, THERE REALLY IS ONLY ONE WAY TO FIND OUT IF THIS NEW VISION OF OUR FUTURE WILL COME TO PASS.
AND I HATE TO SAY IT, BUT THAT IS EXACTLY WHAT RHODEY WOULD SAY.
BUT HEY, IT'S YOUR CALL, CAP.
NO ONE ELSE'S.

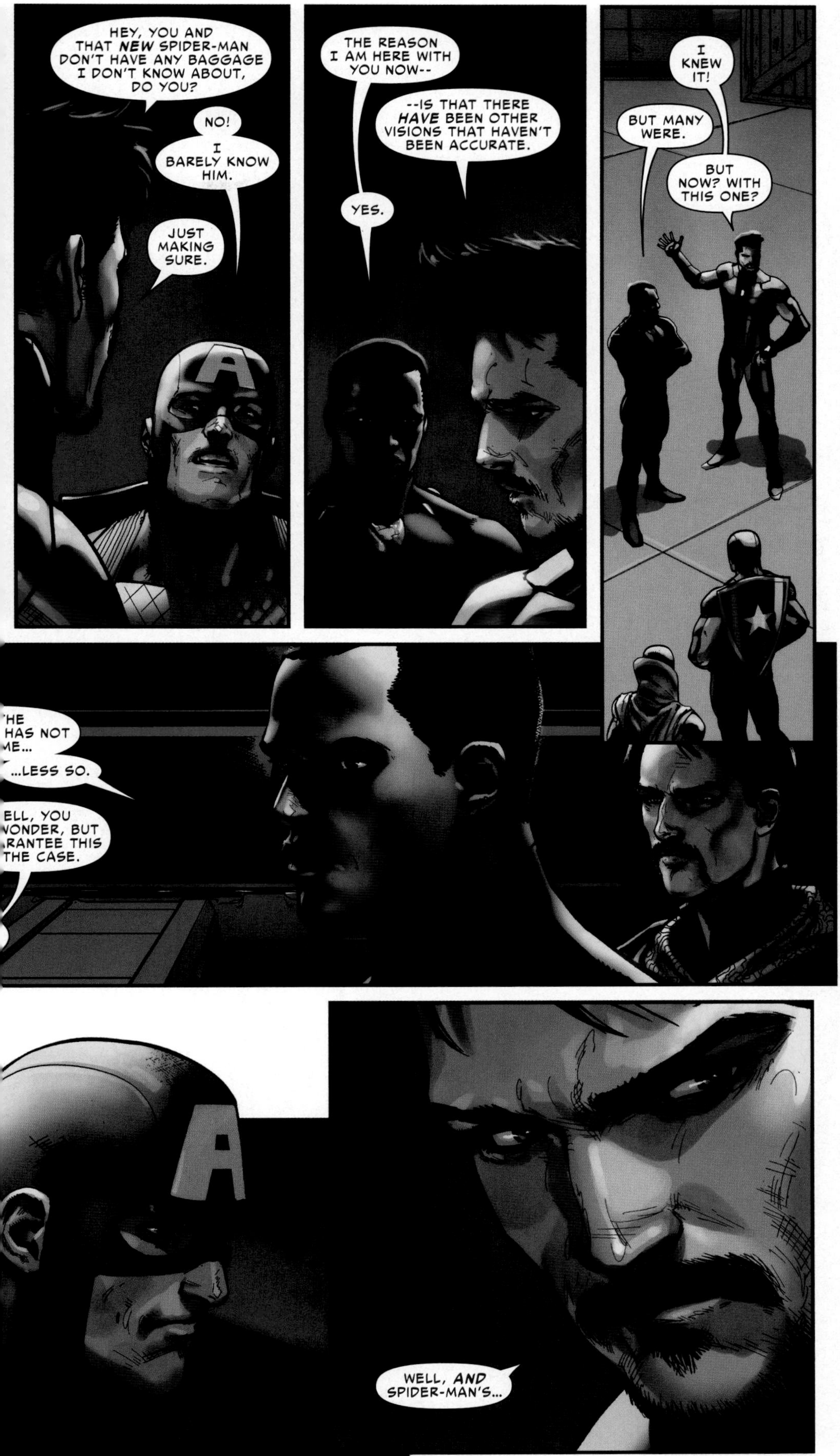
HEY, YOU AND THAT *NEW* SPIDER-MAN DON'T HAVE ANY BAGGAGE I DON'T KNOW ABOUT, DO YOU?
NO!
I BARELY KNOW HIM.
JUST MAKING SURE.
THE REASON I AM HERE WITH YOU NOW--
--IS THAT THERE *HAVE* BEEN OTHER VISIONS THAT HAVEN'T BEEN ACCURATE.
YES.
I KNEW IT!
BUT MANY WERE.
BUT NOW? WITH THIS ONE?
HE HAS NOT ME...
...LESS SO.
ELL, YOU WONDER, BUT ARANTEE THIS THE CASE.
WELL, *AND* SPIDER-MAN'S...

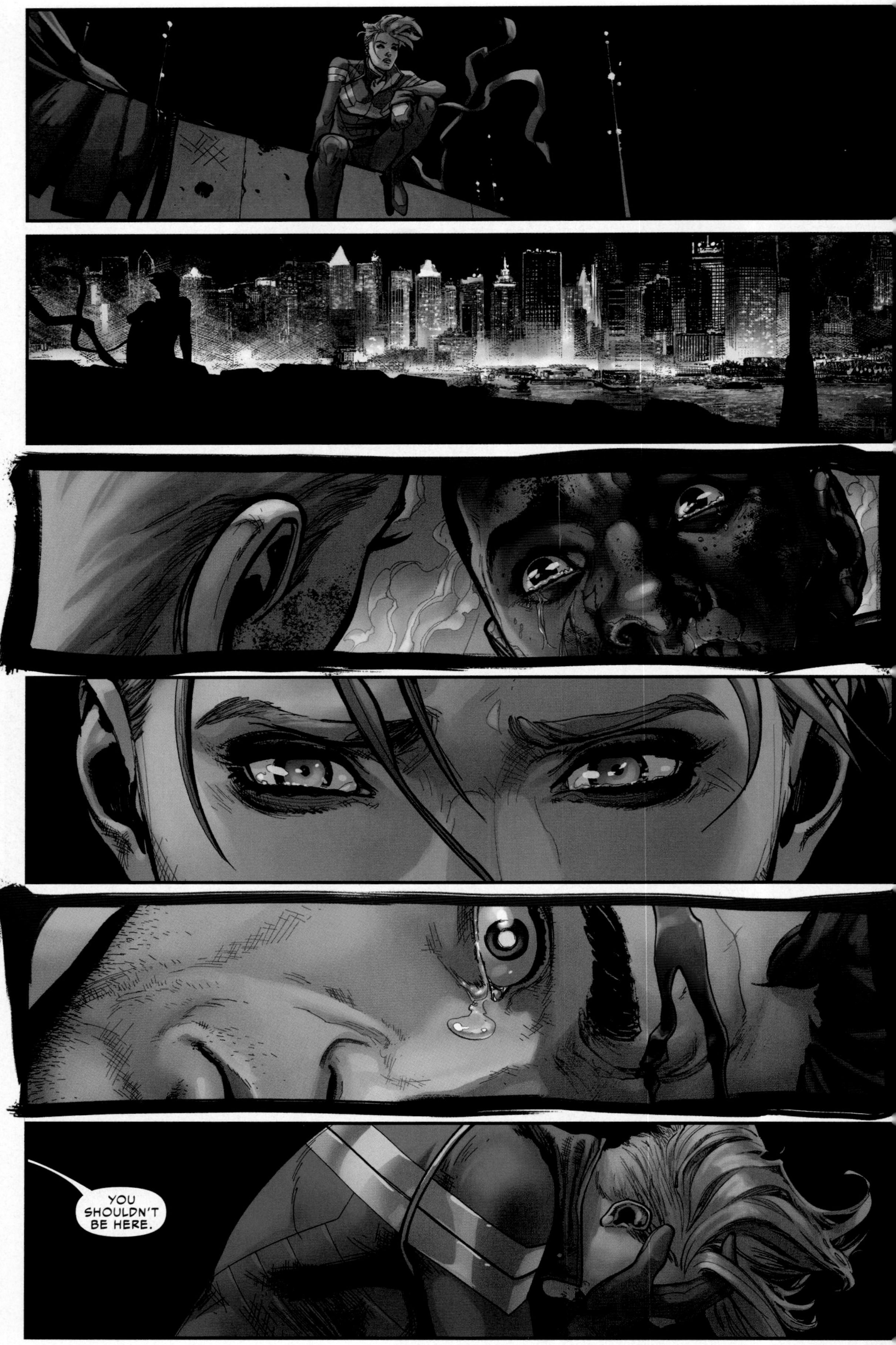
YOU SHOULDN'T BE HERE.

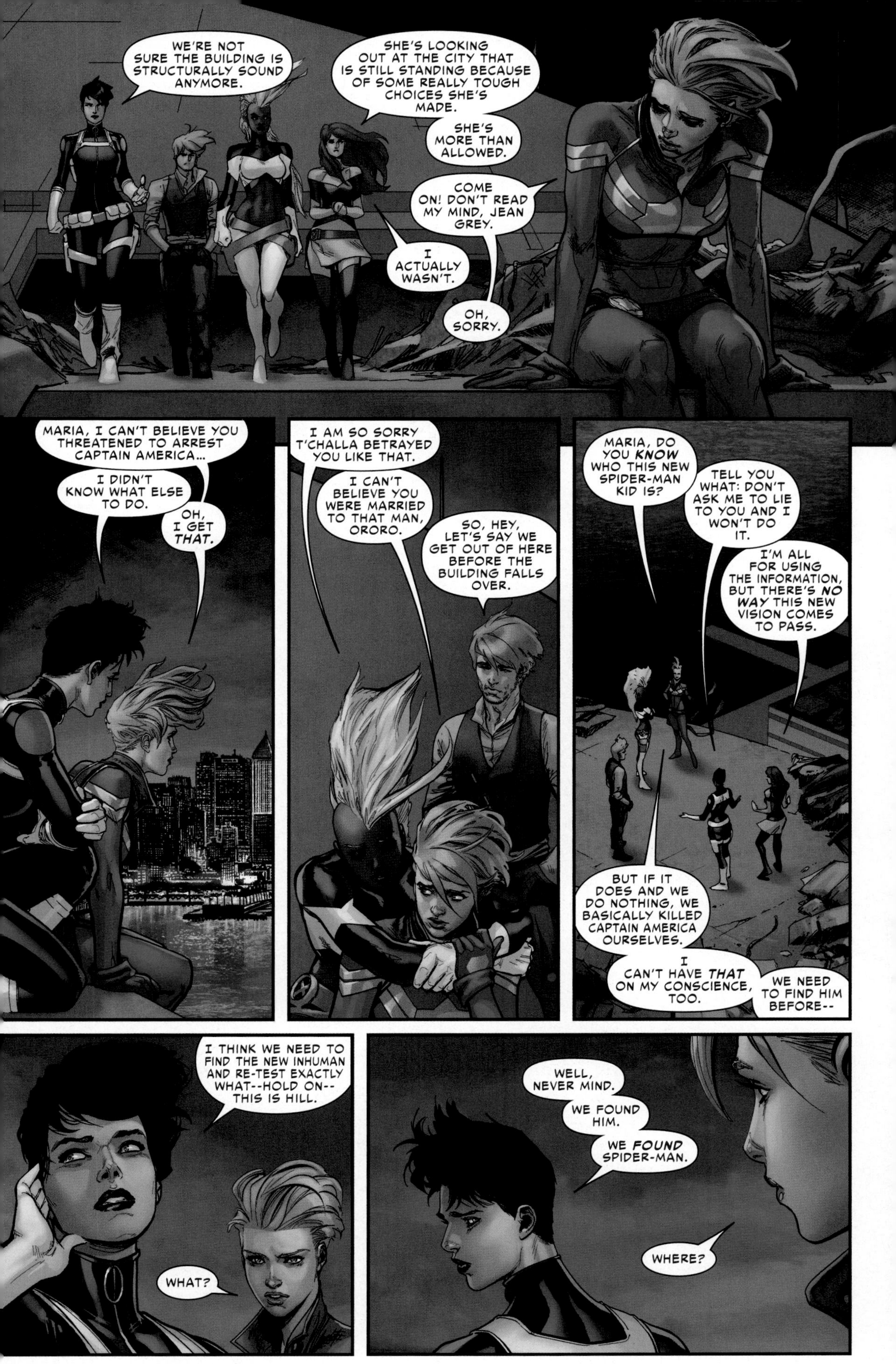
WE'RE NOT SURE THE BUILDING IS STRUCTURALLY SOUND ANYMORE.
SHE'S LOOKING OUT AT THE CITY THAT IS STILL STANDING BECAUSE OF SOME REALLY TOUGH CHOICES SHE'S MADE.
SHE'S MORE THAN ALLOWED.
COME ON! DON'T READ MY MIND, JEAN GREY.
I ACTUALLY WASN'T.
OH, SORRY.
MARIA, I CAN'T BELIEVE YOU THREATENED TO ARREST CAPTAIN AMERICA...
I DIDN'T KNOW WHAT ELSE TO DO.
OH, I GET *THAT.*
I AM SO SORRY T'CHALLA BETRAYED YOU LIKE THAT.
I CAN'T BELIEVE YOU WERE MARRIED TO THAT MAN, ORORO.
SO, HEY, LET'S SAY WE GET OUT OF HERE BEFORE THE BUILDING FALLS OVER.
MARIA, DO YOU ***KNOW*** WHO THIS NEW SPIDER-MAN KID IS?
TELL YOU WHAT: DON'T ASK ME TO LIE TO YOU AND I WON'T DO IT.
I'M ALL FOR USING THE INFORMATION, BUT THERE'S ***NO WAY*** THIS NEW VISION COMES TO PASS.
BUT IF IT DOES AND WE DO NOTHING, WE BASICALLY KILLED CAPTAIN AMERICA OURSELVES.
I CAN'T HAVE *THAT* ON MY CONSCIENCE, TOO.
WE NEED TO FIND HIM BEFORE--
I THINK WE NEED TO FIND THE NEW INHUMAN AND RE-TEST EXACTLY WHAT--HOLD ON-- THIS IS HILL.
WHAT?
WELL, NEVER MIND.
WE FOUND HIM.
WE *FOUND* SPIDER-MAN.
WHERE?

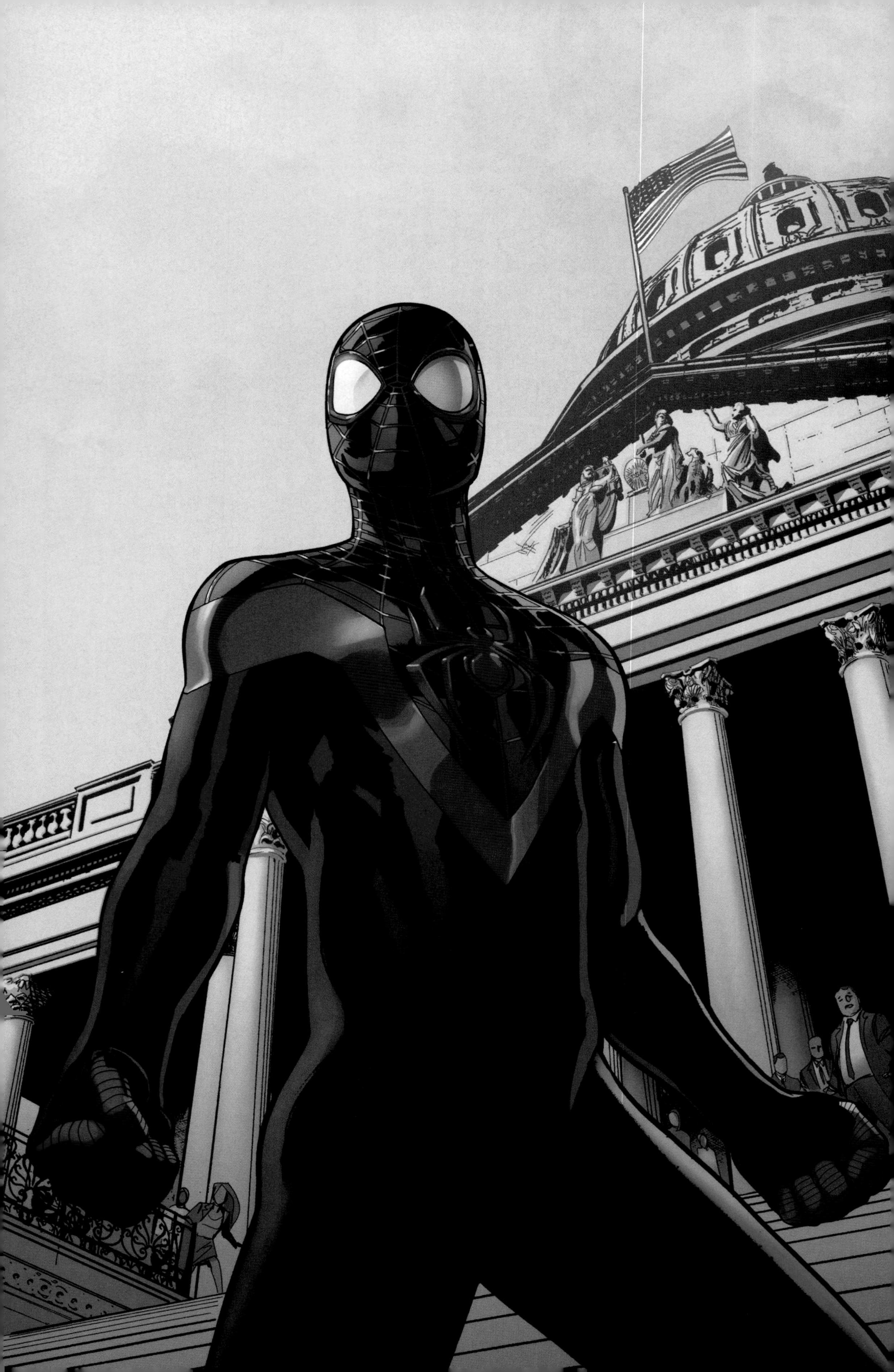

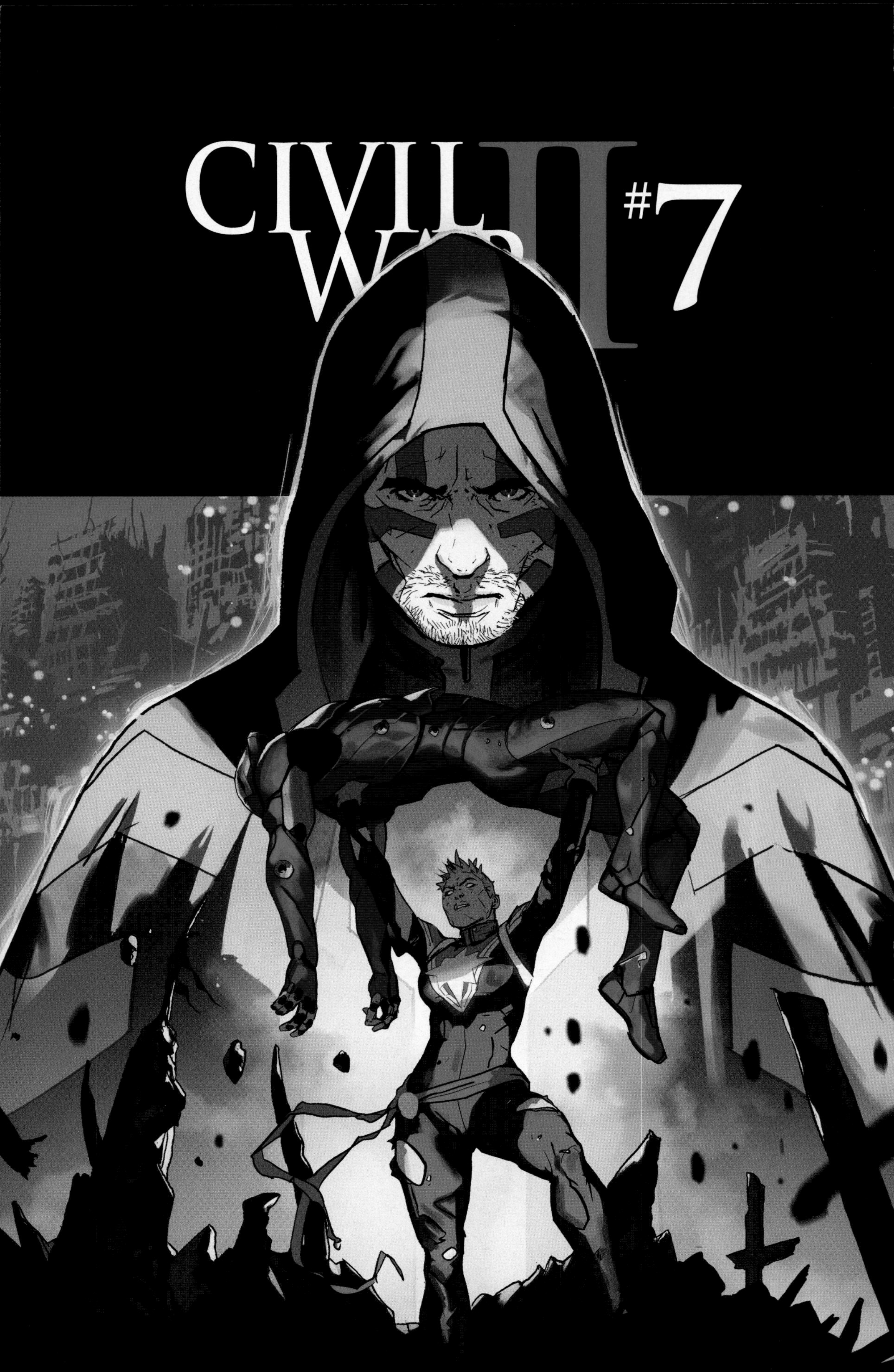
CIVIL WAR II
#7

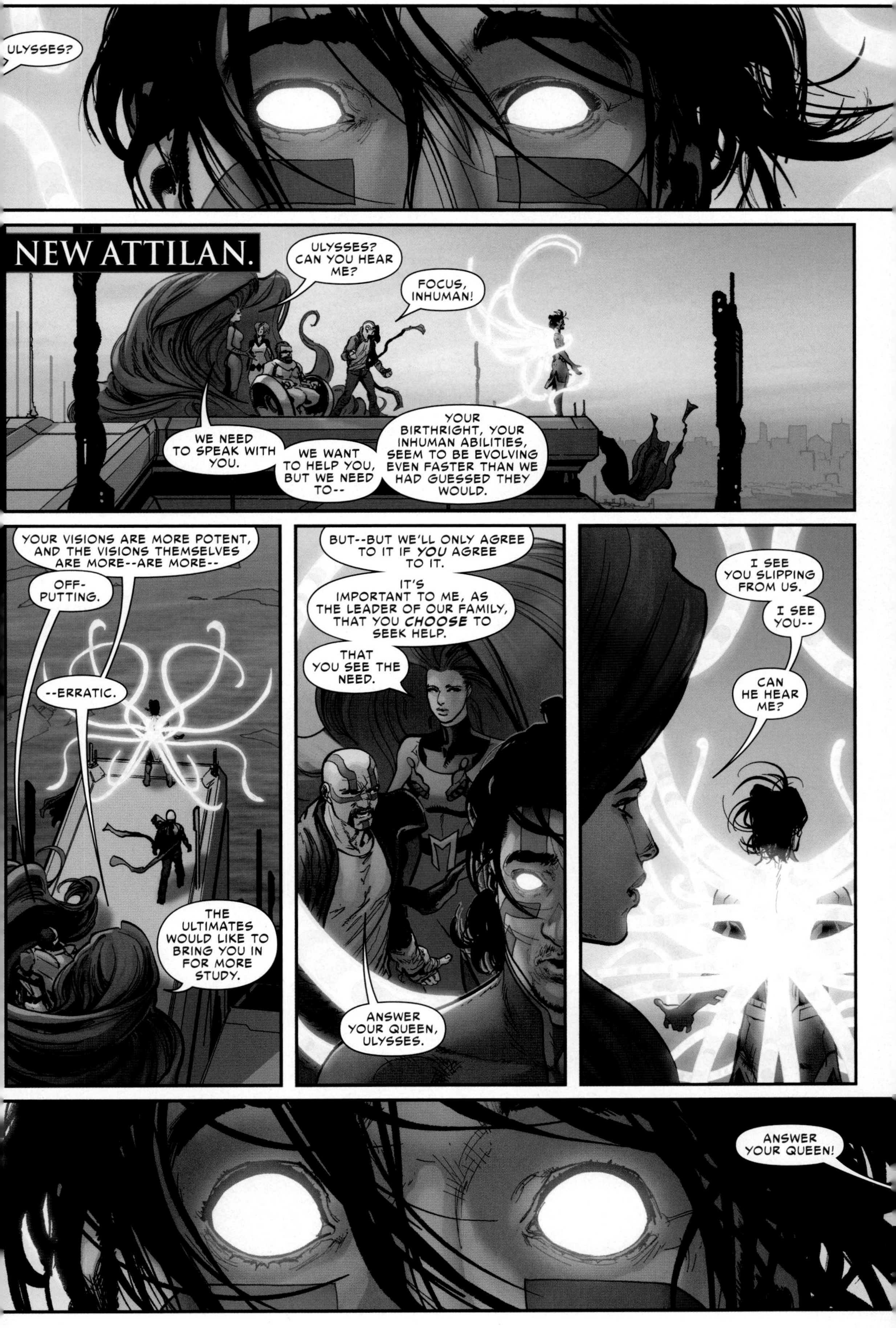
ULYSSES?
NEW ATTILAN.
ULYSSES? CAN YOU HEAR ME?
FOCUS, INHUMAN!
WE NEED TO SPEAK WITH YOU.
WE WANT TO HELP YOU, BUT WE NEED TO--
YOUR BIRTHRIGHT, YOUR INHUMAN ABILITIES, SEEM TO BE EVOLVING EVEN FASTER THAN WE HAD GUESSED THEY WOULD.
YOUR VISIONS ARE MORE POTENT, AND THE VISIONS THEMSELVES ARE MORE--ARE MORE--
OFF-PUTTING.
--ERRATIC.
THE ULTIMATES WOULD LIKE TO BRING YOU IN FOR MORE STUDY.
BUT--BUT WE'LL ONLY AGREE TO IT IF YOU AGREE TO IT.
IT'S IMPORTANT TO ME, AS THE LEADER OF OUR FAMILY, THAT YOU CHOOSE TO SEEK HELP.
THAT YOU SEE THE NEED.
ANSWER YOUR QUEEN, ULYSSES.
I SEE YOU SLIPPING FROM US.
I SEE YOU--
CAN HE HEAR ME?
ANSWER YOUR QUEEN!

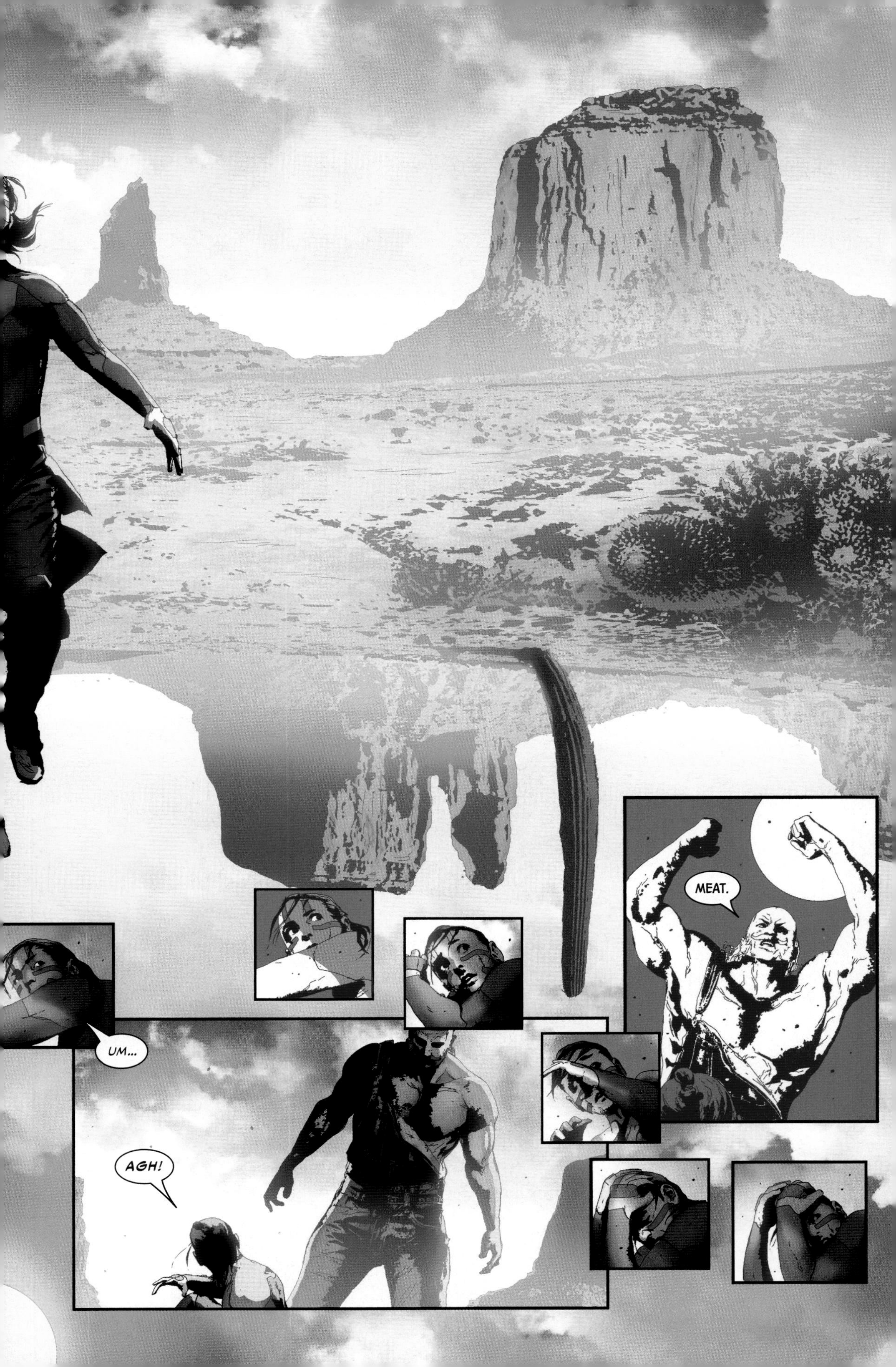
MEAT.
UM...
AGH!

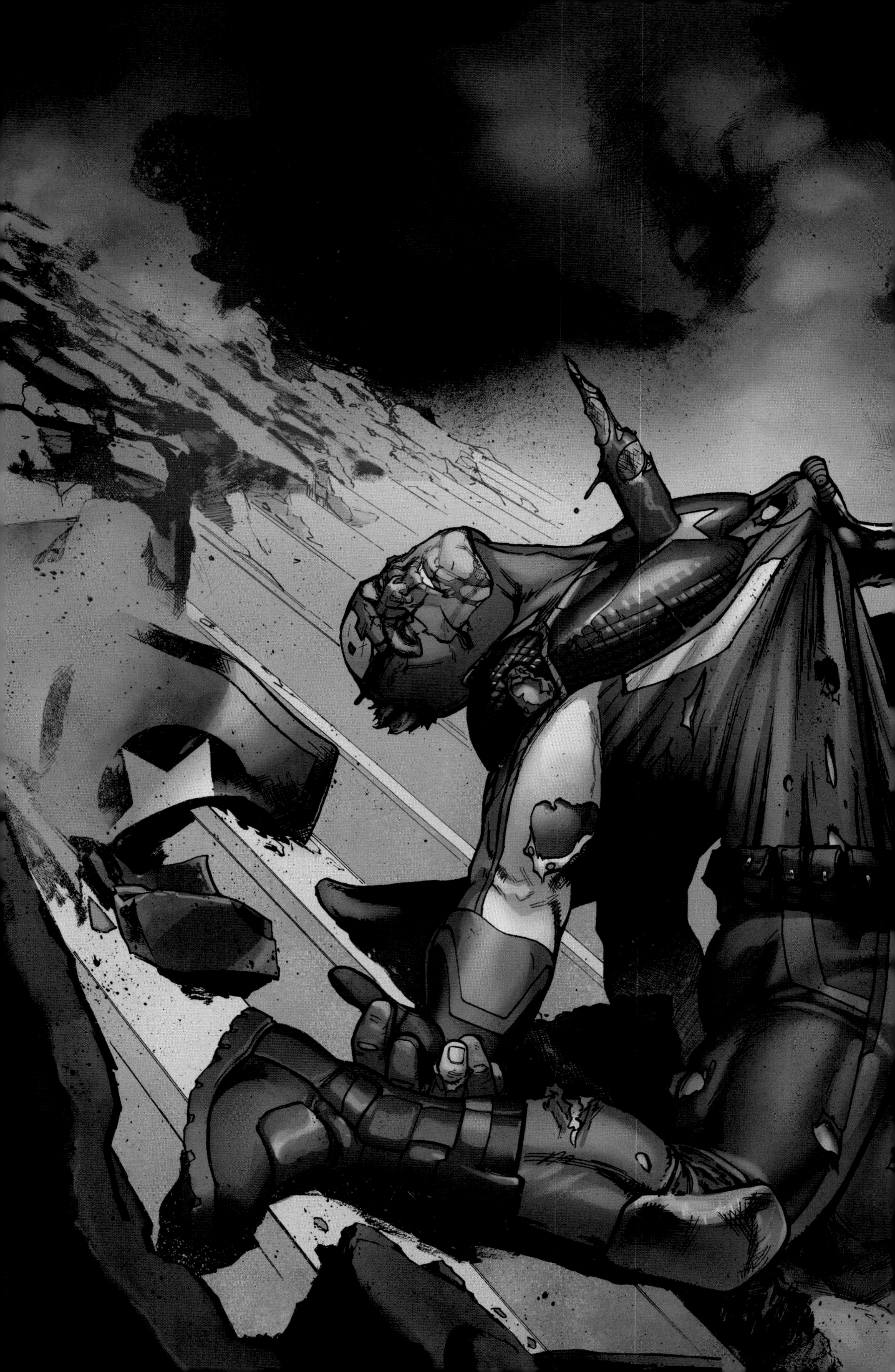

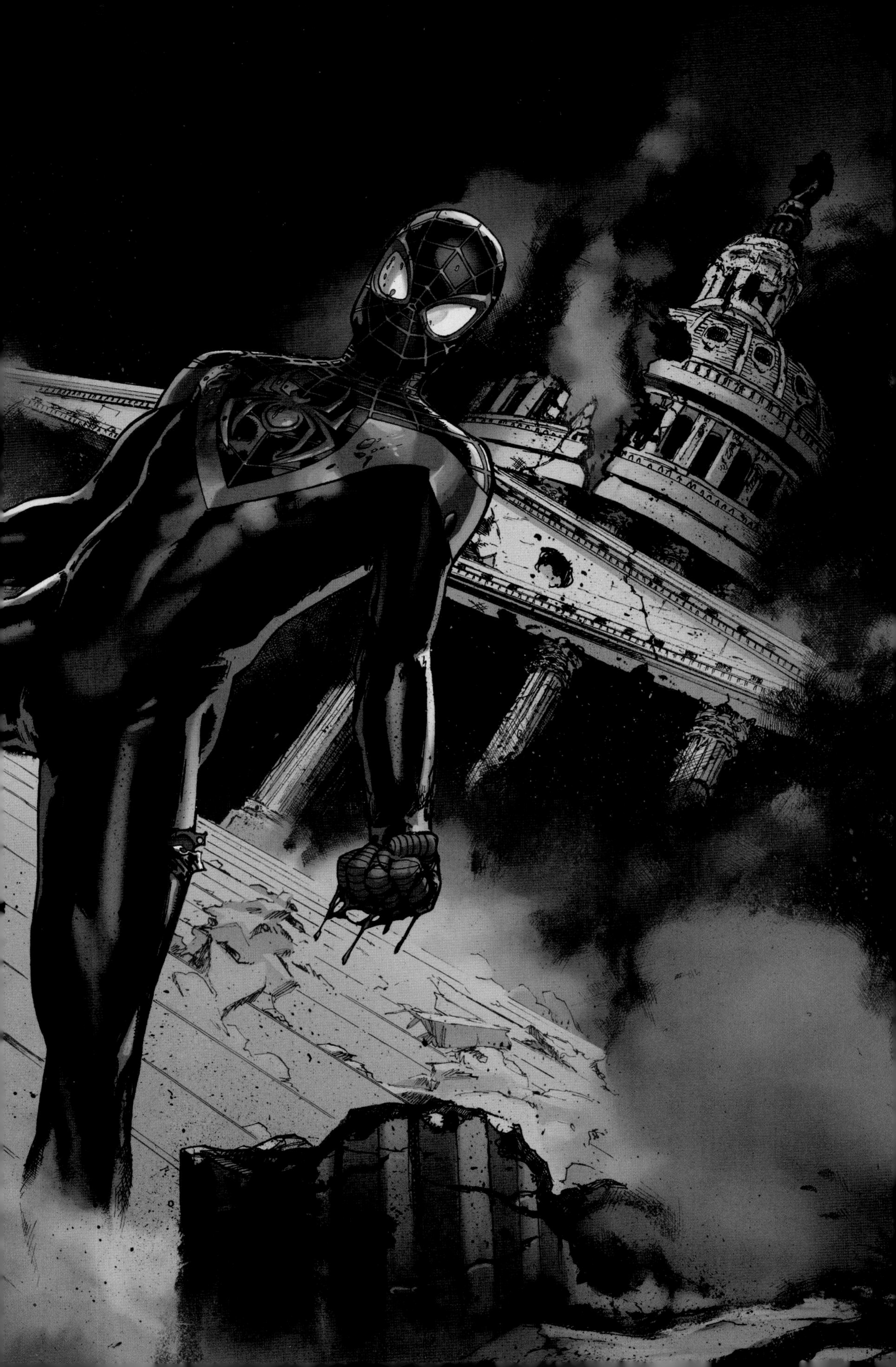

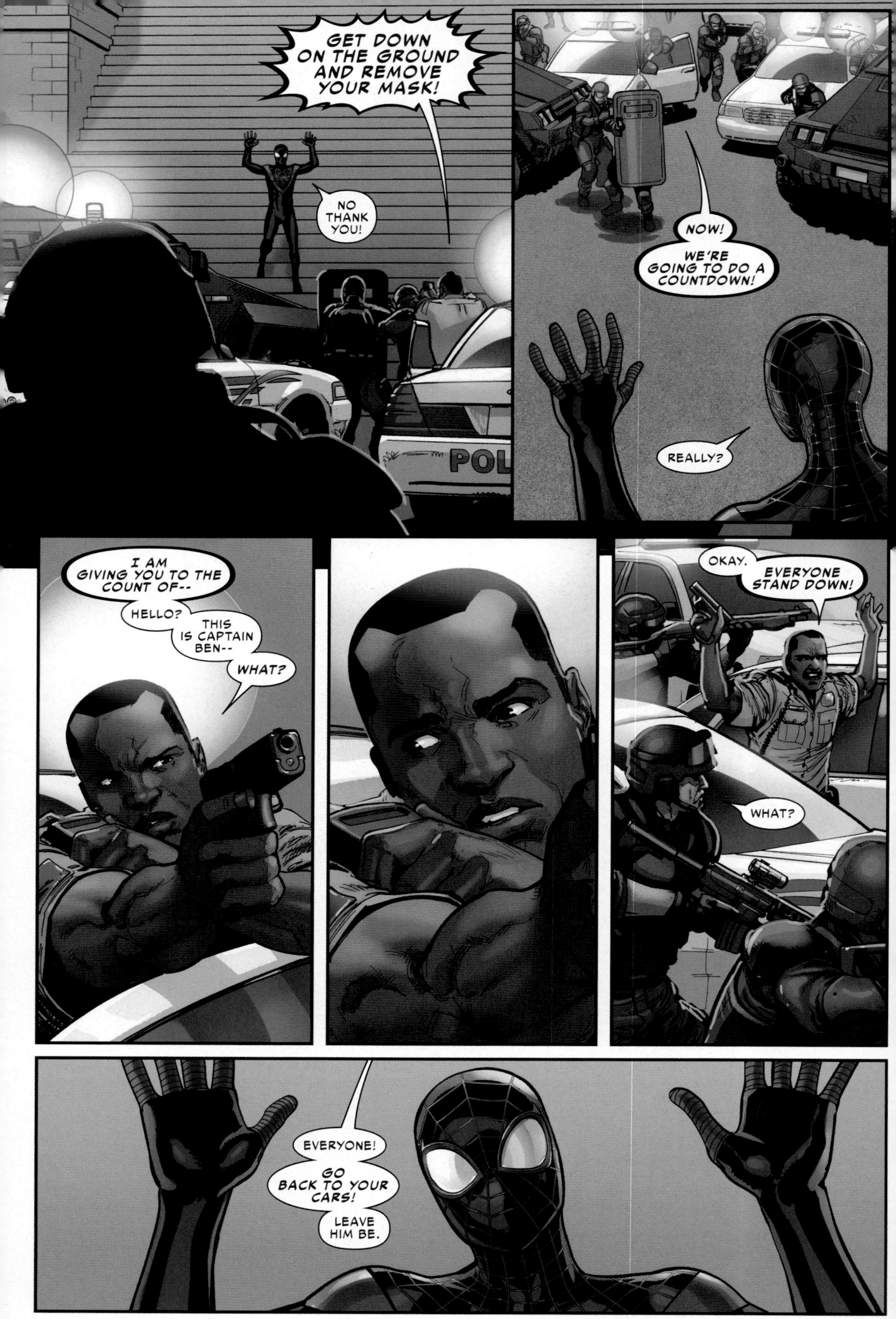
GET DOWN ON THE GROUND AND REMOVE YOUR MASK!
NO THANK YOU!
NOW!
WE'RE GOING TO DO A COUNTDOWN!
REALLY?
I AM GIVING YOU TO THE COUNT OF--
HELLO?
THIS IS CAPTAIN BEN--
WHAT?
OKAY.
EVERYONE STAND DOWN!
WHAT?
EVERYONE!
GO BACK TO YOUR CARS!
LEAVE HIM BE.

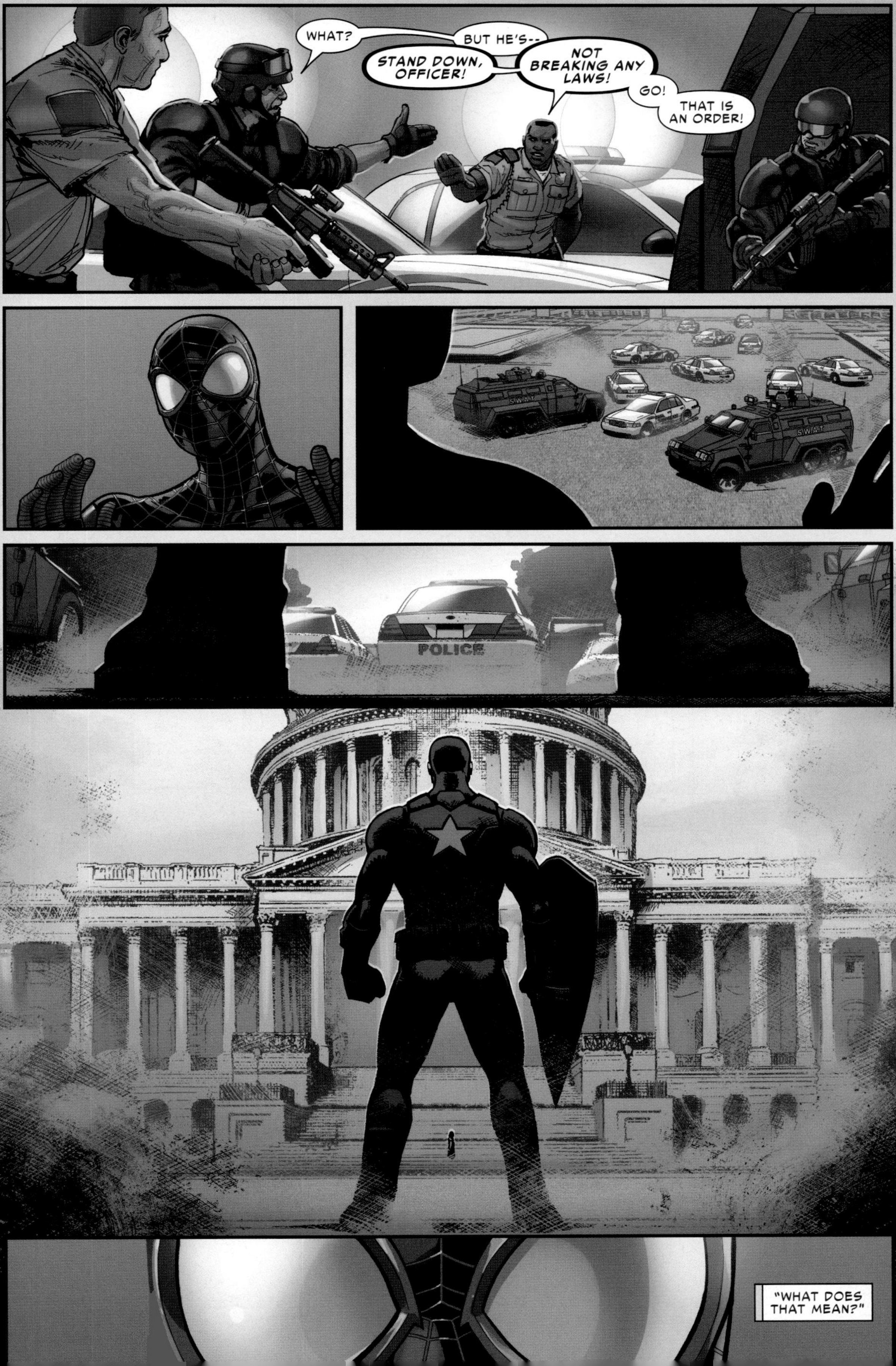
WHAT?
BUT HE'S--
STAND DOWN, OFFICER!
NOT BREAKING ANY LAWS!
GO!
THAT IS AN ORDER!
POLICE
"WHAT DOES THAT MEAN?"

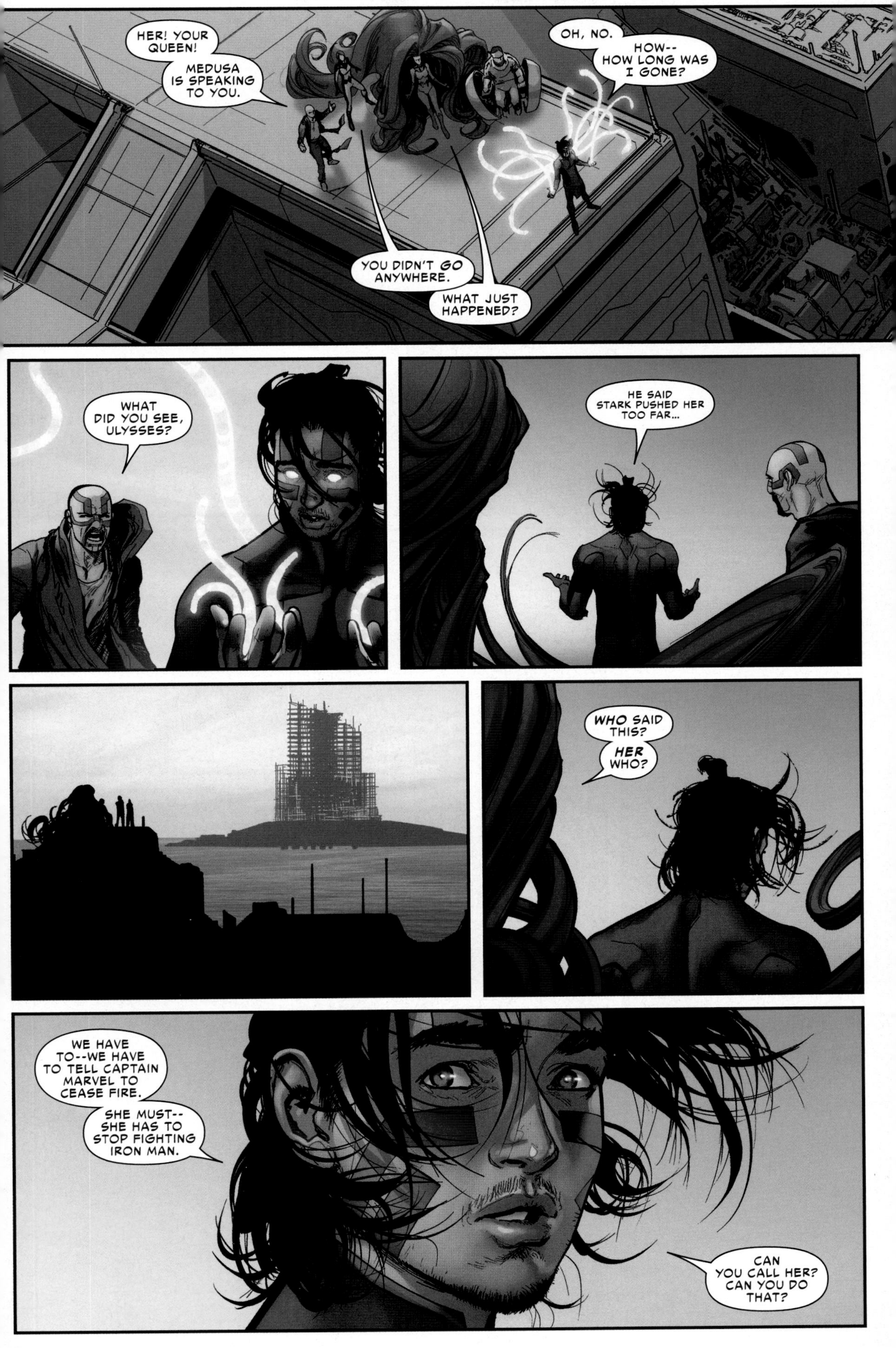
HER! YOUR QUEEN!
MEDUSA IS SPEAKING TO YOU.
OH, NO.
HOW-- HOW LONG WAS I GONE?
YOU DIDN'T GO ANYWHERE.
WHAT JUST HAPPENED?
WHAT DID YOU SEE, ULYSSES?
HE SAID STARK PUSHED HER TOO FAR...
WHO SAID THIS?
HER WHO?
WE HAVE TO--WE HAVE TO TELL CAPTAIN MARVEL TO CEASE FIRE.
SHE MUST-- SHE HAS TO STOP FIGHTING IRON MAN.
CAN YOU CALL HER? CAN YOU DO THAT?

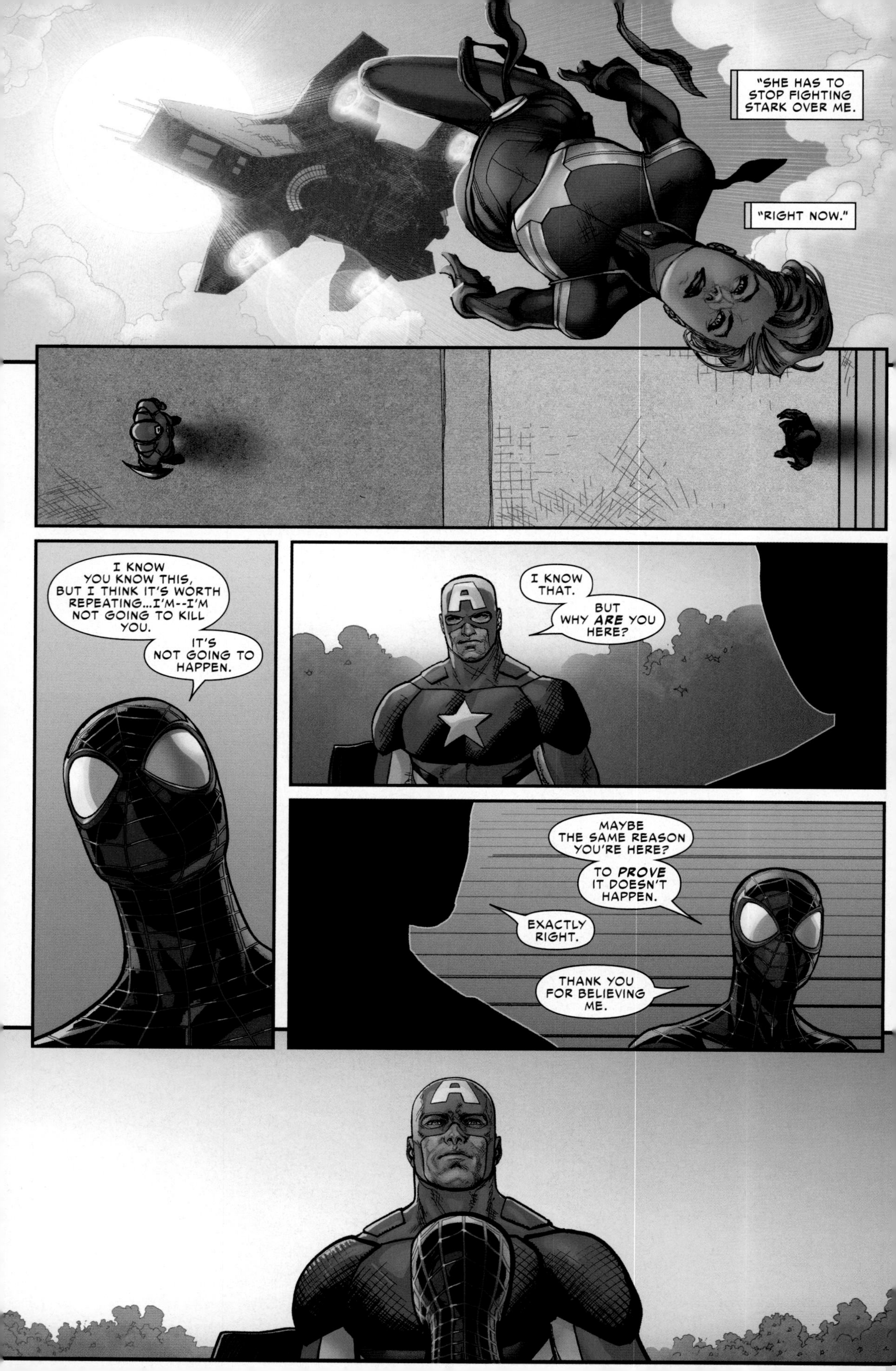
"SHE HAS TO STOP FIGHTING STARK OVER ME.
"RIGHT NOW."
I KNOW YOU KNOW THIS, BUT I THINK IT'S WORTH REPEATING...I'M--I'M NOT GOING TO KILL YOU.
IT'S NOT GOING TO HAPPEN.
I KNOW THAT.
BUT WHY ARE YOU HERE?
MAYBE THE SAME REASON YOU'RE HERE?
TO PROVE IT DOESN'T HAPPEN.
EXACTLY RIGHT.
THANK YOU FOR BELIEVING ME.

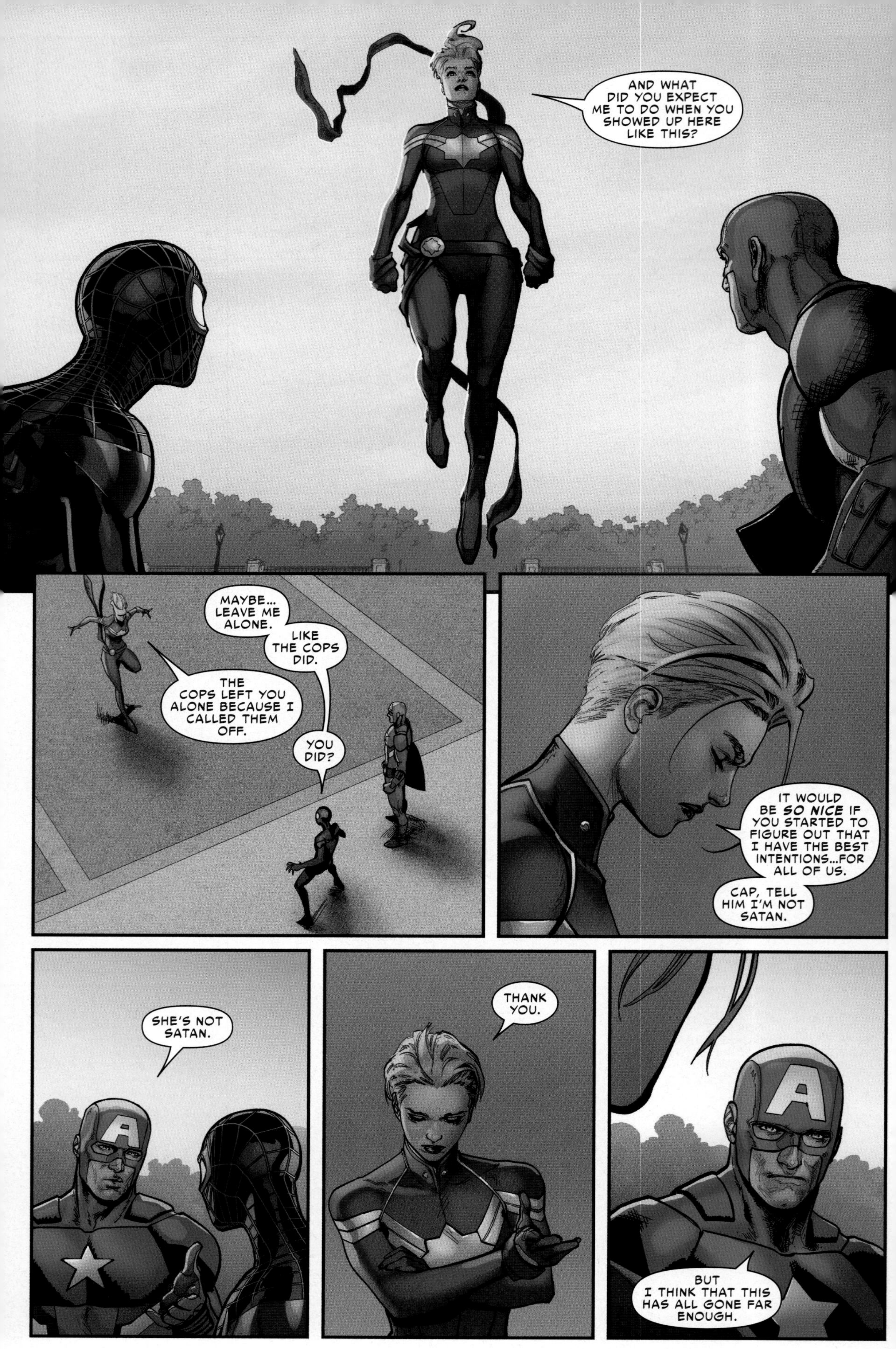
AND WHAT DID YOU EXPECT ME TO DO WHEN YOU SHOWED UP HERE LIKE THIS?
MAYBE... LEAVE ME ALONE.
LIKE THE COPS DID.
THE COPS LEFT YOU ALONE BECAUSE I CALLED THEM OFF.
YOU DID?
IT WOULD BE SO NICE IF YOU STARTED TO FIGURE OUT THAT I HAVE THE BEST INTENTIONS...FOR ALL OF US.
CAP, TELL HIM I'M NOT SATAN.
SHE'S NOT SATAN.
THANK YOU.
BUT I THINK THAT THIS HAS ALL GONE FAR ENOUGH.

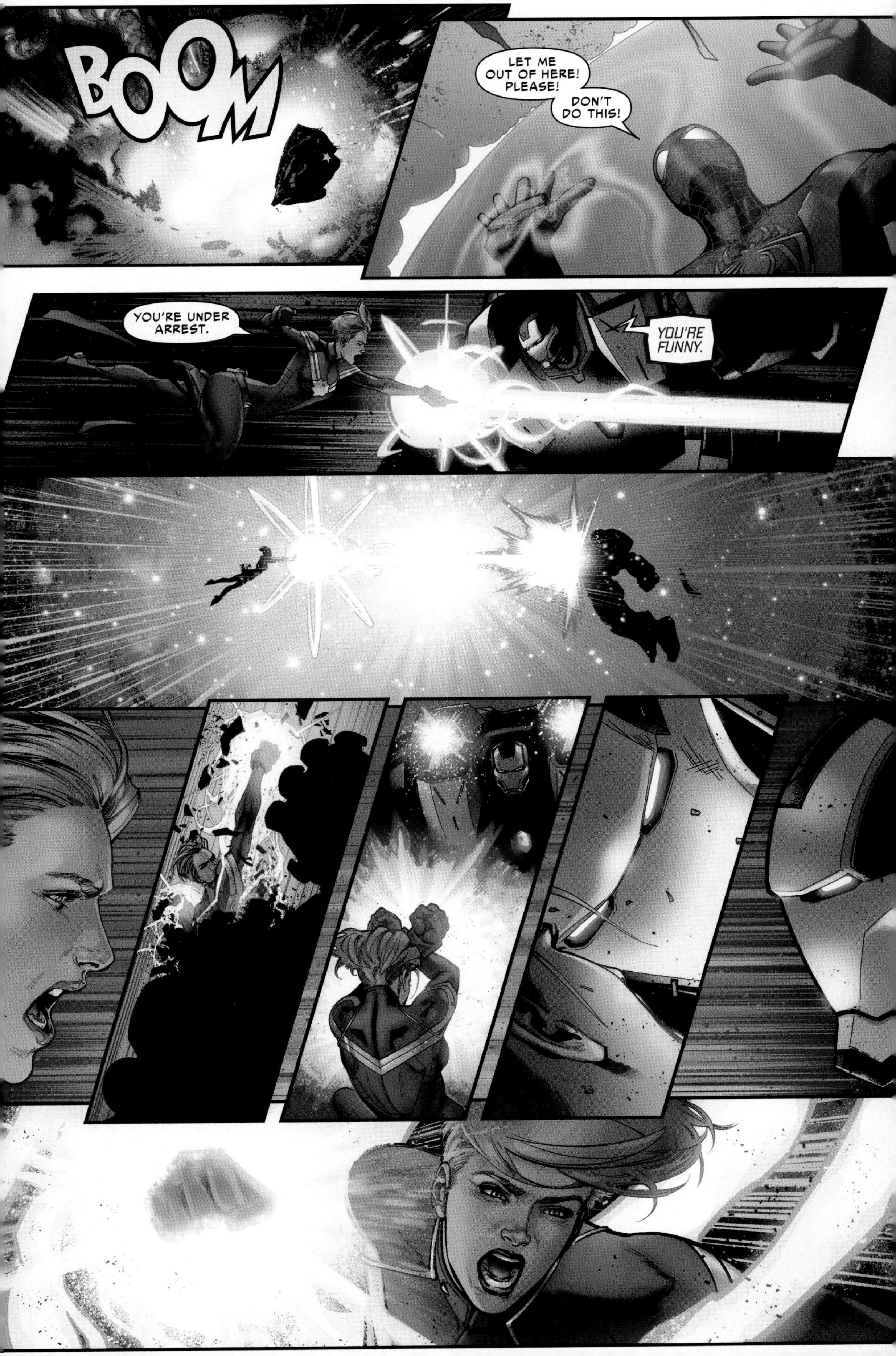
BOOM
LET ME OUT OF HERE! PLEASE!
DON'T DO THIS!
YOU'RE UNDER ARREST.
YOU'RE FUNNY.

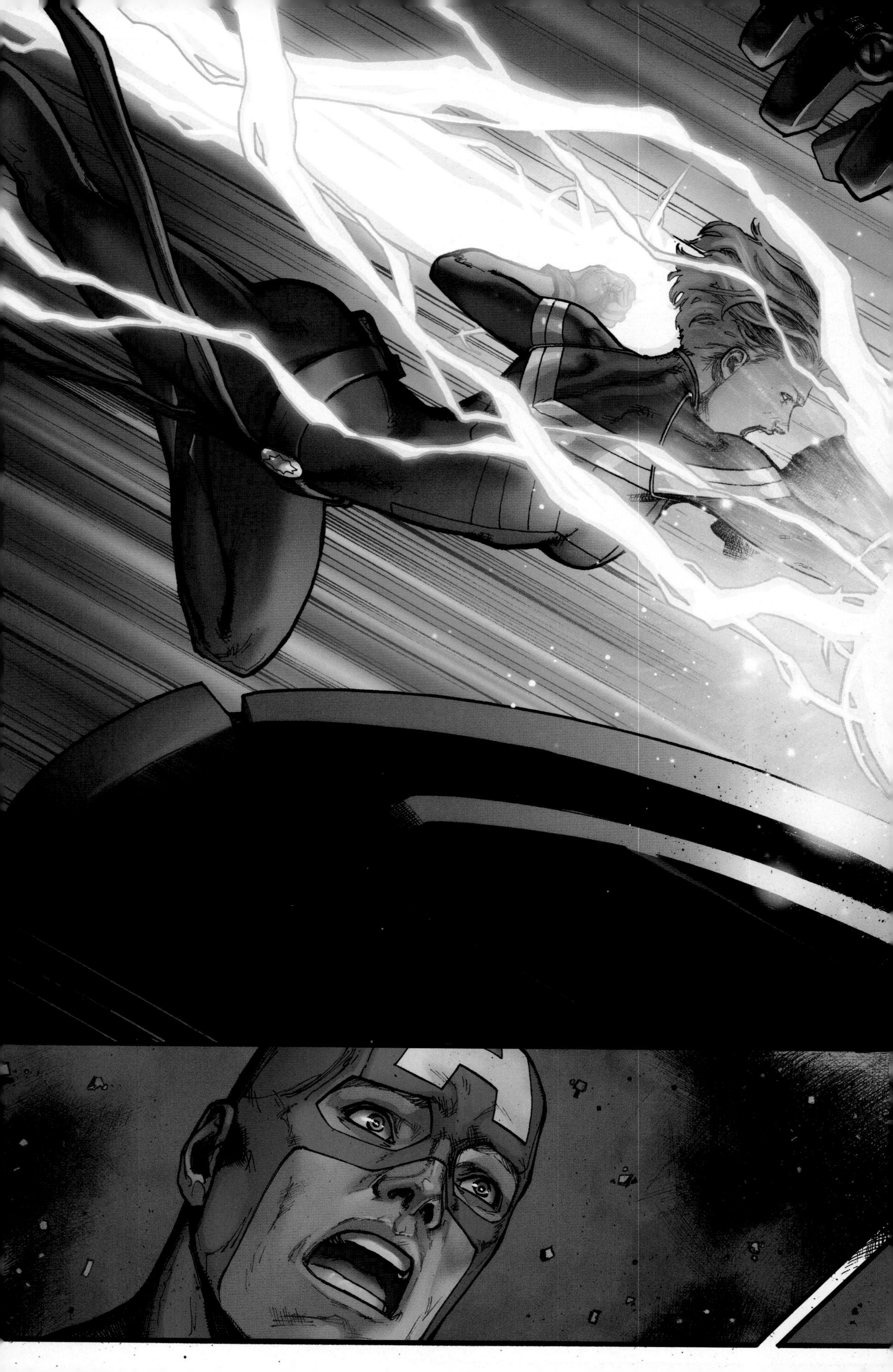

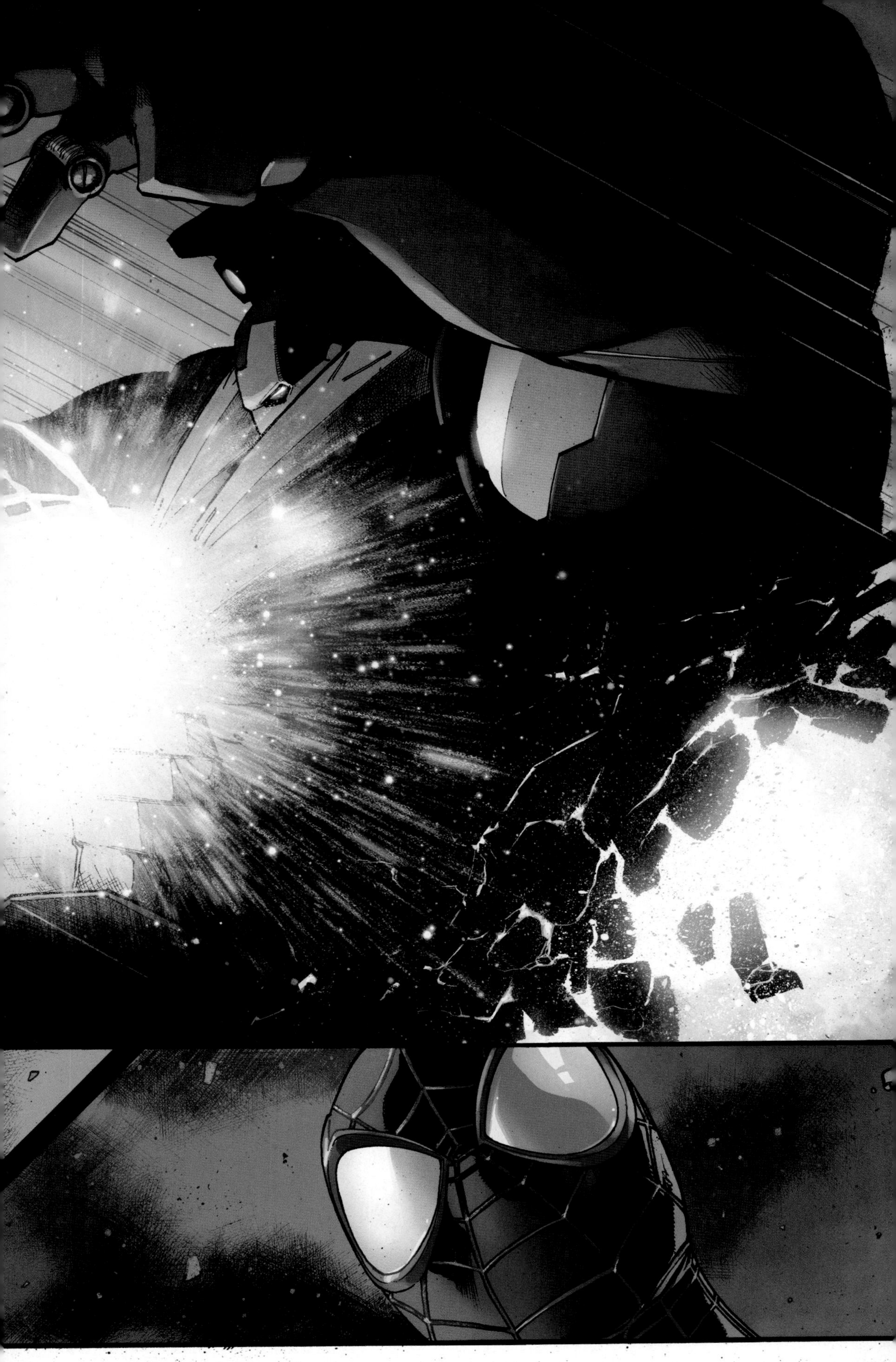

CIVIL WAR II #8

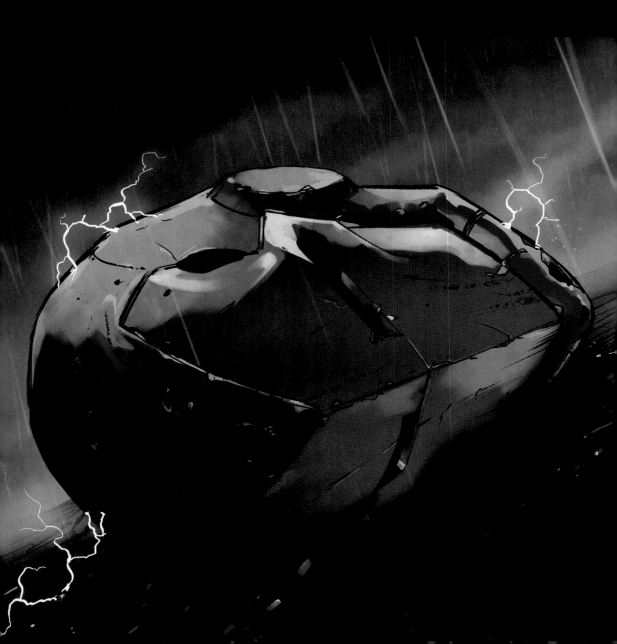

WASHINGTON, D.C.,
DUPONT CIRCLE.

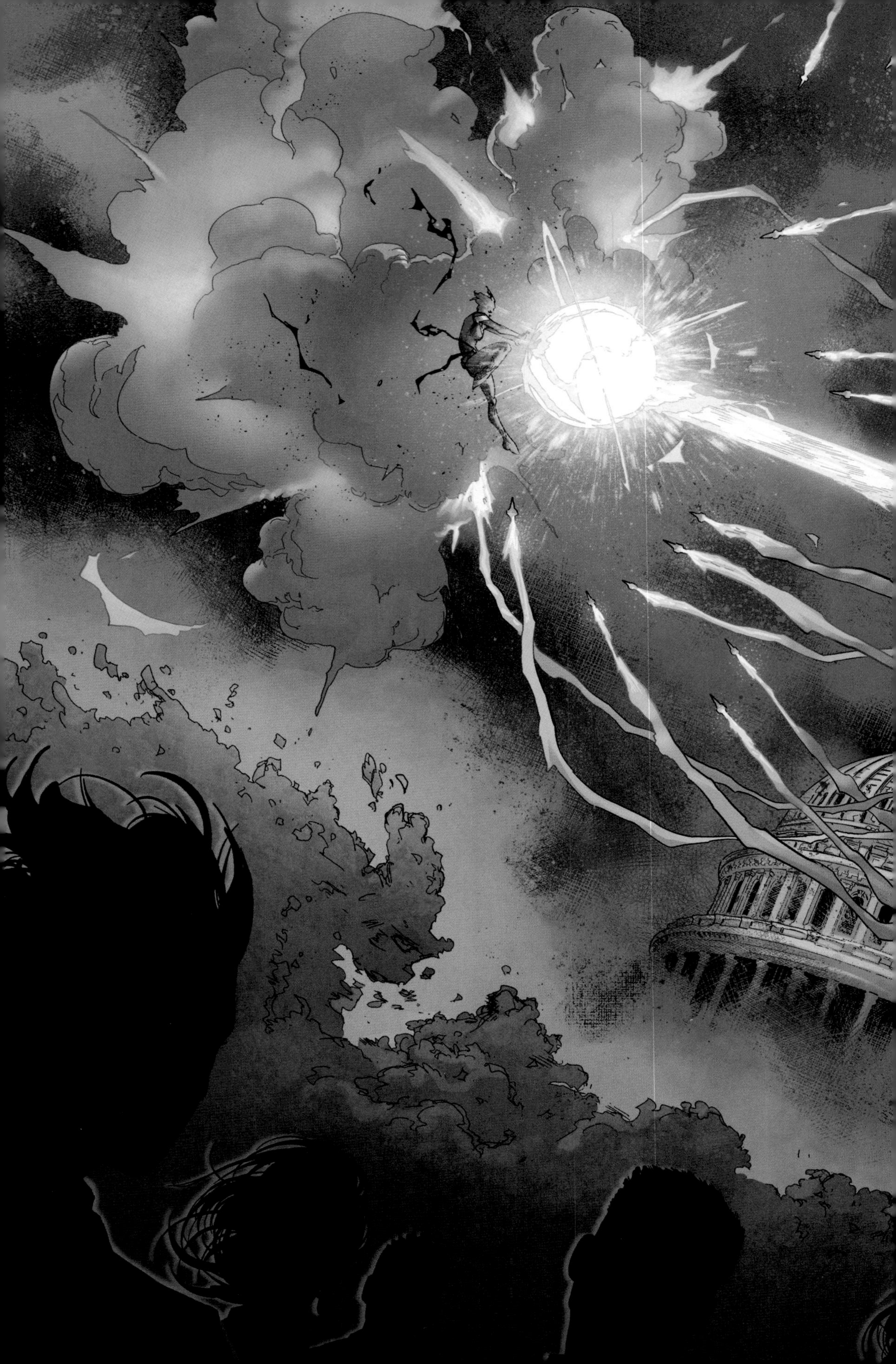

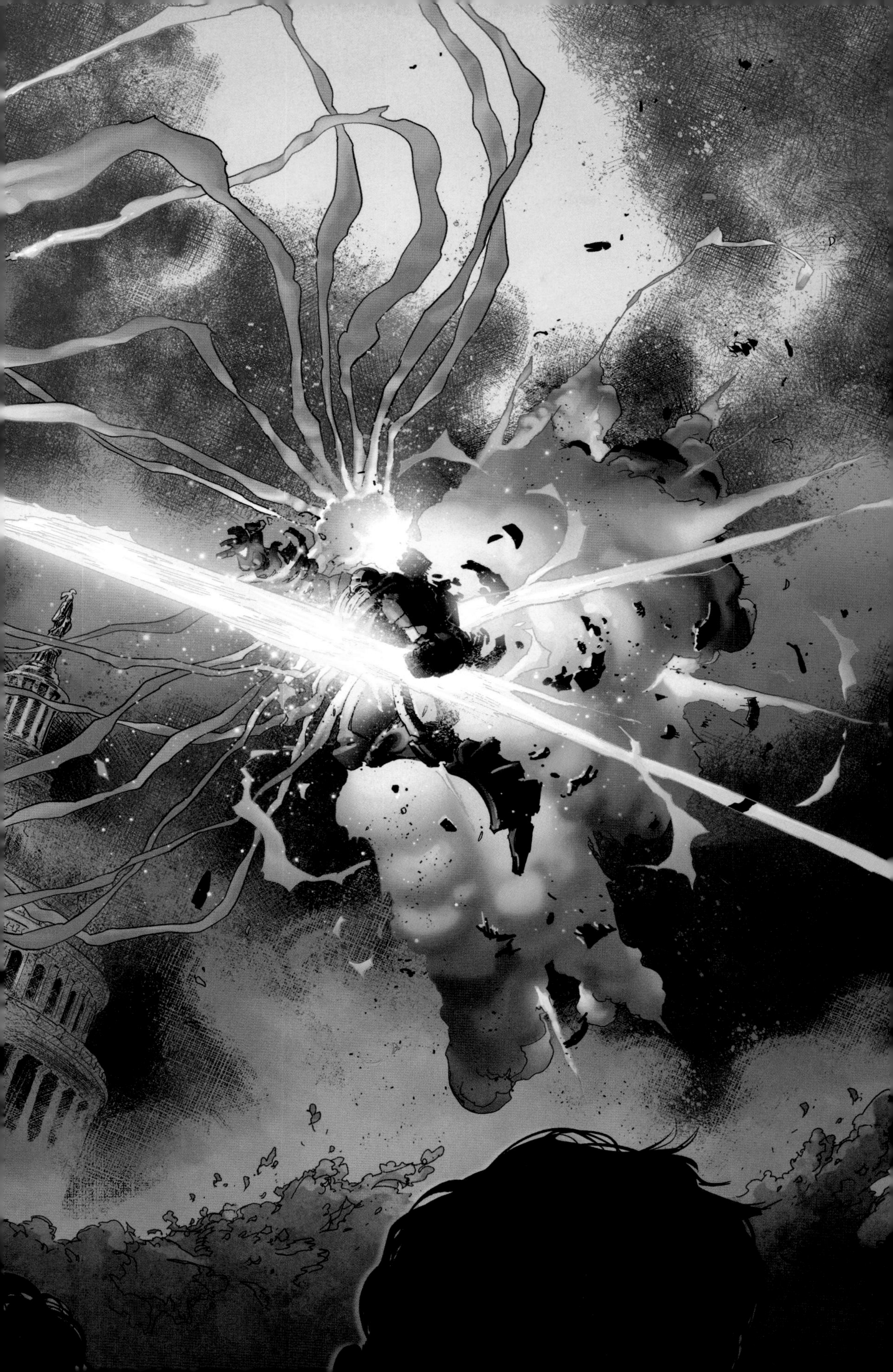

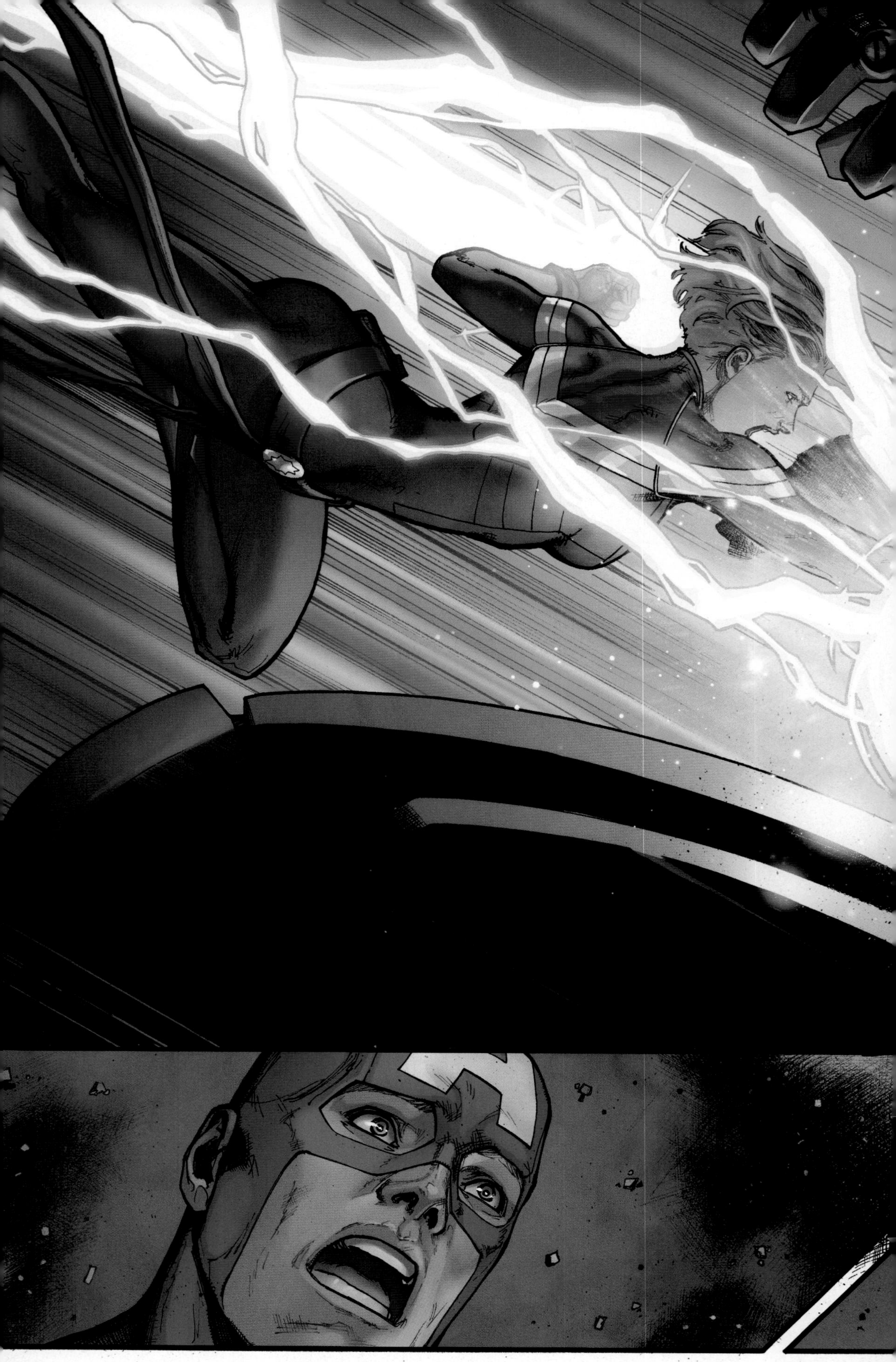

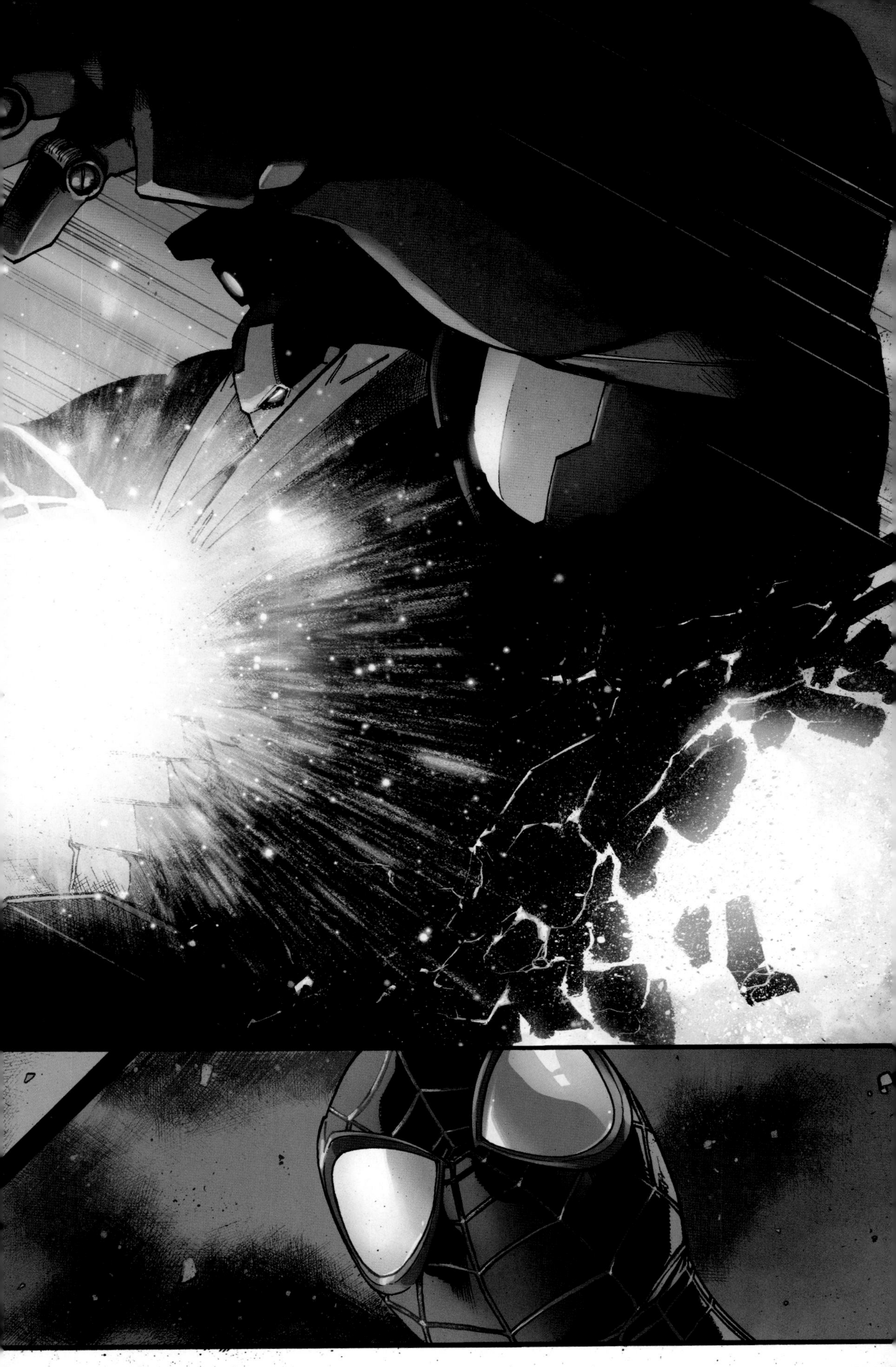

THE ORDER IS *STAND DOWN!*

NO!

I SAID IT'S AN *ORDER!*

BUT--

CAPTAIN MARVEL'S ORDERS *AND* MY ORDERS.

I'M SORRY, ULTIMATES AND ALPHA FLIGHT-ERS, WE'RE NOT HAVING A BIG SUPER-POWERED FIGHT ON THE STEPS OF THE *CAPITOL BUILDING.*

BUT--

SHE CAN *HANDLE* THIS.

STAND. DOWN.

DR. BRASHEAR, ARE WE WORRIED ABOUT STARK'S ABILITY TO IMMOBILIZE HER LIKE HE DID DURING THE TRISKELION BATTLE?

I TOOK CARE OF THAT, BUT WHO KNOWS *WHAT ELSE* HE HAS UP HIS--

AGENT 22, REACH OUT TO THE INHUMANS AND TELL THEM THAT WE'RE STILL AT WAR OVER THEIR ULYSSES.

THEY'RE ON THE COMM, ACTUALLY.

WHO?

THE INHUMANS.

MEDUSA? I'M REALLY VERY--

HILL!

STOP THE FIGHT!

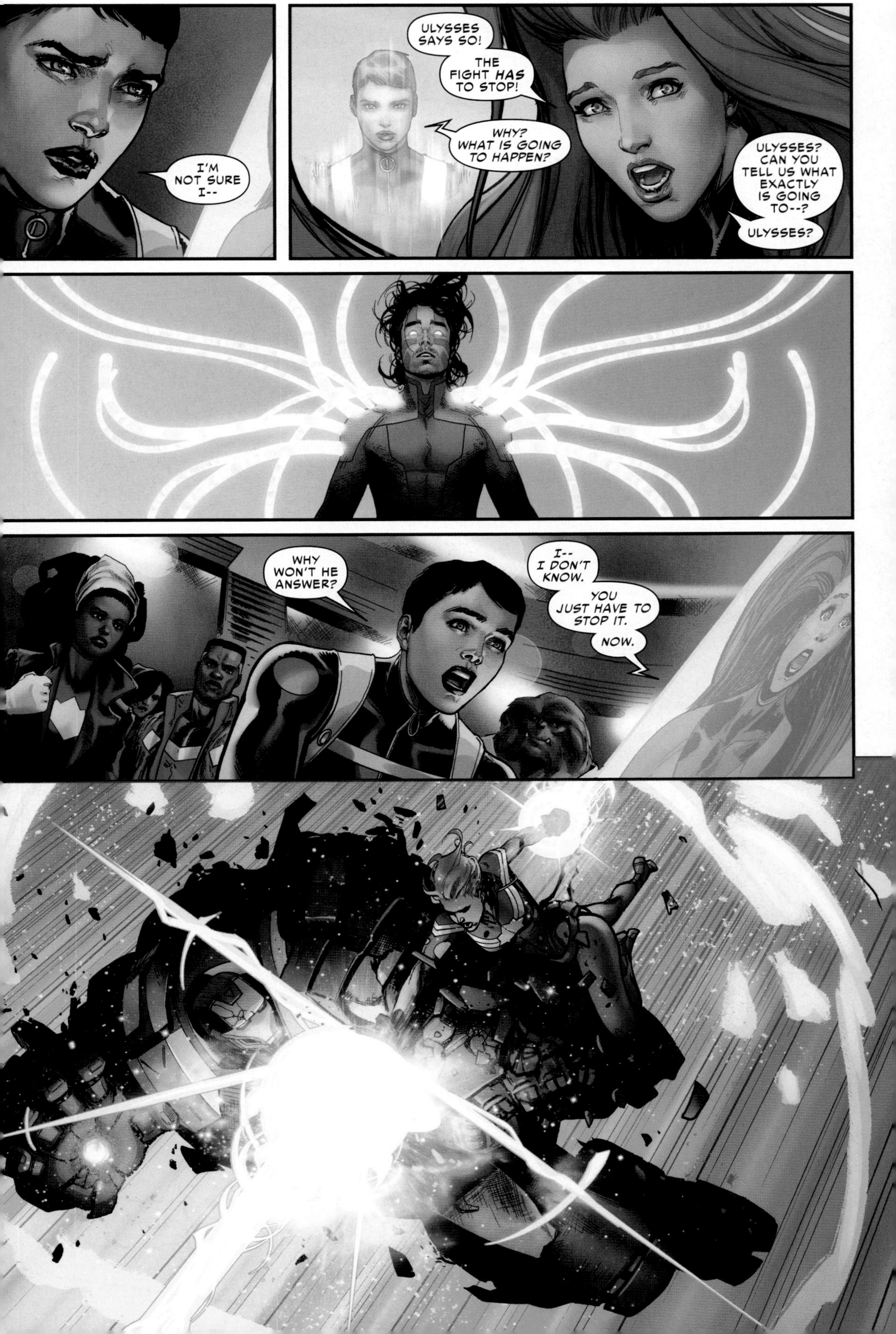
I'M NOT SURE I--
ULYSSES SAYS SO!
THE FIGHT HAS TO STOP!
WHY? WHAT IS GOING TO HAPPEN?
ULYSSES? CAN YOU TELL US WHAT EXACTLY IS GOING TO--?
ULYSSES?
WHY WON'T HE ANSWER?
I-- I DON'T KNOW.
YOU JUST HAVE TO STOP IT.
NOW.

WHAT DID HILL SAY?

SHE HUNG UP.

THEN *WE* NEED TO STOP THE FIGHT, RIGHT NOW.

ULYSSES, YOU NEED TO COME WITH US THIS TIME.

WE CAN'T WASTE ANOTHER SECOND TO--

NEW ATTILAN.

ULYSSES?

ULYSSES? CAN YOU HEAR ME?

GRAB HIM AND LET'S GO.

I'M NOT SURE HE'S ON THE SAME PLANE OF EXISTENCE AS US AT THE MOMENT.

THEY NEED TO HEAR OF THE VISION DIRECTLY FROM HIM, BEAST.

I AGREE, BUT--

LOCKJAW? TELEPORT US THERE.

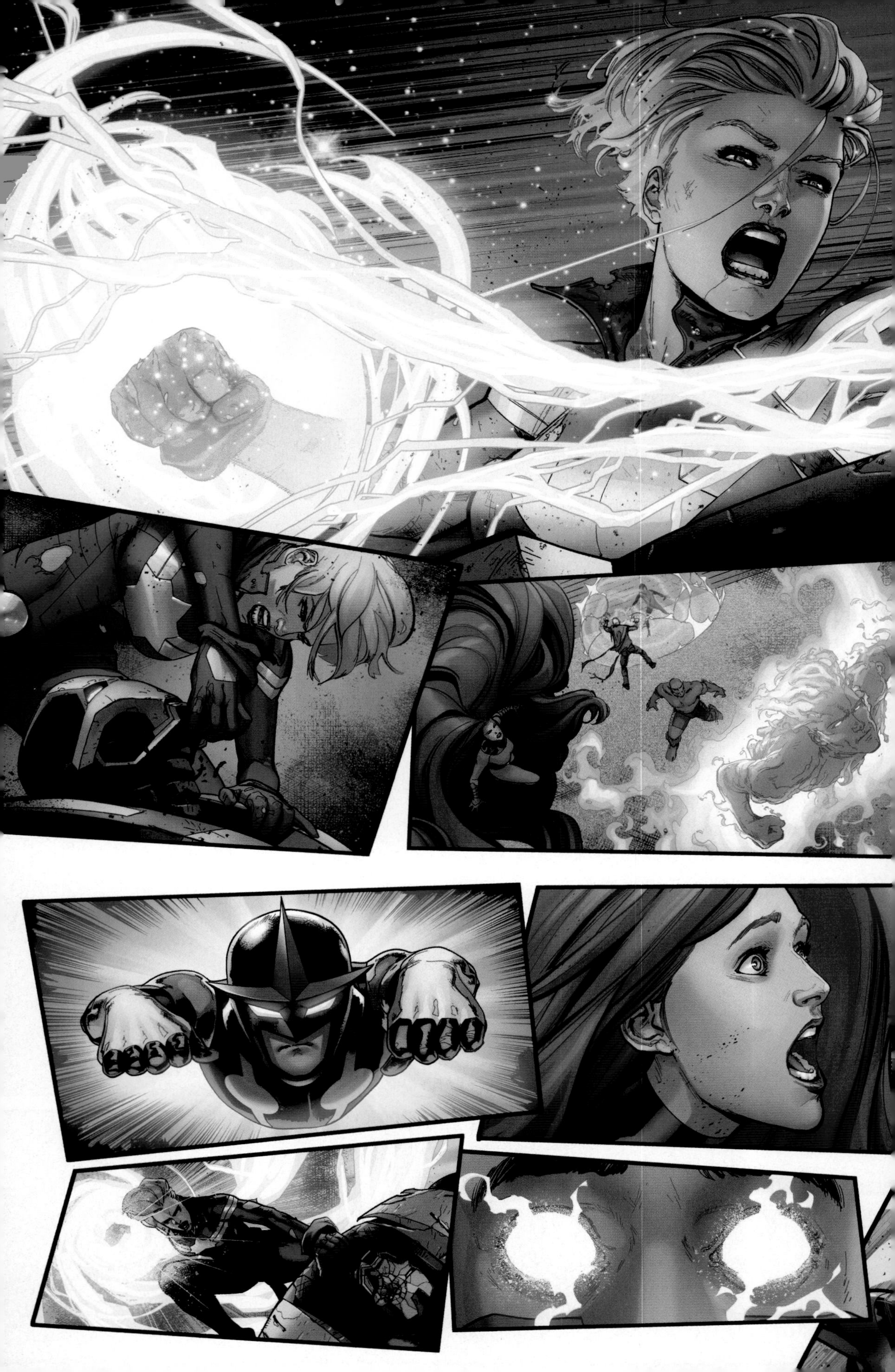

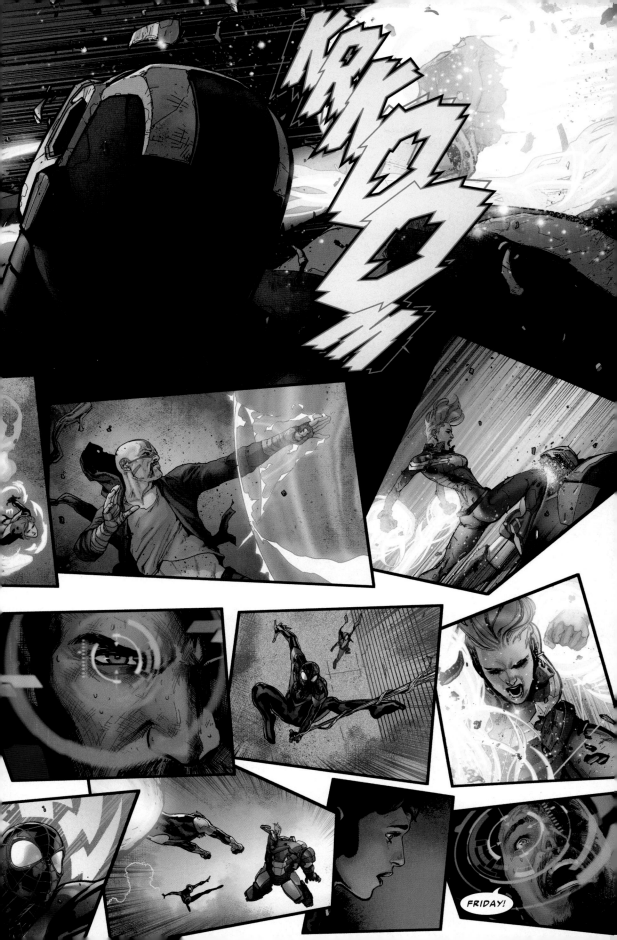

KRKAOOM

FRIDAY!

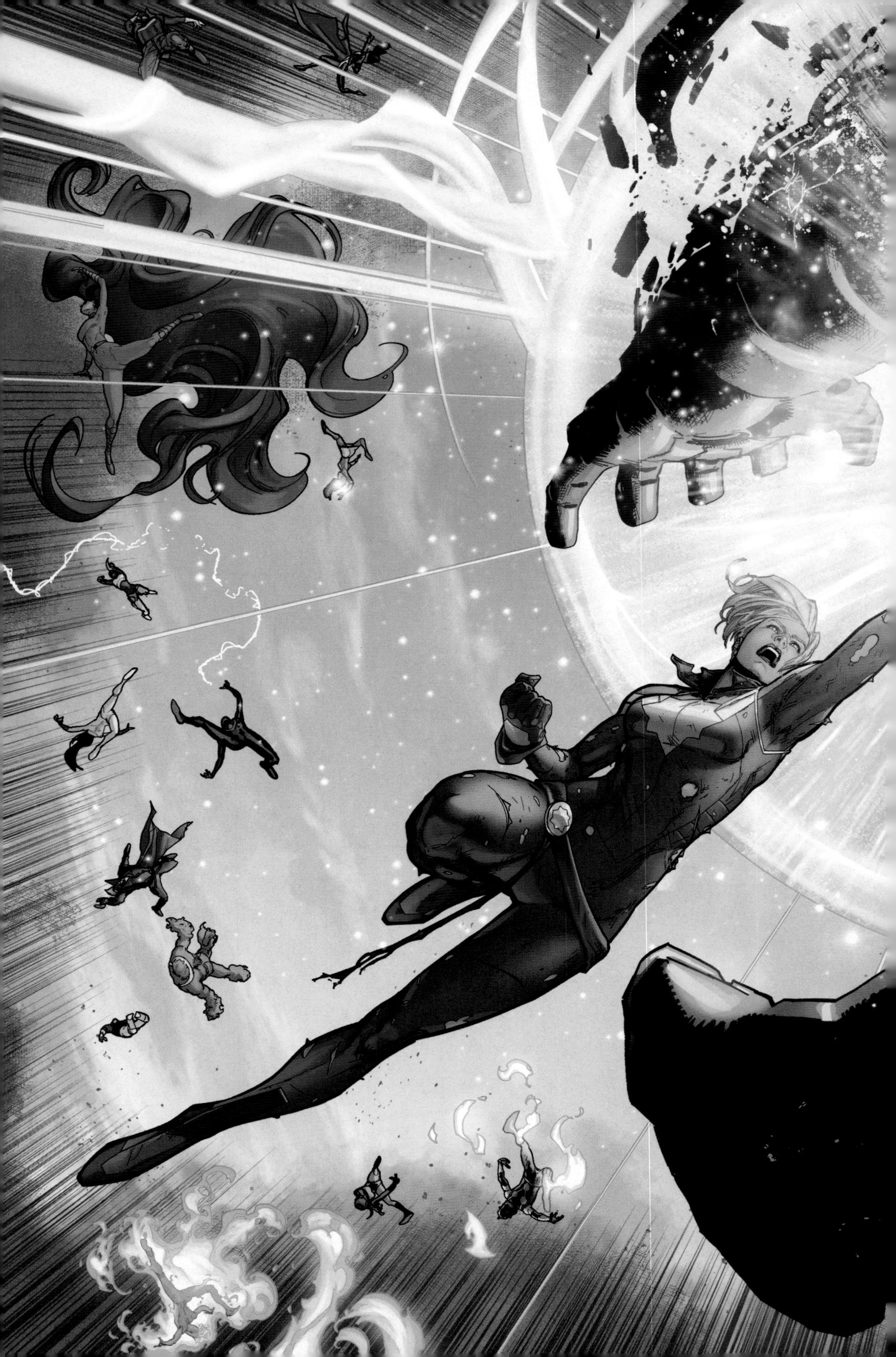

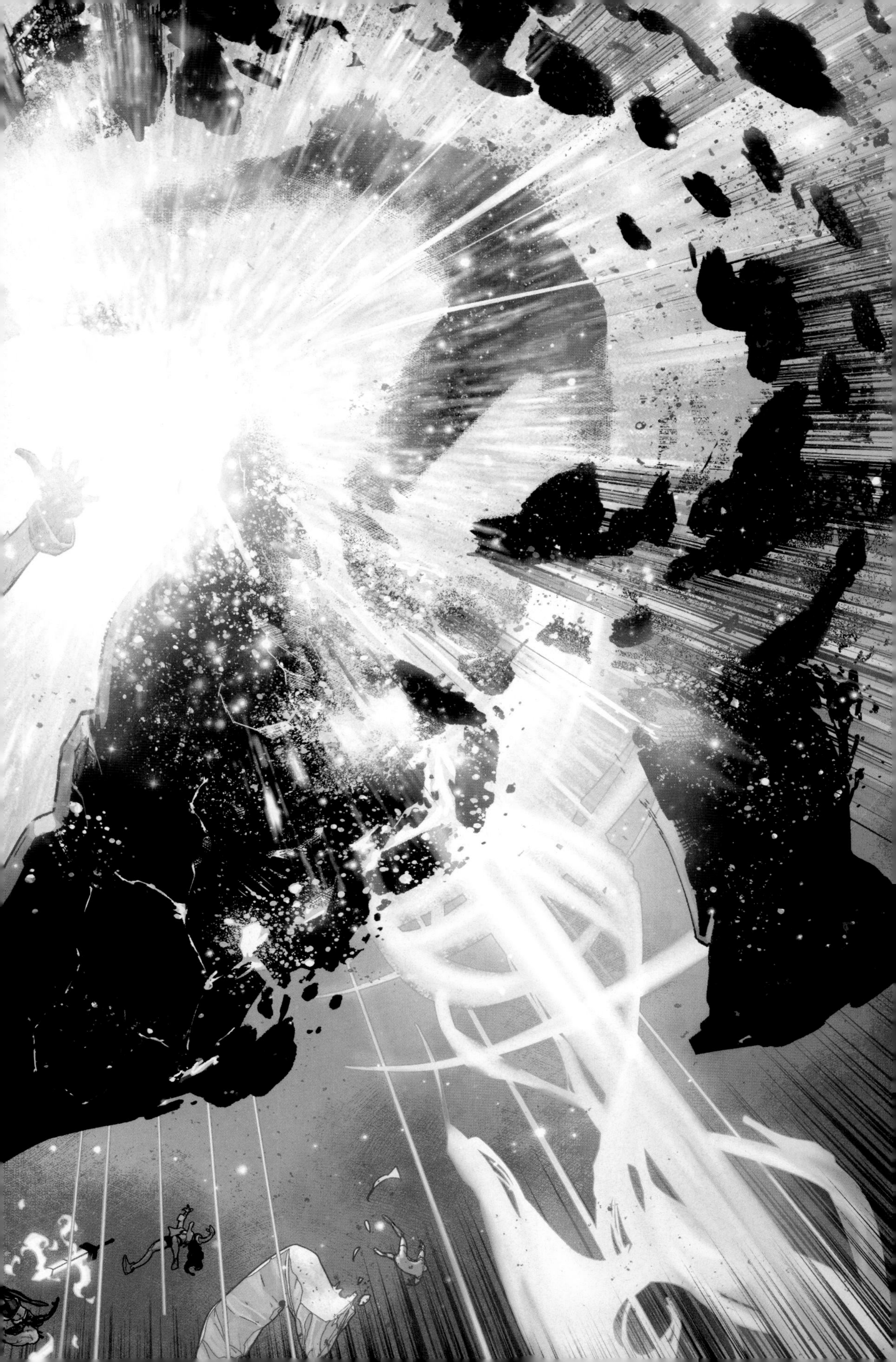

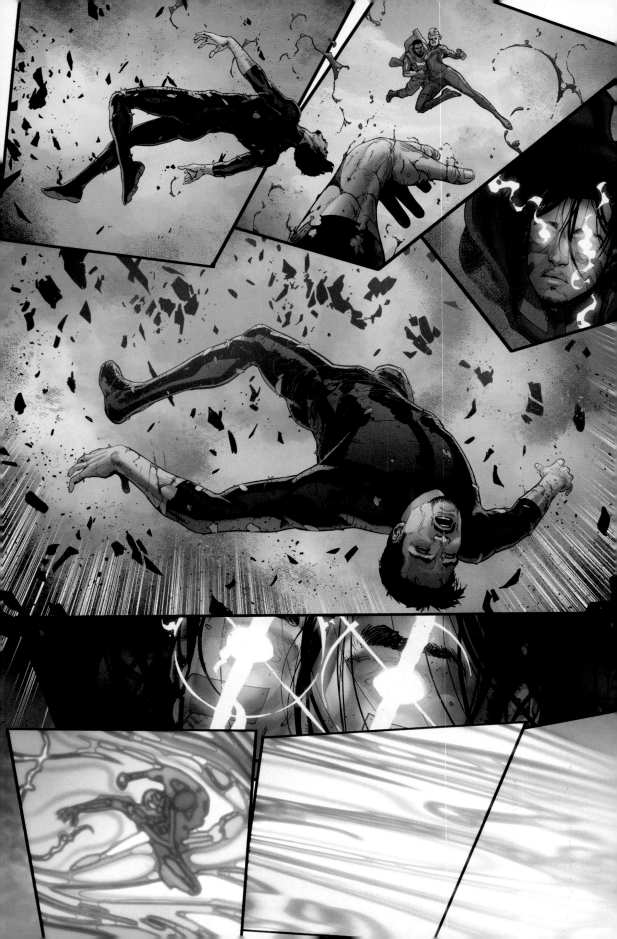

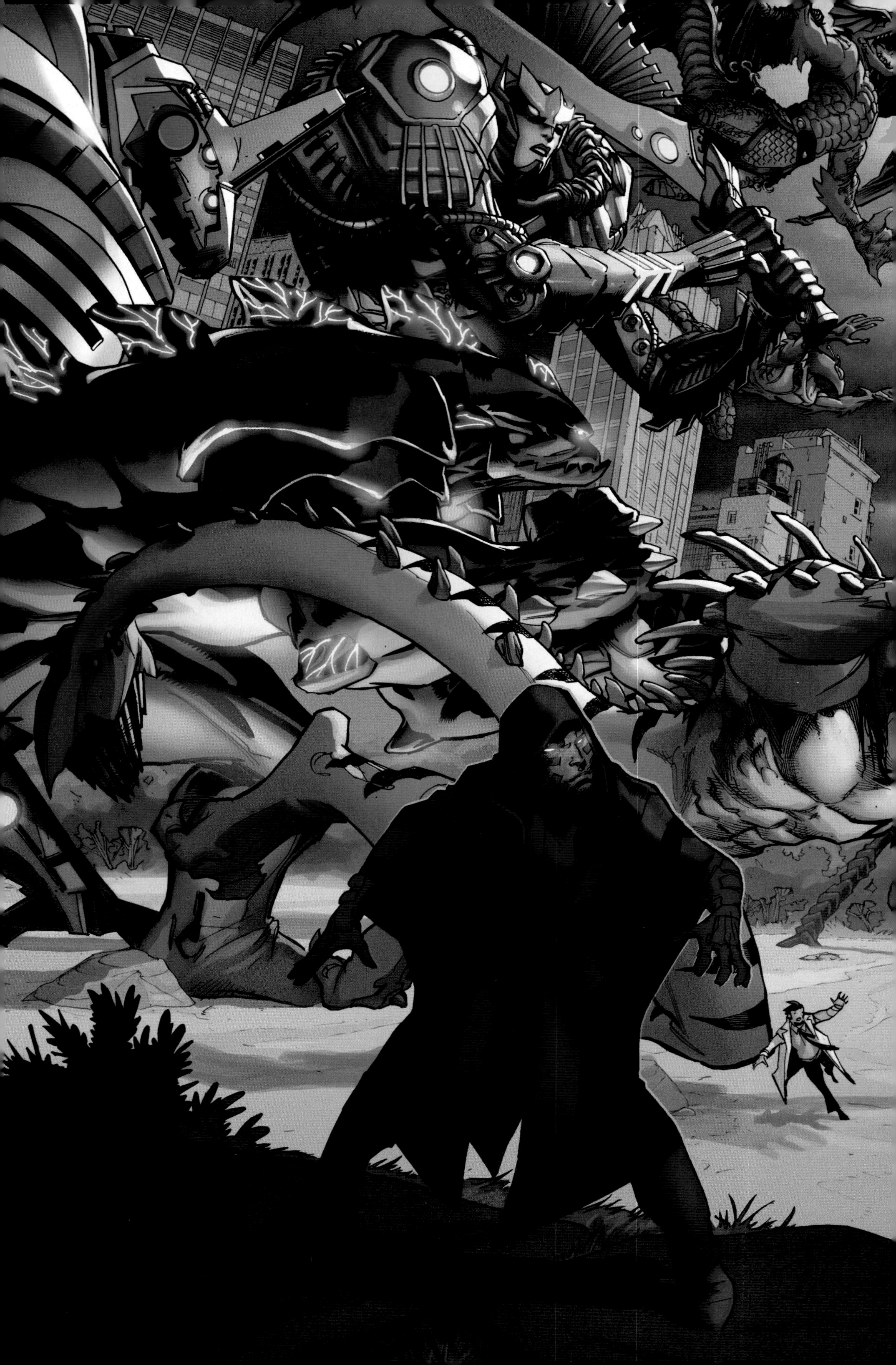

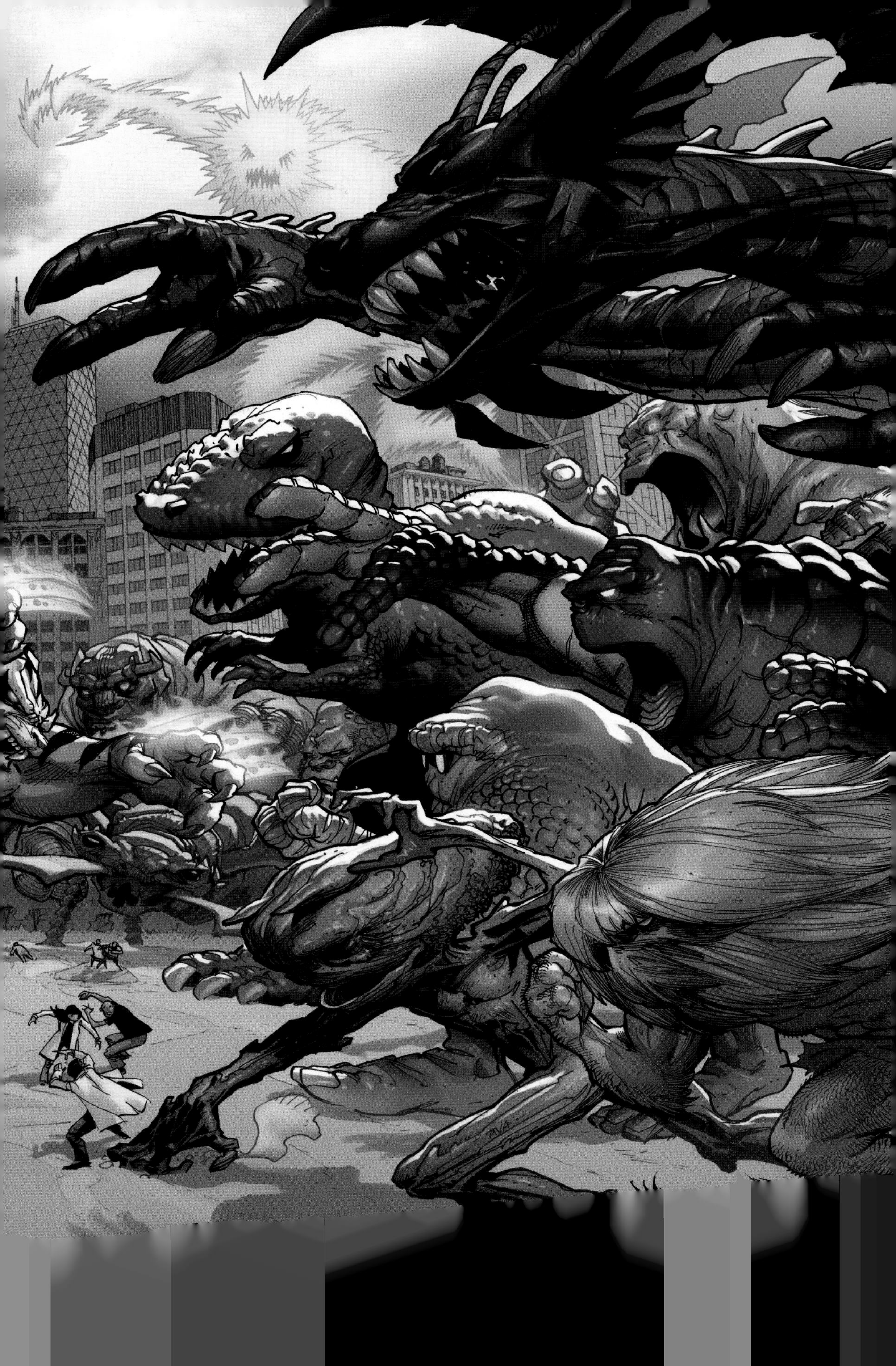

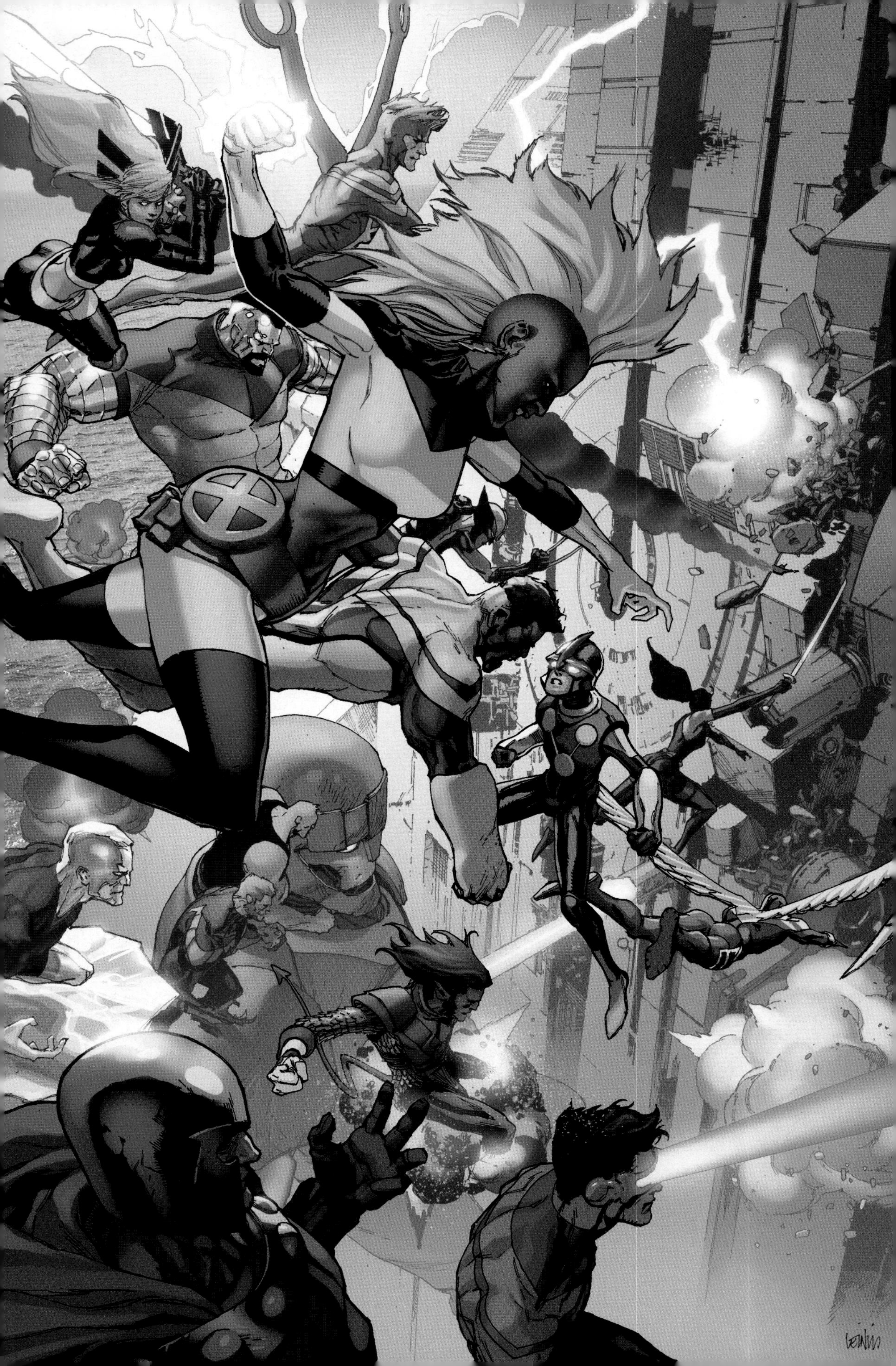

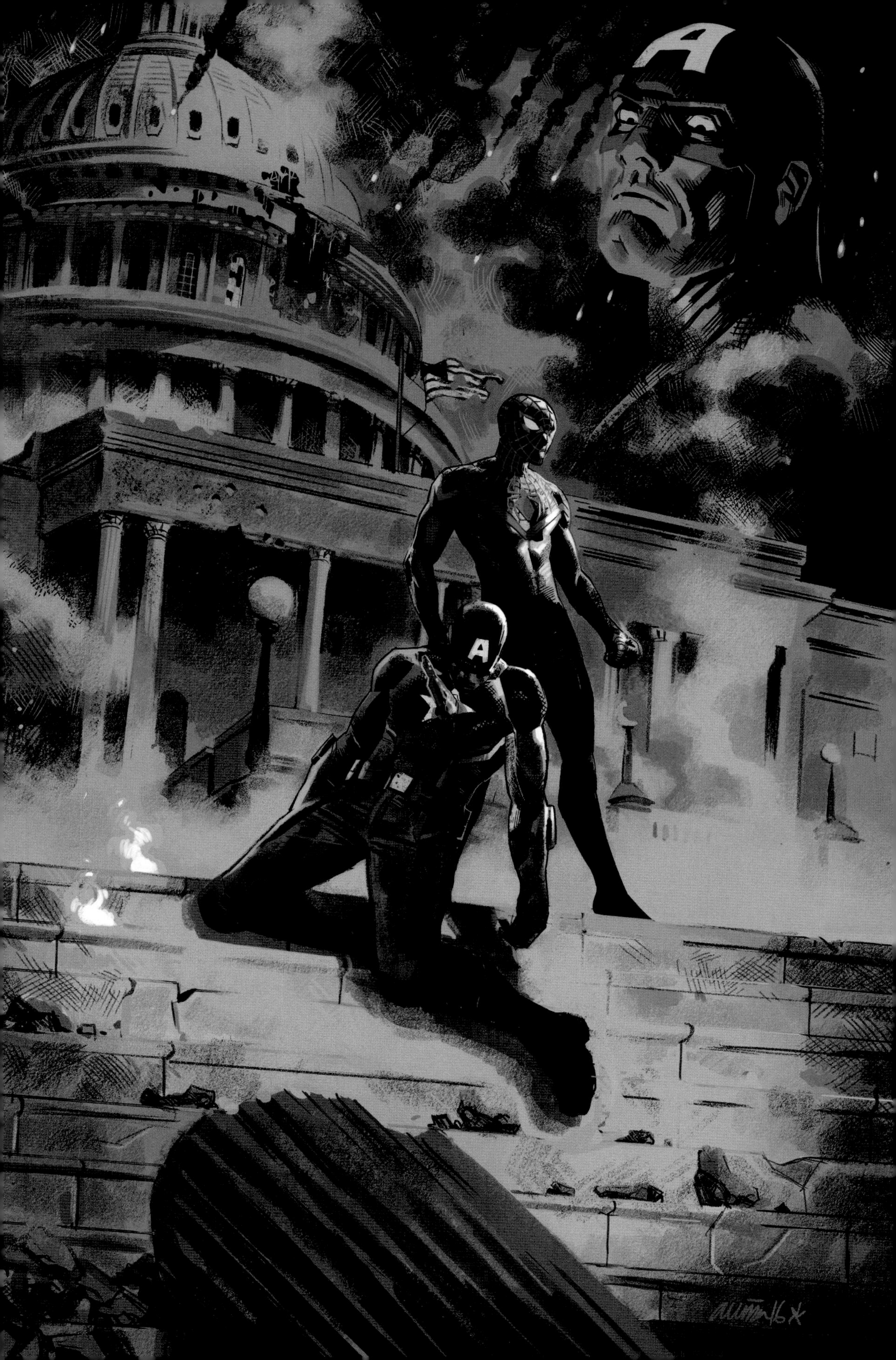

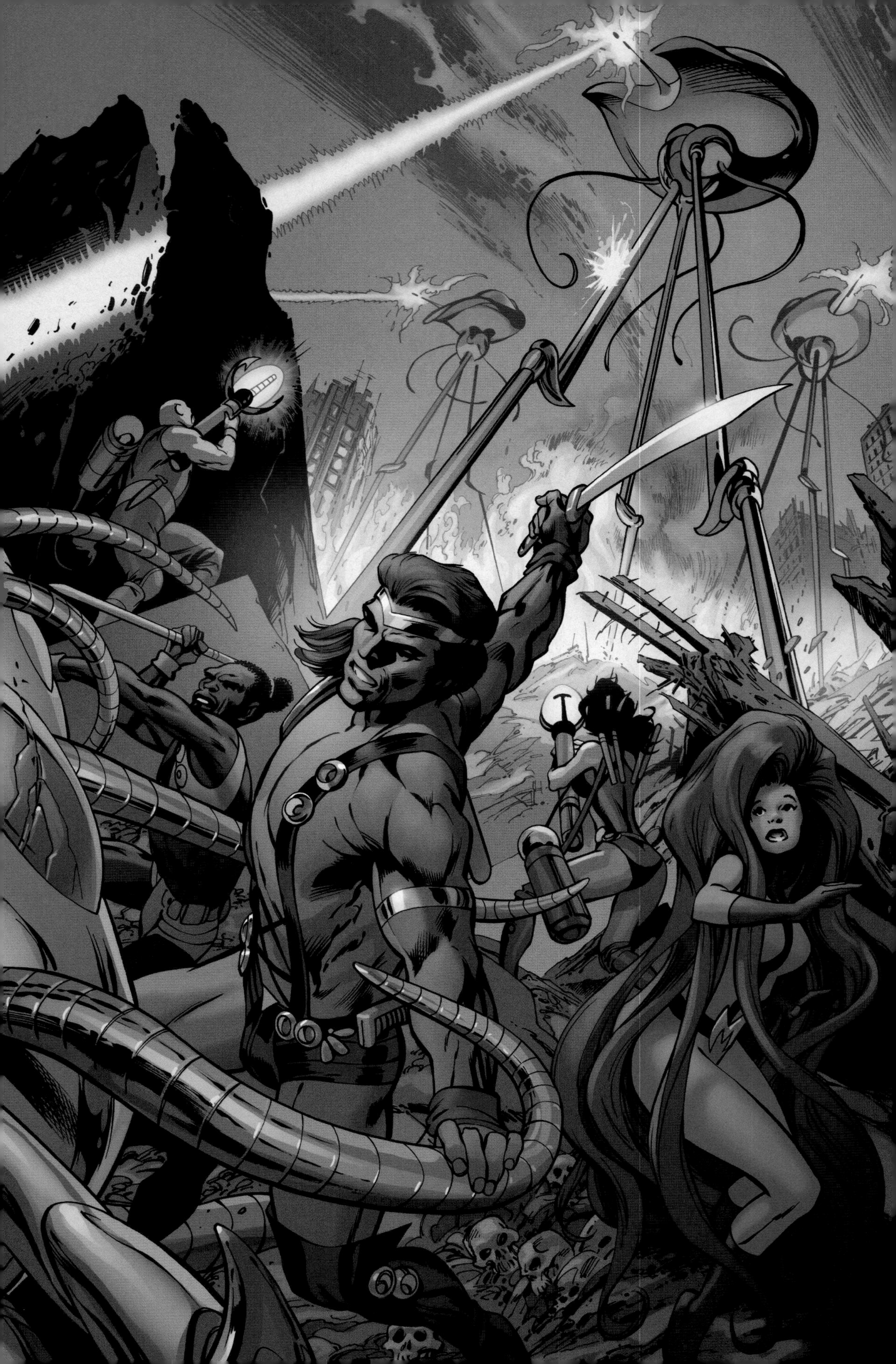

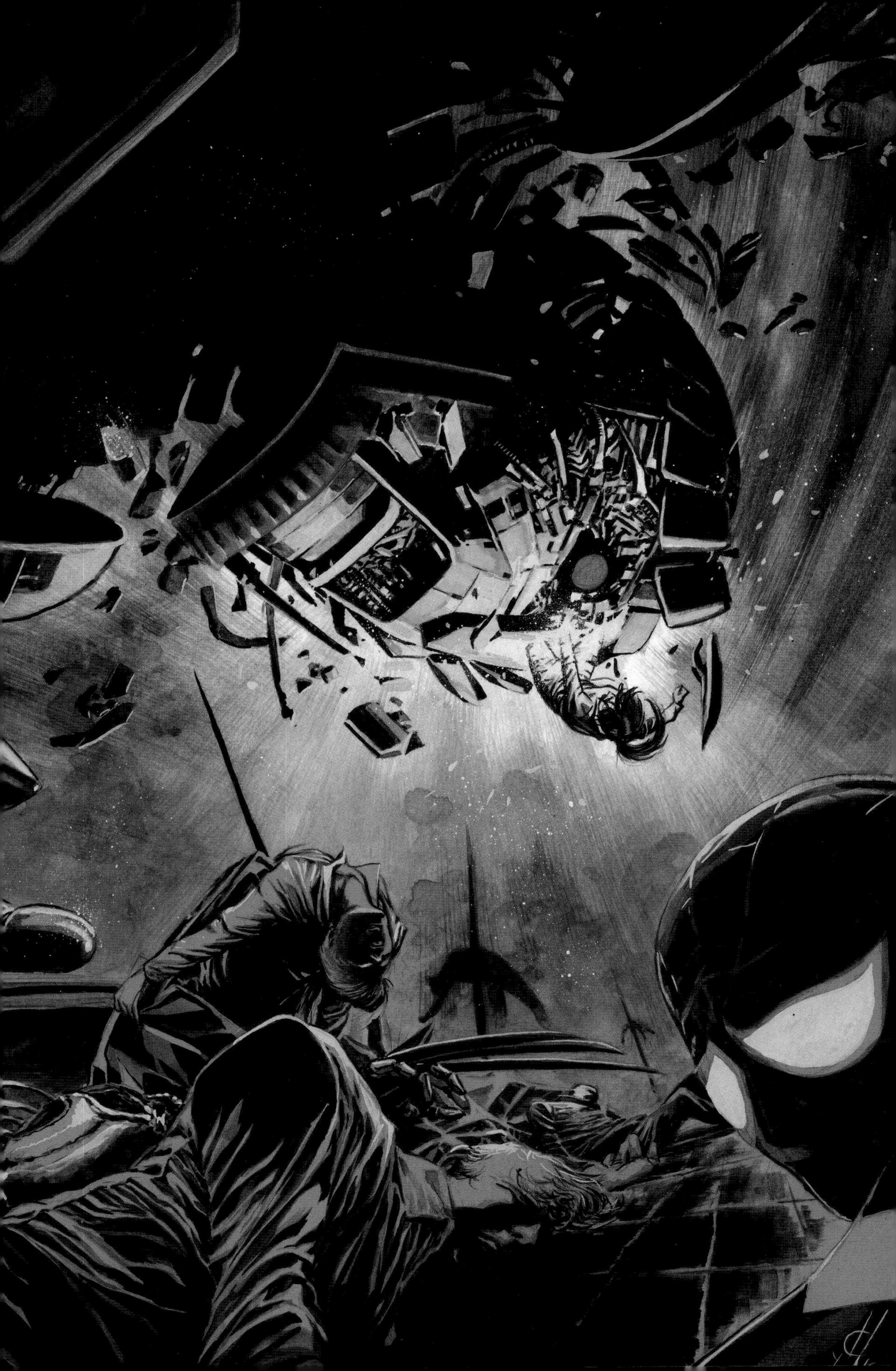

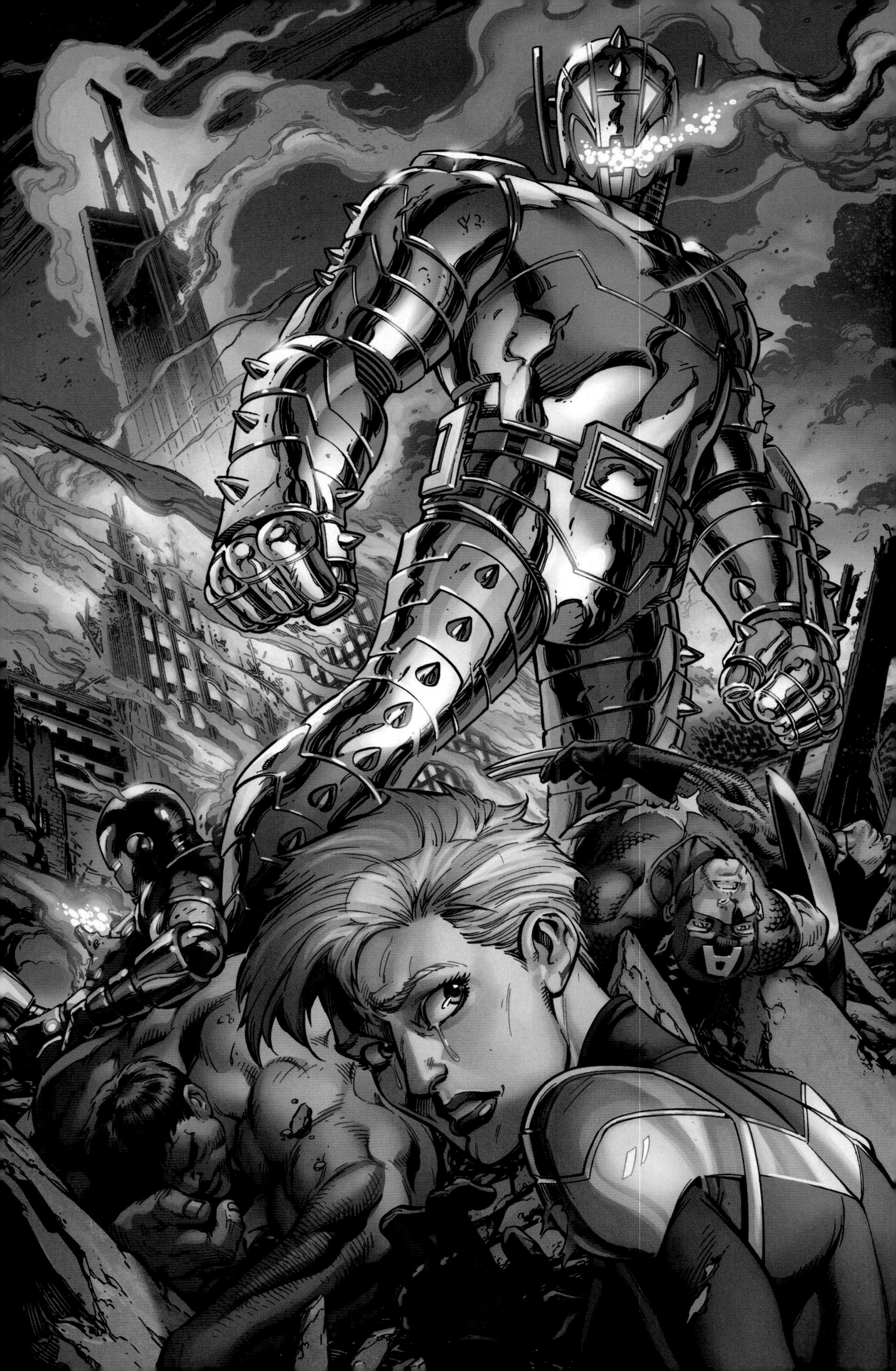

AND HE EVOLVED INTO--?

SOUNDS LIKE HE EVOLVED PAST *US*.

NO, HENRY, YOU REALLY DON'T.

I REALLY WISH I COULD HAVE SEEN THAT.

IT SEEMS AS IF YOU WERE TAKEN TO THE EDGE OF THE UNIVERSE...

...TO THE EDGE OF REASON...

YOU SAW A PERSON FROM EARTH EVOLVE PAST WHAT WE CAN COMPREHEND.

AND I HAVEN'T SLEPT SINCE.

STILL, ALL THINGS CONSIDERED... PRETTY FASCINATING.

IS *HE* GOING TO DIE?

IN THEORY. ONE DAY.

HENRY? IS HE GOING TO *LIVE*?

YOU'RE NOT GOING TO LIKE THIS ANSWER, BUT...

...I'M ACTUALLY UNCOMFORTABLE GOING ANY FURTHER WITH MY EXAMINATION.

WHY?

WHITE HOUSE SITUATION ROOM.

HOW ARE YOU DOING?

I'M FINE, SIR.

YOU HANDLED ALL OF THIS, EVEN WITH THE EYES OF THE WORLD ON YOU, WITH INCREDIBLE GRACE.

THANK YOU, SIR.

AND THE PROFILING, VISION-MAKING INHUMAN?

NO... LONGER WITH US.

THAT IS TOO BAD.

I WAS *REALLY* GETTING USED TO THIS KNOWING-THE-FUTURE-BEFORE-IT-HAPPENS STUFF.

A FUTURE, SIR.

I'M SORRY?

IT WAS *A* FUTURE.

A *POSSIBLE* FUTURE.

ONE-- ONE OF MANY.

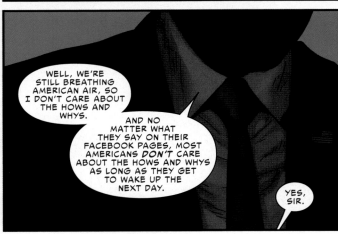

WELL, WE'RE STILL BREATHING AMERICAN AIR, SO I DON'T CARE ABOUT THE HOWS AND WHYS.

AND NO MATTER WHAT THEY SAY ON THEIR FACEBOOK PAGES, MOST AMERICANS *DON'T* CARE ABOUT THE HOWS AND WHYS AS LONG AS THEY GET TO WAKE UP THE NEXT DAY.

YES, SIR.

SO, WHAT DOES IT LOOK LIKE?

WHAT IS THE FALLOUT OVER THERE IN THE SUPER HERO COMMUNITY?

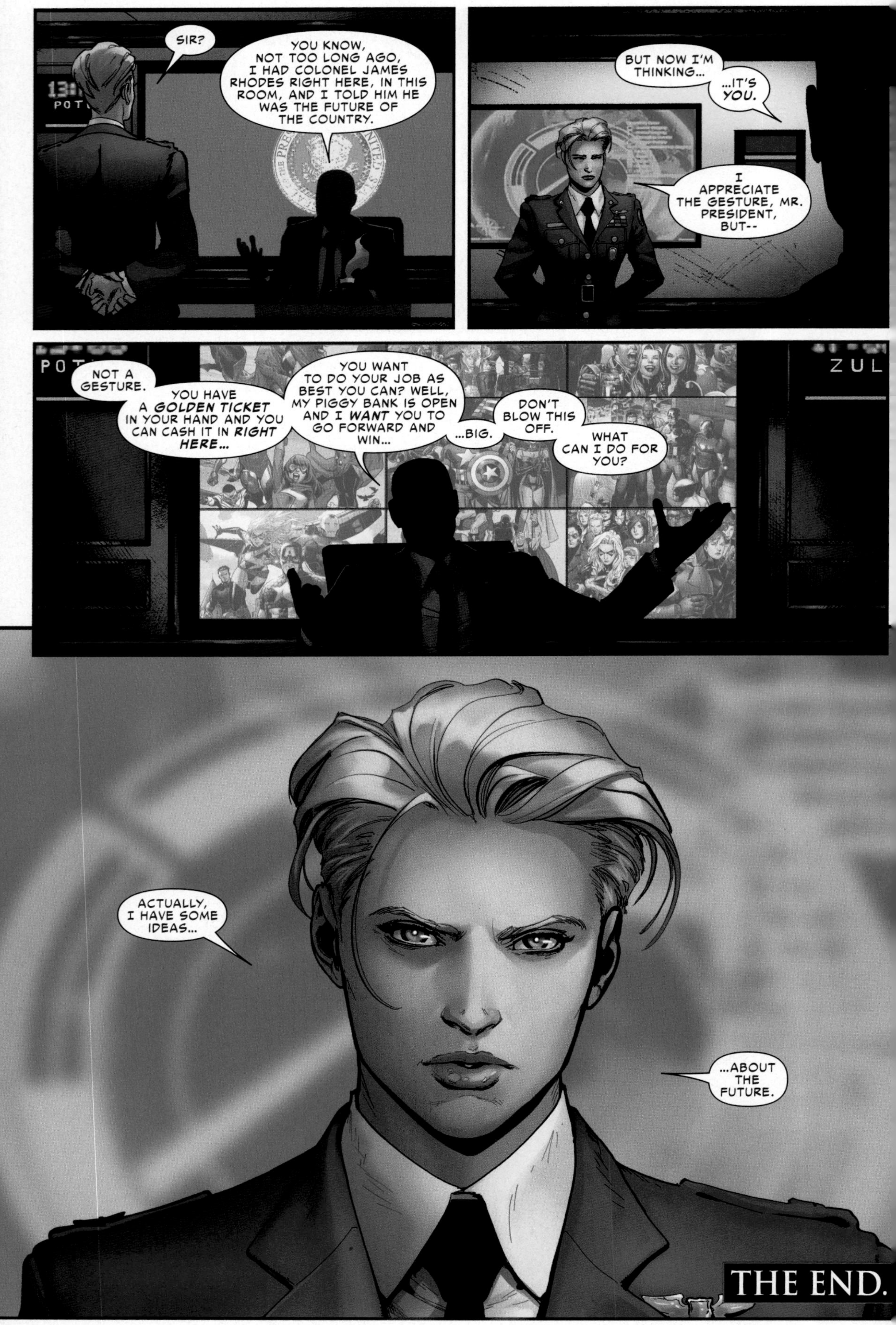

SIR?
YOU KNOW, NOT TOO LONG AGO, I HAD COLONEL JAMES RHODES RIGHT HERE, IN THIS ROOM, AND I TOLD HIM HE WAS THE FUTURE OF THE COUNTRY.
BUT NOW I'M THINKING...
...IT'S *YOU.*
I APPRECIATE THE GESTURE, MR. PRESIDENT, BUT--
NOT A GESTURE.
YOU HAVE A ***GOLDEN TICKET*** IN YOUR HAND AND YOU CAN CASH IT IN ***RIGHT HERE...***
YOU WANT TO DO YOUR JOB AS BEST YOU CAN? WELL, MY PIGGY BANK IS OPEN AND I ***WANT*** YOU TO GO FORWARD AND WIN...
...BIG.
DON'T BLOW THIS OFF.
WHAT CAN I DO FOR YOU?
ACTUALLY, I HAVE SOME IDEAS...
...ABOUT THE FUTURE.
THE END.

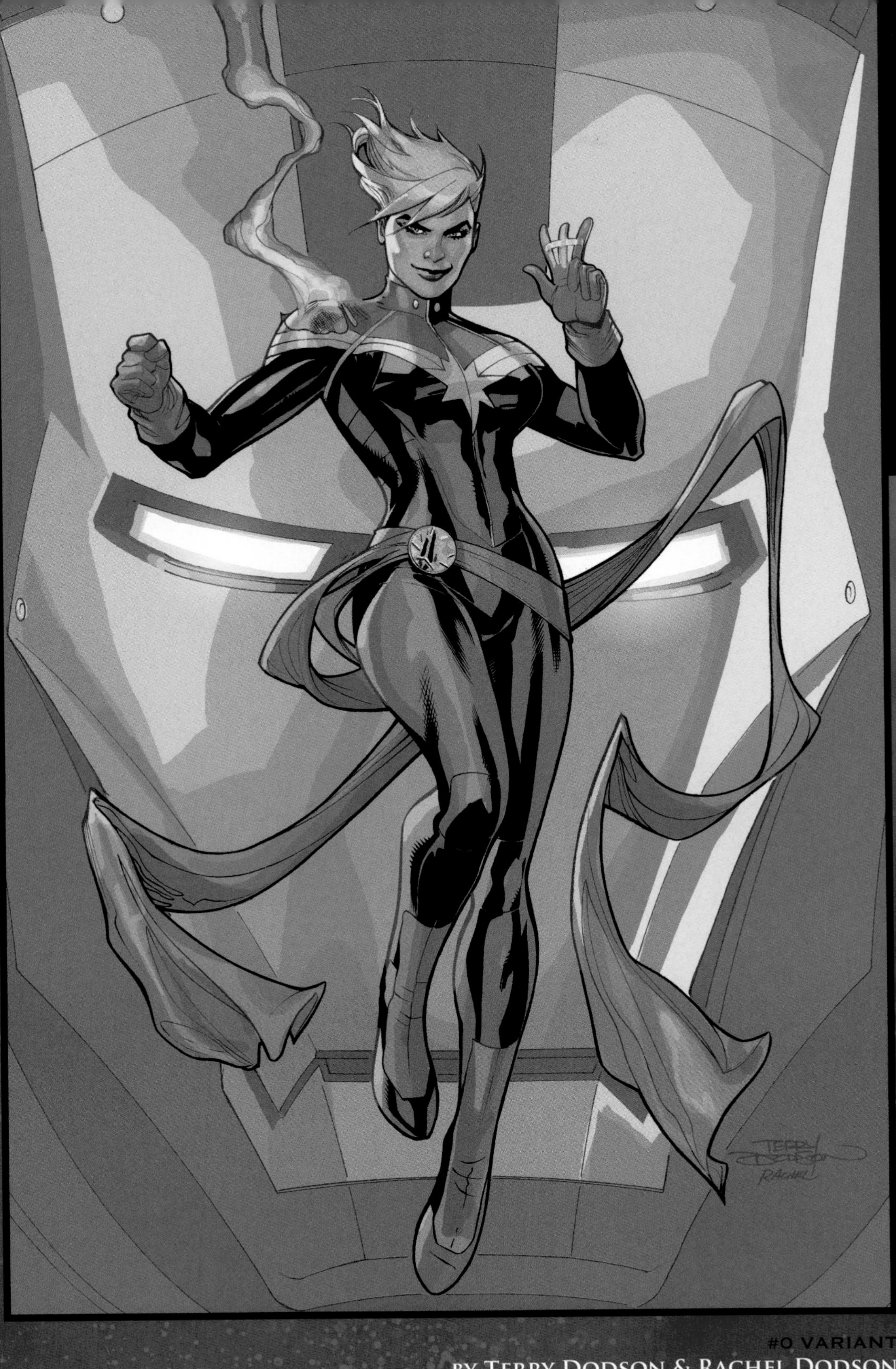
TERRY DODSON
RACHEL

#0 VARIANT
BY TERRY DODSON & RACHEL DODSON

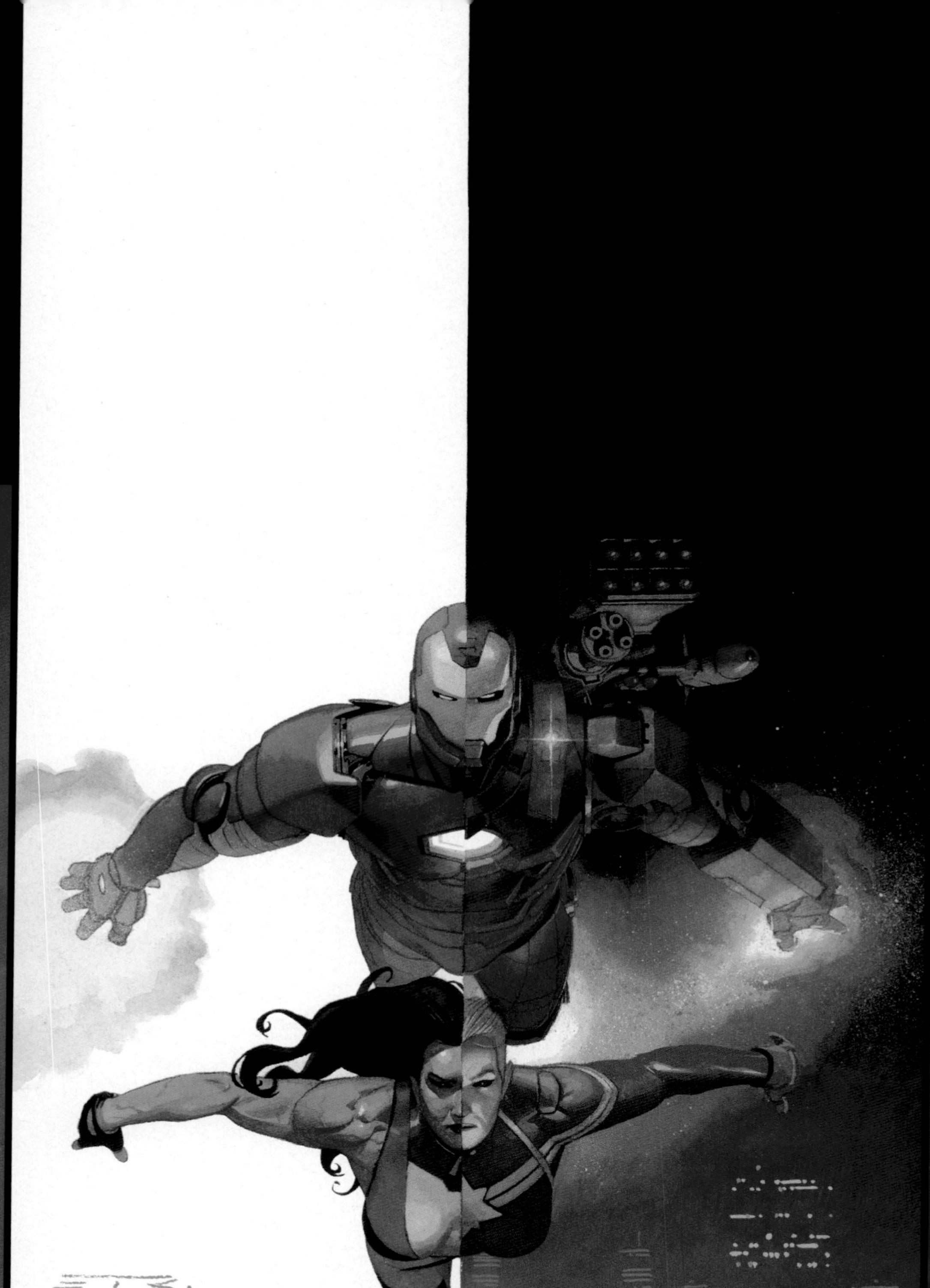

#0 VARIANT
BY ESAD RIBIC

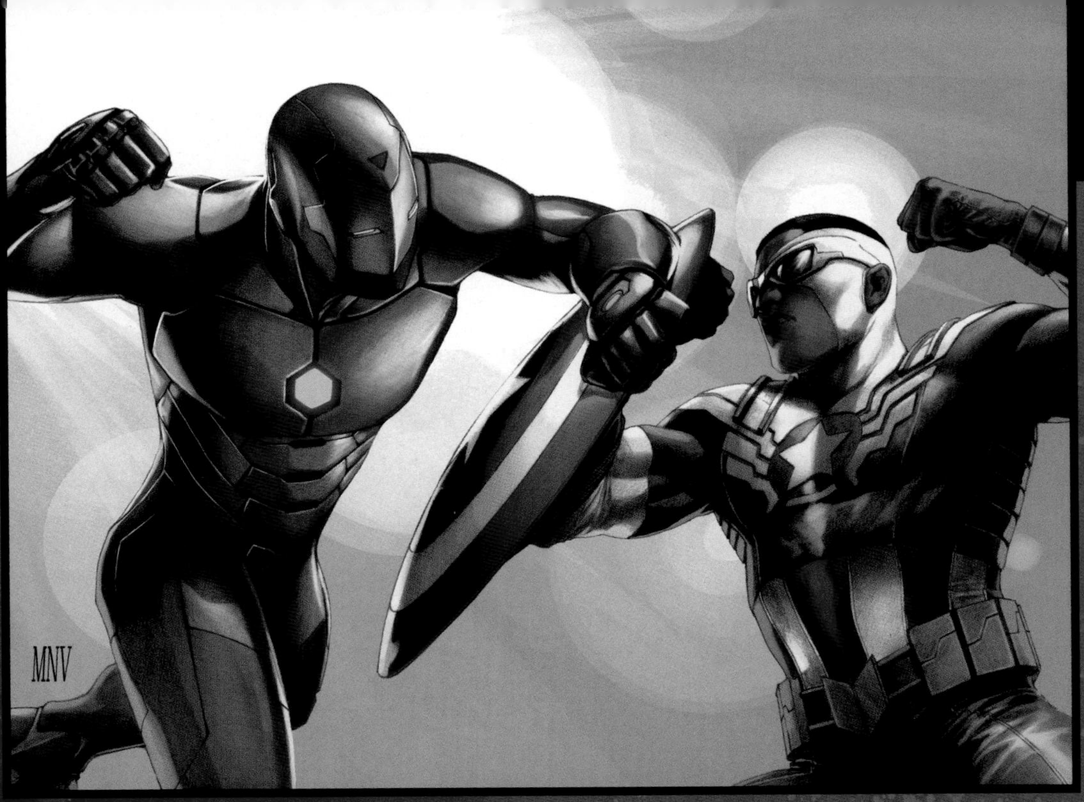
MNV

#1 VARIANT
BY STEVE MCNIVEN

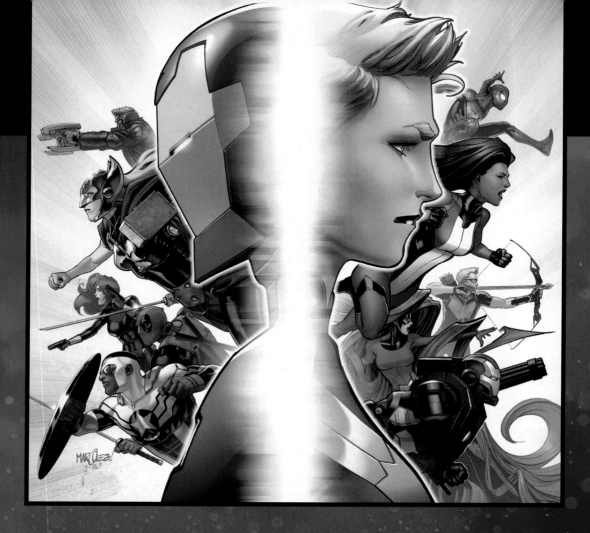

#1 VARIANT
BY MARQUEZ

civil war II
001
jtc negative space
variant edition

rated t+
$5.99 usd
direct edition
marvel.com

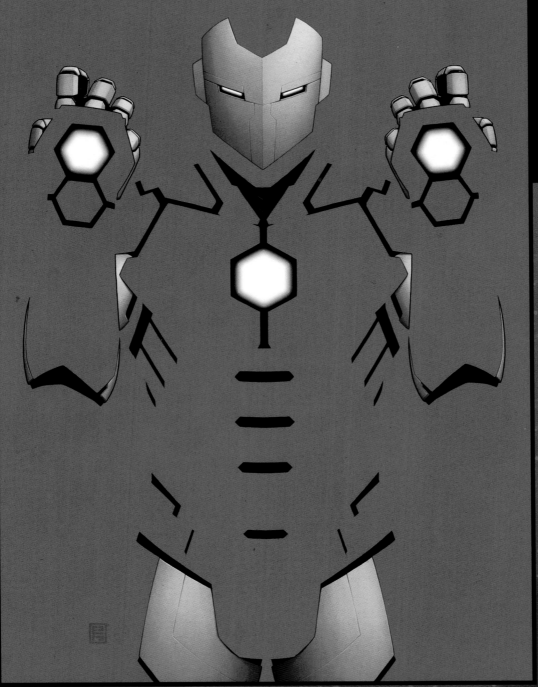

#1 NEGATIVE SPACE VARIANT
BY JOHN TYLER CHRISTOPHER

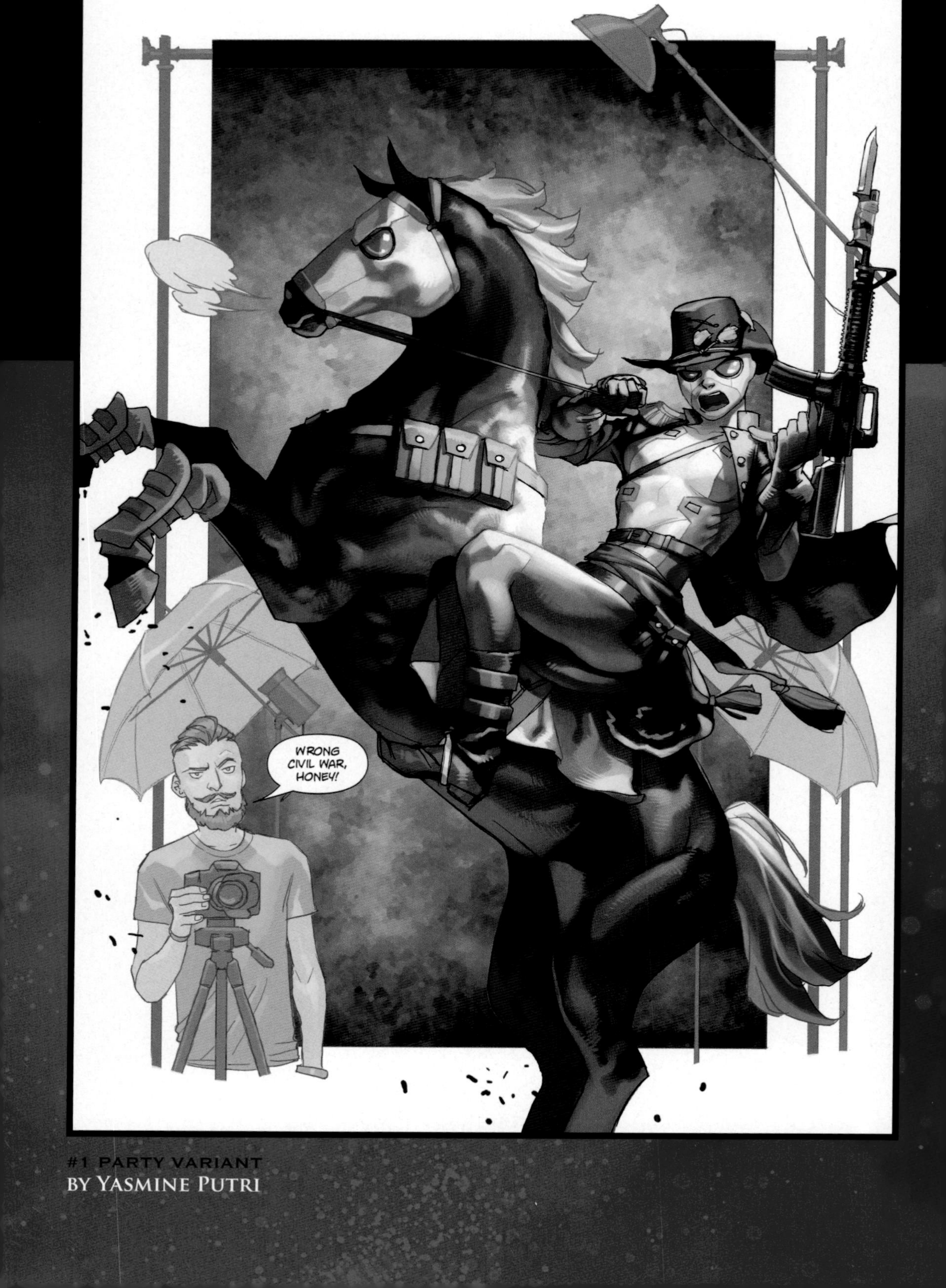
WRONG CIVIL WAR, HONEY!

#1 PARTY VARIANT
BY YASMINE PUTRI

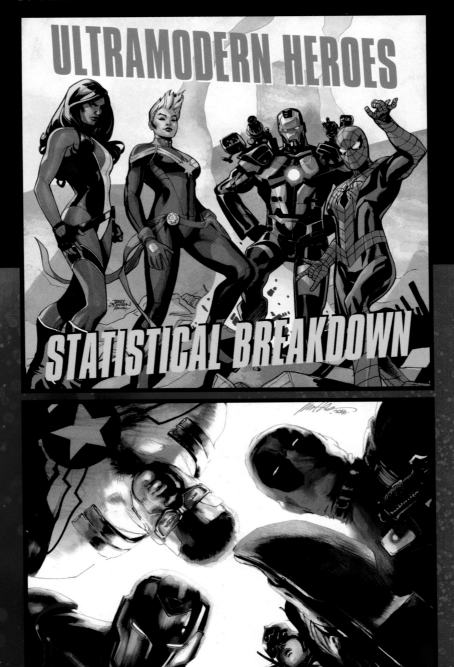

#1 HIP-HOP VARIANT
BY Rafael ALBUQUERQUE

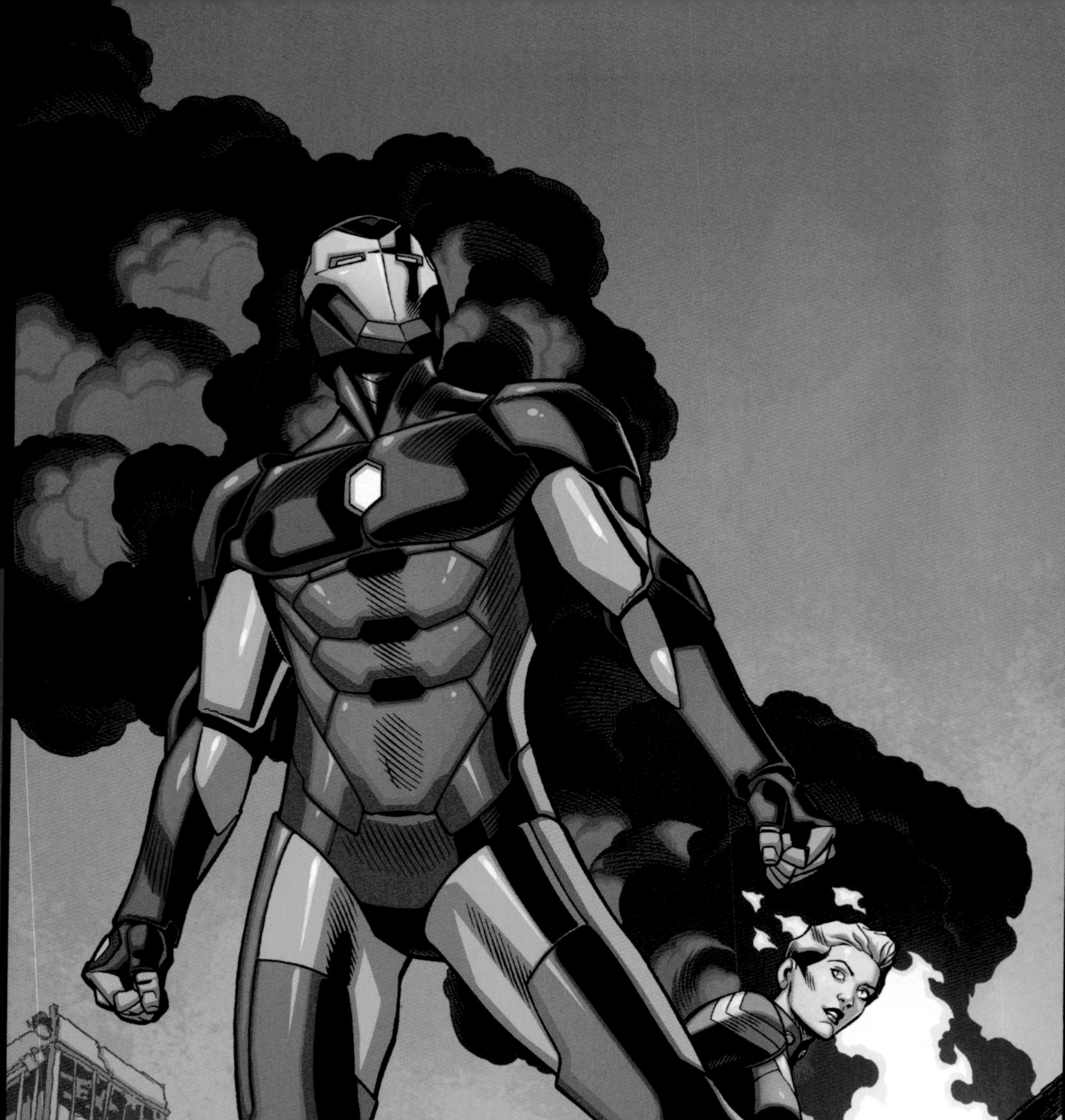

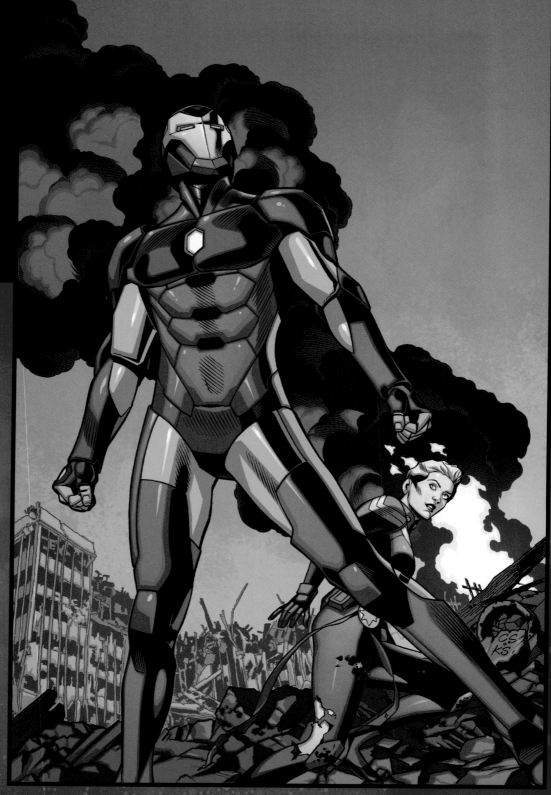

#1 BATTLE VARIANT
BY CHRIS SPROUSE, KARL STORY & DAVE MCCAIG

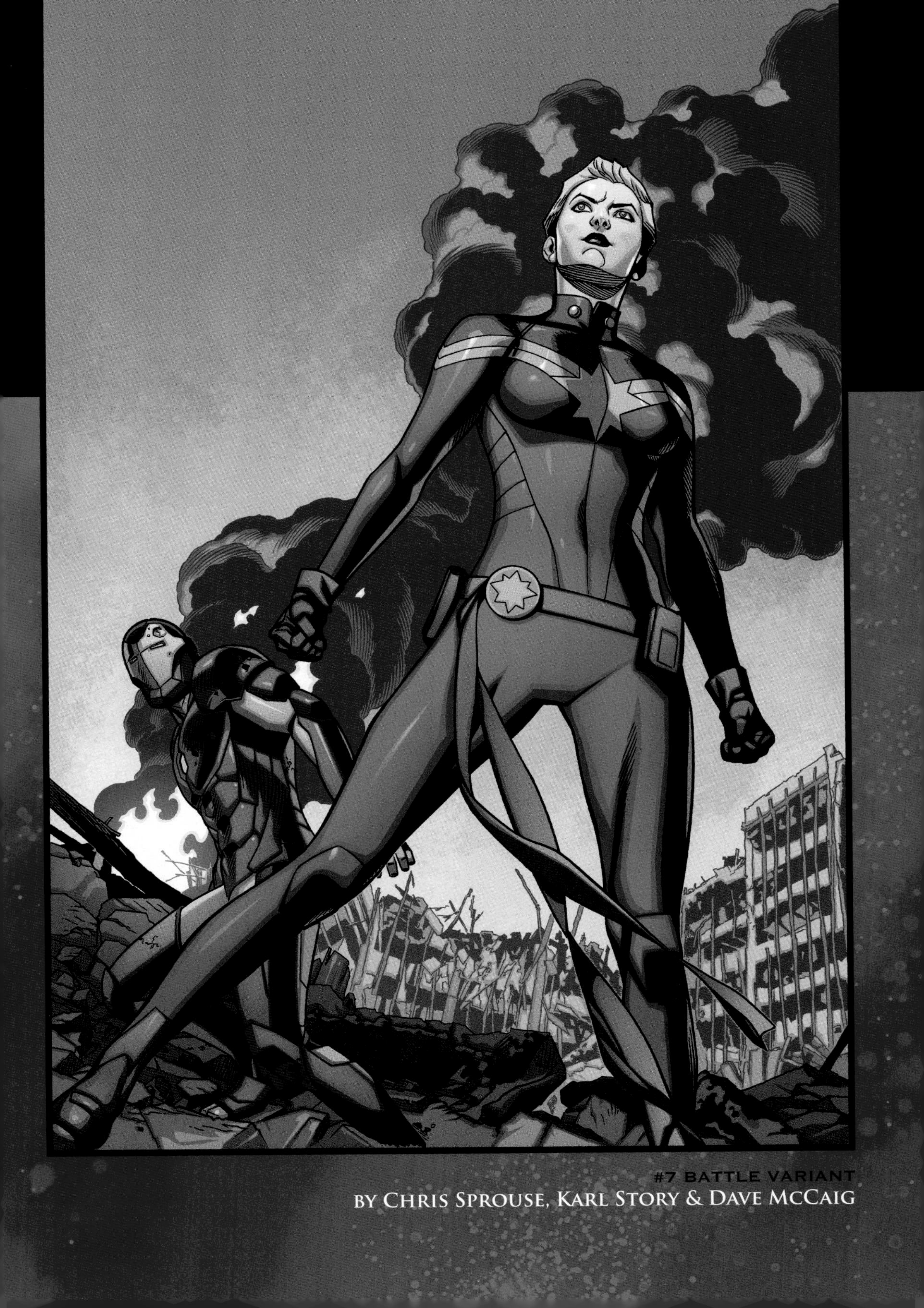

#7 BATTLE VARIANT
BY CHRIS SPROUSE, KARL STORY & DAVE MCCAIG

#1 VARIANT
BY JOHN CASSADAY & PAUL MOUNTS

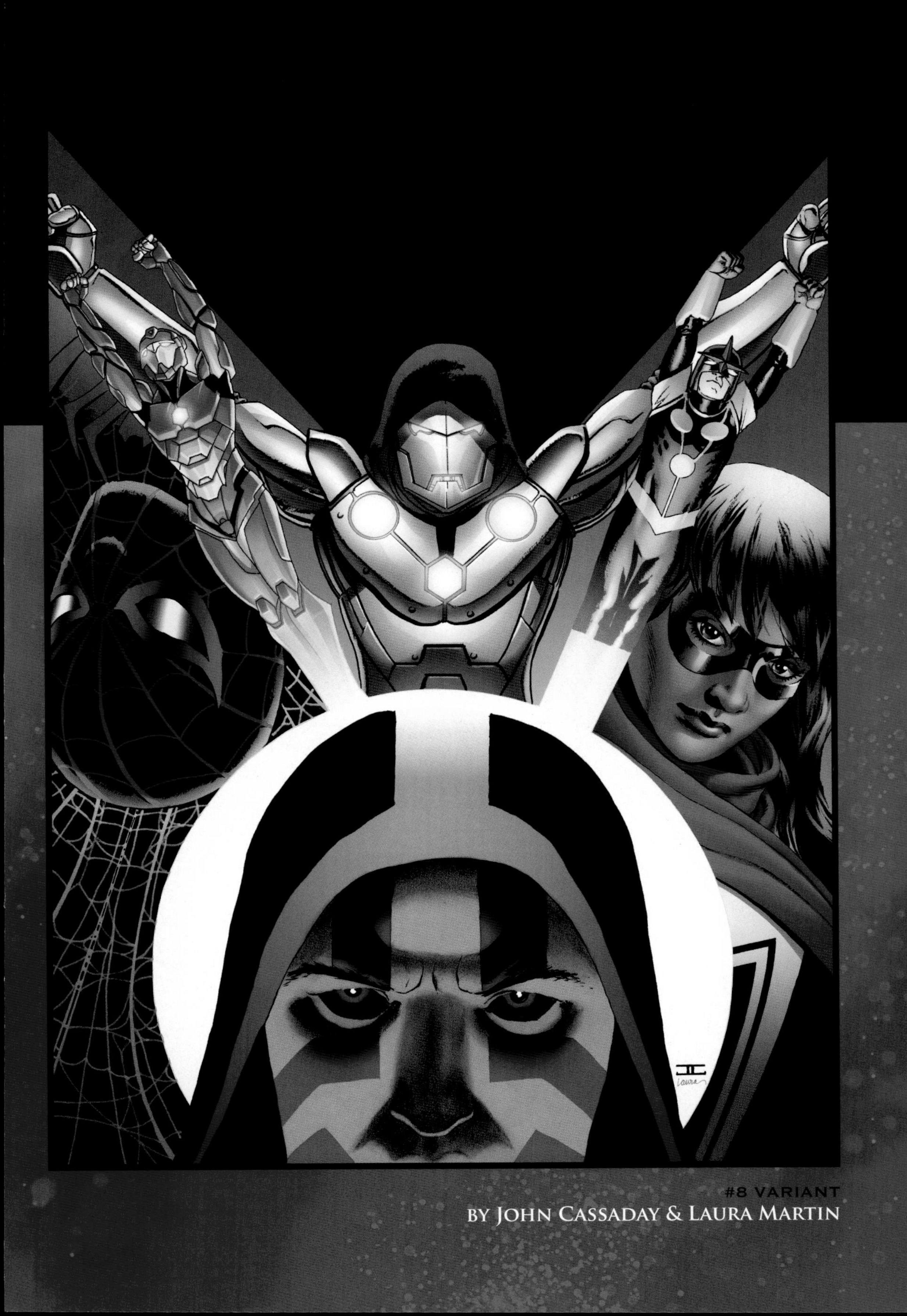

#8 VARIANT
BY JOHN CASSADAY & LAURA MARTIN

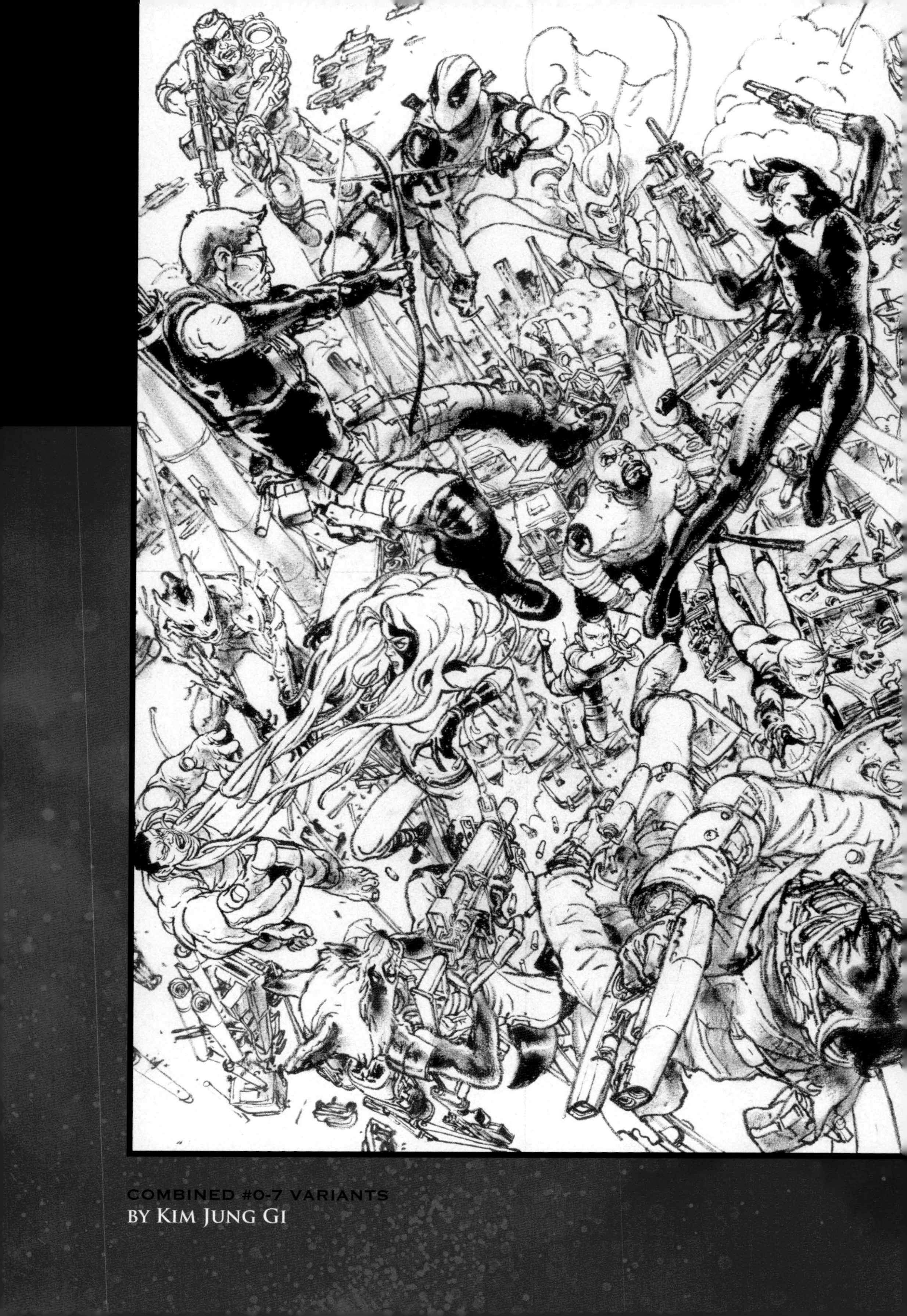

COMBINED #0-7 VARIANTS
BY KIM JUNG GI

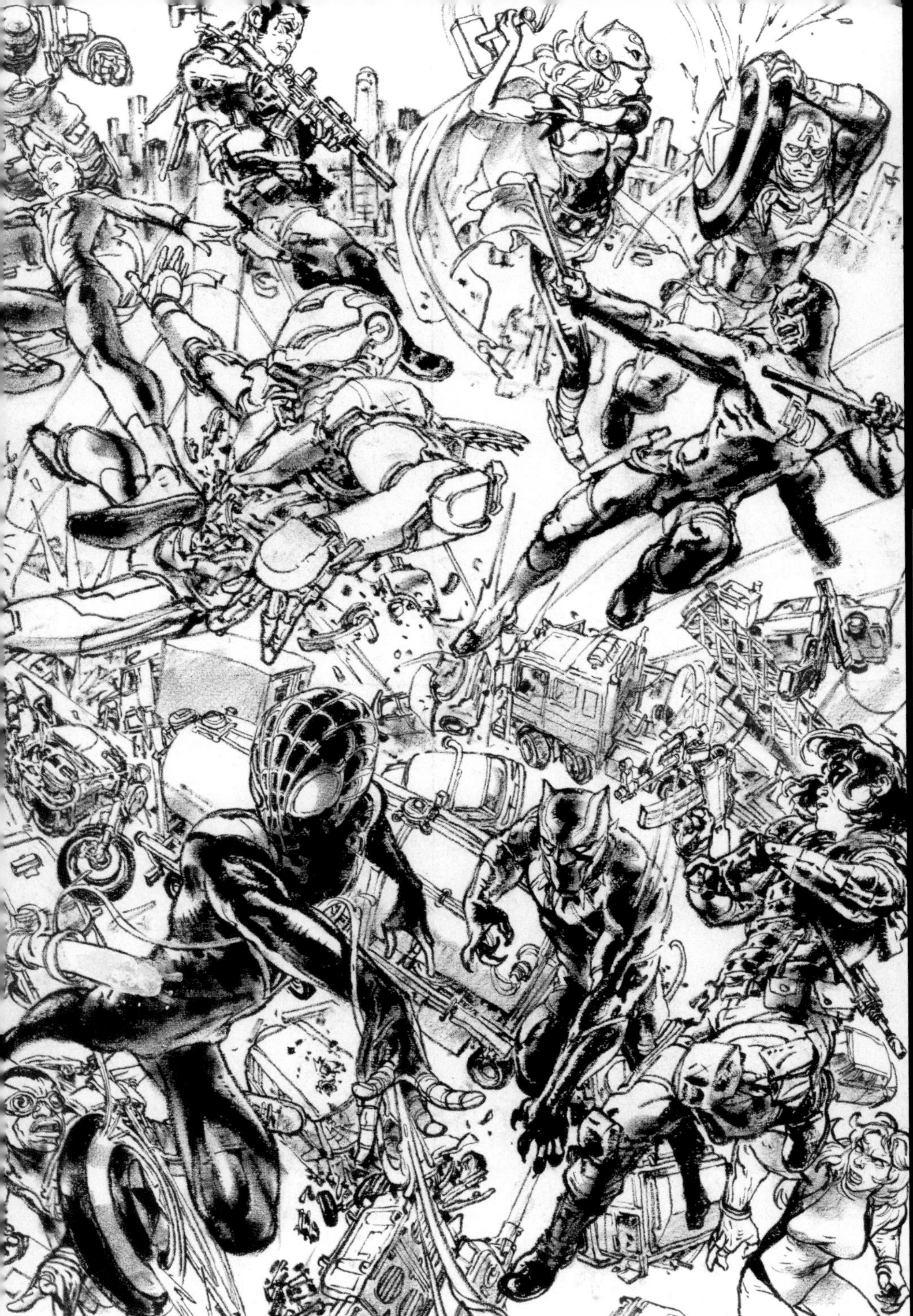

#1 VARIANT
BY MICHAEL CHO

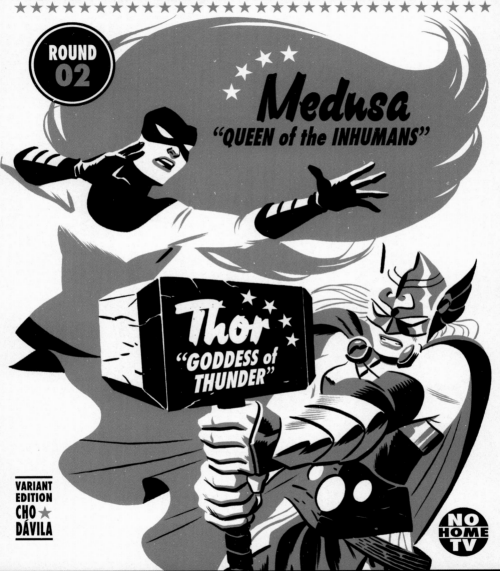

#2 VARIANT
BY MICHAEL CHO

the FIGHT CONTINUES!

SPIDER-MAN
"the WALL-CRAWLER"

CIVIL WAR II

ROUND 3

CAPTAIN AMERICA
"SENTINEL of LIBERTY"

PRESENTED BY
BENDIS
MARQUEZ
PONSOR

VARIANT EDITION BY CHO DÁVILA

#3 VARIANT
BY MICHAEL CHO

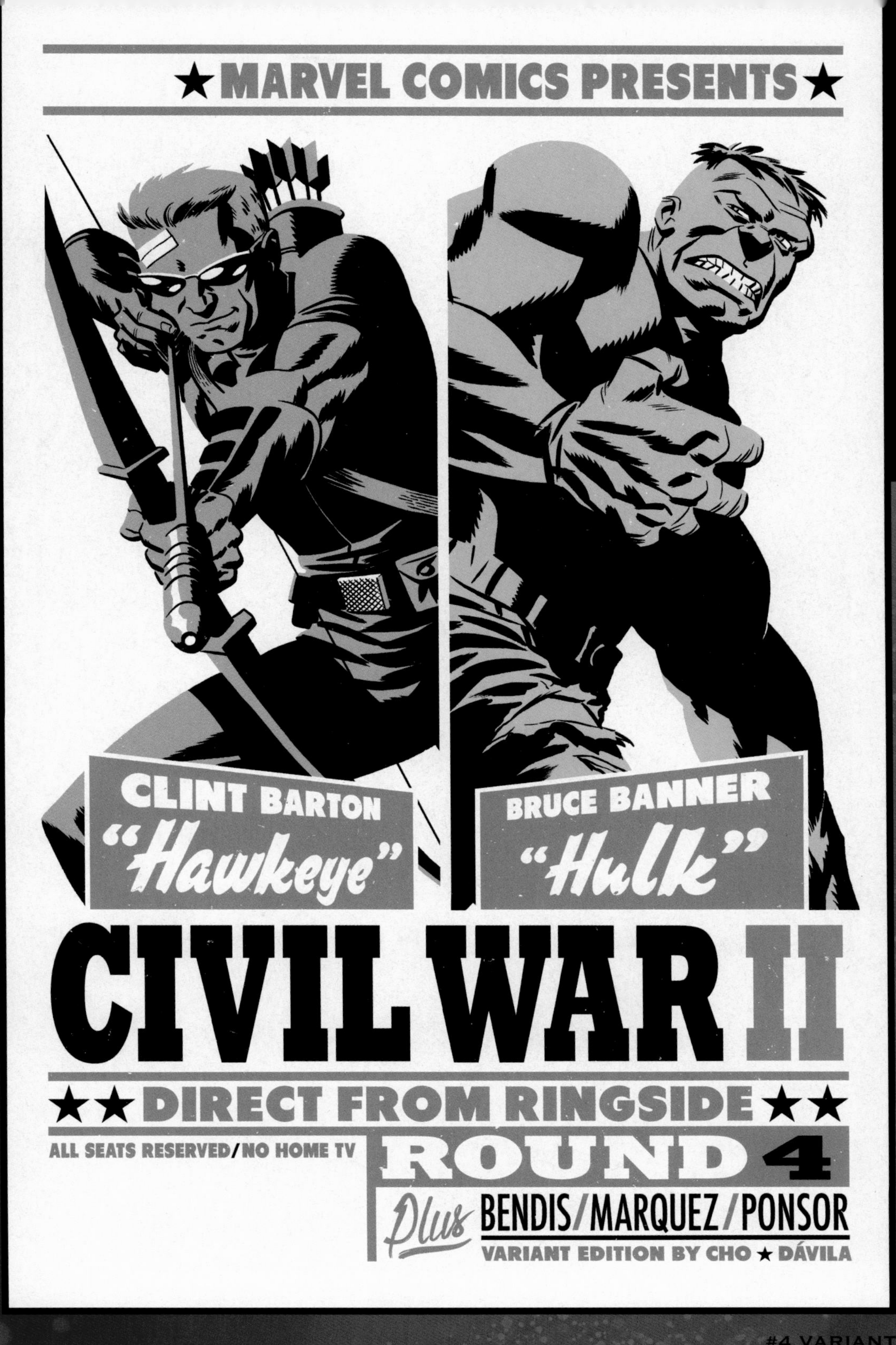
★ MARVEL COMICS PRESENTS ★
CLINT BARTON
"Hawkeye"
BRUCE BANNER
"Hulk"
CIVIL WAR II
★★ DIRECT FROM RINGSIDE ★★
ALL SEATS RESERVED/NO HOME TV
ROUND 4
Plus BENDIS/MARQUEZ/PONSOR
VARIANT EDITION BY CHO ★ DÁVILA

#4 VARIANT
BY MICHAEL CHO

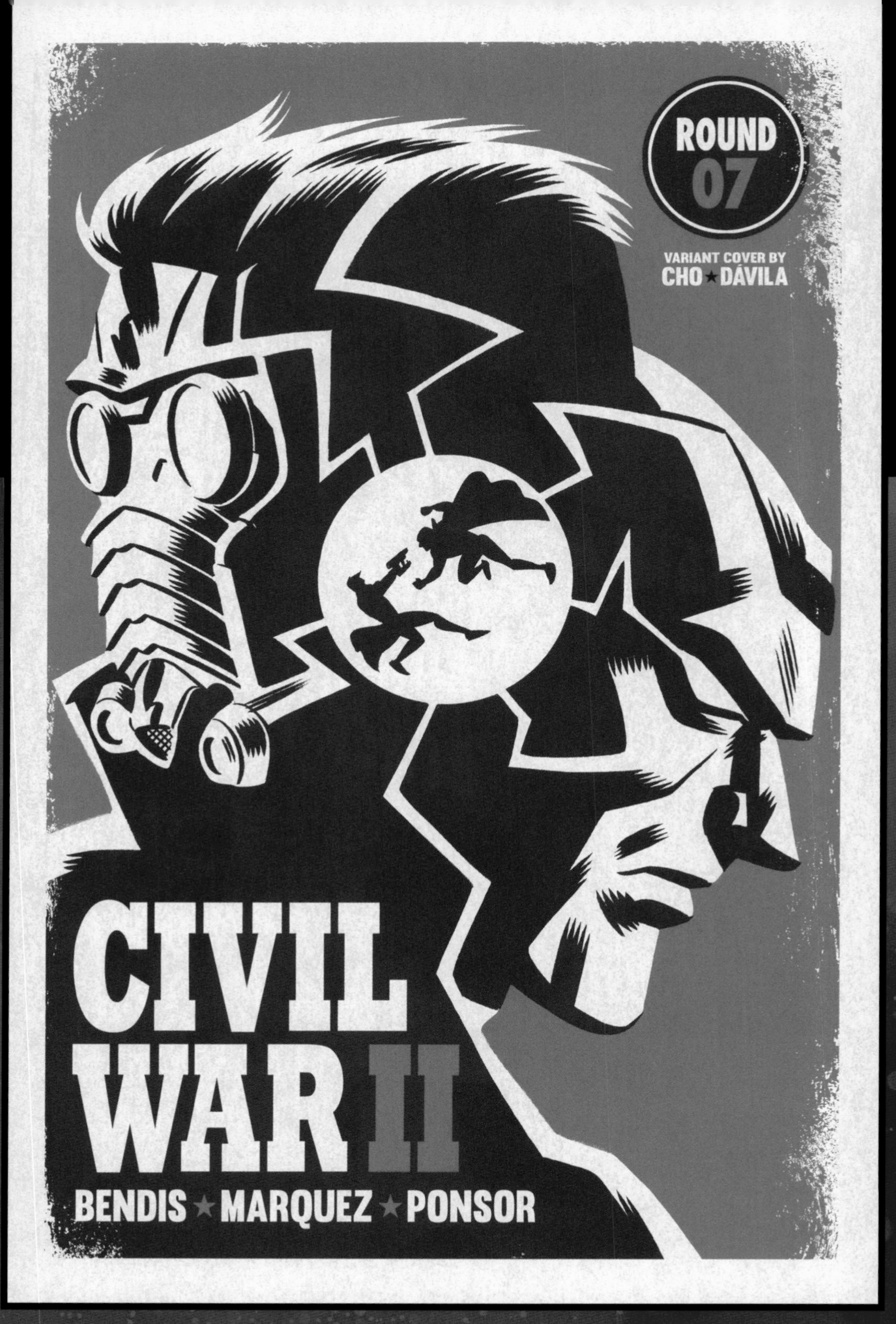
ROUND
07
VARIANT COVER BY
CHO ★ DÁVILA
CIVIL
WAR II
BENDIS ★ MARQUEZ ★ PONSOR

#7 VARIANT
BY MICHAEL CHO

THE REMATCH OF THE CENTURY!

"CAPTAIN MARVEL"
AKA CAROL DANVERS
DYNAMIC POWER IN ACTION

VS

"IRON MAN"
AKA TONY STARK
HEAVY HITTING
TECHNOLOGICAL WONDER

CIVIL WAR II

PRESENTED BY BENDIS ★ MARQUEZ ★ PONSOR | ROUND 8

Plus ADDED ATTRACTION:

"CAPTAIN AMERICA" **VS** "SPIDER-MAN"
STEVE ROGERS   MILES MORALES

THE INHUMAN POWER OF
"ULYSSES" vs THE WORLD
VARIANT COVER BY
CHO ★ DÁVILA

**NO RADIO
NO HOME TV**

GENERAL ADMISSION | EVERY SEAT IS GUARANTEED

#8 VARIANT
BY MICHAEL CHO

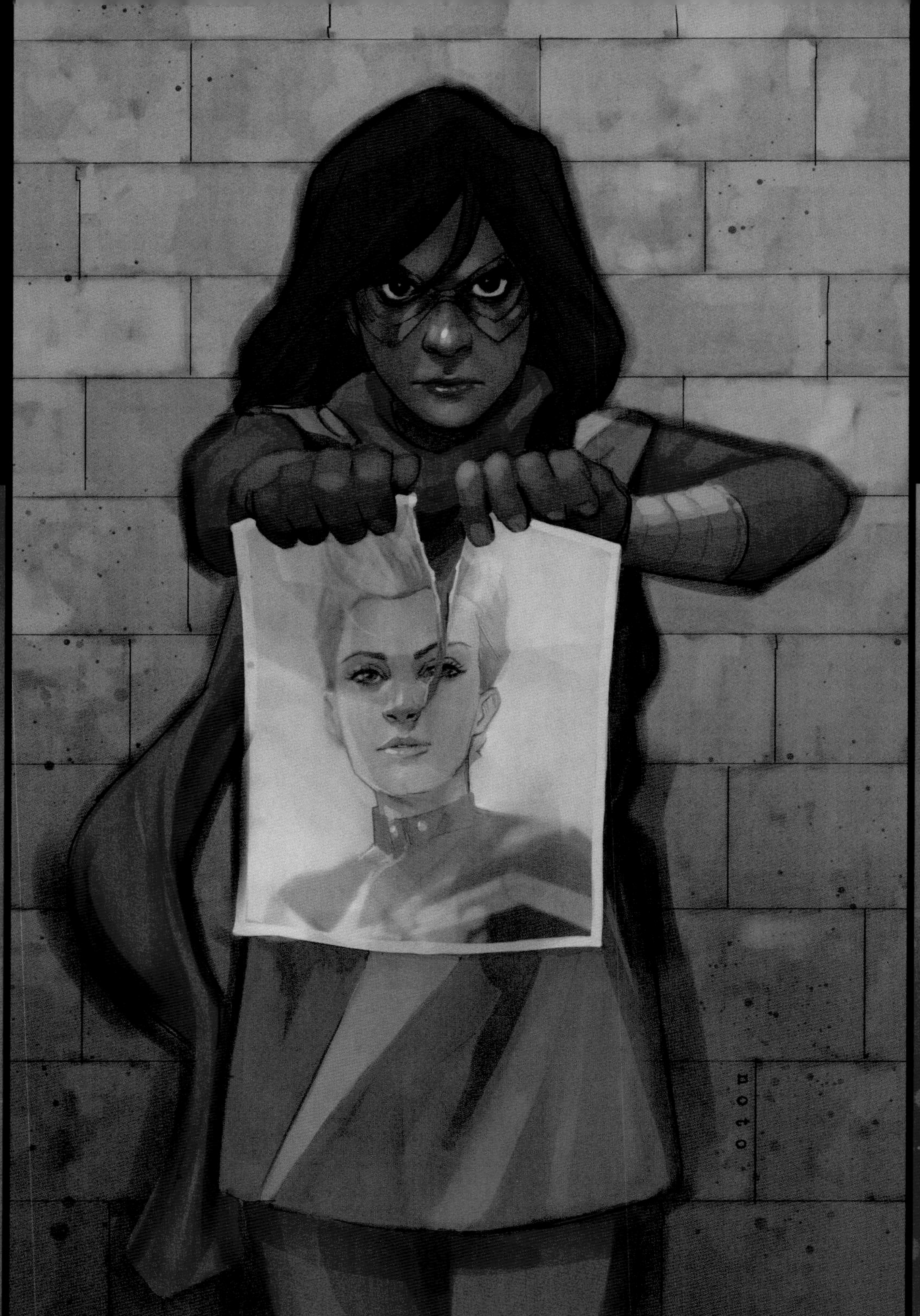

#0 VARIANT
BY PHIL NOTO

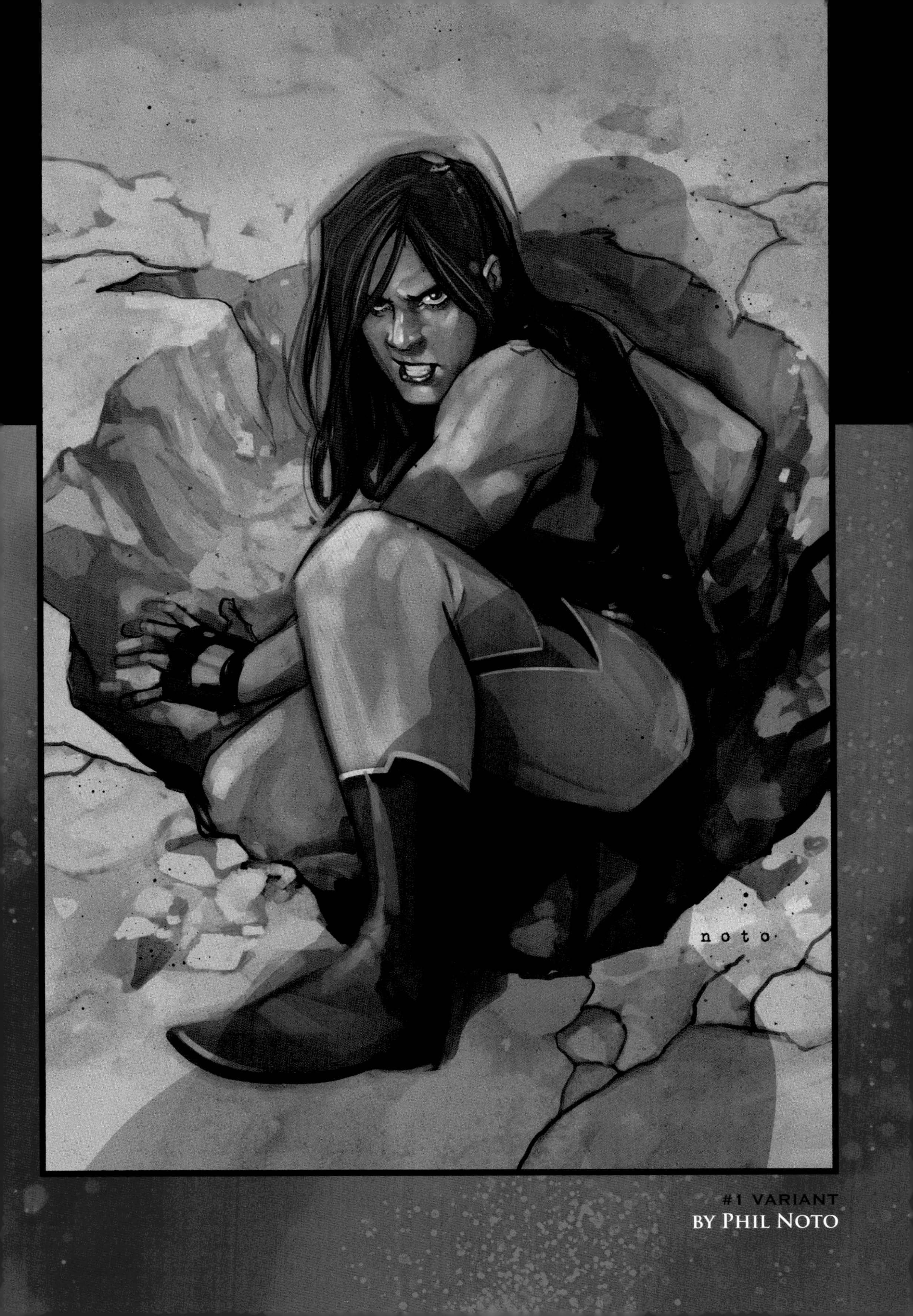
noto

#1 VARIANT
BY PHIL NOTO

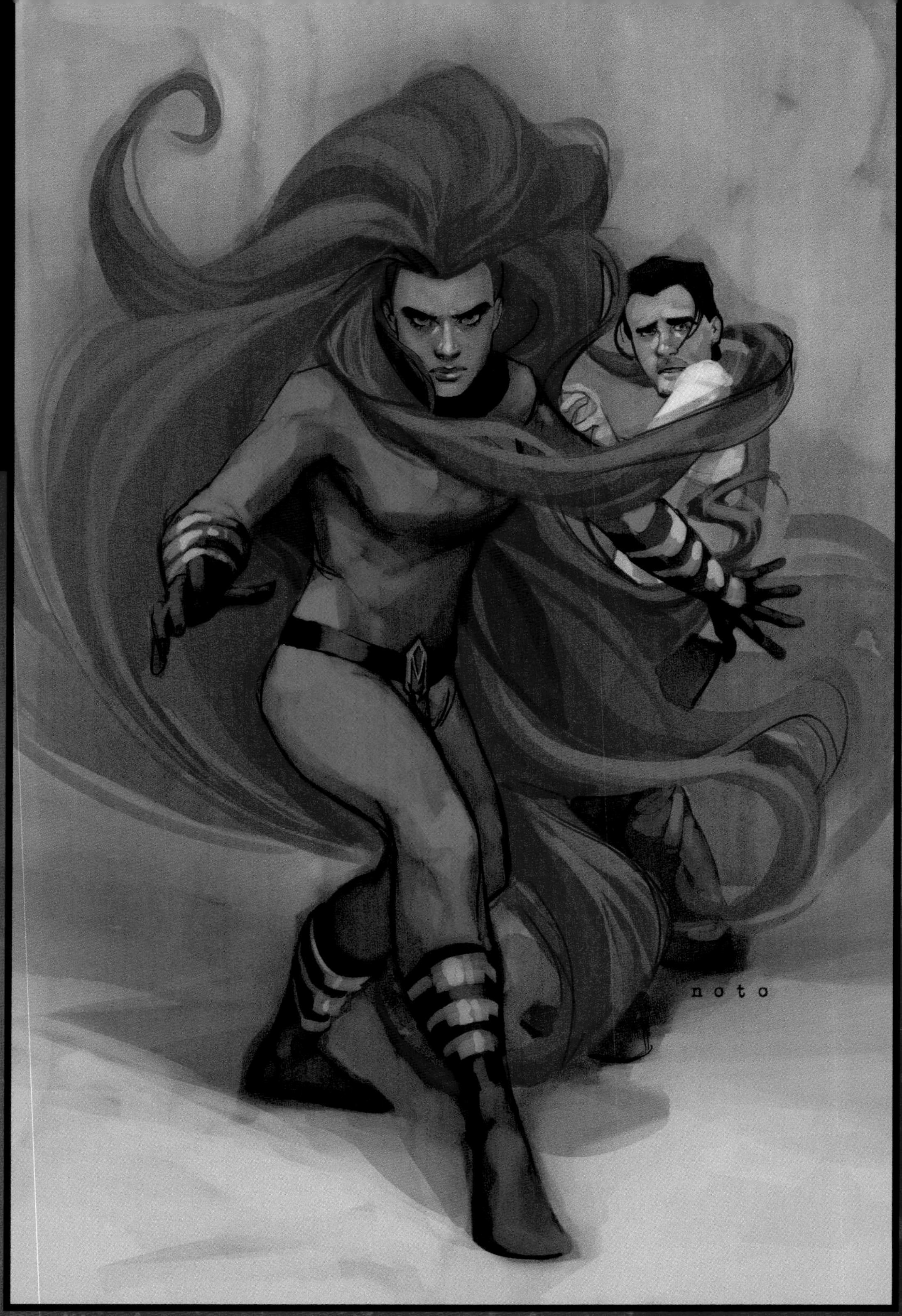
noto

#2 VARIANT
BY PHIL NOTO

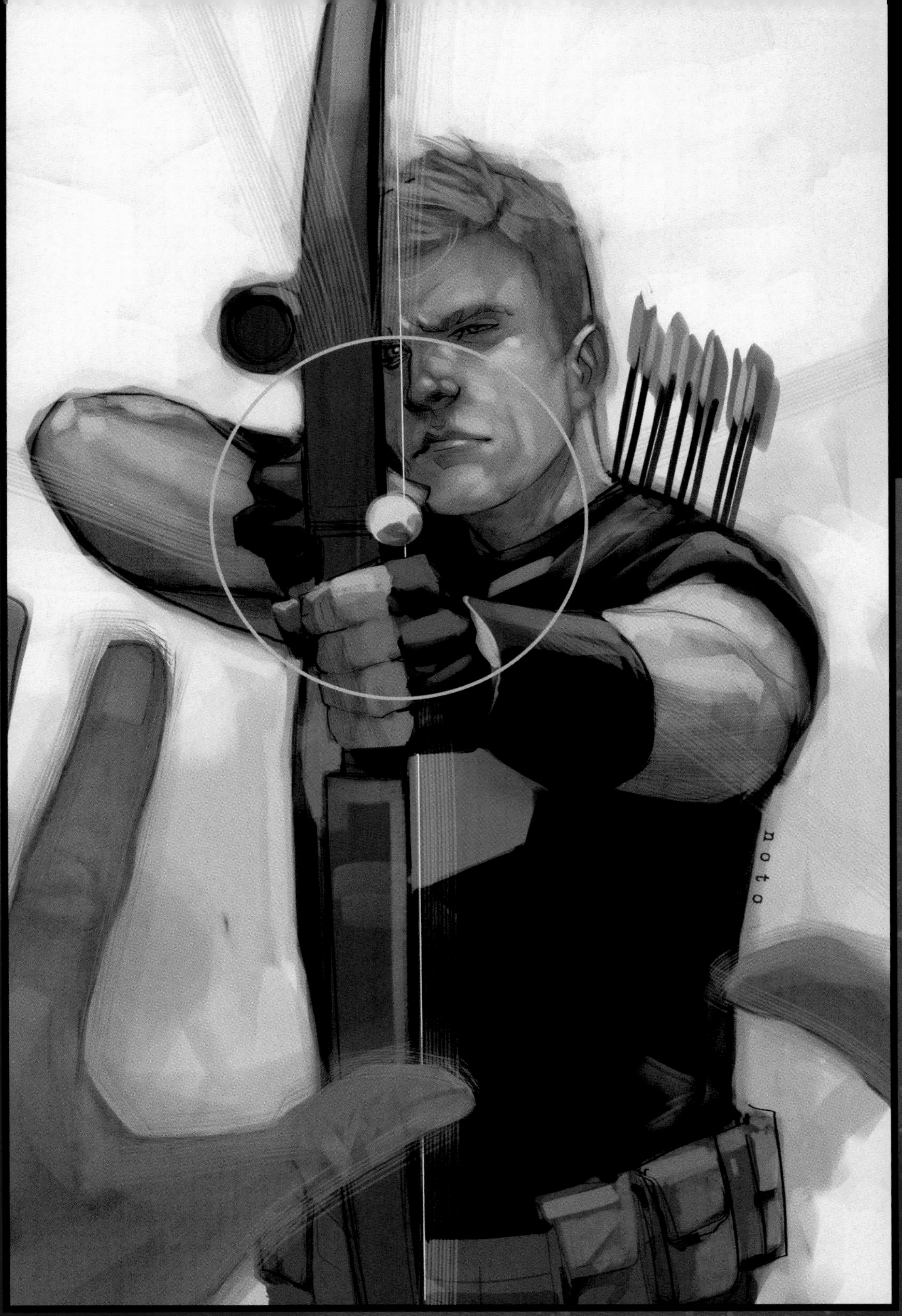
noto

#3 VARIANT
BY PHIL NOTO

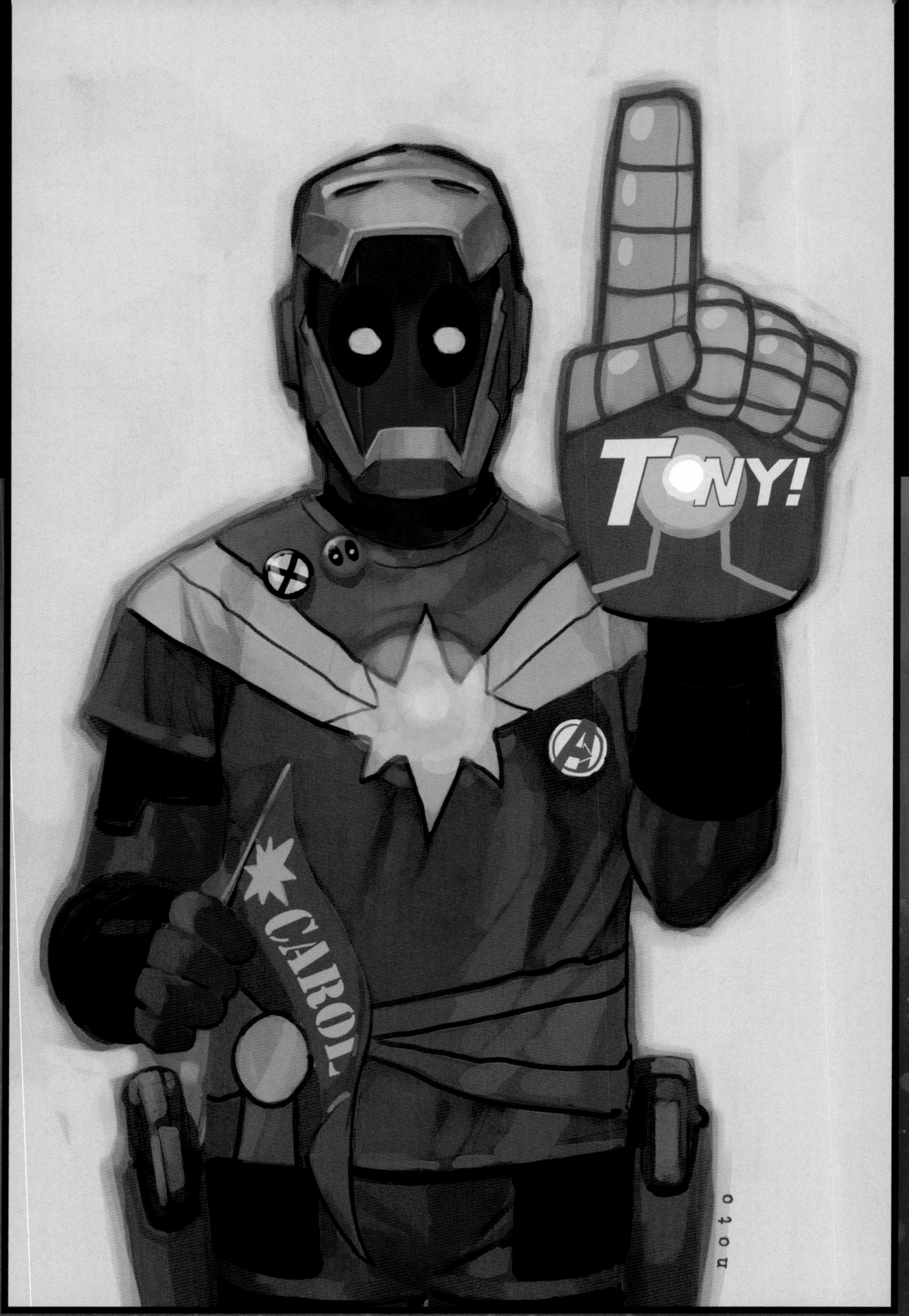
TONY!
CAROL
noto

#4 VARIANT
BY PHIL NOTO

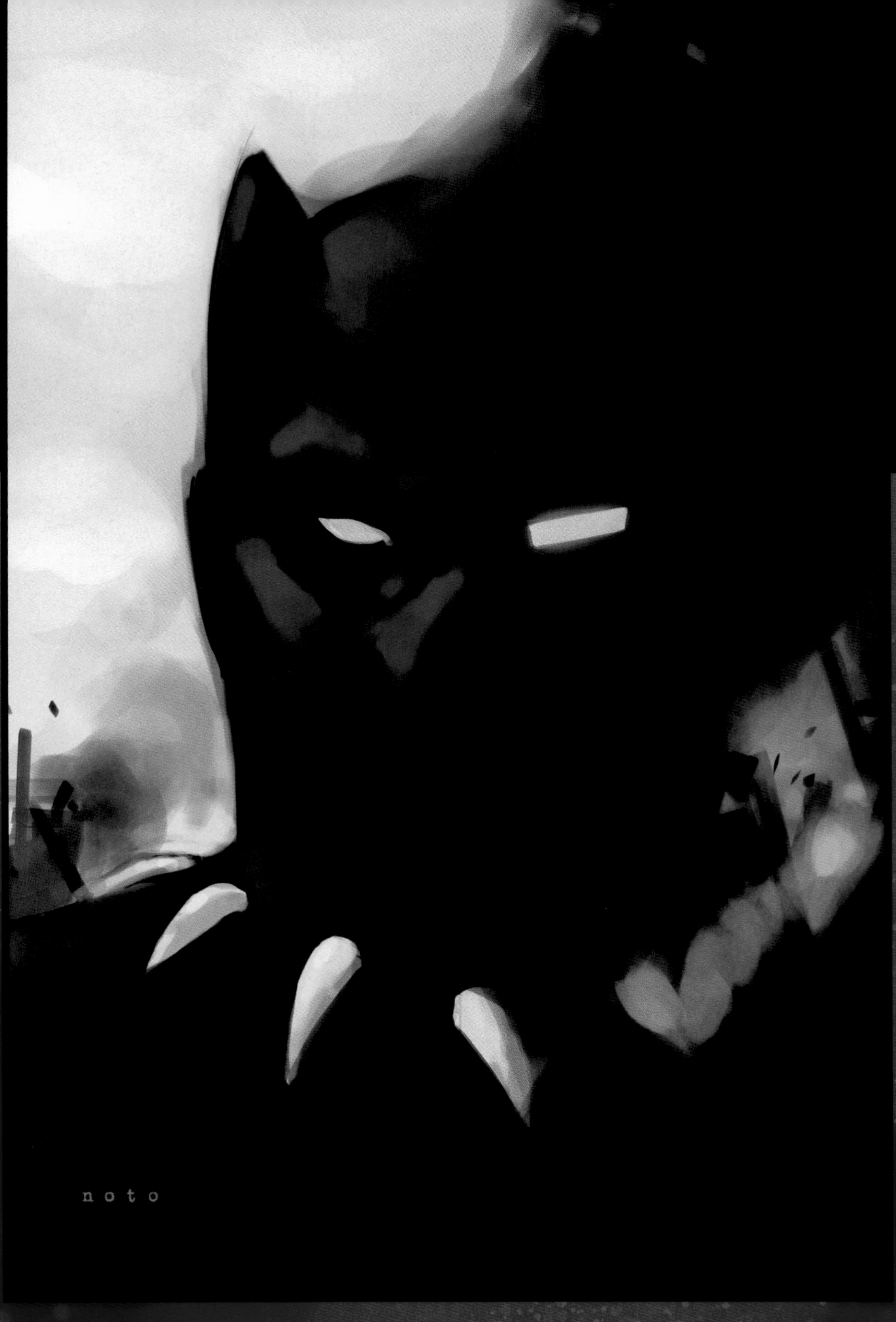
noto

#5 VARIANT
BY PHIL NOTO

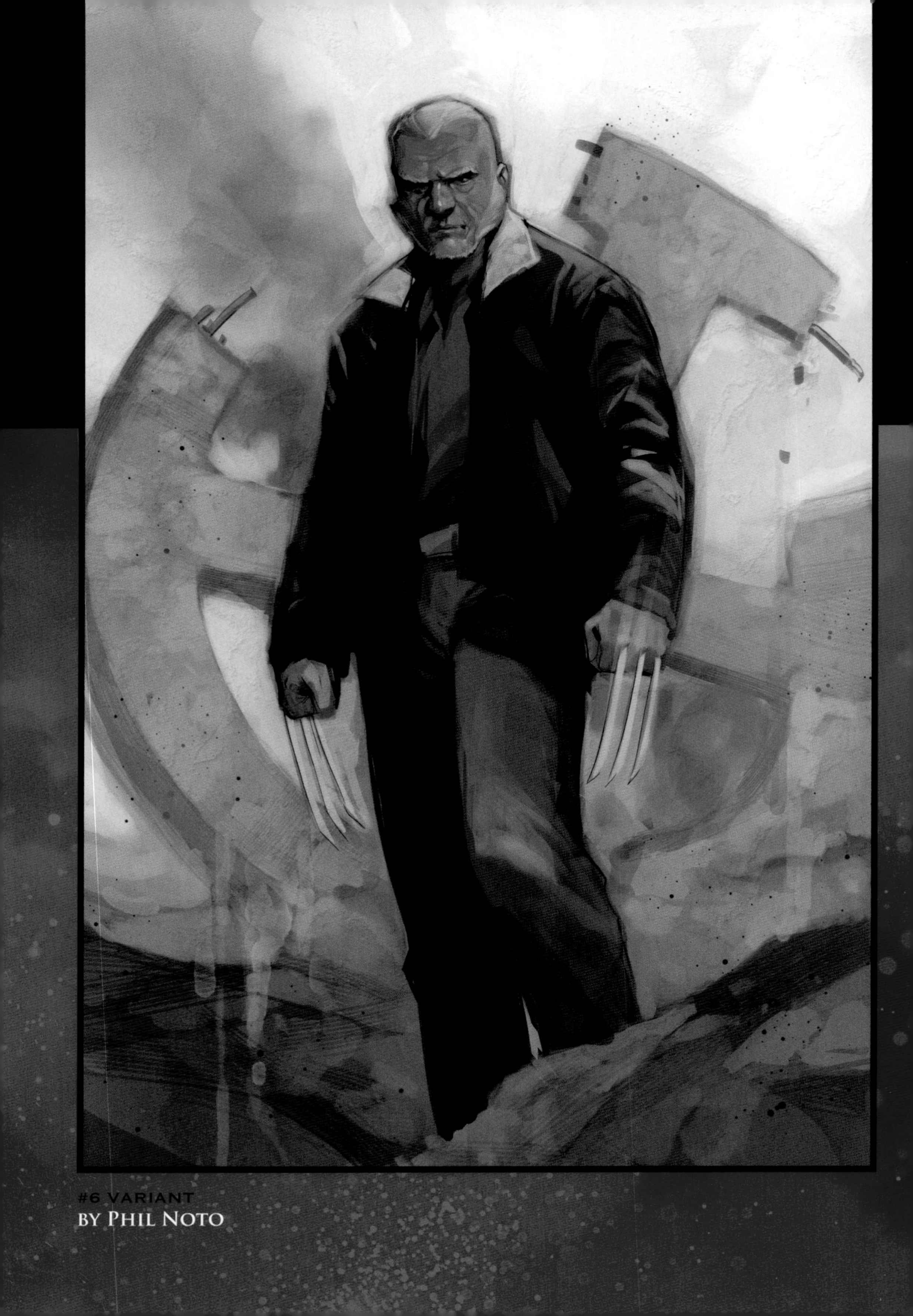

#6 VARIANT
BY PHIL NOTO

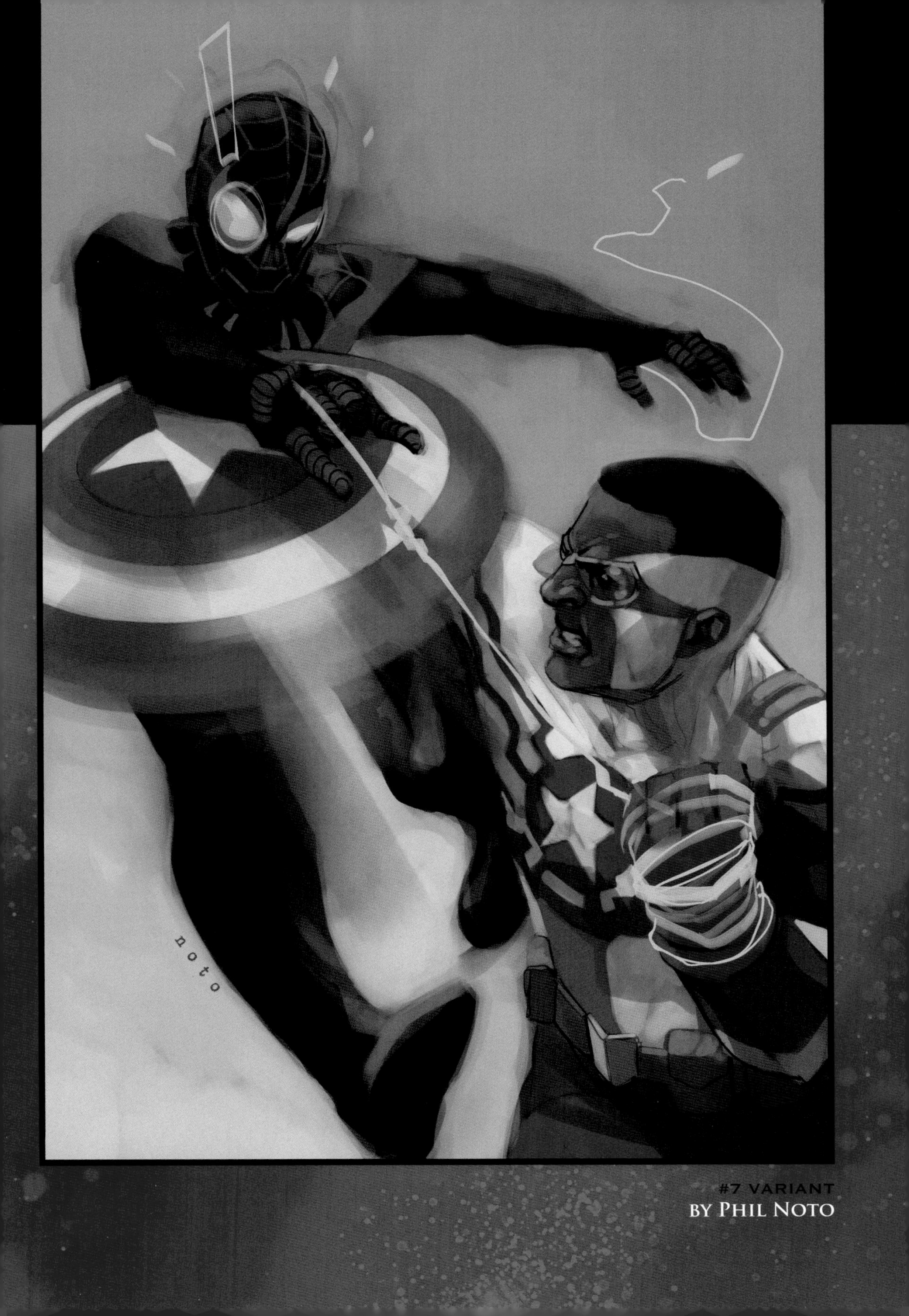
noto

#7 VARIANT
BY PHIL NOTO

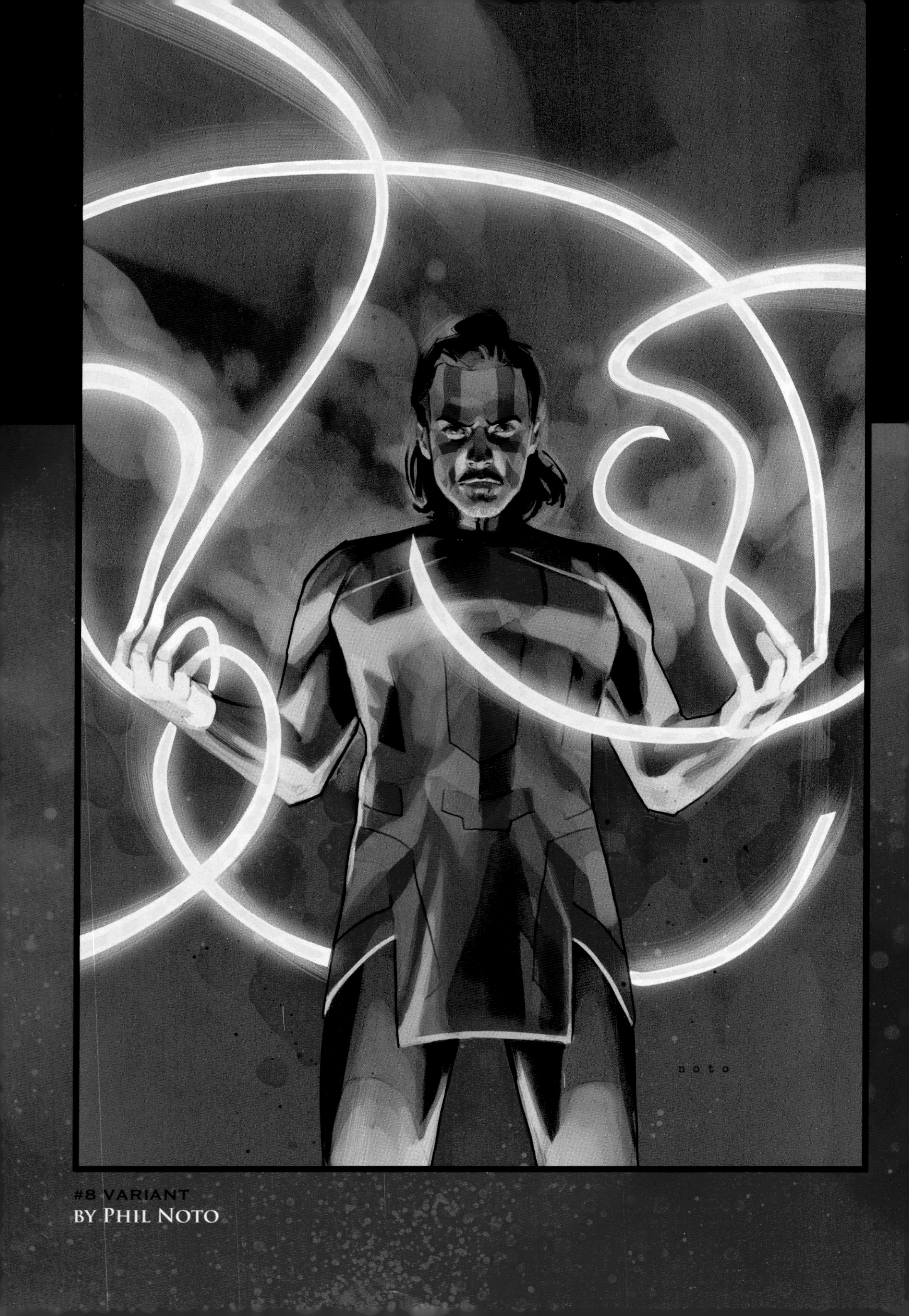
noto

#8 VARIANT
BY PHIL NOTO